www.wadsworth.com

wadsworth.com is the World Wide Web site for Wadsworth Publishing Company and is your direct source to dozens of online resources.

At *wadsworth.com* you can find out about supplements, demonstration software, and student resources. You can also send e-mail to many of our authors and preview new publications and exciting new technologies.

wadsworth.com
Changing the way the world learns®

Emotional Development

A Biosocial Perspective

PETER J. LaFRENIERE
University of Maine

Wadsworth
Thomson Learning™

Australia • Canada • Denmark • Japan • Mexico • New Zealand • Philippines • Puerto Rico
Singapore • South Africa • Spain • United Kingdom • United States

Executive Editor: Vicki Knight
Editorial Assistant: Amy Wood
Marketing Manager: Marc Linsenman
Signing Representative: John Moroney
Project Editor: Jerilyn Emori
Print Buyer: April Reynolds
Permissions Editor: Joohee Lee
Production Editor: Scott Rohr/
  Gustafson Graphics
Art Editor: Kelly Murphy
Photo Researcher: Roberta Broyer

Copy Editor: Linda Ireland
Illustrator: Luis R. Martinez
Compositor: Gustafson Graphics
Cover Designer: Bill Stanton/
  Stanton Design
Cover Image: *Picasso Face,* © 1999
  The Andy Warhol Foundation
  for the Visual Arts/ARS, NY
Printer/Binder: RR Donnelley & Sons/
  Crawfordsville

Printed in the United States of America
1 2 3 4 5 6 03 02 01 00

**Library of Congress
Cataloging-in-Publication Data**

LaFreniere, Peter J.
    Emotional development: a bio-
        social perspective /
Peter J. LaFreniere.
        p. cm.
    Includes bibliographical
references and index.
    ISBN 0-534-34808-4
    1. Emotions in children. 2. Child
development. I. Title.
    BF723.E6L34 1999
    155.4′124—dc21   99-32542

For more information, contact

Wadsworth/Thomson Learning
10 Davis Drive
Belmont, CA 94002-3098
USA
www.wadsworth.com

International Headquarters
Thomson Learning
290 Harbor Drive, 2nd Floor
Stamford, CT 06902-7477
USA

UK/Europe/Middle East
Thomson Learning
Berkshire House
168-173 High Holborn
London WC1V 7AA
United Kingdom

Asia
Thomson Learning
60 Albert Street #15-01
Albert Complex
Singapore 189969

Canada
Nelson/Thomson Learning
1120 Birchmount Road
Scarborough, Ontario M1K 5G4
Canada

The book is printed on
acid-free recycled paper.

Contents

10   Adolescence: Quest for Emotional Maturity   240
Coauthored with Jamie Walter

Foreword

L. Alan Sroufe

Emotion has been described by various scholars as the energy for thought; as that which cognition serves and the window to the mind; as the medium of social exchange and the bond for relationships; as the integrative thread for the continuity and coherence of the self; and as that which gives color to our experience and meaning to our lives. It has been viewed as both an organizing influence and as a potentially disorganizing one.

Emotion is central for understanding an adaptive response to the environment. For humans, it plays the guiding role served by instincts in many animals, granting the flexibility that distinguishes us as a species. Whereas a duckling may automatically follow its mother in response to her movement, the reaction of human infants is mediated by emotion, aroused not only by changes in the caregiver's position but also by the infant's evaluation of such changes based upon context. In an unfamiliar setting, where the infant is ill at ease, the caregiver's increasing distance arouses wariness that prompts proximity-seeking behavior. If more comfortable in the setting, or given a smile or reassuring word by the caregiver, the infant may not be aroused and so may not follow. Salient aspects of context change with age, as do response options, affording this system great flexibility. Louis Breger once wrote that a human without appropriate social emotion is like a hairless polar bear or an antisocial bee; so vital is emotion to human adaptation.

Emotion also plays a critical role in defining psychopathology. Every major psychiatric disorder has as core features the expression or regulation of emotion. Diminished affectivity, inappropriate affect, or uncontrolled emotion are all signs of disturbance. From the split between thought and affect in schizophrenia, to the

ennui in certain personality disorders, to the uncontrolled anger of the oppositional child, emotional disturbances are central.

In developmental psychology, in general, emotion has an absolutely critical
place. Indeed, without understanding emotion it is not possible to fully understand human development. Emotion is the fuel for cognitive growth and the cur-
rency for evolving social relationships. Likewise, without understanding all of
development, one cannot understand emotional life. Emotional life draws upon
perception, cognition, and social experience. At one and the same time, changes
in emotional life reflect changes in cognitive and social development, and in turn,
emotional experience consolidates and prompts advances in these domains. Such
is the centrality of emotion in human behavior.

How timely, then, is the appearance of this extraordinary, beautifully crafted
book. Such a comprehensive, readable text has been long-needed and long-
awaited. It has no predecessor, and there are probably two major reasons for this.
First, as is well documented in the text itself, the study of emotion was banished
from psychology for almost half a century. In recent decades the field of emotional development has matured to the point where such a text is appropriate;
indeed, it is demanded by an outpouring of research and theory. But second, and
equally important, such a text has not been done before because of the very integrative, multidisciplinary nature of this field. Scholarship in numerous domains is
required, as well as a commitment to synthesizing and integrating them into a
coherent piece. It is a monumental task. This is the remarkable achievement of
this book.

All major scholars of emotion agree that it has a social-communicative aspect,
a cognitive aspect, and a physiological aspect. It lies at the intersection of psychology and biology. It is based in both evolution and culture. A comprehensive text,
as this one is, must cover topics as diverse as temperament, theory of mind, brain
evolution and development, peer relationships, attribution theory, early deprivation, primate social behavior, the history of psychology, personality theory, behavior genetics, socialization, and attachment. There is no way around it. This field
must be both multidisciplinary and interdisciplinary. Moreover, in a field where
there are diverse theories, with strong adherents at times taking stands that are at
least on the surface diametrically opposed, there is a great need for thoughtful,
even-handed treatment of controversial topics. This text masterfully presents a balanced interweaving of the diverse facets and viewpoints that characterize this field.
As one example, there was once an active debate about whether individual infant
reactions to separations and reunions with caregivers were due to temperament or
to the history of experience with that caregiver. As it turns out, variation in distress
at separation was related to a variety of temperament assessments, but reactions to
reunion (including ease of settling) were not. The latter were best predicted by
variations in the history of responsive care. Infants with histories of responsive care
may or may not become notably distressed at separation, but they have in common
ease of settling when reunited. A comprehensive understanding of infant emotion
calls upon both temperament and attachment research. Such an integrative perspective is nicely described in this book.

One of the strongest features of the text is the coverage of the evolutionary/ethological perspective. Emotion is deeply rooted in our biological heritage. The presentation on this topic is consistently clear, sophisticated, and engaging. Readers will understand all that this perspective and the comparative study of nonhuman primates have to offer to the study of emotion and its development. At the same time, the author never slips into simple physiological determinism or the fruitless effort to decide how much is in the genes and how much is due to experience. The treatment is "biosocial" from start to finish. Thus, early relationship experiences and their role in emotional development are given ample treatment, along with coverage of behavior genetics and temperament. After all, it is part of our evolutionary heritage that social relationships play such a vital role in development.

A hallmark of this text is the coherence it brings to the field. Not only is emotion complex and multifaceted, so too is emotional development. It includes the orderly emergence of the specific affects (anger, fear, and so forth), their changing manifestations and eliciting conditions across ages, and links between them. It also includes developmental changes in emotional control and emotional regulation, as well as individual differences in these capacities. Finally, it encompasses growth in understanding of the meaning of emotions in self and other and the rules concerning expression and containment of emotions in given circumstances and in the given culture. Heretofore, with rare exceptions, these have been largely separated topics pursued by different researchers with different methodologies. But in this text, all are embraced and the reader is invited to view them as developmentally integrated.

When one deeply understands the development of specific emotions such as fear or joy, as they emerge from precursors and pave the way for more mature emotions such as guilt and pride, processes are uncovered that also are germane for understanding normative and individual aspects of emotion regulation. Fear is not possible without engendering arousal in a rapid manner and attributing a categorical negative meaning, that is, a subjective meaning for the self that entails threat. Because of this meaning component, the "same" event may or may not engender fear in different infants or in different circumstances. The caregiver putting a nylon over her face in an unfamiliar setting (especially following another noxious event) is frightening to a 10-month-old; in the home in a playful context, it produces glee. Once one grants that security of context (and therefore meaning) is at least partly based on experience, a start is made toward understanding individual differences in emotion regulation.

In a real sense, caregivers entrain infants into patterns of physiological and affect regulation, in part by engaging them in stimulating, positively toned play, and in part through the conversion of potentially negative affective experience into neutral or positive affect. The experience of individual infants varies greatly. Some infants routinely are assisted in the task of emotion regulation. Stimulation is geared to the particular infant's mode and momentary readiness for increased arousal. Moreover, when arousal becomes too great, the infant may "signal" via primitive capacities such as turning away. If the infant's caregiver is sensitive to such information, accurately reading the infant's need, the caregiver reduces stimulation and waits until the infant is again ready. Then the stimulation is increased again and positive excitement builds. When such patterns are the routine, not only are infants shaped toward an increased capacity to tolerate arousal, but their developing brain systems are tuned in the service of emotion modulation. For other infants, of course, stimulation may be too sudden, intrusive, or mistimed. When this is the daily diet, the development of emotion regulation may be compromised. With advancing age, of course, the caregiving task becomes more complex. Children initiate much more of their own stimulation, and the caregiver is called upon not only to react to signals from the child but also to anticipate frustration and to help the child restore equilibrium should strong affect temporarily overwhelm the child.

Likewise, the growth in understanding of the meaning of emotion and the rules for its expression underlies both normative changes in emotional regulation and individual differences. Emotions such as shame and guilt require the emerging awareness of standards for behavior followed by internalizing such standards as guides for behavior. Shame and guilt, like fear and anger, are of course a normal part of human development. They are part of our evolutionary heritage as a group living, highly social species. They have been described by some scholars as playing an important role in socialization and in the beginnings of morality. But there also is an attendant vulnerability in such emotional capacities. Children who are harshly punished or shamed for expressions of anger will, in time, learn to camouflage or conceal such emotions, perhaps even from themselves.

All these issues are treated in this text. In addition, to be complete, the interface between emotion and personality, peer relationships, and self-development is also explored. Early differences in dyadic emotional regulation are among the strongest predictors of later self-esteem, resiliency, and social competence. Moreover, emotions play a vital role in the child's subsequent encounters with peers, shaping the nature and ultimate success of such relationships. The author of this text has extensive knowledge about all these topics. His treatment of peer relationships itself makes the book worth reading. Rich details are provided of the role of affect in the world of peers and how peer relationships contribute to emotional life.

Thus, you are about to begin a journey that traverses our evolutionary heritage, as well as the history of the psychology of emotion. And you will follow the life of the child from the newborn period to adolescence. It is a well-told tale. At the end, you will understand a great deal about emotional development.

Preface

The goal of this book is to define and describe a biosocial perspective on emotional development. This perspective emphasizes the necessity of reuniting nature and nurture in any attempt to fully understand the development and function of human emotions. From a functional perspective, emotions signal needs, attitudes, anticipations, and impulses toward action. Human emotions such as joy, love, anger, fear, and sadness become evident in infancy and are generally recognized across cultures, not just as verbal labels for emotional experience, but as core species-specific motivational systems that organize behavior and development across the life span.

Unlike biological reductionistic theories of emotion that ignore the role of culture or social constructivist theories that ignore human biology, a biosocial perspective assumes that socialization, learning, and cognition are just as inherent to the process of human adaptation as the phylogenetic structures that support these behaviors. Indeed, it is the unique biological evolution of Homo sapiens that creates the imperative to recognize that in our species only, language, symbolism, and culture provide the means and the medium by which humans create new adaptations and new understandings of their world. Emotions are central to that adaptation, representing a vital link with our primate heritage, and providing a basis for understanding the human family and communicating across cultural and linguistic barriers. In particular, human nonverbal communication and emotional expression provide a rich domain for research illustrating the interpenetration of biology and culture. The key to integrating such a broad, interdisciplinary domain is to abandon the conceptualization of nature versus nurture as a zero-sum game.

A biosocial perspective posits essential roles for both factors, not as parallel strands of human experience, but as an interwoven tapestry.

WHY A TEXTBOOK ON EMOTIONAL DEVELOPMENT?

The need for a synthetic textbook on emotional development has been apparent to me since 1983 when I first started teaching undergraduate and graduate courses on the topic. My own interest in the topic stems from my undergraduate days at the University of Michigan. But, as a psychology major, I could not find a single course dealing with emotion per se. As a graduate student at Minnesota's Institute of Child Development, I began a series of naturalistic observational studies under the direction of William Charlesworth, in which I investigated the social ecology of children's peer groups, with an emphasis on children's affective expression. When the infants in the Minnesota Longitudinal Study came of age, I continued this work with a sample of preschoolers selected on the basis of their attachment history. In the research articles that derived from my thesis, co-authored with Alan Sroufe, affective expression and emotion regulation were highlighted as central to the individual's social adaptation. This remains a dominant theme of this book.

After graduation, I accepted a faculty position at the University of Quebec and the University of Montreal from 1982 to 1993. My Peace Corps French came in handy as I taught all my courses on emotional development in French and conducted research using Francophone subjects. This immersion in the French culture both solidified my interest in emotion and retarded the writing of this book. Though it was apparent early on that a textbook on emotional development was greatly needed, my intention to write it did not crystallize until after I returned to the United States and taught my first course on emotion in English at the University of Maine.

I have tried to write the kind of textbook that I would have appreciated as a student. It is written equally for graduate and advanced undergraduate students, because in teaching this material to graduate students, I have found that they generally lack a foundation in the topic, though they may be well grounded in cognitive and social development. This is hardly surprising, since, like scholars of my generation, they too have completed their undergraduate degree in developmental psychology without a single course dealing specifically with emotion. I hope that this situation will be different for the next generation of graduate students. Thus, altering the undergraduate curriculum is a key reason for writing this textbook.

Of course, the reason that this textbook could be written at all is the tremendous explosion of scientific information on the topic of emotion. The number of books and research articles published annually on emotion has been doubling every decade since the 1960s. This exponential growth of information has resulted in a pressing need to organize and integrate knowledge from the neurosciences, genetics, ethology, and primatology with emotion research in the many subfields of psychology and other social sciences, particularly anthropology. It is unrealistic to expect any student to synthesize such diverse information scattered across so many disciplines and specialized areas of inquiry. An interdisciplinary approach to understanding emotion may help counter the trend in American higher education toward forming increasingly specialized experts who are unable to communicate with one another, even across subfields within a discipline, much less across different disciplines.

The first part of this book is an open invitation for students of emotional development to adopt a broad perspective of their own field. It is designed to assist them in analyzing and synthesizing knowledge by casting a broad net that extends beyond developmental psychology to allow them to learn about various points of view in perspective, both historical and interdisciplinary. The book is also intended to complement other advanced texts dealing with adjacent areas of developmental psychology. Chapter 1 provides a historical background to contemporary debates in the field of emotion research and embraces the idea that those who are ignorant of history are condemned to repeat the errors of the past ad infinitum. The next two chapters on biology provide a context for understanding functionalist thinking about emotion by presenting evolutionary, ethological, and neuropsychological perspectives on emotion. Chapter 4 briefly recapitulates some of the major theories of emotion and emotional development that inform and guide current research in psychology.

The second part of this book covers emotional development from birth through adolescence. It is organized with respect to two interrelated goals: (1) describing patterns of normative growth; and (2) understanding the origin and significance of individual differences. Within each of the four broad developmental periods, I have attempted to introduce and rework a number of common questions and themes relating to how emotions are expressed, how they are recognized and understood, and how they are regulated and socialized within a given culture. All these aspects of emotion undergo profound developmental change. I have consistently related these changes to cognitive and social advances, illustrating the interpenetration of all three aspects of the whole child during each major period of development.

These same aspects of emotional development animate the discussion of the origins and significance of individual differences. Just as individuals in different developmental periods differ in their expression, regulation, and understanding of emotions, so, too, do individuals of the same age differ in these qualities. Throughout the book it is argued on the basis of longitudinal research that such differences arise as the result of complex transactions with inputs from the child's own genotype interwoven with socialization influences. In particular, the child's close relations with family and peers are examined, as well as influences from the broader sociocultural milieu.

Emotional development is now viewed as central to the adaptation of children in our society, as it is in any society. Many of the problems children face have an important emotional component, if not an emotional basis. It follows that emotional development deserves to be a central topic in the training of undergraduate students in psychology, as well as graduate students in the traditional subfields of developmental, social, and clinical psychology. I invite faculty to continue to innovate and rethink the organization of their curriculum and to move forward into an exciting new millenium of research and teaching on human emotion.

ACKNOWLEDGMENTS

The realization of a project as vast as this one could not have been accomplished without several years of professional assistance from the Wadsworth editorial staff. I would especially like to thank the Psychology editors and their editorial assistants for their help and encouragement throughout this project. I am grateful to Jim Brace-Thompson for his support at the inception of this project and his assistance in getting me through the first phases of its realization. For her enthusiastic support and knowledgeable assistance in the middle phases I'd like to thank Stacey Purviance. And for help in completing the book on time, a special thanks to Wadsworth's senior production editor, Jerilyn Emori. For her meticulous care and considerable expertise in copyediting, I'd like to thank Linda Ireland. For their efficiency and expertise in the production of the book, my heartfelt thanks to Scott Rohr and Sara Dovre Wudali at Gustafson Graphics in St. Paul, Minnesota. Also many thanks to Kelly Murphy for help with the artwork, Roberta Broyer for help in the photo research, and Joohee Lee for her advice in securing the necessary permissions.

In the early stages of the project the editors at Wadsworth wrote to the following scholars who agreed to read a substantial section of the book and provide expert commentary. I would like to thank them now for their many insightful and constructive remarks which have been carefully considered in revising the final draft of the book:

Karen Barrett, Colorado State University
Joyce Benenson, McGill University
Susan Calkins, University of North Carolina at Greensboro
Linda Camras, DePaul University
Jude Cassidy, University of Maryland College Park
William Charlesworth, University of Minnesota
Susan Crockenberg, University of Vermont
Susanne Denham, George Mason University
Michelle Dunlap, Connecticut College
Robert Emde, University of Colorado Health Sciences Center
JoAnn Farver, University of Southern California
John Gaa, University of Houston
Amy Halberstadt, North Carolina State University
Carroll Izard, University of Delaware
Kevin MacDonald, California State University–Long Beach
Kathy Stansbury, University of New Mexico Main Campus

I would also like to thank the following colleagues who each read a draft of a chapter for their helpful comments: Cynthia Erdley, Marie Hayes, Marcelle Ricard, and Janice Zeman. Also a special thanks to Kathy McAuliffe for providing assistance in the laborious task of typing the reference list. This was greatly appreciated. Sincere thanks to my colleagues Frans de Waal at Emory University in Atlanta, Georgia, and Irenäus Eibl-Eibesfeldt at the Max-Planck Institute for Human Ethology in Andechs, Germany, for allowing me to publish their wonderful photos. Finally, a special thanks to the teachers at the University of Maine's Child Study Center, Barb Guidotti and Karen Belknap, and the parents and children at the center who graciously permitted me to sneak about on the outskirts of their play, snapping photographs.

About the Author

Peter J. LaFreniere is Professor of Developmental Psychology and Director of the Child Study Center at the University of Maine. LaFreniere graduated from the University of Michigan in 1975 and received his Ph.D. from the Institute of Child Development, University of Minnesota, in 1982 after a two-year stint in the Peace Corps in West Africa. He is an internationally recognized expert on social and emotional development in young children and has worked with typical and atypical preschoolers throughout his career, publishing over 60 articles in developmental and clinical journals in English and French. Besides basic research in child development, LaFreniere has published articles, films, and assessment instruments on social competence and behavior problems in young children that are widely used in North and South America and Europe. He is currently editor of the *Human Ethology Bulletin,* reflecting a career-long interest in the integration of evolutionary biology with developmental psychology. He has received a Fulbright grant to conduct research at the Laboratoire de Psycho-Biologie du Developpement in Paris, France, in the year 2000.

1

Philosophical and Historical Foundations of a Science of Emotion

Philosophical Foundations

Greek and Roman Philosophical Views of Emotion

  Aristotle

  The Stoics

Emotion in the Age of Reason

  Descartes

  Hume

  Rousseau

Early Scientific Foundations

Darwin's Evolutionary Theory of Emotional Expression

James, Cannon, and the Mind–Body Problem

Pavlov, Watson, and Classical Conditioning of Emotions

Freud's Psychoanalytic Theory of Affect

Bridge's Theory of Emotional Differentiation

Lorenz, Harlow, Bowlby: The Origin of Emotional Bonds

Tomkin's Affect Theory

PHILOSOPHICAL FOUNDATIONS

This chapter introduces the topic of emotion by considering some of the landmark contributions and debates that have shaped our present scientific understanding of emotion. From at least the time of the Greeks, Western philosophers have embraced a dualistic vision of human experience by separating mind and body, reason and passion, cognition and emotion. We begin the chapter by reviewing the ideas of Aristotle who identified the study of emotion with the tradition of ethical philosophy where it remained until Descartes and Darwin linked the study of emotions to natural philosophy. By the nineteenth century, psychology emerged as the science of the mind, including cognition, motivation, and emotion, and inherited earlier philosophical debates.

Early psychologists were also profoundly influenced by Darwin's theory, which viewed human emotions as products of natural selection that served the adaptive functions of regulating the body's response to different challenges and communicating with others. However, the study of the adaptive functions of emotion did not become the focus of psychological research on emotion until much later. Instead, psychologists like William James focused on the study of emotion as internal states and debated whether emotions originated in the mind or the body. We discuss this debate as the basis for the emergence of neuroscientific research on how the brain initiates and organizes emotion physiology and subjective experience.

With the emergence of radical behaviorism in the early twentieth century, psychologists like Pavlov, Watson, and Skinner turned their attention to the study of objective stimuli and behavioral responses, relegating emotion, along with cognition, to a "black box" of phenomenon unsuitable for scientific inquiry, except as a conditioned response. Outside academic psychology, the psychoanalytic tradition initiated by Freud continued to view emotions as central to human

functioning, and elaborated concepts concerning personality development, moral development, dreams and the unconscious, infantile sexuality, and defense mechanisms.

By the mid-twentieth century, after decades of scientific neglect, psychological theorists such as Tomkins and Bowlby revisited biological models, reinstating emotion as central to the process of human adaptation. We present some of the key ideas associated with their work that, along with research in the neurosciences, eventually helped create the conditions for a renaissance for the scientific study of emotion.

Greek and Roman Philosophical Views of Emotion

The early Greek philosophers Socrates (470–399 BC) and Plato (428–327 BC) are an important source of the perennial Western tradition of elevating reason over passion or emotion. An enduring metaphor in Western philosophy casts reason and emotion as master and slave, with the ideal of enlightened reason firmly in control of the disruptive influence of the emotions. It is perhaps remarkable that in this context, Aristotle (384–322 BC) developed the first, and surprisingly modern, theory of emotions that anticipated many of the features of contemporary theories.

Aristotle (384–322 BC) As Solomon (1993) argues, it is critical to view Aristotle's theory of emotions as emanating from his broader concern with human ethics. Thus, for two millennia, from Aristotle in the fourth century BC until Darwin in the nineteenth century, the analysis of emotion is identified with the tradition of ethical philosophy rather than natural philosophy. As a natural philosopher, Aristotle spent considerable time developing taxonomies based on observation and description of various phenomena, such as the virtues and various kinds of birds. However, we see no comparable inductive approach to the phenomena of emotions, but rather insightful

Figure 1.1 Aristotle

(Photo from Corbis)

commentary within essays on rhetoric, drama, and ethics. In his *Rhetoric* (Aristotle, trans. 1941), he views emotion "as that which leads one's condition to become so transformed that his judgment is affected, and which is accompanied by pleasure and pain. Examples of emotion include anger, fear, pity and the like, as well as the opposites of these." Curiously these "opposites" are never made explicit, and Aristotle never mentioned "feelings," which was a topic of so little interest for the Greeks that it played no significant role in their language or psychology (Solomon, 1993).

Aristotle's ethical analysis of emotion considered both the mind and body, subject and object. When the subject perceives an object, real or imagined, as being good or having the potential to produce pleasure, this evaluation produces desire, which may be manifested by attraction, positive expressions, approach behavior, and action to satisfy the desire. If the real or imagined object is evaluated as negative or likely to produce pain, repulsion, negative expressions, and avoidance of the object are activated.

The emotions that were important for Aristotle were the emotions that must be mastered by reason in the service of ethical conduct, chiefly anger and fear. Anger interested Aristotle deeply. He viewed this emotion as a natural response to provocation ("scorn, spite, or insolence"), and as a moral force that could be cultivated by reason. According to Solomon (1993):

> Anger (and several other emotions, notably pride) are also prominent in Aristotle's classical list of virtues in his *Nicomachean Ethics* (1941), where he discussed in some detail those circumstances in which it is appropriate to get angry, those in which it is not, and what amount or intensity of anger is justified. He suggested that forgiveness may be a virtue, but only sometimes. He also insisted that only fools don't get angry, and that although overly angry people may be "unbearable," the absence of anger (aimed at the right offenses) is a vice rather than a virtue. In this, as in all else, Aristotle defended moderation, the mean between the extremes." (p. 5)

In the *Rhetoric,* Aristotle (trans. 1941) demonstrated his insight and understanding of anger. His analysis breaks anger down into a number of important components. He was the first emotion theorist to emphasize a cognitive component in the evaluation of the stimulus that aroused anger. For Aristotle, the arousing stimulus could even be an imagined slight, incorrectly interpreted, but the unwarranted anger arising from such a misinterpretation is nevertheless the genuine emotion. This is the strongest logical argument that we have today for analyzing the subject's perception of the stimulus, rather than the stimulus itself, as the source of anger. It leads directly to contemporary attributional and information processing models of emotion. Aristotle goes further by insisting that not only do cognitive evaluations influence emotions, but emotional states may influence later cognitions or judgments. Thus, Aristotle advised that it would be unethical to move a judge to anger through rhetoric and so distort his judgment.

The key behavioral component of anger is vengeful action, so that the emotion provides the basis of the behavioral response. Aristotle considered the relational context of emotion, stating that "anger is always directed towards someone in particular." He also recognized a physiological component and mentioned that physical distress accompanies strong anger, as well as noting that the physiological context (for example, sickness and pain) may predispose one toward anger. Predisposing contexts may also be psychological, such as duplicity or ingratitude, or sociological, such as conditions of poverty or war. Finally, Aristotle viewed the regulation of anger, not in terms of its negation through control, but rather in terms of its adaptive expression through reason and moderation. Ultimately, one gets a clear sense of a modern, insightful, and above all, balanced analysis of the emotion of anger.

The notion of achieving a balanced or well-regulated emotional state that neither stifles the emotional arousal nor gives it full or unreasonable expression also characterizes Aristotle's analysis of fear. Courage (presumably one of his unnamed "opposites") does not consist of overcoming fear, but in having just the right amount—enough fear not to be a fool, but not the uncontrolled fear of the coward. In this view it is not the presence of the emotion per se that is adaptive, but its modulation through reason.

Summarizing Aristotle's theory of emotion, we see many contemporary qualities that are all the more remarkable given that he is considered to be the first person to think systematically about the topic, and that he inherited prevailing wisdom that consigned the emotions to the dark and dangerous side of human nature. For Aristotle, the emotions are an essential part of the self, and this insight lends further meaning to the slogan at Delphi made famous by Socrates: "Know thyself."

The Stoics The analysis of emotion in relation to the broader problem of human ethics continued with the work of the Roman Stoics, Seneca and Chryssipus, four centuries after Aristotle. They developed the Aristotelian notion that emotion and cognition are intimately linked, but returned to the older view that emotions are generally a source of misery and error. The Stoics viewed emotions as arising from misguided judgments about one's society and one's place in it. As Solomon (1993) points out, it is important to understand Roman society under Nero as a context for the development of this philosophy. Life in Roman society was often irrational, unhappy, unpredictable, and sometimes brutal. For example, Seneca, a Roman statesman and senator was buffeted about by the capricious will of those in political power. After a brilliant political career he was sentenced to exile in Corsica from 41 to 49 AD, at which time he was recalled to Rome and charged with the education of young Nero, who later ordered him to commit suicide in 65 AD for his alleged involvement in a conspiracy.

In this context, the Stoics formulated a somewhat cynical and pessimistic worldview. Their analysis of different emotions emphasized the presumptuous quality of indignation and moral anger, the heightened sense of vulnerability in love, and the self-absorbing dependency arising from fear. Because they viewed emotions as the source of frustration and misery, they preached maintaining a "higher reason" that emphasized the pointlessness of emotional attachments and involvement, and called instead for an impassive or indifferent attitude to the vagaries of the world. Such an attitude, it was argued, would lead to transcendence of the vanities of society.

The philosophy of stoicism remained influential in European culture after the fall of Rome and has found expression in art and literature up

Figure 1.2 Rodin's *The Burghers of Calais* (1884–1886)

"The central figure is the aged Eustache, whose venerable head with its long hair is bowed, but not with fear or hesitation; he seems rather, in sorrowful resignation, to be in deep contemplation in the spirit of his own words, 'I have so good trust in the Lord God.' If his step is a little halting, it is from the privations of the long siege; his firmness is calculated to inspire his fellows. 'He was the one who said "we must",' Rodin remarked. The one next to him, who is probably Jehan d'Aire, holding the key which he is to hand to the King, also has no fear or hesitation, but his whole body is tense with the effort to get the strength sufficient to go through the ordeal and humiliation. His face—a clean shaven, lawyer-like face—is set in grim sorrow at the pass to which his city is reduced. Behind him is the figure known as the 'Weeping Burgess,' whose face is covered by his two hands, as if he were indeed faltering or regretting his decision, and were thinking of wife and children. Just behind Eustache, one of the men looks back to the city, while he passes his hands before his eyes as if to drive away some terrible vision, for his resolution is evidently not as stern as that of the two leaders. Of the final two, who may be the two brothers, the one in advance, whose movement is more hasty and nervous than that of Eustache, as if he would fain have the ordeal over, may be encouraging by his gesture the one behind him, the youngest of the group, who hesitates at now leaving life and its sweetness behind."

(Photo from Art Resource, NY)

to the twentieth century. For example, stoicism as a response to the uncontrollable brutality of the wars that wracked European history was given artistic form in Rodin's celebrated masterpiece, *The Burghers of Calais* (see Figure 1.2). The work was inspired by the heroic sacrifice of Eustache de Saint-Pierre and his five comrades after their surrender to the English army in 1347. Because of the long and spirited defense of the city, the terms of the surrender were particularly harsh for the burghers who led the resistance. The people of Calais were to be spared only if the chief burghers agreed to come to the king barefoot, bareheaded, with ropes about their necks and the keys to the city in their hands. They were to be first humiliated, and then executed, as an example to those who considered further resistance.

In his classic work, Rodin placed the burghers so each is visible from any leading point as if to recreate the collective gaze of the original witnesses, the survivors of the siege. It is not merely a group of men marching off to execution, but a detailed, expressive study of the group as individuals, each of whom is infused with a different emotion that can be read from facial, gestural, and postural expressions. In *The Burghers of Calais,* Rodin embraces a modern psychology of emotion that recognizes that emotions arise from the individual's appraisal of an event, not from the event itself. Moreover, Rodin gives artistic form to the idea that the expression of powerful emotions is influenced by the individual's attempt at regulation, which may be more or less successful.

Emotion in the Age of Reason

The ideas of Aristotle and the Stoics remained an undercurrent of European thought over the next millennium and resurfaced in the writings of the **Enlightenment** philosophers Descartes and Hume. The duality of human experience and the relation between reason (cognition) and passion (emotion) remained a central theme for each of these philosophers, as it is today in psychology, which has inherited the debate from them.

Descartes (1596–1650) By all accounts, René Descartes is considered to be the first modern philosopher. He was well versed in mathematics and the seventeenth-century sciences and was sharply critical of ancient and medieval views of emotion. Indeed, his appraisal of everything that had been previously written on the subject was dismissive (Solomon, 1993). Despite this, Descartes epitomized the mind–body dualism that was the hallmark of the Western tradition that preceded him. Nowhere is this more apparent than in his attempt to deal with the topic of emotion. As described by Solomon (1993), Descartes attempted a resolution of this problem

Figure 1.3 René Descartes

(Photo from Archives of the History of American Psychology, University of Akron)

in his famous treatise, *On the Passions of the Soul* (1649/1989):

> [T]he mind and body "meet" in a small gland at the base of the brain (known as the pineal gland), and the latter effects the former by means of the agitation of "animal spirits" (minute particles of blood), which bring about the emotions and their physical effects in various parts of the body. But the emotions involve not only sensations, but perceptions, desires, and beliefs as well.
>
> (SOLOMON, 1993, P. 6)

This was clearly a new vision and represents the earliest attempt to relate emotion to an underlying neurophysiology. It also reintegrated the cognitive appraisal component of Aristotle's theory into a new intellectual context. For Descartes, an emotion was a specific type of passion closely related to higher thought processes that he referred to as the soul. Just as the physiological passions of hunger or pain relay information about the well-being of the body, emotions can inform one about the state of the inner self or soul. Descartes was the first theorist to organize the emotions into basic and complex types. He listed six primitive passions—wonder, love, hatred, desire, joy, and sadness—which he viewed as an essential part of human experience. Complex blends of these primitive emotions, such as pride, envy, disdain, hope, and fear, are also an inevitable part of human experience. One can detect a note of ambivalence in Descartes's view of emotion; emotions can be either disturbing or gratifying. Descartes considered both their functional and dysfunctional aspects:

> The utility of the passions consists alone in their fortifying and perpetuating in the soul thoughts which it is good that it should preserve, and which without that might easily be effaced by it. . . . The harm is that they fortify these thoughts more than necessary, or they conserve others on which it is not good to dwell.
>
> (SOLOMON, 1993, P. 6)

Thus, for Descartes, like Aristotle before him, reason was the key to regulating the emotions. If the emotions can undermine our judgment and render it confused, reason can elevate the passions and harness them in the service of the self. *Cogito, ergo sum*—"I think, therefore I am"—was the central premise of his philosophy and with it he laid the groundwork for the Age of Reason.

Hume (1711–1776) If Descartes, along with his seventeenth-century contemporaries Bacon, Galileo, and Newton, brought mathematics, deductive logic, and empirical science into the forefront of Enlightenment thought, David Hume brought the movement to its zenith in the late eighteenth century. The **Age of Reason,** sometimes referred to as the Enlightenment, spanned roughly two centuries and shaped the modern intellectual tradition of the West, including the concept of the university and its three major branches of learning—the natural sciences, the social sciences, and the humanities. The essential difference was that the Enlightenment of the seventeenth and eighteenth centuries was a *unified* vision of knowledge in the service of humanity. Enlightenment scholars were defiantly secular and skeptical of all forms of religious and civil authority, and embraced instead a spirit of free and open inquiry into all branches of knowledge. As one of the movement's most outspoken defenders, Hume went so far as to question reason itself.

In his *A Treatise on Human Nature* (1739/ 1972), Hume grappled with many of the same questions that Aristotle and Descartes had attempted to resolve. His interest in moral behavior led him to question the role of reason in ethics and to defend the passions as the faculty of mind that motivates us to engage in moral (or immoral) conduct, with reason left on the sidelines as an innocent (or guilty) bystander. Of all the passions, Hume was particularly interested in the "moral sentiments," and the most human of these is sympathy. Sympathy, the ability to feel and appreciate the suffering of another, is a universal quality of human nature. Rather than opposing sympathy with reason, or elevating reason over it, Hume argued that sympathy counteracts excessive self-interest and is essential in establishing human society and morality (Solomon, 1993).

Rousseau (1712–1778) The French philosopher, Jean-Jacques Rousseau, stands as a counterpoint to the elevation of reason above emotion in European philosophy. Although Rousseau is remembered primarily as a political philosopher, he was also a social reformer famous for his sensitive understanding and concern for children. He proposed that education should be natural, guided by emotions rather than rigidly constrained by logic and reason. In *Emile* (1762/1956), he offers surprisingly modern advice on early childhood education:

> Your first duty is to be humane. Love childhood. Look with friendly eyes on its

games, its pleasures, its amiable dispositions. Which of you does not sometimes
look back regretfully on the age when
laughter was ever on the lips and the heart
free of care? Why steal from the little
innocents the enjoyment of a time that
passes all too quickly?

Rousseau's ideas quickly gained acceptance
and spread throughout Western culture, bringing
an end to the Enlightenment movement. The
philosophical, literary, and artistic movement that
Rousseau founded, known as **Romanticism,**
flowered for about one hundred years as a reaction to the formal and impersonal style of the
rational and classical movements that preceded
it. During this period, poets and novelists
throughout Western Europe, including Balzac,
Byron, Keats, Shelley, Schiller, Goethe, and
Hugo, explored emotion and nature as their
principal themes, and were critical of high culture as artificial. They disdained the cultivated
artistic sensibilities of the aristocrats as false,
pompous, and corrupting, and they began to
explore the world around them instead, finding
much new ground to cover in the drama of
everyday life. In politics, populist revolutions
were in the air on both sides of the Atlantic. In
music, the Romantic movement led by
Beethoven and including composers like
Chopin, Schubert, Schumann, Brahms, Wagner,
and Tchaikovsky celebrated a free and unrestrained return to natural forms and dramatic
expression. These composers often drew from
folk traditions and used large orchestras and col-
orful instrumentation to probe into emotion and
psychology in a manner uncharacteristic of the
more orderly, restrained compositions of the
classical and baroque periods. This countercur-
rent to the Age of Reason expressed by
Rousseau in *Emile* has remained a perennial
theme in Western culture, especially Rousseau's
vision of the essential goodness of nature, the
innocence of childhood, and the corrupting
influence of society. An example of twentieth
century Romanticism may be found in the films

of Francois Truffaut, notably his autobiographi-
cal account of a young boy's search for freedom
in *Quatre Cents Coups* ("Four Hundred Blows").

EARLY SCIENTIFIC FOUNDATIONS

Darwin's Evolutionary Theory of Emotional Expression

By the mid-nineteenth century, the Romanticism
of Rousseau that had spread throughout Europe
was on the wane and eventually gave way to a
new form of Realism in the humanities. As part
of a literary and artistic movement, Realists
rejected the sentimental ideas of Romanticism
and were instead inspired by the emerging scientific age and its exacting attention to detail. One
of the most influential scientists of this era was
Charles Darwin, who stands out as having made
some of the most enduring contributions to a
diversity of fields, including developmental psychology and the study of emotion.

Darwin's status among history's truly great
scientific discoverers is ensured by virtue of his
uncanny ability to reason on the basis of
hypotheses, deducing ultimate consequences
from a broad array of descriptive facts. As Lorenz
(1965) notes in his introduction to the reprinting
of Darwin's *The Expression of the Emotions in Man
and Animals,* "many different branches of biological research have been inspired by him, and each
is claiming him, with equal right, as its particular
originator and pioneer. What is surprising is the
extent to which further research, based on
Darwin's hypotheses and pursuing them in every
conceivable direction, has invariably proved him
right on every essential point."

Lorenz goes on to claim Darwin as the
founder of ethology because he anticipated the
essential problems that confront contemporary
ethologists and mapped out methods to their
solutions. Darwin was the first to appreciate the
basic biological fact that behavioral adaptation is

realized through the same process of natural selection as that which leads to the morphological and physiological characteristics that support the behavior pattern. "Darwin shows in the most convincing manner that analogous processes (to the evolution of organs) have taken place in the evolution of motor patterns, as for instance, in the case of snarling, in which an expressive movement with a purely communicative function has developed out of the motor pattern of actual biting which, as a means of aggression, has practically disappeared in the human species" (Lorenz, 1965, p. xii).

Darwin also anticipated the key debates of early twentieth-century psychologists between central and peripheral theories of emotion. (See the discussion on James later in this chapter.) He was aware of the dynamic interaction of the central and autonomic nervous system that generates the spontaneous expression of strong emotions. He speculated that there must be specific neural pathways whose function is to provide a channel of communication between brain structures and the pattern of autonomic activity that characterizes a specific emotion. According to Darwin,

> When the mind is strongly excited, we might expect that it would instantly affect in a direct manner the heart. . . . When the heart is affected it reacts on the brain; and the state of the brain again reacts through the pneumo-gastric [vagus] nerve on the heart; so that under any excitement there will be much mutual action and reaction between these, the two most important organs of the body.
>
> (1872/1965, P. 69)

Recognizing that the study of emotional expression is difficult, Darwin adopted a multi-methods approach "in order to acquire as good a foundation as possible." Darwin proposed that the evolutionary foundations of emotion can be deduced from a variety of independent sources of information. These include careful observation of infants, independent judgments of expression in photographs, cross-cultural research, the study of

Figure 1.4 William James

(Photo from Corbis)

expression in painting and sculpture, the study of emotional expression in psychiatric patients, and most importantly, the comparative analysis of expression in different species. These methods did indeed prove to be a good foundation for modern observational research on emotional expression, as will become apparent throughout this book.

James, Cannon, and the Mind–Body Problem

The search for the emotional centers in the brain have occupied neuroscientists for most of the twentieth century, and our understanding of the anatomical organization of the emotional brain has increased dramatically as a result of this sustained scientific attention. One of the earliest debates in the psychology of emotion concerned whether emotions originate in the mind or the body, or in modern parlance, in the central or autonomic nervous system. This was a major debate among ancient Greek philosophers as well. The dominant view of the Greeks, championed by Aristotle, was that the heart was the organ most responsible for our emotions. The minority view, that the brain was chiefly responsible for all thought and feeling, pleasure and pain, was first advocated by the Greek physician Hippocrates, who deduced this from observing the effects of head trauma on his patients. As we shall see, this idea—that the brain rather than the heart is the key determinant of our emotions—is the view of contemporary neuropsychology.

At the end of the nineteenth century, peripheral theories of emotion, as first advocated by William James (1884, 1890) and Carl Lange (1885), assigned a central role to organs, muscles, and the vascular system, under the control of the **autonomic nervous system** (ANS). In this view, emotions originate in different parts of the body, including the heart and the arteries and vessels of the vascular system, the stomach and organs of the interior of the body, and sweat glands. James saw the feeling of a particular emotion as the mind's perception of the "bodily changes" that occur as a direct result of an "exciting fact," the object or event that elicits the emotional response. Under this view, researchers should concentrate their attention on ANS indices such as heart rate (HR), galvanic skin response (GSR), and other measures pertaining to physiological changes in the body.

In contrast, central theories hold that emotions originate in the **central nervous system** (CNS), composed of the brain and the spinal column. The first central theorists to challenge the James–Lange theory of emotions were Cannon (1927) and Bard (1928) who proposed that various brain mechanisms account for emotional experience, including the physiological changes identified as central by James and Lange. In Cannon's view, feelings arise from neural impulses originating in the thalamus and relayed to the cortex, which are then relayed from the thalamus to various motor systems, resulting in emotional expressions.

Cannon criticized the James–Lange position by noting that emotion may be unimpaired when the viscera are separated from the CNS in animal research and that the diffuse visceral changes associated with emotional states are also present as a result of physical exertion, fever, or exposure. This makes it clear that no clear isomorphism between physiology and emotion exists, and that the presence of an emotion cannot be inferred on the basis of physiological response alone. Cannon also suggested that the viscera are too slow to be the source of emotion and that artificial induction of visceral changes known to occur in specific emotions does not produce that emotion. Both points have since been confirmed by modern research (LeDoux, 1993; Schachter, 1966). In general, visceral feedback (while vaguely related to arousal) is only a part of a complex process and is not, by itself, sufficient for the occurrence of emotion. However, peripheral mechanisms under the control of the ANS still figure prominently in neurological theories of emotion, as we shall see in Chapter 3.

Pavlov, Watson, and Classical Conditioning of Emotions

Like many scientists of his era, the eminent Russian physiologist Ivan Pavlov was suspicious of the subjective element in the scientific analysis of emotions and so removed it from the chain of events that account for emotional behavior. In his experiments on **classical conditioning** in dogs, Pavlov discovered an important mechanism that can account for individual differences in the stimuli that elicit particular emotions. Pavlov observed that dogs salivated at the sound of a bell if the bell was rung consistently while they were being fed meat. The association of the natural stimulus (meat) with the natural response (salivation) is unlearned or, to use Pavlov's terminology, unconditioned. The systematic pairing of the bell with the presentation of meat results in a learned association between them. The proof that this connection has been formed in the brain of the dog is the capacity of the bell alone to elicit salivation. In Pavlovian terminology, the ringing bell is now a **conditioned stimulus,** and the salivation that is activated by this sound is the **conditioned response.** This provided Pavlov with an adequate explanation of the new chain of events without invoking mentalistic or anthropomorphic concepts.

The American behaviorist, John Watson, was equally suspicious of emotion and even expressed his aversion to emotionality in a popular manual on child rearing. Watson believed that human infants possess just three unlearned emotional reactions—fear, rage, and love. Each of these basic emotions can be elicited naturally by just a few unconditioned stimuli. For example, Watson believed that an unlearned fear response can be elicited by just two unconditioned stimuli, a loud noise and sudden loss of support. It is then a simple matter to explain emotional development: "These unconditioned stimuli with their relatively simple unconditioned responses are our starting points in building up those more complicated patterns we later call our emotions . . . our emotional life grows and develops like our other sets of habits" (Watson, 1920, pp. 130–131).

Watson chose to focus his research efforts on fear conditioning, a methodological decision that has been vindicated by modern researchers as possibly the best choice he could have made to investigate emotional processes. In 1918 he set out to study the conditioning of a fear response to a white rat in an 11-month-old boy named Albert. He first demonstrated that loud noises and removal of support both elicited fear responses. At the same time, Albert became accustomed to playing with a white rat over a period of several weeks. On the first trial in the conditioning experiment, Albert was presented with a basket containing the familiar white rat:

> He began to reach for the rat with his left hand. Just as his hand touched the rat the bar was struck immediately behind his head. The infant jumped violently and fell forward, burying his face in the mattress. [On the second trial later that day] just as

his right hand touched the rat the bar was again struck. Again the infant jumped violently, fell forward and began to whimper. On account of his disturbed condition no further tests were made for one week.

(WATSON, 1920)

After a week the rat was presented without sound, and Albert refused to reach out and touch it. After five more trials with the rat and loud noise paired, Albert responded to the rat by crying and crawling away from it.

What was learned by this experiment? Watson provides a straightforward interpretation based on Pavlov's principles of conditioning. First, it is clear that the form of the fear response is unlearned. The same response occurs first to the unconditioned stimulus (the loud noise) and later to the conditioned stimulus (the white rat). The child has learned to associate the two stimuli and thus the fear response can be elicited by presenting either of them. As we shall see in Chapter 2, associational learning or classical conditioning continues to play an important role in understanding how the brain attaches emotional significance to incoming sensory information.

Somehow Watson extrapolated on his research with little Albert to a general theory of child development that included advice to parents on how to apply the principles of behaviorism to child rearing. Compare his advice to that offered by Rousseau two centuries earlier and decide for yourself which best represents the "modern" view:

> There is a sensible way of treating children. Treat them as young adults. Dress them, bathe them with care and circumspection. Let your behavior always be objective and kindly firm. Never hug and kiss them, never let them sit in your lap. If you must, kiss them once on the forehead when they say good night. Shake hands with them in the morning. . . . In conclusion won't you then remember when you are tempted to pet your child that

mother love is a dangerous instrument? An instrument which may inflict a never healing wound, a wound which may make infancy unhappy, adolescence a nightmare, an instrument which may wreck your adult son or daughter's vocational future and their chances for marital happiness.

(WATSON, 1928, P. 87)

As a scientist, Watson scorned the idle speculation of the Freudians regarding the role of childhood emotional bonds in shaping the adult personality. In the clarity and purity of Pavlov's concept of classical conditioning, he embraced what he viewed as a scientific and objective methodology for understanding human behavior. Watson was also a true believer in "logical positivism," a philosophical purge of the traditional questions raised in ethical philosophy as essentially meaningless and unscientific. "Emotivism" became briefly fashionable, even dominant, at this time and dismissed inquiry into ethical questions because it consisted of nothing but expressions of emotion (Solomon, 1993).

One of the central themes of this book is that a science of human emotions will not progress very far if its sole objective is to reduce complex phenomena to simpler and simpler elements. Though analytical **reductionism** is a useful tool, scientists must also respect the different levels of analysis of complex systems and seek to integrate them hierarchically, formulating laws at all levels of the system. As applied to Watson's theory of emotion, we can assert that classical conditioning is a valid level of analysis, while understanding that it is unrealistic to deduce all the laws underlying emotional behavior from this one mechanism. Each higher level of analysis has its own laws that cannot be reduced to those of the lower level. To understand the whole child, one must take into account the various hierarchically organized levels of analysis when interpreting findings at any given level. Keeping the levels of analysis in mind will help safeguard against formulating unfounded applications in the name of science.

Figure 1.5 Sigmund Freud

(Photo from Corbis)

Freud's Psychoanalytic Theory of Affect

The **psychoanalytic theory** of emotion or affect is based upon Freud's view of human motivation as determined by biological instincts or drives and primarily unconscious. Freud's theory of instincts, which evolved throughout his career, was rooted in nineteenth-century biology and neurology. Initially, he divided the instincts into two classes, sexual instincts and ego instincts (hunger, thirst, avoiding pain and danger), and later he added death instincts that included aggressive drives. Freud believed that humans are motivated by unconscious, biological impulses that seek continuous release (the id), but are often checked by the demands of socialization (the superego). He viewed a healthy personality in terms of the success of the self (the ego) in regulating a harmonious balance between these opposing forces.

Within this tripartite model of personality, the affects were conceived as the energy component of the instinctual drive that continuously seeks some form of expression. The affect associated with any particular drive will be expressed more or less directly, depending upon the life experience of the individual. Psychoanalytic theorists often distinguish three components of affect: (1) the "charge" or energy component, (2) its discharge, and (3) the perception of its discharge, which corresponds to the subjective aspect of felt emotion. Because the expression of an affect will often be transformed or displaced from one object onto another, psychoanalytic theory emphasizes intrapsychic conflict and defense. Examples of this emphasis may be found in the Freudian concepts of repression, denial, and other defense mechanisms. In Freud's view, if the discharge of affect is blocked by the superego, its underlying energy will still seek some form of expression. Dreams, drawings, jokes, slips of the tongue (Freudian slips), free associations, and unguarded facial expressions, body postures, or tone of voice were all considered by Freud as keys to unlock and reveal the individual's suppressed affect. In unbalanced personalities, the indirect expression of repressed affect can take the form of phobias, obsessions, or compulsive rituals. Psychosomatic illnesses and other mental health problems can arise when the affective and ideational (cognitive) components of an instinctual drive are disassociated.

Like Darwin and later developmental theorists, Freud saw the emotions of guilt and shame as arising during the course of socialization. Freud associated the emotion of guilt with conflict over aggressive impulses, while viewing shame and disgust as control mechanisms for the expression of sexual impulses. In his view, guilt, shame, and disgust emerge from conscious or unconscious conflict resulting from the suppression of impulses arising from the id. "The tension between the harsh super-ego and the ego that is subjected to it, is called by us the sense of guilt; it expresses itself as a need for punishment" (Freud, 1930/1961, p. 70).

Although this synopsis of Freud's ideas concerning affect does not do justice to the full range of his thinking, a more complete account of Freud's work and the hundreds, if not thousands, of significant revisions and modifications by psychoanalytic theorists is beyond the range of this book. The intent here is to note that emotion was central to Freud's views concerning human motivation and mental health. In his theory of neurosis, Freud developed the idea that our emotions may be obscure to us because of the unconscious processes of psychological defense. The aim of psychoanalytic therapy is to uncover latent emotions and understand their significance in order to relieve the symptoms associated with their repression. Because of his emphasis on unconscious psychic structures as the primary forces of human emotion and motivation, his ideas have proven difficult to substantiate with scientific evidence. Despite this problem, Freud was undoubtedly the most influential psychological theorist of his time, and the legacy of Freud is still pervasive in psychology. Many of his original ideas concerning personality development, moral development, dreams and the unconscious, infantile sexuality, and his concept of defense mechanisms have continued to evolve, even as they did during his lifetime.

Bridge's Theory of Emotional Differentiation

Though Freud formulated the first developmental theory of human personality, the first theory that directly addressed the question of when specific emotions emerge in infancy and early childhood was formulated by Kathleen Bridges (1930, 1932), who based her theory on naturalistic observation of young children. In her classic paper, Bridges argued that emotions differentiate from a single state of general excitement to excitement and distress at 1 month, with fear, disgust, and anger emerging from general distress at about 6 months. According to Bridges, "The genetic theory of emotions is thus that excitement, the undifferentiated emotion present at birth, becomes differentiated and associated with certain situations and certain motor responses to form the separate emotions of later life. This process of differentiation and integration takes place gradually, so that at different age levels different emotions are distinguishable" (Bridges, 1930, p. 517).

Bridges used the term *genetic,* as most developmental psychologists did in her day, as synonymous with *developmental.* She also invoked the leading theory of her time, namely Watson's idea that emotions arise from learned associations. Finally, she applied basic developmental concepts such as **differentiation** and **integration.** Early developmental psychologists based much of their thinking on principles borrowed from biology that described the fundamental properties of living systems that account for their growth and development. Because the differentiation of global structures into specific structures is a common process in biology, it is reasonable to consider this possibility as the basis for the gradual unfolding of the human emotions. Bridges listed a total of 10 distinct emotions presumed to derive from this process by the age of 18 months, as shown in Figure 1.6.

Modern proponents of a developmental model of emotions as products of a process of differentiation include Emde, Gaensbauer, and Harmon (1976), Lewis (1993), and Sroufe (1979, 1996). Differentiation theorists differ in terms of the importance they accord to biological versus social factors, though most concede that emotions differentiate as a function of some combination and interaction among maturation, socialization, and cognitive development. Much consensus exists regarding which emotions may be observed during infancy, although considerable debate remains concerning the factors that contribute to this orderly unfolding of the emotions.

The simplest developmental model posits a maturational clock regulating the timing and rate of the differentiation of specific emotions according to a physiological timetable. Early developmental theories, such as that formulated by Bridges, did not specify what developmental processes were implicated, nor did they describe changes in any given emotion system over time

(Sroufe, 1979). As we shall see in Chapter 3, more recent developmental theories have dealt more extensively with these issues.

Lorenz, Harlow, and Bowlby:
The Origin of Emotional Bonds

Konrad Lorenz is best known for his work on imprinting in the greylag geese and, along with Tinbergen and von Frisch, won the 1973 Nobel prize for establishing the foundations of **ethology,** the branch of biology that concerns animal behavior. In 1935 Lorenz published "Der Kumpan in der Umwelt des Vogels" or "The Companion in the Bird's World." In this seminal paper, Lorenz introduces the new science of ethology, articulates its basic concepts and methods, and provides a comprehensive treatment of the different types of relationships systematically observed among birds. These relationships are organized from the bird's point of view, and include the parental companion, the infant companion, the sexual companion, the social companion, and siblings. According to Lorenz, these relationships are essential for survival and reproduction, and as a result they are highly stereotyped. The bird's individual experience plays a key role in the emergence of these relationships, but there are important elements of each of them that are not learned. As Lorenz later asserted in response to his American critics, to say that they are innate is about as much of an exaggeration as to say that the Eiffel Tower is made of metal.

Some years later, Harry Harlow began his classic book entitled "Learning to Love" with a similar listing, not of avian companions, but of five basic primate relationship types. Harlow's relationship or affectional systems are made up of (1) maternal love (the love of the mother for her child); (2) infant love (the love of the infant for the mother); (3) peer, or age-mate, love; (4) heterosexual love; and (5) paternal love. Harlow (1971) adds:

> Our description of five separate and discrete love systems is not to imply that each system is physically and temporally

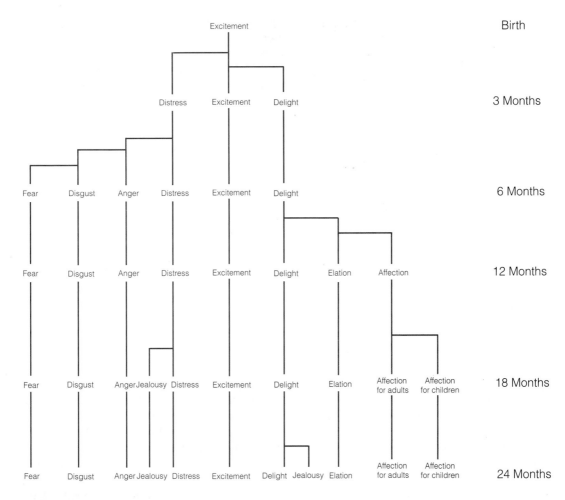

Figure 1.6 An early model of emotional development. The first model outlining the emergence of specific emotions in infancy was formulated by Bridges in 1932. Basing her theory on observation of infant emotional expression, she argued that human emotions were not present at birth but gradually differentiated from basic states of excitement and distress. (See photo illustrating dendritic branching in nature.)

Source: Bridges, 1932. Used by permission of the Society for Research in Child Development (SRCD).

(Photo by LaFreniere)

separate. Actually, there is always an overlap . . . affectional motives are continuous . . . each love system prepares the individual for the one that follows, and the failure of any system to develop normally deprives him of the proper

Figure 1.7 Lorenz and goslings

(Photo by Nina Leen, © Time Warner, Inc.)

foundation for subsequent increasingly complex affectional adjustments. (p. 4)

Both the Lorenzian view of the relationship systems that characterize the social ecology of birds and the primate affectional systems formulated by Harlow played a pivotal role in the theoretical development of the British attachment theorist John Bowlby. Theoretically, in both early psychoanalytic and behaviorist approaches, attachment was viewed as a secondary drive, derived from primary drives like hunger. Prior to Bowlby, few scientists questioned the idea that the infant became attached to the mother because she supplied food. Bowlby was skeptical of this view and instead considered the attachment process to be primary, but he had little scientific support for his intuition. He found this support outside psychology in the emerging discipline of ethology. From Lorenz, Bowlby found a model for the formation of the parent–offspring bond that did not depend upon associating the mother with food. The **imprinting** of chicks to the maternal figure during a critical period in early infancy could not be interpreted as association of the mother with a food source, because the chicks were born with the innate ability to forage for themselves, and at no point in their development after birth did they rely on the mother as a source

of food. Rather, the behavioral system underlying the formation of the mother–offspring bond evolved in goslings through natural selection in order to increase the viability of the defenseless juvenile.

Of course, imprinting in greylag geese is only analogous to the formation of attachment bonds in primates. They are not at all the same mechanism, and the two systems are not derived from a common ancestor. But if one species evolved a primary mechanism for establishing the crucial bond with the parent that did not derive from learned associations, was it possible that other species did so as well? Bowlby turned to Harlow's research for the answer to this question. Using an ingenious paradigm involving surrogate "mothers," Harlow was the first to test the notion that attachment to the monkey mother forms as a result of feeding (Harlow & Harlow, 1966; Harlow & Zimmerman, 1959). It is important to notice that despite the fact that the idea of attachment as a secondary drive based on learned associations was never directly tested, it was nevertheless installed as dogma in psychology over a half century ago, and defended until quite recently. One elegant experimental demonstration proved to be its undoing. Harlow separated infant monkeys from their mothers at birth, then reared them with two surrogate mothers, one

Figure 1.8 Harlow's cloth surrogate monkey mother

(Photo from Harlow Primate Lab, University of Wisconsin)

made of stiff wire equipped with a bottle for feeding, the other covered with soft terry cloth, but without the bottle. If an infant monkey became attached by associating the mother with food, we would expect to see attachment behaviors exhibited toward the wire surrogate with the bottle. Instead the infant monkeys all showed a clear preference for the soft, cuddly surrogate without the bottle, spending most of their time (when not feeding) clinging to it and leaping into its "lap" when frightened or distressed.

Fortunately for emotion researchers today, Bowlby was less influenced by the dominant ideas of his era and more persuaded by the elegant experimentation and observation of Lorenz and Harlow in formulating his seminal theory of attachment. The animal models of relationship systems supplied the theoretical basis for his central hypotheses: that infant–mother attachment is basic to humans as an evolved system, not dependent upon learned associations for its

appearance, and is vital to survival and reproduction. The attachment relationship is viewed as central to human adaptation, not only because it protects the offspring during infancy, but also because it provides an internal working model for the construction of other vital relationships throughout development. As Harlow clearly perceived, conceptualizing the variety of relationship or affectional systems that comprise our primate heritage does not imply that they are somehow functionally distinct. Indeed, the evolution of the brain would be neither parsimonious nor efficient if it were unable to draw upon the same basic emotional/behavioral systems for the various types of relationships that are vital to our survival and reproduction. This cycle of affective continuity in interpersonal relations from infancy to parenthood will be elaborated in subsequent chapters.

Tomkin's Affect Theory

Though he worked in relative obscurity for most of his career, the seminal writings of Silvan Tomkins can be viewed from our contemporary vantage point as a key influence on the current renaissance of emotion in psychology. The son of Russian Jewish immigrants, Tomkins majored in playwriting as an undergraduate, began graduate school in psychology in 1930, but soon abandoned academic psychology for philosophy. By 1940, Tomkins renewed his interest in psychology at Harvard under the tutelage of the eminent personality theorist Henry Murray, but he remained a philosopher at heart (Brewster Smith, 1995).

During the 1950s and 1960s, Tomkins developed the core of ideas on affect theory in virtual isolation from mainstream psychology, which was dominated by behaviorism and was just beginning to reentertain the notion that cognition might have an important influence on human behavior. If affect was recognized at all, it was only outside academic psychology within the psychoanalytic tradition. However, despite the richness of insight contained in this tradition regarding conflict-defense, anxiety, and aggression, the theoretical linkage of affect with drive led to a theoretical cul-de-sac when Freudian drive theory was abandoned as scientifically untenable.

A way out of this impasse was formulated by Tomkins, who essentially revived Darwin's contention that affect and emotions are central to human motivation and adaptation. In contrast to drives, an emotion cannot be reliably elicited by any single stimulus, but is a more flexible, motivational system dependent on the evaluation of the significance of the stimulus for the individual. During an era in which academic psychology was dominated by Skinner and clinical psychology by Freud, Tomkin's script theory explicitly rejected the S-R (stimulus–response) view of radical behaviorism and the energy metaphors of Freud's drive theory. Rather than attempting to formulate a synthesis of the two dominant theories, as Dollard and Miller (1950) did, Tomkins abandoned both:

> In *Affect, Imagery, Consciousness* (Tomkins, 1962, 1963), I argued that American psychology had lost both its heart and its mind from a fear of methodological impurity, from excessive reliance on primary drives as motivators, and from attention to behavior rather than the complex transformations that make behavior possible. Against psychoanalysis and behaviorism, I argued for the centrality of consciousness rather than the unconscious, and rather than behavior.
>
> (TOMKINS, 1981/1995, P. 306)

Building upon Darwin's description of the role of facial and bodily expressions in relation to the evolved, fundamental, discrete human emotions, Tomkins proposed that specific positive and negative affects amplify any response that they may recruit and prompt, whether cognitive or motoric. Facial expression was seen by Darwin as an important amplifier of emotion, not just a means of social communication. According to Darwin, "the free expression by outward sign of an emotion intensifies it" (Darwin, 1872/1965, p. 365). In their article entitled "What and Where Are the Primary Affects? Some Evidence for a Theory,"

Tomkins and McCarter (1964) developed this idea far beyond Darwin's initial conjecture. Ekman summarizes the main theoretical points:

1. The face is central and has priority over visceral changes because of its speed, visibility, and precision.

2. The face informs the self, not just others. Feedback of the facial response *is* the experience of affect.

3. Emotion is guided by innate inherited programs.

4. We learn the language of the face partly through correspondence between what a face looks like and what it feels like.

5. Every face has a predominant expression which shines through poses and spontaneous expressions.

6. Individual differences in the interpretation of facial expression reflect the personality of the perceiver, which resulted in the idea of examining affect sensitivity contours.

7. Particular emotions are commonly confused because of shared neurophysiology, shared situational contexts, response overlap, and the likelihood of occurring together. (1995, p. 210)

Besides his influence on Paul Ekman's research on facial expressions of affect, Tomkins also exerted an influence on Carrol Izard's research on facial expression of affect. Tomkins was an astute observer of affective expression, and like Darwin before him, and Ekman and Izard after him, he made extensive use of photographs of facial displays of affect to investigate issues related to the cross-cultural universality of facial expression and recognition of expressions by different observers.

SUMMARY

Although emotion research has come of age only recently, the topic of emotion has had a long history in philosophy, biology, and the social sciences. From at least the time of the early Greeks, Western philosophers conceptualized human experience in terms of the dualities of mind and body, reason and passion, cognition and emotion. Of all the Greek philosophers, Aristotle developed the most advanced theory of emotion. Though he introduced the idea that emotions were an essential aspect of human nature, he retained the earlier view that emotions must be dominated by reason in order to be adaptive. Aristotle identified the study of emotion with the tradition of ethical philosophy where it remained until Descartes and Darwin linked the study of emotions with natural philosophy.

Roman philosophers, such as the Stoics, carried forward some of Aristotle's ideas, but returned to an earlier view that regarded the emotions as a disruptive force, a source of misery and error. Enlightenment philosophers like Descartes and Hume continued this essential debate into the eighteenth century when reason began to be questioned as the sole basis for a moral society. In reaction against the domination of reason, Rousseau initiated the Romantic movement, which embraced the expression of emotion in literature, music, and the arts.

By the nineteenth century, psychology emerged as the science of the mind—including cognition, motivation, and emotion—and inherited the philosophical debates initiated by the Greeks. Early psychologists were also profoundly influenced by Darwin's theory that viewed human emotions as products of natural selection that serve the adaptive functions of regulating the body's response to different challenges and communicating with others. However, the study of the adaptive functions of emotion did not become the focus of a large amount of research until much later. Instead, psychologists studied emotion as an internal state and debated whether emotions originated in the mind or the body. This debate eventually led to the emergence of a neuroscientific tradition concerned with how the brain initiates and organizes emotion physiology and subjective experience.

With the emergence of radical behaviorism in the early twentieth century, psychologists turned their attention to the study of objective stimuli and behavioral responses, relegating emotion, along with cognition, to a "black box" of phenomena unsuitable for scientific inquiry. If emotions were discussed at all, they were reduced to nothing more than learned associations or conditioned responses. Outside academic psychology, this reductionistic view was countered by the psychoanalytic tradition initiated by Freud that continued to view emotions as central to human functioning, and elaborated influential concepts concerning personality development, moral development, dreams and the unconscious, infantile sexuality, and defense mechanisms. However, Freud's identification of emotion with drives and his focus on the unconscious aspects of human experience did not foster a climate for empirical research on emotions.

A return to empirical investigations of emotions within psychology was initiated by developmental psychologists like Bridges who were interested in how different emotions emerged during infancy and childhood, and by psychoanalytically inspired researchers like Spitz who began to observe the emotional behavior of children with the goal of understanding how and why individuals differ in their emotional makeup. By the mid-twentieth century, after decades of relative neglect, psychological theorists such as Tomkins and Bowlby revisited the biological models of Darwin, Lorenz, and Harlow as a source of inspiration for their theories, each casting a central role for emotions in the process of human adaptation. This focus eventually created the conditions for a renaissance within psychology for the study of emotion as a central topic.

FURTHER READING

Aristotle. (1941). *The basic works of Aristotle* (R. McKeon, Ed.; J. I. Beare, Trans.). New York: Random House.

Aristotle's works contain some surprisingly modern insights on emotion, and his theory of emotion is more comprehensive than many current theories.

Darwin, C. R. (1872/1965). *The expression of emotions in man and animals.* Chicago: University of Chicago Press.

This is the most enduring and influential book ever written about emotions and their expression, and it is still required reading for serious students of emotion.

Solomon, R. C. (1993). The philosophy of emotions. In M. Lewis & J. Haviland (Eds.), *The handbook of emotions* (pp. 3–15). New York: Guilford.

This essay is an excellent and concise historical treatment of the topic of emotion within philosophy.

2

Evolutionary Perspectives

Evolutionary Theory

Darwin and Natural Selection
Mendel and the Laws of Inheritance
The Synthetic Theory of Evolution

Ethological Perspectives

Classic Period: Lorenz and Tinbergen
Evolution of Primate Facial Expressions
Conceptual Advances
Human Ethology

It is strange how little attention the philosophy of science has paid to the overwhelming importance of concepts. For this reason, it is not yet possible to describe in detail the processes of discovery and the maturation of concepts. This much is evident, however, that the major contribution of the leaders of biological thought has been the development and refinement of concepts and occasionally the elimination of erroneous ones. Evolutionary biology owes a remarkably large portion of its concepts to Charles Darwin, and ethology to Konrad Lorenz.

ERNST MAYR (1982)

This chapter and Chapter 3 are intended to provide students of the social sciences with an introduction to the major concepts of the biological sciences as applied to the problem of emotion. In this chapter, we begin our discussion with key concepts from evolutionary biology and ethology, which may be thought of as the biological sciences that deal primarily with the whole organism in relation to its environment. Within the framework provided by evolutionary theory, ethologists describe observable components of emotional responses and seek to understand the evolution of expressive behavior and its functional significance. A functionalist approach to emotion has recently emerged as the dominant paradigm within psychology, and it is useful to understand where this approach originated. Because of the scope and diversity of the biological sciences presented in these two chapters, only a general introduction with specific illustrations of each branch may be presented, since they differ widely in their content, concepts, and methods. However, despite these differences, they are unified by the synthetic theory of evolution, which is the necessary and logical starting point for our review.

EVOLUTIONARY THEORY

The modern theory of evolution owes its existence to two remarkable nineteenth-century scientists, Charles Darwin and Gregor Mendel. It is widely recognized as one of the greatest accomplishments of the human mind with implications that have yet to be fully grasped. Its relation to the many diverse fields of biology has been summed up quite succinctly by Dobzhansky (1973): "Nothing in biology makes sense except in the light of evolutionary theory."

Darwin and Natural Selection

Darwin's theory embraces a vision of immense grandeur, but it can also be reduced to relatively few explanatory principles. The main goal that Darwin set for himself while still an intrepid naturalist on a five-year voyage aboard the H.M.S. Beagle was to account for the marvelous adaptive fit between species and their environments and to explain the origins of such diverse forms of life that seem to fill all the habitats on earth. His extraordinary powers of observation and deduction resulted in one of the most influential scientific works ever produced, *On the Origin of Species* (1859). In essence this work can be abstracted to the principles of variation, selection, and retention, and can be summarized in just five points:

1. The starting point for the theory was derived from Malthus's essay (1798/1826) on human population. It begins with the rather common observation that despite the fact that offspring in any generation outnumber parents, the total number of individuals in a species remains somewhat stable across generations. One may thus deduce that a certain percentage of offspring die and/or never reproduce.

2. Individuals within any species vary in terms of their morphology, physiology, and behavior.

3. Certain variants are more likely to survive and leave more offspring than others as a function of the demand characteristics of the environment that is inhabited. This is Darwin's principle of **natural selection.**

4. Offspring somehow inherit the characteristics of their parents. Certain characteristics will be retained more often than others, and natural

Figure 2.1 Charles Darwin

(Photo from Corbis)

spoke first and preached "for full half an hour with inimitable spirit, emptiness, and unfairness." The Bishop then concluded his remarks:

> In a light, scoffing tone, florid and fluent, he assured us there was nothing in the idea of evolution; rock-pigeons were what rock-pigeons had always been. Then turning to his antagonist with a smiling insolence, he begged to know, was it through his grandfather or his grandmother that he claimed his descent from a monkey?
>
> Huxley slowly and deliberately arose. A slight, tall figure, stern and pale, very quiet, very grave, he stood before us and spoke those tremendous words—words which no one seems sure of now, nor, I think, could remember just after they were spoken, for their meaning took away our breath, though it left us in no doubt as to what it was. He was not ashamed to have a monkey for his ancestor; but he would be ashamed to be connected with a man who used great gifts to obscure the truth. No one doubted his meaning and the effect was tremendous. One lady fainted and had to be carried out; I, for one, jumped out of my seat.

(HUXLEY, 1898, PP. 433–434)

Debates such as this remain, though not among scientists. After 140 years and many challenges, Darwin's theory of evolution by natural selection has revolutionized our thinking about the natural world and the place of humans in it. It has restructured and energized the biological and behavioral sciences, and continues to do so as we enter a new millennium. Its impact on psychology in particular has never been stronger than it is today.

Mendel and the Laws of Inheritance

As originally proposed in 1859, Darwin's theory had one important weakness. Though Darwin could observe individual variation in species-typical characteristics, he had no explanatory mechanism to account for the transmission of

selection ensures retention of those characteristics that best fit the environment.

5. Throughout the history of life on earth, environmental conditions have changed, different species have moved into new environments, and species have gradually changed to fit the new conditions. All life forms are thus related and can be traced through a series of common ancestors back to the origin of life.

Although Darwin formulated this solution to the problem of the adaptive design and origin of species relatively early in his career, he was reluctant to publish his ideas knowing that they would create quite a stir. And they did. Emblematic of the contentious nature of their reception is a famous debate that took place a few months after the publication of *On the Origin of Species*. On the side of orthodoxy in religion and science was Bishop Samuel Wilberforce, while Thomas Henry Huxley represented Darwin and the new scientific order. As retold in 1898, the Bishop these characteristics from one generation to the next. If natural selection was the key to determining which traits were adaptive in a given environment, how were these traits retained in the species? Because the complex characteristics that interested Darwin appeared to blend in the offspring, producing an intermediate form, he speculated that the hereditary material was some fluidlike substance that could be blended in various proportions. Such was the practical knowledge of naturalists in his era who, after all, had been successfully breeding traits in dogs and other domestic species for many years. Although this solution was reasonable and seemed to fit the facts, it was nevertheless incorrect. The problem of retention in Darwin's model was to be remedied by simple experiments of growing peas in the garden of an Austrian monk.

Key breakthroughs in science are often made when scientists choose to tackle simpler problems first, and there is no better example of this principle of the "art of the soluble" than the research of the Austrian monk Gregor Mendel. Mendel chose to work with simpler organisms and focused his research on characteristics that were expressed as simple dichotomies in both parent and offspring. Unlike crossbreeding in dogs, crossbreeding different pea plants produced offspring that were either tall or short, yellow or green, with no intermediate forms. Working with such simple structures allowed Mendel to use straightforward quantitative methods to test his ideas about heredity.

After a series of ingenious breeding experiments, Mendel was able to deduce a more parsimonious account of the origin of individual characteristics and their transmission to the next generation. According to this view, each individual's characteristics, or **phenotype,** result from the unique combination of genes that are contributed by both parents, referred to as the **genotype.** Mendel's key observation was that crossbreeding plants of dissimilar genotypes resulted in first-generation offspring of only one type, referred to as **dominant.** However, the next generation of crossbreeding resulted in 75 percent tall plants (the dominant form) and 25 percent short plants (the **recessive** form). From this experiment, Mendel correctly deduced that the dominant gene, when paired with itself or with the recessive gene, will yield the dominant phenotype. Only the recessive gene paired with itself (a 25 percent probability) will yield the recessive phenotype. Simple **experimentation** enabled Mendel to discover the laws of inheritance that Darwin had postulated as necessary but was unable to find through **naturalistic observation.** This illustrates an important methodological point that remains just as true today: the combination of fieldwork and laboratory experimentation can be extremely effective in generating and testing scientific hypotheses.

Despite the fact that no scientist in Mendel's era had ever seen a **gene,** the existence of genes could be deduced from careful observation and systematic experimentation. In a sense, genes are a scientific construct. They can be thought of as indivisible units of heredity and are more formally defined as a segment of **DNA** that contains the code for constructing one specific type of protein molecule. Genes accomplish this through replication of one strand of the DNA as RNA, as shown in Figure 2.2. Genes are replicated in each parent and recombined in infinite variety in each offspring, except in identical twins who inherit the exact same genotype from their parents. As will be seen in Chapter 6 when we introduce the modern science of behavioral genetics, this fact makes twin research critical to a scientific understanding of heritability in humans. For the present, it is sufficient to understand that genes are responsible for building proteins, which in turn structure the organism's physiology. As shown in Figure 2.3, the route by which genes influence behavior is indirect and always influenced by interaction with the organism's internal and external environment.

The Synthetic Theory of Evolution

Though Mendel was a contemporary of Darwin, they were unaware of each other's

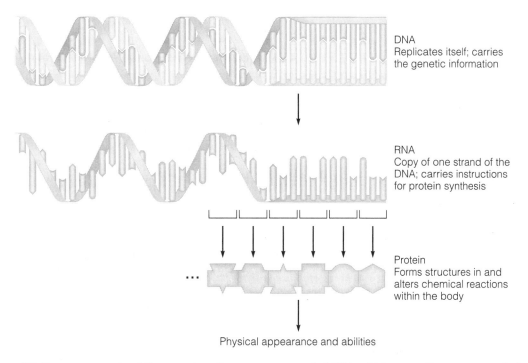

Figure 2.2 How genes construct the organism. Genes are composed of DNA, which can replicate one strand of itself, called RNA, which contains instructions for synthesizing protein. Proteins represent fundamental building blocks of physical structures of the body and are capable of altering the body's chemistry to aid in processes like digestion.

Source: Kalat (1999, p. 640). Reprinted with permission of Wadsworth Publishing, a division of Thomson Learning.

work. Without an Internet or other means of connection, Mendel's ideas lay dormant in the scientific world until they were rediscovered in the early twentieth century. Initially, they were put forward in opposition to Darwin's theory, rather than as a complement to it. The modern synthesis arose in the 1930s as a result of the efforts of Wright, Fisher, and Haldane, who proposed a workable integration of Darwin's theory of evolution with Mendelian genetics. This integration posits that heritable traits are determined by genes and that natural selection and sexual selection, rather than mutation, are the principal means of evolution. Key debates following this important advance have focused on the definition of a species (Mayr, 1942), determining the level or unit of selection (that is, the gene,

organism, or group) (Dawkins, 1976; Hamilton, 1964; Williams, 1966), and conceptualizing evolution as a gradual, continual process or one that is dominated by long periods of equilibrium punctuated with periods of rapid change (Eldredge & Gould, 1972).

Most textbooks depict evolution as a branching tree, suggesting an ever-increasing diversity of life forms. But this view of evolution is clearly wrong. Indeed, it appears that five major phases of extinction have struck the planet in the past 500 million years, and we have currently entered a sixth phase with estimates of approximately 27,000 species lost each year in the rain forests alone (Wilson, 1992). Thus, a branching tree must be redrawn to reflect both "diversification and decimation" (Gould, 1989). The models in

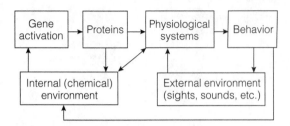

Figure 2.3 How genes influence behavior. The proteins produced by genes directly affect physiological systems in the organism, which in turn influence behavior. All aspects of this process are open to inputs from the internal or external environment as indicated by the arrows.

Source: Adapted from *Psychology* by Gray. © 1999 by Worth Publishers.

Figure 2.4a illustrate different assumptions about the evolutionary process. Model a is drawn without this assumption of extinctions and reflects diversification only, whereas models b, c, and d each depict extinction as lines that end abruptly without reaching the end point of growth (representing currently living species). As Hodos and Campbell (1969) pointed out, model a correctly depicts the order in which different groups arose during the course of evolution, but it should indicate clearly that no currently living species is ancestral to any other. Finally, the gradually sloping branches in models b and c reflect evolution as a process of gradual change. In contrast, model d, with branches at sharp right angles to the trunk, depicts the process as long stable eras punctuated with abrupt periods of change, or *punctuated equilibrium* (Eldredge & Gould, 1972). Whatever the form of the model, all living organisms can be traced back to one another, and together they represent less than 1 percent of all the species that have ever evolved. Competing ideas about the nature of the evolutionary process, and the level at which selection occurs (to be discussed later in this chapter), are central to the process of scientific progress. As with scientific theories in general, the synthetic theory of evolution continues to be refined and reexamined in light of new evidence.

ETHOLOGICAL PERSPECTIVES

Classic Period: Lorenz and Tinbergen

Historically, the term *ethology* has been widely employed since the 1930s in relation to the naturalistic observation and description of animal behavior. Although it is clear that an ethological approach owes much to Darwin and the subsequent work of zoologists like Heinroth, Whitman, and Craig around the turn of the century, it was not until the publications of Lorenz and Tinbergen (Lorenz, 1935, 1941; Lorenz & Tinbergen, 1938; Tinbergen, 1951) that ethology emerged as a systematic and coherent discipline. In his early publications, Lorenz focused on species-typical behaviors that could be used for taxonomic purposes, much like morphological characteristics, to compare different species and trace ancestral relationships (Eibl-Eibesfeldt, 1997). A fundamental distinction in the comparative analysis of behavior must be made between a similarity between species that can be traced to a common origin (**homology**), and one that has been produced through independent but convergent lines of evolution (**analogy**). Analogous features often appear to be similar in their function, but differ in terms of underlying mechanism. Both birds and bats fly, but the similarities end there, since bats, as mammals, belong to a different taxonomic group altogether. Although both animals have wings that sustain intricate patterns of flight, their wings differ markedly in the neural and muscular mechanisms responsible for flying. In contrast, the wings and flight patterns of different species of bats are homologous. Homologous features may sometimes differ in outward appearance and even function, but they always retain underlying similarities in the details of their construction owing to a common genetic foundation, even when later evolution creates substantial divergences. As we shall see, the line of inquiry initiated by Darwin into the homologous nature of human facial expressions was to become a central battle ground between those who viewed humans as purely cultural beings and

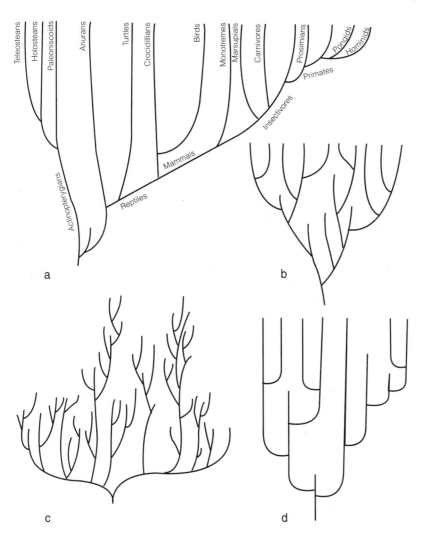

Figure 2.4a Different types of branching trees depicting evolution

Source: Hodos and Campbell (1969). © 1969 The American Psychological Association. Used by permission of Hodos.

those who viewed human behavior in comparative perspective. Unlike Darwin, the classical ethologists focused exclusively on simpler organisms for the first few decades of the evolution of their discipline.

By 1935, Lorenz was able to formulate the basic concepts of ethology, including the idea of an innate template by which specific behaviors (**fixed action patterns**) are released by triggers (**sign stimuli**). A classic example of such a lock-key mechanism is the release of aggressive behaviors involved in territorial defense in the male

stickleback (a small fish common to Europe) caused by the red underbelly of other male sticklebacks (Tinbergen, 1951).

Naturalistic observation of sticklebacks during the breeding season revealed that males build a nest and defend it from encroachment by other male sticklebacks, relentlessly attacking them if they approach too close to the nest. In his classic experiments, Tinbergen tested the hypothesis that male aggression was released by the bright-red coloration of the male's underbelly (which is gray outside the breeding season). He presented

various models to male sticklebacks who were defending their nest. Some of the models closely resembled a male stickleback in size and shape, but without red coloration, while other models did not look anything like a stickleback, but did have a red belly. These experiments clearly demonstrated that males only attacked the models with a red underbelly. Later research showed that this aggression was context-specific, and could not be elicited in males outside their home territory.

Several important points can be drawn from this classic example of ethological research. First, it illustrates that an ethological approach is not synonymous with naturalistic observation. Tinbergen's hypotheses were generated as a result of careful fieldwork guided by evolutionary theory, and were subsequently tested in experiments. Rather than being identified with a particular method, the discipline of ethology is more appropriately defined according to its questions. Tinbergen provides a succinct account of an ethological orientation to the study of behavior in his fourfold scheme of basic questions concerning (1) evolution, (2) development, (3) causa-

tion, and (4) function (see Table 2.1). Within this framework, an ethologist seeks to understand behavior from a broad perspective that combines the concerns of the developmental psychologist (How does a particular behavior develop? What causes it to occur?) with those of the zoologist (How did a particular behavior evolve? What are its adaptive functions?). In the example of stickleback territorial defense, the proximate cause of male aggression is the sign stimulus (the intruding male's red underbelly during breeding). This type of territorial aggression is unique to males, and occurs only when they are in their home territory and another male approaches. In other words, the aggressive response has evolved in the male of the species as a conditional strategy and shows much greater flexibility than a simple reflex. Its adaptive function is to protect the male's reproductive investment and ensure the survival of his offspring.

Tinbergen's four questions provide a deceptively simple framework for analyzing the behavior of any species, but maintaining a balanced concern for these different questions is not easy. According to Lorenz (1978):

Table 2.1 Tinbergen's Four Questions

	Proximate	Ultimate
How	Development	Evolution
Why	Causation	Function

Many students of animal behavior have become so fascinated with its directedness, with the question "What for?" or "Toward what end?," that they have quite forgotten to ask about its causal explanation. Yet the great question . . . "How?" [is] quite as fascinating as the question "What for?"—only [it] fascinate[s] a different kind of scientist. If wonder at the directedness of life is typical of the field student of nature, the quest for understanding of causation is typical of the laboratory worker. It is a regrettable symptom of the limitations inherent to the human mind that very few scientists are able to keep both questions in mind simultaneously. (p. 122)

An important philosophical foundation of classic ethology is the notion of **critical realism** (Eibl-Eibesfeldt, 1989; Lorenz, 1973/1977; Popper, 1965), which assumes that species-typical adaptations mirror external reality. As an epistemological system, the idea of critical realism builds upon Kant's transcendental idealism in the following manner. Kant understood that an organism's knowledge of the external world is determined not so much by the features of external reality, but by its perceptual faculties. But he did not see how the organism's perceptual faculties were related to these external features. Evolutionary scientists were able to make this important leap forward by realizing that the sensory/perception systems and brains of organisms evolved to respond to, or adapt to, those features of external reality that were critically involved in the organism's survival and reproduction. The philosophical view of critical realism is expressed by Karl Popper in *The Logic of Scientific*

Discovery (1945/1962): "The thing-in-itself is unknowable: we can only know its appearances, which are to be understood (as pointed out by Kant) as resulting from the thing-in-itself and from our own perceiving apparatus. Thus appearances result from a kind of interaction between the things-in-themselves and ourselves" (cited from Lorenz, 1973, p. 18).

Phylogenetic adaptations, such as a finch's beak or the human brain, are "shaped" over time by environmental demands and opportunities. Likewise behavioral adaptations represent the accumulation of information about features of the environment that have at some time been critical in enhancing survival and reproductive success. Lorenz viewed the innate structures of thought, language, and emotional expression in humans to be excellent examples of phylogenetic adaptations, and recent neurobiological studies support this view by identifying specific structures in the human brain that map onto these important functions. Darwin supplied two major mechanisms by which such evolution occurs: natural selection and sexual selection. The behavior patterns that have proven to be successful in terms of inclusive fitness become codified genetically, and this "information" is transmitted to future generations. In the realm of emotion, organismic responses that have been shaped by critical environmental stimuli include the neurological, physiological, motivational, and behavioral components of the emotion system. Ultimately, selection can operate only on the behavioral consequences of the system for the individual organism. For this reason, ethologists have been primarily interested in the functional significance of expressive behavior in a social context rather than the investigation of unobservable psychological states (Charlesworth, 1982).

During its classic period, European ethology had little in common with the work of early American comparative psychologists. European ethologists were interested in observing the spontaneous behaviors of diverse species, each in their natural habitats, in order to pose questions about evolution and function. In contrast, American psychologists studied only a few species, such as rats and pigeons, under a few experimental conditions, such as mazes and Skinner boxes, in order to understand animal learning. However, it was not long before these two groups of scientists, each studying animal behavior, began to intersect.

One of the earliest examples of research in the interface between these disciplines can be found in the pioneering work of Karl Lashley (1930, 1951). After early training with Watson, Lashley followed up Watson's analysis of the stimulus–response learning of various animals in order to understand the contribution of the organism's inherited neural systems to its behavior. After years of experimentation, he concluded that learning operates by modifying species-typical neural programs, rather than by erecting complex chains of conditioned reflexes. By the 1960s and 1970s, comparative psychologists such as Harlow, Mason, and others began exploring a wider range of complex behaviors, such as attachment, exploratory behavior, and play, in various species of primates, in order to pose questions about evolution and function, as well as questions concerning the role of learning and biological preparedness in these behaviors. In a recent address, Mason (1997) advocated the description of spontaneous behavior as critical to comparative psychology, illustrating his case with examples drawn from the study of emotional attachments in nonhuman primates. The orientation advocated by Mason no longer resembles the orientation of animal psychology of the 1950s and is only faintly distinguishable from the ethological approach advocated by Lorenz and Tinbergen.

In later chapters of this book, we will explore a number of human behavioral systems involving emotions that ethologists view in comparative perspective. These include physical features and behaviors that act as releasing mechanisms and ultimately serve the individual's adaptation. An example of a physical feature that functions in this manner is the infant's appealing **kindchenschema** (Lorenz, 1943). Lorenz used this term (literally baby-schema) to refer to the relatively large head, large eyes, and soft, rounded features of the typical infant's face, which are thought to elicit an emotionally based caregiving response from the adult. As Gould (1980) pointed out, Walt Disney grasped this principle intuitively in the creation of his endearing cartoon characters. The artistic evolution of Mickey Mouse over a period of 50 years reveals a progressive adoption of the typical kindchenschema features. The size of Mickey's head and eyes increased dramatically over this span, and the contours of the body became soft and cuddly (Gould, 1980). This gradual progression indicates a kind of market selection toward a more visually appealing character, mimicking the natural selection that shaped the visual appearance of infants of a wide range of species. See Figure 2.5 for an example of kindchenschema in primates.

Of course, the key insight of ethology is to extend the operation of natural selection beyond physical features to behavior. According to Lorenz (1978/1981), the discovery that behavior patterns are homologous is the point from which ethology marks its origin. A good example of an homologous expressive behavior that has been selected for in human infants is smiling. As a congenitally organized behavior, the smile requires no prior learning in its production and functions to elicit caregiving immediately after birth, before the expression is fully integrated into an emotion system. Thus, from an ethological point of view, the child is not born a **tabula rasa,** or blank slate, upon which the environment acts. Rather, the child is capable of actively engaging the environment from birth, with inborn predispositions, preferences, and reflexes that have been shaped by natural selection to provide an adaptive advantage in the **environment of evolutionary adaptedness** (EEA).

One means to dramatically illustrate the inborn nature of the infant's expressive repertoire is to observe the facial expressions of children born deaf and blind. Such children exhibit the full range of facial expressions, though the expressions may be less refined than those of sighted children (Eibl-Eibesfeldt, 1973). They smile when their mother caresses them, laugh excitedly

Figure 2.5 Cuddly features of a rhesus infant. The term *kindchenschema* was coined by Lorenz to refer to the relatively large head, large eyes, and soft, rounded features of the typical infant's face, which are thought to elicit an emotionally based caregiving response from the adult.

(Photo by Frans de Waal, 1996)

during stimulating play, cry when hurt, and frown and clench their teeth when angered. These expressive behaviors exhibited by deaf-and-blind children are the same as those that have been shown to be universal across cultures. Many other sources of data that support this general view of the nature of infancy will be presented in detail in Chapter 5.

Evolution of Primate Facial Expressions

Little is known about the genetic basis of primate facial displays, though careful study of the pat-

terns of variation between species and among members of the same species strongly suggests a genetic basis, in that a peculiar variation from a common general form may be found in just one species, but is present in all of its adult members (Chevalier-Skolnikoff, 1973). Ethologists have long assumed that closely related species have more similar patterns of facial expressions than more distantly related species. Indeed, the similarities and differences in the expressive displays of different species, breeds, phyla, and classes noted by Whitman and Heinroth gave rise to the idea that behavioral patterns can be used as reliably as morphological features to indicate genetic relatedness (Lorenz, 1973).

One of Darwin's most enduring contributions to the study of facial expressions was his exacting description of the precise movements that contribute to the overall expression and his emphasis on the underlying muscular anatomy of the expression. Over a century later, Darwin's work is still considered to be the most encompassing on the subject because of his insight regarding the relationship between the form and function of the muscles involved in the evolution and production of facial expressions. The details of this analysis are beyond the scope of this text, but the ideas will be summarized because they are central to his hypothesis that human facial expressions have evolved from our primate heritage.

The general trend in the evolution of facial displays from the most primitive primates, the prosimians, to monkeys, apes, and humans involves an increase in the number of muscles in the midface and the diversity of expressions that they permit. Because they are generally nocturnal, prosimians rely primarily on smell, sound, and touch rather than vision for vital information about their environment. Moreover, they do not share the general primate characteristic of group living, and instead lead relatively solitary lives. Consequently, they make only a few facial expressions, and their facial muscles function mainly for movements associated with eating and biting.

In contrast, the old world monkeys have adapted to a very different environment, one that is diurnal, arboreal, and highly social. Keen vision is essential to their adaptation, and they also have evolved somewhat different facial muscles. There is a reduction in the size and number of muscles involved in smelling and hearing, and an increase in the size and number of midface muscles that allows a greater range of movement in the lip and cheek. Compared to prosimians, old world monkeys are much more expressive, although the two groups share some expressions that are similar in form and function, primarily expressions of fear, threat (anger), and affection. Rhesus monkeys (Figure 2.5) and Hamadryas baboons (Figure 2.6) are members of the old world monkeys.

As shown in Figure 2.7, the ancestral line leading to humans and the great apes split off from that leading to old world monkeys about 20–25 million years ago. The great apes (chimpanzees, bonobos, orangutans, and gorillas) show a continuation of the trend toward an increase in midfacial musculature and a decrease in ear, scalp, and forehead musculature. In particular, the size and number of muscles in the area around the mouth and lip show an increase. Primatologists consider the chimpanzee to be more expressive than any other nonhuman primate. However, many of the expressions of the great apes are also found in similar form among the old world monkeys, and appear to be clearly homologous (Chevalier-Skolnikoff, 1973). Indeed, an experienced observer of macaque expressions would be capable of recognizing many of the chimpanzee expressions, and vice versa. See Figures 2.8 and 2.9 for a comparison of the facial expressions of macaques and chimpanzees.

Based on recent DNA analyses, the line leading to Homo sapiens diverged from that of chimpanzees and bonobos about five or six million years ago. In humans, the trend toward an increase in midfacial musculature and a decrease in ear and scalp musculature continued, with one exception. Rather than increasing in size and number, the midface muscles increased in number but decreased in size. The jaw bones and teeth are smaller as well, probably as a result of hominid tool use and less reliance on strength of jaws, teeth, and lips than in the great apes (Washburn, 1960).

The complex muscular anatomy of the human face supports a vast number of possible expressions, though the number of expressions that is considered to be homologous to chimpanzees is limited to six or eight basic expressions, each of which is discussed in detail in Chapter 5. Ethologists like Chevalier-Skolnikoff (1973), Eibl-Eibesfeldt (1972, 1989), and van Hoof (1972) have attempted to develop models of the evolution of typically human social signals such as the smile, laugh, and the eyebrow flash. The initial behavior pattern has a species-typical form and is assumed to be reliably associated with a specific emotional state. Among primates, there has been selection for facial markings, in the form of hair patterns and skin color, in order to enhance the signal. A good example of this enhancement is the distinct line of hair above the eye that allows for a social signal that may be observed pan-culturally in humans, the **eyebrow flash.** This signal may be observed during distal greetings between familiar partners in many cultures and has been extensively studied and filmed by Eibl-Eibesfeldt during greetings in cultures as diverse as Western Europe, Bali, Papua New Guinea, Kalahari, South American Indian, and so on. According to Eibl-Eibesfeldt (1972), when greeting friends and acquaintances over a distance, people all over the world raise their eyebrows rapidly for about one-sixth second, as shown in Figure 2.10. Though they may not be fully conscious of this behavior, people respond strongly to the signal by smiling recognition and responding with the same signal in return. Eibl-Eibesfeldt notes that the basic behavior pattern is overlaid with cultural prescriptions that in some cases may suppress its use, as in Japan where it is used by adults when greeting children. Alternatively, among Samoans, it is used by nearly everyone. In most cultures, it is used along with a smile to signify a positive attitude associated with recognition and approach.

As shown in Figure 2.11, Eibl-Eibesfeldt speculates that this signal evolved from the raising

Figure 2.6 Birth of a baboon. The interest and sensitivity of adult apes to the arrival of the newborn is evident in this photo. The attribution of so-called "human" emotions to the great apes was once considered anthropomorphic, but this taboo is breaking down, especially among ethologists like Goodall, de Waal, and others who work closely with these primates.

(Photo by Frans de Waal, 1996)

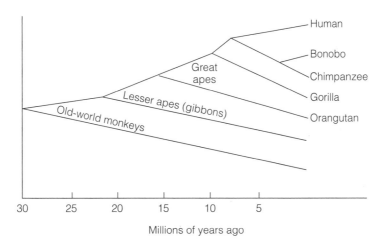

Millions of years ago

Figure 2.7 Hominoid evolution. This diagram represents the ancestral line of primates that eventually led to hominoid evolution, including African apes (gorillas, chimpanzees, and bonobos) and humans. Recent DNA analyses indicate that the hominid line diverged from that of the African apes more recently than was previously believed.

Source: Adapted from de Waal (1996).

and opening of the eye during the experience of surprise. This represents the initial state starting point of a process of ritualization leading to several distinct signals involving the eyebrow lift. Two distinct forms can now be observed in humans. In the first, the eyebrow flash evolved from friendly surprise to requesting or approving social contact, where it is often accompanied by nodding and smiling. It may be displayed in a variety of contexts, such as flirting, seeking attention or confirmation during conversation, and thanking or expressing approval. In the second

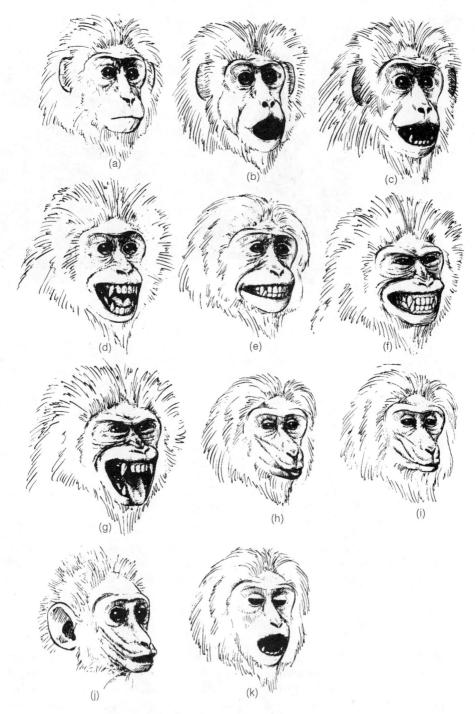

Figure 2.8 Various facial expressions of macaques

(From *Darwin and Facial Expression: A Century in Review,* edited by Paul Ekman, page 65. © 1973 Academic Press. Reprinted by permission)

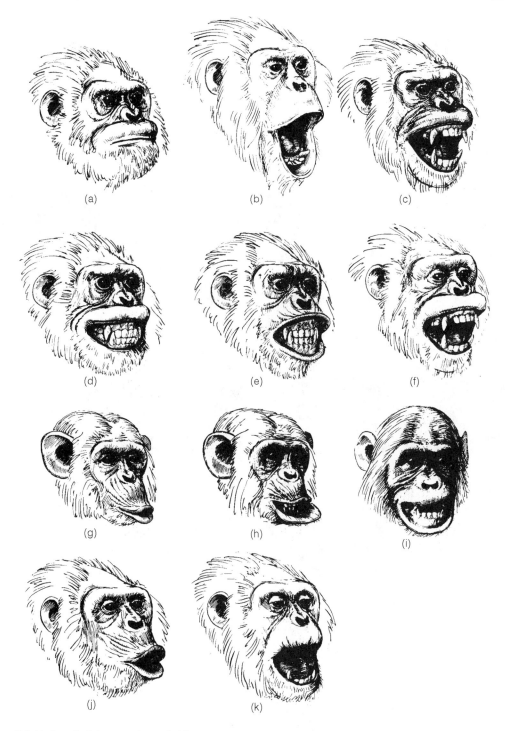

Figure 2.9 Various facial expressions of chimpanzees

(From *Darwin and Facial Expression: A Century in Review,* edited by Paul Ekman, page 73. © 1973 Academic Press. Reprinted by permission)

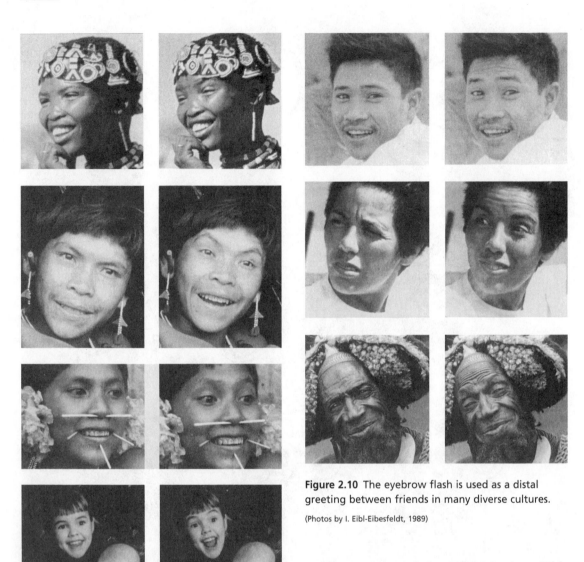

Figure 2.10 The eyebrow flash is used as a distal greeting between friends in many diverse cultures.

(Photos by I. Eibl-Eibesfeldt, 1989)

instance, the raised eyebrow may be held in place and accompanied by a continuous stare, signifying disapproval or indignation and eventual withdrawal or rejection. The many differences in form and context that serve to differentiate the two displays make it unlikely that they would be confused. Although heuristic in terms of research

on human nonverbal communication, Eibl-Eibesfeldt's evolutionary model remains somewhat speculative and difficult to substantiate with comparative evidence. It does appear to be the case that eyebrow raising in nonhuman primates is associated with alertness (Hinde, 1974) and, at least in chimpanzees, with greeting behavior (Fouts, 1997).

Another example of a homologous expression is the universal human display of smiling and laughing. These expressions are thought to have evolved from two originally independent primate displays that have become closely related in

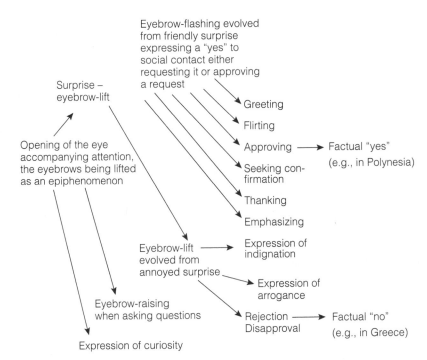

Figure 2.11 Hypothetical model of the evolution of the eyebrow flash

Source: Eibl-Eibesfeldt (1989). Reprinted with permission.

Homo sapiens. As depicted in Figure 2.12, the bared-teeth display and the relaxed open-mouth display occur in existing primate species like monkeys (for example, rhesus and crab-eating macaques) and chimpanzees (pan-troglodytes). The figure indicates a plausible phylogenetic pathway, but should not be interpreted as suggesting that one currently living species evolved from another. The silent bared-teeth display is the probable evolutionary precursor of human smiling, and the relaxed open-mouth display is the precursor of laughing. This speculation is supported by a cluster analysis of chimpanzee behavior conducted by van Hoof (1972). According to van Hoof, the open, silent bared-teeth display was observed in affinitive or friendly social interactions, while a slight variation of the same was observed in submissive contexts involving appeasement. The relaxed open-mouth display was predominantly observed during social play.

Because chimpanzees are more closely related to humans than they are to gorillas, sharing between 98 and 99 percent of our genes, they have received a great deal of scientific attention. Those primatologists (Fouts, 1997; Goodall, 1986) who have adopted the Lorenzian approach of actually living and communicating with the animals that they are studying seem to have the most insight into the emotional behavior of chimpanzees. They all agree that chimpanzees express their emotions in ways that are so similar to those of humans that no specialized translation of their emotional behavior is required. Roger Fouts (1997), who trained **Washoe,** the first chimpanzee to master sign language, comments on understanding her facial expressions:

When it comes to non-human primates, much of their facial repertoire is similar to our own. Apes flash their eyebrows just as we do. When Washoe was unhappy she wrinkled up her face, pulled back the corners of her mouth, and curled her lips outward—which made her look like she was crying. When she was happy she drew back her lips and exposed her bottom

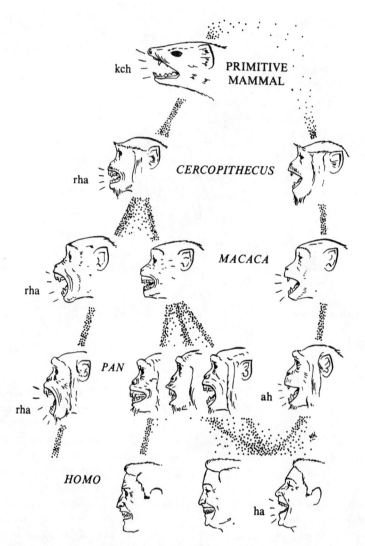

Figure 2.12 Evolution of laughter and smiling. This hypothetical model is suggested by homologies present in existing species of primates. On the left is a line linking the silent bared-teeth display with the bared-teeth scream. On the right is a line of relaxed open-mouth displays associated with play.

Source: van Hoof in Hinde (1972). Reprinted with the permission of Cambridge University Press.

teeth in a big smile. When she was really happy to see me she pursed her lips and gave me a small kiss. . . . When I used to tickle Washoe, she made an open-mouth "play face" and a sound like the wheezing laughter of a human child. . . . When Washoe was frustrated she would throw a tantrum by screaming. Before opening her birthday presents she would start panting and hooting in anticipation. Neither one of us needed sign language to figure out the other's moods. (pp. 67–69)

Because of the extensive fieldwork of Goodall (1971, 1986) and others, we can assert that all of these behaviors are typical of the wild chimpanzee. Of course, these species-typical emotional displays involve more than just facial expressions. They include body movements, gestures, and vocalizations as well. Consider the resemblance between a toddler's full-blown tantrum and that of a young chimp. The chimp will throw itself to the ground, screaming and flailing about, and may pound the ground or throw objects for added emphasis. Goodall (1986) notes a number of typical chimpanzee emotions and the contexts in which they occur, including anger and fear in the context of aggression, wariness in response to a stranger, distress when lost, irritation when bothered by a juvenile, social excitement, sexual arousal, tenderness during reconciliation, sadness during mourning, and many others.

Although it was once considered **anthropomorphic** to attribute such humanlike emotions to animals, even closely related primates, most primatologists today consider this view to be outmoded, if not downright antiscientific. The Dutch ethologist Frans de Waal considers the anthropomorphic critique to be one-sided as well. Although it is perfectly acceptable, and quite common in practice, to describe aggressive, competitive, and deceitful behavior in nonhuman primates in anthropomorphic terms (for example, the Machiavellian hypothesis), it becomes unacceptable when applied to affectionate, loving, or peaceful behaviors. According to this double standard, if two chimpanzees come together after a fight and seal their desire for reconciliation with a kiss, it must be described scientifically as "a post-conflict interaction involving mouth-to-mouth contact." De Waal (1996) defends the more user-friendly description by noting that

> [a]nimals, particularly those close to us, show an enormous spectrum of emotions and different kinds of relationships. It is only fair to reflect this in a broad array of terms. If animals can have enemies they can have friends; if they can cheat they can be honest, and if they can be spiteful they can also be kind and altruistic. Semantic distinctions between animal and human behavior often obscure fundamental similarities. (p. 19)

This point of view has gained ascendancy among those scientists who not only are studying the great apes but are also engaged in a desperate attempt to safeguard the continued existence of the apes in their native habitats. According to Fouts, "drawing an all-or-nothing line between species is completely futile. Nature is a great continuum. With every passing year we discover more evidence to support Darwin's revolutionary hypothesis that the cognitive and emotional lives of animals differ only by degree, from the fishes to the birds to monkeys to humans" (1997, p. 372). Or as the early ethologist Heinroth put it a century ago, "animals are emotional persons with very little understanding."

In conclusion, it is apparent that the primate face has been the site of intensive selective pressure for tens of millions of years. This selection pressure has produced an intricate set of facial muscles responsible for controlling the facial expressions of the great apes and humans. In particular, the social ecology of primates, with its challenging flux of coalitions and alliances, has led to finely tuned abilities to produce and conceal subtle expressions, and to detect such subtleties in the course of social interaction (de Waal, 1982, 1996). In addition, neurobiological studies reveal that the primate brain has evolved specialized collections of neurons responsible for processing sensory information sensitive to faces, including the recognition of familiar faces and emotional expressions (Hauser, 1997). These evolutionary achievements suggest that the expression and recognition of emotional cues are of central importance for primate adaptation.

Conceptual Advances

Since its emergence during the classic period from 1935 to about 1965, ethologists have continued to

Figure 2.13 A kiss is just a kiss—Chimpanzee reconciliation

(Photo by Frans de Waal, 1996)

evolve broader, more heuristic concepts to explain animal behavior than the first notions proposed by Lorenz and Tinbergen. Research on social behavior has become increasingly sophisticated involving analyses at multiple levels including individual action, dyadic interactions, and group structures. For example, Lorenz's early conceptualization of aggressive behavior postulated an innate drive that seeks release, and is thus difficult to control. In many respects this idea was no more testable than Freud's concept of Thanatos, or the death instinct. Perhaps both scientists were unduly pessimistic regarding human aggression, having witnessed world wars from close proximity. Today, ethologists no longer regard aggression as the expression of an internal state or drive. Rather, aggression is studied in a relational context and is viewed as a conditional strategy that may be employed, depending upon the individual's assessment of a conflict situation.

Another example of an advance in basic concepts may be seen in the recent debate in evolutionary theory over group selection. Prior to this debate, classic ethological theory on the evolu-

tion of emotional expressions was based upon Darwin's principles (1872/1965). Tinbergen (1952), Marler (1959), Huxley (1966), and other ethologists developed and refined the Darwinian notion that signals evolved from incidental and involuntary expressions of emotions, a process known as ritualization. If an incidental result of emotional arousal and autonomic state activity involved an observable effect (for example, a facial expression or erection of hair or feathers), through **ritualization** this movement could evolve into an effective signal that provides clear information to the receiver. Most often the "information" pertains to the animal's internal state, rather than some external condition of the environment, hence Darwin's title *The Expression of the Emotions in Man and Animals* (1872/1965).

The key difficulty of the classical explanation of the evolution of signal systems is its assumption of mutual benefits of increasingly accurate information transfer from sender to receiver. This view is summarized by Tinbergen (1964): "One party—the actor—emits a signal, to which the other party—the reactor—responds in such a way that the welfare of the species is promoted." However, the assumption of mutual benefit of truthful signals is deeply problematic from the standpoint of modern views of natural selection emphasizing individual (Hamilton, 1963; Williams, 1966) or gene selection (Dawkins, 1976) rather than group selection (that is, "the welfare of the species"). From this more recent perspective, signals that accurately convey one animal's intentions can be used by the receiver to gain a strategic advantage over the sender, especially in situations involving assessment, competition, or conflict. If by sending a clear signal, the sender stands to lose ground in the Darwinian struggle to survive and reproduce, how did signal systems evolve?

One answer to this puzzle involves rethinking signal function. The beginnings of a shift in thinking is expressed in the following analysis of signals and emotional states by Brannigan and Humphreys:

> The biological function of an activity can be defined in terms of selective advantage, in which case the biological function of signals is to modify a reactor's behaviour so that this behaviour will mesh more adaptively with the future behaviour of the actor. Signals should then be regarded as giving information about future likely behaviour and to signal how another person's previous behaviour has been received. To the extent that future behaviour correlates with subjectively experienced emotional states, signals may well indicate particular emotions. But in terms of natural selection, as well as ethological objectivity, it is the signal itself and the ensuing behaviour of the actor and reactor which alone are of primary importance. (1972, p. 48)

Today most ethologists believe that signals have evolved toward greater persuasiveness rather than toward increasingly accurate readouts of inner emotional states and intentions. This newer position proposes that expressions that exaggerate or minimize internal emotional states may be strategically advantageous to their sender on some occasions, particularly if they are likely to be accepted as true (Dawkins & Krebs, 1978). Individuals' adaptation within the social group may depend upon their ability to manage their own signals and assess the veracity of signals directed to them. In their recent account of animal communication, Owings and Morton (1998) argue that the tension between management and assessment issues drives the evolution of communicative systems to new heights by fostering successive adjustments in both the subtlety of displays and the ability to interpret them. This "evolutionary arms race" is thought to have supported the evolution of primate social intelligence. Although different forms of deception are widespread in the animal world, the ability to consciously manipulate the behavior of a partner to one's own advantage is an aspect of higher intelligence that is quite limited phylogenetically. It can be observed in chimpanzees in laboratory tests (Premack & Woodruff, 1978) and naturalistic settings (Byrne & Whitten, 1988), and is present in human children as young as 4 years (LaFreniere, 1988).

The shift in thinking about the basic evolutionary processes responsible for signal systems has important implications for an ethological perspective on the communicative function of emotional expressions. The classical view of signal systems has been reformulated using more recent concepts derived in part from Game Theory. **Game Theory** provides a means for conceptualizing conditional strategies in which the optimal strategy is not fixed, but requires a consideration of the strategies most likely to be encountered by other gameplayers (Maynard Smith, 1982). These ideas have been fruitfully applied to the study of human cooperation and competition (Axelrod, 1984; Charlesworth, 1996; LaFreniere & MacDonald, 1996) and to the analysis of human facial expressions in social interaction (Fridlund, 1994).

Human Ethology

As Tinbergen (1963) anticipated regarding the application of ethology to the study of humans,

Figure 2.14 (a) Eibl-Eibesfeldt filming social interaction unobtrusively with the reflex lens; (b) reflex lens showing the window in the dummy lens placed in front of the true lens; (c) lens removed to allow direct filming

(Photos by I. Eibl-Eibesfeldt, 1989)

investigators need to attend primarily to the attitudes, methods, and concerns of the discipline, rather than the specific theories and constructs of its classic period. Observation and careful description of the behavior of animals in their natural ecology has remained the dominant methodology in modern ethology; however, it should not be equated with the ethological approach itself. Indeed, if ethologists were to observe humans in their natural habitat, where on earth could they do so?

For a quarter of a decade beginning in the 1960s, the Austrian ethologist Eibl-Eibesfeldt (1989) produced an astonishing archival record containing approximately 275 km of 16-mm film of unstaged social behavior in many diverse hunter–gatherer, agrarian, and fishing societies that will continue to provide insight into the origins of human culture even as these once intact societies are forever lost. As shown in Figure 2.14, traditional filming techniques were abandoned in favor of a reflex lense in order to reduce the reactivity of the people being filmed, an ingenious technique developed by Hass (1968).

Biologically oriented anthropologists, such as Konner (1982a) and Chagnon (1968), have made seminal contributions by studying cultures such as the !Kung and Yanomamö, thought to resemble the ecology of earlier hominid evolution. However, generally speaking, contemporary human ethologists have been much more concerned with the direct observation of how people in modern societies are adapting to their environment, an environment that has been transformed in significant ways from that of our evolutionary origins.

Because of the developmental focus of this book, we shall be particularly interested in the application of ethology to the study of human infants, children, and adolescents. In Great Britain, several influential books on human ethology were published in the early 1970s that generated enormous interest, in that country and abroad, on the potential of applying the concepts and methods of ethology to the study of humans, particularly children (Blurton-Jones, 1972; McGrew, 1972). Other British researchers such as Hinde, Smith, and Connolly established pioneering research programs on the structure and function of children's play and social relations among peers. In the United States and Canada, human ethology gained a foothold in various research centers like the Universities of Chicago, Minnesota, and Virginia during the 1970s, with inroads by Freedman, Charlesworth, Ainsworth, and their students. Research topics, students, and ideas were shared across different laboratories, and a number of important studies were conducted on attachment, play, cooperation and competition, and the structure and function of peer groups from early childhood to adolescence. At about the same time, American psychologists with a Darwinian perspective, led by Tomkins, Ekman, and Izard and their students, were engaging in systematic cross-cultural research on facial expressions that eventually evolved into a complex and diverse research agenda, spanning all of Tinbergen's questions. Two aspects of research in human ethology that bear directly on the scientific study of emotions will be discussed at length in subsequent chapters: (1) ethological studies of infancy and early childhood that examine the functional significance of emotion systems in promoting individual adaptation, and (2) the cross-cultural study of facial expressions.

SUMMARY

We began this chapter with a brief introduction to key concepts from evolutionary biology and ethology, which may be thought of as the biological sciences that deal primarily with the whole organism in relation to its environment. The modern theory of evolution owes its existence to two remarkable nineteenth-century scientists, Charles Darwin and Gregor Mendel, who provided the key mechanisms of evolution and heredity, respectively. Within the framework provided by evolutionary theory, ethologists describe observable components of emotional responses and address the four basic questions of evolution,

development, causation, and function within a comparative perspective.

An important philosophical foundation of classic ethology is the notion of critical realism, which assumes that the sensory/perception systems and brains of organisms evolved in response to the demands of the environment that were critical to the organism's survival and reproduction. Classical ethologists focused on species-typical behaviors that could be used for taxonomic purposes, much like morphological characteristics, to compare different species and trace ancestral relationships. A fundamental distinction in the comparative analysis of behavior must be made between a similiarity between species that can be traced to a common origin (homology), and one that has been produced through independent but convergent lines of evolution (analogy).

One of Darwin's most enduring contributions to the study of facial expressions was his exacting description of the precise movements that contribute to the overall expression and his emphasis on the underlying muscular anatomy of the expression. Ethologists have long assumed that closely related species have more similar patterns of facial expressions than more distantly related species. The primate face has been the site of intensive selective pressure for tens of millions of years. The social ecology of primates, with its challenging flux of coalitions and alliances, has led to finely tuned abilities to produce and conceal subtle expressions, and to detect such subtleties in the course of social interaction. This selection pressure has produced an intricate set of facial muscles responsible for controlling the facial expressions of the great apes. The complex muscular anatomy of the human face supports a vast number of possible expressions, though the number of expressions that is considered to be homologous to chimpanzees is limited to six or eight basic expressions. Neurobiological studies reveal that the primate brain has evolved specialized collections of neurons responsible for processing sensory information sensitive to faces, including the recognition of familiar faces and emotional expressions. These evolutionary achievements suggest that the expression and recognition of basic emotions are of central importance for primate adaptation.

Thus, from an ethological point of view, the child is not assumed to be born a tabula rasa, or blank slate, upon which the environment acts. Rather the child is capable of actively engaging the environment from birth, with inborn predispositions, preferences, and reflexes that have been shaped by natural selection to provide an adaptive advantage in the environment of evolutionary adaptedness (EEA).

Biologically oriented anthropologists and human ethologists have made seminal contributions by studying cultures such as the !Kung and Yanomamö, thought to resemble the ecology of earlier hominid evolution. Many expressive behaviors and social signals may be observed pan-culturally in humans. For example, the eyebrow flash may be observed during distal greetings between familiar partners in many cultures. Though they may not be fully conscious of this behavior, people respond strongly to the signal by smiling recognition and responding with the same signal in return. Generally speaking, contemporary human ethologists have been much more concerned with the direct observation of how people in modern societies are adapting to their environment, an environment that has been transformed in significant ways from that of our evolutionary origins.

Classical ethological concepts have been continually reappraised and sometimes modified in light of theoretical or empirical advances. An example of this renewal concerns the Darwinian notion that signals evolved from incidental and involuntary expressions of emotions, a process known as ritualization. Today most ethologists believe that signals have evolved toward greater persuasiveness rather than toward increasingly accurate readouts of inner emotional states and intentions. From this more recent perspective, signals that accurately convey one animal's intentions could be used by the receiver to gain a strategic advantage over the sender, especially in situations involving assessment, competition, or conflict. This newer position proposes that expressions that exaggerate or minimize internal emotional states may be strategically advantageous to their sender on just those occasions, particularly if they are likely to be accepted as true. Thus, individuals' adaptation within the social group may depend upon their ability to manage their own signals and assess the veracity of signals directed to them. The tension between management and assessment issues drives the evolution of communicative systems to new heights by fostering successive adjustments in both the subtlety of displays and the ability to interpret them. This "evolutionary arms race" is thought to have supported the evolution of primate social and emotional intelligence.

FURTHER READING

Byrne, R. W., & Whitten, A. (1988). *Machiavellian intelligence: Social expertise and the evolution of intellect in monkeys, apes and humans.* Oxford: Oxford University Press.

This entertaining anthology examines the basis of the hypothesis that human intelligence evolved as an adaptation to the politics of primate social existence.

Dawkins, R., & Krebs, J. R. (1978). Animal signals: Information or manipulation? In J. R. Krebs & N. B. Davies (Eds.), *Behavioral ecology* (pp. 282–309). Oxford: Blackwell.

This was the key theoretical article that led to a reconsideration of the basic theory of the evolution of animal signals, by viewing signal function from a "selfish gene" point of view.

Eibl-Eibesfeldt, I. (1989). *Human ethology.* New York: Aldine de Gruyter.

Still the most authoritative account of the emerging discipline of human ethology, this text includes hundreds of original photographs of expressive behavior from the author's archival films of traditional peoples.

Goodall, J. (1986). *The chimpanzees of Gombe.* Harvard: Belknap.

This is a masterful and sympathetic account of chimpanzee emotions and social life from the point of view of someone who pioneered the naturalistic observation of primate societies.

3

Psychobiology of Emotion

Neurological Analysis of Emotions

Localization of Function in the Brain
- Brain Anatomy
- Accidental Lesions
- Experimentally Induced Lesions
- Electrical Stimulation
- Biochemical Stimulation
- Brain Pathology
- Functional Brain Imaging

MacLean's Limbic System Theory
- The Reptilian Brain
- The Paleomammalian Brain
- The Neomammalian Brain

Emotion Lateralization
LeDoux's Amygdala Theory of Fear

Physiological Analysis of Emotion

Heart Rate
Vagal Tone
Cortisol

NEUROLOGICAL ANALYSIS OF EMOTIONS

One of the outstanding achievements in all of twentieth-century science is the systematic exploration of the brain and how it works. In this chapter we divide our discussion of the psychobiological foundations of emotion into research on the central nervous system, including the brain and spinal cord, and the peripheral nervous system, which extends the operation of the brain throughout the entire body. Together these two systems provide interactive feedback loops that are ultimately responsible for the behavior of the organism in relation to sensory input from the environment. This first section provides a brief overview of the key methods and findings in neuropsychology that will be needed to understand current theoretical positions on the neurology of emotion.

Localization of Function in the Brain

Research on the **localization of function** in the brain involves the oldest and most basic questions in neuroscience. Investigating how nearly 100 billion neurons of the human central nervous system function in order to create thought and emotion is an enormous challenge to scientists. During the twentieth century, neuroscientists developed a considerable array of methods to map the human brain and to understand how it functions. In this section we explore the contribution of neuroscience to our understanding of the role of the brain in our experience of emotion. We shall begin by organizing our discussion in terms of the methodological evolution of the field, since theoretical progress has been directly related to the refinement of the technology used to assess the neuropsychological underpinnings of emotion.

Brain Anatomy Darwin's theory of evolution provided nineteenth-century neuroscientists like John Hughlings-Jackson and Paul Broca with a strong reason for expecting structural and functional continuity in the basic brain structures of various animals, including humans. We now know that there is a great deal of structural similarity among various vertebrate brains, which is due to the essentially conservative nature of the evolutionary process.

A useful metaphor for thinking about brain evolution is the pioneer homestead. Before the first winter sets in, the goal may be the construction of a basic house made of sod. The following year a wooden construction may be built with more rooms, and the original dwelling converted to a storage shed. Eventually more rooms may be added and even a porch for sitting and looking at the sunset. In this metaphor, nothing is wasted or thrown away once it is built, and the order of the construction is not random, but guided by functional concerns. The first constructions may be crude, but they are effective in promoting survival. As time passes, more refined structures serving a broader range of more specialized functions are added to the whole. When we state that brain evolution is essentially conservative we mean that the most basic systems in the brain responsible for controlling behavior that promote survival are phylogenetically ancient, having been preserved throughout vertebrates despite important evolutionary advances.

Anatomical studies of vertebrate brains are consistent with this view. Brain anatomists would begin their comparative analysis by organizing each type of brain into three basic units: **hindbrain, midbrain,** and **forebrain.** Within each of these units, one can identify all of the major structures and neural pathways that are common to a wide range of vertebrates. In particular, the forebrain or cerebrum is progressively larger as one compares fish to reptiles to mammals, culminating in the human brain. Not only is this portion larger in the human brain than in all other animals, it is also more differentiated, containing elements not found in other animal brains. Despite the more recently evolved specializations of the human neocortex, we shall argue that the brain systems that regulate emotional behavior have been preserved throughout many phylogenetic levels. The evidence in support of this view begins with an understanding of brain anatomy.

As early as 1878, the French neuroanatomist Paul Broca demonstrated that the area of the limbic lobe immediately surrounding the brain stem is common to the brains of all mammals. As can be seen in Figure 3.1, the limbic lobe (the dark area) remains a common element, but it accounts for progressively less of the total cortical mass in the cat or monkey compared to the rabbit. This progression across these mammals reflects the growth of the neocortex, which reaches its zenith in the human brain where it accounts for more than 90 percent of the total cortical mass. Nevertheless, the older central core retains its original functions, as later studies have shown. As neuroscientists began to develop the necessary research tools, the comparative description of brain structure led to systematic research on the function of the different structures of the brain.

Accidental Lesions An early tool for understanding how the different components of the human brain work together was the study of the mental and emotional sequelae of brain trauma caused by accidents that affect brain functioning. Since the famous case of Phineas Gage, who in 1848 was involved in an explosion that drove an iron spike through his forebrain, brain scientists have attempted to understand the function of specific areas of the brain by recording the results of such trauma. Prior to his accident, Gage had been one of the railroad's best liked and most responsible foremen, described by family and friends as amiable in character. However, after the injury to his brain, he became capricious and subject to sudden fits of ill temper. His physician commented that the "balance, so to speak, between his intellectual faculties and his animal propensities seems to have been destroyed" (Harlow, 1868/1963, p. 277). If it was possible to gain insight into the function of different areas of the brain by describing the effects of accidental lesions, which are essentially uncontrolled experiments of nature, it might be possible to build a science of the brain by

conducting more controlled experiments involving systematic brain lesions.

Experimentally Induced Lesions Philip Bard (1928), who worked in Cannon's laboratory, was a pioneer in developing the strategy of conducting systematic lesions to gather information about the localization of function in the brain. His initial experiments involved the surgical removal of the entire cerebral cortex of cats. These decorticate cats were observed to exhibit species-typical emotional arousal linked to the behavioral system of aggression. When provoked these cats would respond with a display called "sham rage," which involved crouching down, arching their backs, pulling back their ears, and unsheathing their claws, while hissing, snarling, and biting any object nearby. In addition, they also displayed clear signs of ANS arousal, such as pupil dilation and elevated heart rate and blood pressure. These observations led Bard and Cannon to suspect that the **hypothalamus** was the emotional center of the brain, while the **neocortex** functioned to check or inhibit unrestrained emotional expressions. Guided by this hypothesis, Bard made progressively larger lesions, starting with the cortex and moving downward until he was able to eliminate the display of "sham rage." After removing the hypothalamus, the emotional reactions were essentially eliminated and the cats exhibited only sporadic fragments of the display that lacked the coordination of the more integrated behavioral system.

Another influential approach to understanding how the brain assigns emotional significance to incoming stimuli involved surgical lesions to study the emotional behavior of monkeys. Following the surgical removal of the temporal lobe, Kluver and Bucy (1937) reported that the animals lose their fear of stimuli to which they previously reacted with fear. They also attempt indiscriminant sexual and feeding behaviors that are maladaptive, such as eating rocks. The loss of coordinated function in these basic systems as a result of damage to the temporal lobe came to be known as the Kluver-Bucy syndrome. Later studies determined that lesions

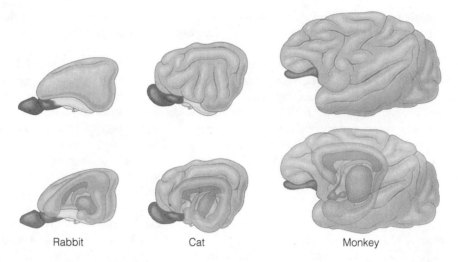

Rabbit   Cat   Monkey

Figure 3.1 The neocortex in mammalian evolution. The brains of these four mammals all contain the same structures. However, a comparison of the association areas reveals a progression in the total mass of the neocortex that reaches its zenith in the human brain.

Source: Gray (1999). Used by permission of Worth Publishers.

confined to the **amygdala,** an almond-shaped structure located in the temporal lobe, but sparing surrounding structures, were sufficient to produce the emotional components of the syndrome (Weiskrantz, 1956).

Electrical Stimulation An important experimental technique that complements studies involving brain lesions is electrical stimulation. This technique, pioneered by the Swiss scientist Hess in the 1920s, involves sending small amounts of electric current through an electrode attached to the skull and inserted into a specific area of the brain. This artificial stimulation can reproduce the chain of events that occurs due to natural stimulation. If a particular set of **neurons,** or nerve cells, in the brain are stimulated in this manner, and a certain type of behavior follows, then neuroscientists assume that those neurons are the part of the brain that controls that behavior.

We know that the brain communicates on the basis of chemical and electrical signals transmitted from neurons in one area of the brain to another.

For example, certain areas of the frontal cortex can be electrically stimulated to produce corresponding movements of certain bodily parts. This happens because the motor cortex is connected to the spinal cord which in turn sends messages to control the movement of limbs. If the same area of the motor cortex is surgically removed, corresponding deficits in motor movements will occur. The combination of surgical lesions and electrical stimulation in animal research is referred to by LeDoux (1996) as the yin and yang of brain science methodology. Along with the imaging and tracing techniques introduced in the following text, activating specific areas of the brain through artificial stimulation, or deactivating areas by surgical lesions, remains a key tool for understanding brain function.

Researchers are sometimes able to combine experimental techniques with more naturalistic methods. For example, Delgado (1969) implanted electrodes in the brains of macaque monkeys that could be stimulated telemetrically while the animal was interacting with cage-mates. Using this technique, Delgado found that stimulating a particular brain site elicited threat expressions when the animal was placed with a group of subordinates, but submissive behavior if the same animal was placed with more dominant monkeys. Thus, even when using techniques of artificial electrical stimulation, the behavior that is elicited is open to influences from the social context.

Biochemical Stimulation The discovery of the brain's chemical messengers was made by the German scientist Otto Loewi in his research on electrical stimulation of the vagus nerve in frogs (Loewi, 1960). This discovery opened a whole new area of research on the brain, and Loewi was awarded the Nobel prize in physiology in 1936 in recognition of this breakthrough. Loewi observed that he could slow the frog's heartbeat by electrical stimulation, but he went one step further in his inquiry. He decided to transfer the fluid surrounding a frog's heart that had been slowed by stimulation to a second frog's heart. When the heartbeat of the second frog slowed down as a result, he deduced that some chemical agent must have been released from the nerve endings of the first frog. After many thousands of more sophisticated experiments, we now know that almost all neuronal communication depends upon chemical messengers. They are generally classified into three types—neurotransmitters, neurohormones, and hormones—according to their function.

The electrical stimulation artificially induced by Loewi instigated the brain's natural communication flow. When sufficiently stimulated, a neuron will release a wave of electrical charge, or **action potential,** down the output **axon** where it branches off into many axon terminals, as shown in Figure 3.2. When the action potential reaches a terminal it causes a chemical, called a **neurotransmitter,** to be released. The neurotransmitter flows across the **synapse** (the space between the axon terminal of one neuron and the **dendrites** of its neighbor) to the dendrites of surrounding neurons where it contributes to the release of electrical energy, and so on throughout an area of the brain. In this manner, both electri-

cal and chemical stimulation form the basis for communication between nerve cells. Serotonin is an example of a neurotransmitter. Antidepressants are designed to relieve depressive moods by making certain transmitter substances, such as serotonin, more available for use at synapses.

Another group of neurochemicals that is quite distinct from neurotransmitters are hormones. Hormonal systems, like the hypothalmic-pituitary-adrenocortical (HPA) system, are activated by the **pituitary gland** or other glands located in the body, which are controlled by outputs from the hypothalamus. Once activated, the pituitary gland secrets stress **hormones** that stimulate the production and release of adrenaline or **cortisol** that circulates in the bloodstream to reach the specific organs that respond to its presence. For this reason, hormones usually require more time to have an impact on the body than neurotransmitters.

In comparing hormones and neurotransmitters, it is useful to understand their evolution. The current evolutionary model (Snyder, 1985) is presented in Figure 3.3. The first and most basic form of chemical communication (model a) evolved to provide a primitive form of intracellular communication so that the organism could behave as a unit rather than a collection of uncoordinated cells. As organisms evolved into more complex forms, two lines of chemical communication evolved from this simple system. Neurotransmitters evolved to equip the organism with the ability for rapid and specific behavioral adjustments. As shown in model b, they travel an extremely short distance (measured in nanometers or billionths of a meter) to produce their effects. The second line of evolution produced hormones that must travel much longer distances in the circulatory system, and thus provide for much slower and more generalized behavioral adjustments, as shown in model d. Another important difference between hormones and neurotransmitters is that the effects of hormones can be felt over the life span of the organism, and some effects are irreversible and occur before birth. In later

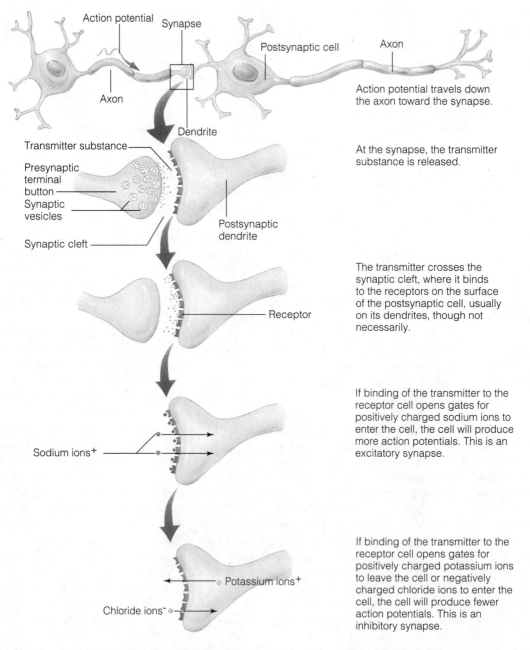

Figure 3.2 Neurons are composed of a cell body, axon, and dendrites. When stimulated by enough inputs at the same time, a neuron will emit an electrical charge that travels along its axon, spreading through the cell's dendrites. When the electrical charge reaches the axon terminal, it causes a neurotransmitter to be released. This chemical messenger diffuses across synapses to the dendrites of adjacent cells. In this manner, electrical and chemical processes sustain communication between neurons in the brain.

Source: Kalat (1996). Reprinted by permission of Wadsworth Publishing, a division of Thomson Learning.

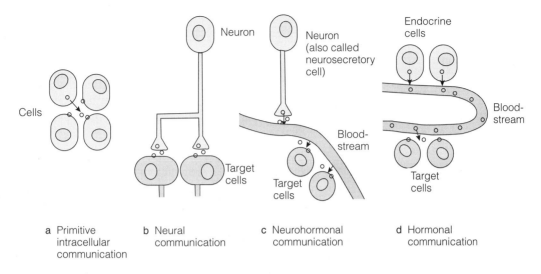

Figure 3.3 Evolution of chemical communication between cells. From a common ancestor (a) three distinct modes of chemical communication have evolved. In neural communication (b) chemicals diffuse across a short synapse to other cells. In neurohormonal communication (c) chemicals travel a longer route via the bloodstream to reach target cells. And in hormonal communication (d) endocrine glands release chemicals that reach target cells via the bloodstream.

Source: Adapted from *Psychology* by Gray © 1999, 1994, 1991 by Worth. Used by permission.

chapters, we shall distinguish between their organizing influence during prenatal development and their activating influence during biological events such as puberty.

Although different in terms of their function, neurotransmitters and hormones are quite similar in their chemical structure. In some unusual cases, they may have identical chemical structures. For example, the chemical norepinephrine can act either as a hormone in the bloodstream, where it increases the heart rate, or as a neurotransmitter in the brain, where it produces an alert state.

Other evidence of a commonality between neurotransmitters and hormones comes from the discovery of a special class of chemical messengers that fall midway between these two types. Known as neurohormones (model c in Figure 3.3), they are produced from neurons and released from axon terminals (like neurotransmitters), but are absorbed into the bloodstream

(like hormones). This group includes peptides that appear to modulate synaptic transmission in a wider diffusion than neurotransmitters. It also includes natural opiates that, like artificial drugs, can modulate pain or other emotional systems. Research on neurohormones is still in its infancy, and much remains to be learned about their role in influencing emotional moods and other states of consciousness. The role of chemical messengers, particularly hormones, in emotional functioning will be treated more extensively in the section on emotion and physiology later in this chapter.

Brain Pathology A number of diseases may be used to shed light on brain function, including rabies, psychomotor epilepsy, and Huntington's chorea. To illustrate this methodology, consider the early research on psychomotor epilepsy. In 1948, Gibbs, Gibbs, and Fuster published an article in which they described this condition in which the patient experiences emotional feelings followed by amnesia and automatisms, rather than the convulsions more commonly associated with other epileptic seizures. This report was followed up by Penfield and associates in Montreal and yielded a dramatic experimental demonstration of the integration between limbic and neocortical functions. Penfield and Jasper (1954) found that it is possible to electrically stimulate precise sites in the limbic area of the brain to reproduce the subjective emotional states, subsequent automatism, and associated amnesia characteristic of an epileptic seizure. They also observed that the electrical discharges that occur in psychomotor epilepsy do not spread outside the limbic system. This finding, confirmed by animal research, was considered to be evidence for the physiological distinctness of the limbic system. The procedures developed by Penfield and associates provided a means to literally pinpoint those limbic structures involved in the generation of emotional feelings during the course of therapeutic neurosurgery. These striking results have led neuroscientists like MacLean (1993) to view psychomotor epilepsy as the key to understanding the cerebral evolution of emotion.

In psychomotor epilepsy there is generally an aura at the onset of an epileptic attack that is accompanied by feelings that can range from ecstasy to extreme terror. MacLean (1993) lists six general affective states: feelings of desire, fear, anger, dejection, affection, and gratulance. The latter may include profound feelings of discovery or revelation similar to drug-induced feelings of euphoria or enhanced reality. All these emotional feelings are, according to MacLean, detached from any particular emotion elicitor and instead perceived as free-floating affects.

As the nerve impulse associated with the seizure discharge spreads further into the limbic system, the patient exhibits automatic behavior that can range from simple to complex automatisms. These automatisms often correspond to the particular feeling experienced during the aura. MacLean (1993) provides the following examples:

Following a horrifying feeling of fear or terror, for example, a patient may run screaming to someone for protection. Or after a feeling of anger, there may be angry vocalization and pugilistic behavior, with the arms flailing somewhat like those of a fighting chimpanzee. Or there may be a gorilla-like hooting and striking of the chest. An opposite sort of behavior is that of a woman who would walk around the room showing marked affection for anyone present, or that of a 20-year-old woman in whom "each slight seizure was followed by a paroxysm of kissing." (p. 79)

Functional Brain Imaging Over the past decade there has been an explosive growth in the use of brain imaging techniques such as **positron emission topography** (PET scan), **Magnetic resonance imaging** (MRI), and **magnetoencephalography** (MEG). These techniques give neuroscientists the opportunity to study the human brain at work by identifying those brain structures that are activated while subjects perform various tasks that call on specific abilities. A PET scan provides a color image of the brain displayed on the screen of a computer monitor. The test consists of injecting a small quantity of glucose that is tagged with a radioactive substance that can be used to trace where the glucose is consumed in the brain. For example, on the basis of PET scans we know that certain areas of the right hemisphere are activated when a person is asked to identify different faces (Sergent, Ohta, & MacDonald, 1992).

The MRI technique uses magnetic detectors to measure the amounts of hemoglobin, with and without oxygen. This allows physicians and scientists to study the living brain by viewing it at different depths as if in slices. Brains areas that have been highly active can be identified because they have used up the oxygen bound to hemoglobin.

Finally, MEG also provides a color image of the brain at work that is based on electromagnetic fields that are created as electrochemical information passes between neurons. During a MEG test, a patient may be told to move the right index finger, and an instant readout of the brain's activity is provided in the form of concentric colored rings that pinpoint the signals in the brain even prior to moving the finger! Currently, these techniques provide a noninvasive methodology that is beginning to bridge the gap between animal and human studies.

MacLean's Limbic System Theory

A number of contemporary investigators in the neurology of emotion such as MacLean (1993) and LeDoux (1993, 1996) trace the development of their thinking back to an influential paper by Papez (1937) titled "A Proposed Mechanism of Emotion." This proved to be an important conceptual advance over earlier research models because it moved beyond the search for a single brain structure and proposed instead that emotion is mediated by several cortical structures. From this point on, all neurophysiological theories of emotion have generally agreed that multiple brain structures are involved in emotion. Papez proposed a circuit theory of emotion that implicated several distinct brain structures that are serially connected and operate together as a system. The structures he identified were the hypothalamus, anterior thalamus, cingulate gyrus, and the hippocampus. The loop connecting these structures came to be known as the Papez circuit. Papez speculated that sensory impulses travel to the thalamus, which then reroutes them into three pathways, each responsible for a different dimension of the total emotional response. Thus, the impulse traveling to the striatal region instigates movement, that to the neocortex instigates thought, and that to the hypothalamus gives rise to the feeling and expressive components that make up emotion. This tripartite structure of the emotional brain was the immediate conceptual ancestor of the next important advance.

The next major step in the development of a neural model of emotion was taken by MacLean who renamed the structures of the Papez circuit,

together with the amygdala, septal nuclei, orbito-frontal cortex, and the basal ganglia, the **limbic system** (see Figure 3.4). In 1949, MacLean initially chose the term *visceral brain* to convey the difference between what we feel (strong inward feelings) and what we know (verbally mediated logic). MacLean (1949) argued that the visceral brain gives sensory impulses their emotional tone, and unlike information processed in the neocortex, it "eludes the grasp of the intellect because its animalistic and primitive structure makes it impossible to communicate in verbal terms" (p. 348). Because of the ambiguity and misinterpretations arising from the use of the term *viscera,* MacLean eventually borrowed Broca's descriptive term *limbique* and introduced *limbic system* to refer to the limbic cortex and its primary brain-stem connections (MacLean, 1952). These extensions to the Papez circuit, particularly the amygdala, have proven to be of enduring value to modern structural/functional analyses of the emotional brain.

A key idea that was emphasized by MacLean was the concept that the brain, as a product of a long evolutionary history, is modular in its design, composed of a hierarchy of three major developments. These three steps in the evolution of the human brain correspond to phylogenetic adaptations common to reptiles, early mammals, and late mammals, as shown in Figure 3.5. According to MacLean, "there results a remarkable linkage of three cerebrotypes which are radically different in chemistry and function and which in an evolutionary sense are eons apart. There exists, so to speak, a hierarchy of three-brains-in-one or what I call for short, a triune brain" (from LeDoux, 1996, p. 98).

The Reptilian Brain In order to reach an understanding of the brain–behavior connections and the contribution of each of the three components of the triune brain to the experience of emotion, MacLean needed to integrate information from evolutionary biology and ethology with neurophysiology. He began this task by carefully examining the fossil record detailing the

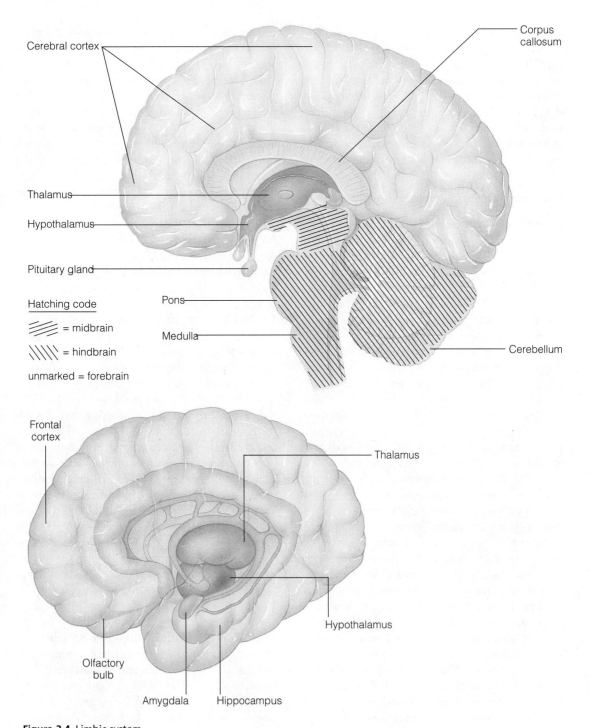

Figure 3.4 Limbic system

Source: Kalat (1996). Reprinted with permission of Wadsworth Publishing, a division of Thomson Learning.

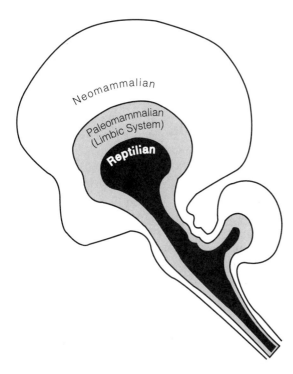

Figure 3.5 MacLean's triune brain. This evolutionary model of the brain is composed of three major divisions: The reptilian brain includes the striatal region, the paleomammalian brain includes the limbic system, and the neomammalian brain includes the neocortex. Each part is named for the era in which it is thought to have originated.

Source: MacLean (1967).

evolution of reptiles. Unlike fish and amphibians, reptiles evolved a mode of reproduction involving the amniote egg that permitted them to adapt to life on land. This fundamental change permitted an adaptive radiation into a new terrestrial environment that eventually led to an evolutionary line of mammal-like reptiles called therapsids. The fossil remains of these mammal-like reptiles have been uncovered on every continent, indicating a very successful adaptation from the mid-Permian period, about 250 million years ago, to the mid-Triassic period, about 200 million years ago. During this long period, an evolutionary line emerged from the therapsids that is considered to

be the prototype of the mammalian class. The critical changes of this period involved the acquisition of a mammalian posture, five-digit fingers and toes, mammalian-like jaws and teeth, the mammalian ear, and the gradual transition from a cold-blooded to warm-blooded organism (MacLean, 1990).

In order to understand the behavioral repertoire of these primitive mammal-like reptiles, MacLean chose to focus his behavioral analysis on lizards because they are the closest living relative of these ancient reptiles. Turning to ethology, he identified about 25 forms of behavior that constitute the **ethogram,** or general profile of species-typical behavior patterns. The ethogram includes a wide variety of animal behaviors that have evolved within a species (or group of species) in order to promote the organism's adaptation to its ecological niche and to ensure its survival and reproduction. For lizards, the ethogram includes basic behaviors such as nesting, foraging, territorial behavior, hunting, hoarding, greeting, grooming, flocking, migration, and mating. In addition to these basic behaviors, four rudimentary displays are used in social communication involving (1) signature or identification of the individual, (2) dominance or challenge, (3) submission or appeasement, and (4) courtship. Because these groups of behavior programs are very old, phylogenetically speaking, they are also expressed in various species-typical forms in more recently evolved animals, such as birds and mammals. As with development, earlier forms of behavior are not discarded with further evolution, but rather they are integrated within more recently evolved structures.

In order to test the hypothesis that the reptilian brain remains functional in higher animals, MacLean chose to study the distinctive species-typical greeting display in squirrel monkeys. This display, which is exhibited when a new monkey comes into view, involves elements of signature, dominance, and courtship displays associated in lizards with the striatal region of the brain. In one type of squirrel monkey (gothic type), this display is readily elicited by presenting the monkey with its mirror image, thus facilitating experimental work. In a series of experiments performed on 120 gothic-type squirrel monkeys, MacLean found that only the removal of portions of the striatal region eliminated the display behavior, whereas removal of limbic or neocortical systems did not result in an elimination of the display. Analagous experiments on lizards showed the same overall pattern of results, thus demonstrating continuity of structure and function in the oldest portion of the brain in animals as diverse as reptiles and primates.

The idea that the **striatal** region of the brain functions to schedule species-typical behavior patterns in order to promote the adaptation of the organism has been supported by clinical observations of patients suffering from a genetic disease known as Huntington's chorea. This hereditary disease does not have known effects in childhood, but later in life patients become incapable of organizing and planning even simple daily routines. They can be engaged in these activities if directed to do so by others, but appear to lack the self-organizing capacity for such actions. Without external direction, they appear to be listless and apathetic, but this striking passivity is simply a lack of initiative, due to the damage caused by the disease to the striatal region of the brain responsible for organizing daily routines and motivating the individual.

The Paleomammalian Brain A similar comparative analysis underlies MacLean's assertion that the limbic system has evolved as the common denominator in the paleomammalian brain. Again the first step in the analysis involved the comparative analysis of mammalian behavior in relation to the evolutionary advances already present in the reptilian ethogram. Such a comparison yields only three broad classes of behavior that are universally present in mammals, but completely absent in reptiles: vocal signal systems, attachment systems, and juvenile play. At first glance this may not appear to be such a monumental leap forward, but let us consider the implications of the addition of these three behav-

ioral systems to the lives of mammals, as distinct from reptiles. Together these changes provided a major impetus for the evolution of social life, and with it a primary role for emotions in regulating social interaction.

From a comparative perspective, the major unifying component of the mammalian order is the universality of maternal nursing and caregiving. In contrast to the reptilian order, mammals invest heavily in the care and protection of their offspring. Early separation from the parent inevitably results in the death of the offspring, and this intensive selective pressure led to the evolution of behavioral systems "designed" to maintain proximity between parent and offspring. MacLean speculates that the earliest vocalizations in the evolution of mammals were the infant's cries of separation distress in order to restore the vital contact with the parent. In contrast, reptiles like lizards and turtles are mute. Unlike mammals, the only investment reptile parents provide to their offspring is the fertilized egg. Unlike birds, the eggs are laid and left to hatch on their own. Not only are lizards "remiss" in the care and protection of their offspring, the young must actually hide from their parents and other adult lizards to avoid being eaten by them! Considering the behavioral and social ecology of lizards, it should be clear that selection pressures in this line lead away from infant vocalization, parental care, and the evolution of family cohesion and group living, all vital characteristics of mammals in general, and primates in particular.

The physical structure in the brain thought by MacLean to be responsible for regulating the evolving behavioral programs related to maternal care, infant attachment, vocal signaling, and play is the limbic system. He argued that with the emergence of these new behavioral systems, the limbic system evolved in mammals as the brain's primary emotional and motivational system. This portion of the brain, referred to in Figure 3.5 as the paleomammalian brain, is closely connected with the hypothalamus, which in turn controls the ANS. The term *limbic system* was inspired by Broca's term *limbique,* derived from the Latin word *limbus* or *rim,* which he used to describe the oval-shaped rim of the medial cortex. Based on both organizational structure and clinical findings, MacLean asserts that these two phylogenetically older modules (the striatal region and the limbic system) lack any capacity for verbal communication with those areas of the human brain that are responsible for speech. This is the physiological substrate for MacLean's insight that much of what is processed in these areas cannot be easily processed in verbal reasoning. This idea concerning the duality of the heart and mind is a perennial theme in literature and is elegantly captured by the famous phrase "The heart has reasons of which reason knows nothing," attributed to the French author Blaise Pascal.

The Neomammalian Brain The third major division in MacLean's evolutionary model of the human brain is the neomammalian brain. This outer layer or **cortex** is considered to be the most recently evolved portion of the brain and for this reason is often referred to as the neocortex. As can be seen in Figure 3.4, it is more substantial in higher mammals, particularly primates. Within the primate order, this portion of the brain is much larger in humans than in our closest relative, the chimpanzee. The anterior cortical region has shown the most dramatic expansion in size over the course of phylogeny, and the large frontal lobes appear to be the most distinctive feature of the human brain.

This area of the brain plays an important role in many distinctive human behaviors such as reasoning, language, and metacognitive abilities such as planning and anticipating events. For our purposes the anterior cortical areas are also critically implicated in emotional behavior and experience (Davidson, 1993). The frontal cortex adds a dimension of emotional life to humans that may not be present in most primates. This dimension may be thought of as the interface of the cognitive and emotional functions that produces more complex human emotional states. Some human emotions are linked to the ability to anticipate outcomes of

future events that are unknown or uncontrollable, but important to the individual. For example, emotions like anxiety, concern, and empathy often involve anticipating consequences that have not yet been realized, and the frontal cortex has been identified as a neural substrate for these characteristically human feelings. An understanding of the role played by the cortex in human emotional experience begins with an account of the functions of the cerebral hemispheres.

Emotion Lateralization

Much current research on the neural influences on emotion in humans addresses the question of asymmetries in anterior cortical function that underlie various forms of emotional behavior and expression (Davidson, 1993). Three different hypotheses have been proposed regarding the role of the cerebral hemispheres in emotional behavior and expression: (1) the right hemisphere hypothesis; (2) the valence hypothesis; and (3) the approach–withdrawal hypothesis.

The first hypothesis proposes a general role for the right hemisphere in all emotion processing. Support for this idea comes from split-brain research and a number of other empirical studies suggesting that the right posterior region is implicated in recognizing emotional states based on the perception of facial expressions. These data also provide support for the more general concept of the modular brain. Data derived from studying accidental brain damage in humans suggest that a specific area of the brain is specialized in the recognition of different faces, and that damage to it results in the loss of this specific function only. Patients suffering from this deficit, known as prosopagnosics, are capable of recognizing familiar nonfacial visual stimuli, and they can recognize the voices of familiar individuals, but not their faces. Prosopagnosics generally have little difficulty in identifying faces as faces, distinguishing human and nonhuman faces, and identifying the expression, gender, and age of the face (Damasio, Damasio, & Tranel,

1990). Comparative neurobiological studies support the notion of modularity by identifying neurons that respond selectively (have higher spike rates) to faces over other visual stimuli. Moreover, there are groups of neurons that respond to individual faces, independent of their expressions, and other groups of neurons that respond selectively to particular expressions, independent of identity (Hauser, 1996). These face-sensitive cells, together with those found in the amygdala, are likely to play a significant role in face-to-face communication.

Research on the production (as opposed to recognition) of emotional expressions provides substantial support for both the valence and the approach–withdrawal hypotheses (Camras, Holland, & Patterson, 1993). The valence hypothesis predicts lateralization as a function of the valence of the emotion expressed, with the left hemisphere mediating positive emotions, while the right hemisphere is thought to mediate negative emotions (for example, Dimond, Farrington, & Johnson, 1976). A somewhat different formulation hypothesizes that the frontal regions of the left and right hemispheres are specialized to mediate approach and withdrawal, respectively (for example, Davidson, 1984, 1993; Kinsbourne, 1978). According to this latter view, approach and withdrawal are fundamental behavioral/motivational systems found at any level of phylogeny where behavior has evolved. Because of this primacy, it is reasonable to suggest a corresponding duality in the structure of the brain responsible for controlling and coordinating these behaviors. Because positive emotions motivate interest and approach, and negative emotions often motivate avoidance and withdrawal, it is not often possible to differentiate these closely related hypotheses in empirical terms. As a result a great deal of data exist in support of either of these two hypotheses, while very little data successfully discriminate between them.

Early researchers, such as Hughlings-Jackson (1878/1959), reported differential symptoms in patients with unilateral cortical lesions suggesting that damage to the left hemisphere is more often associated with depression than damage to the right hemisphere. More recent research confirms and elaborates on this basic finding. For example, Robinson and associates (Robinson, Kubos, Starr, Rao, & Price, 1984) reported that the closer the lesion is to the left frontal lobe, the more severe the depressive symptomatology. In contrast, unilateral damage to the right hemisphere is more often associated with mania. A review of 122 clinical cases by Sackeim et al. (1982) indicated a greater likelihood of pathological laughter associated with damage to the right hemisphere, while left-sided damage is associated with pathological crying. In rare cases of hemispherectomy, the entire left or right hemisphere is surgically removed. In reviewing 19 such cases, Sackeim found that 12 out of 14 patients with right removal were judged to be euphoric following surgery, while 3 out of 5 with left removal were judged to be depressed. Of course, our understanding of the specialized functions of the human brain cannot be systematically mapped by experimental lesions as it has been in animals.

In humans, surgical lesions involving the permanent removal of critical brain regions are extremely rare. The frontal lobotomies routinely performed on emotionally disturbed psychiatric patients have been abandoned since the onset of drug therapies in the 1950s, and ethical questions are now being raised regarding the use of such procedures with nonhuman primates and other animals. However, in cases of severe epilepsy, surgeons routinely perform an operation on the brain to sever the nerves connecting the two sides or hemispheres of the brain. After the operation, so-called "split-brain" patients are able to enjoy life without experiencing the devastating effects of violent epileptic seizures, but they pay a price. After surgery, information that reaches one hemisphere is trapped on that side and is inaccessible to the other hemisphere. In general, split-brain patients can function quite well in their daily lives because all the sensory systems have dual inputs to the brain, which needs just one input to process the incoming information.

However, under controlled experimental conditions, it is possible to present such patients with stimuli that reach only one side of the brain. The study of split-brain patients by Gazzaniga (1970) is particularly interesting with respect to the debate regarding the independence of cognition and emotion. Because language is usually produced in the left hemisphere, split-brain patients can talk about stimuli presented to the left hemisphere only. Stimuli presented to the right hemisphere cannot be verbally described, but split-brain patients can demonstrate that nonverbal processing of the stimuli has taken place in experiments involving touch. They are able to successfully sort through a bag of objects and select the object that matches the picture seen by the right hemisphere, even though they cannot describe its features. However, because the right hemisphere is thought to be more involved in processing emotional stimuli, experiments involving the presentation of such stimuli to split-brain patients can be especially informative. For example, Gazzaniga (1988) showed a film segment of a person being engulfed by flames to the right cortex of a split-brain patient. While unable to verbally describe or even form a mental image of the event, the patient was clearly frightened by it. The language centers of the left cortex received a fear signal but were unable to link it to the stimuli seen by the right cortex. Could this fear have been processed by some deeper, subcortical area of the brain? We shall answer this question later in this section.

In special cases, a split-brain patient may be able to read words in both hemispheres but speak only through the left hemisphere. This situation allows scientists to ask even more intriguing questions concerning the relation between verbal thought and emotion. In one celebrated case reported by Gazzaniga and LeDoux (1978), the patient was asked to say what the word was and tell how he felt about it. When the emotional stimulus was presented to the left hemisphere, the patient could respond to both instructions. When the same stimulus was presented to the right hemisphere, the patient could not verbalize the

stimulus, but could assign some emotional significance to it. Somehow the patient's emotional reactions could be manipulated by a stimulus that he could not process verbally and claimed not to have seen.

Another line of research that indicates emotion lateralization in the brain stems from clinical reports of patients involved in neurosurgery to remedy intractable epilepsy. During the operation, patients often receive an injection of sodium amytal into the left or right cartoid artery. A recent review of studies reporting the emotional reactions of such patients to these injections establishes a systematic relation between the type of emotional reaction and the side of the injection. Left-sided injections were associated with dysphoric reactions such as feelings of emptiness and despair, crying, and fearful, pessimistic, or negative thoughts. In contrast, right-sided injections elicited euphoria, as evidenced by feelings of well-being, smiling, and optimism (Lee, Loring, Meader, & Brooks, 1990).

Finally, supportive data for emotion lateralization also come from studies of facial expression using observer judgments and using **electromyographic** (EMG) and **electroencephalographic** (EEG) recordings of posed and spontaneous facial expressions. Observations of facial asymmetries from videotapes or photographs of posed and spontaneous expressions may reflect other factors than muscle activation, and these data are less consistent than EMG or EEG data. Using the EMG assessments, lateralized responses have been consistently found for the zygomatic muscles, with positive emotions eliciting greater muscle activity on the left side of the face (Schwartz, Ahern, & Brown, 1979). Similarly, consistent support for the approach–withdrawal and valence hypotheses comes from EEG studies showing greater left-frontal cerebral activation for positive emotions, and greater right-frontal activation with negative affect (Fox & Davidson, 1988).

These diverse sources of data clearly indicate that the left and right frontal hemispheres of the brain are involved in different ways in the experience and expression of emotion. In understanding this relationship between hemisphere and emotion, it may be important to consider whether the hemisphere has been damaged or whether it has been activated. This idea contributes to a finer understanding of the type of affect that is expressed as a result of excitation or disinhibition (release from inhibition). Robinson et al. (1984) and Sackheim et al. (1982) believe that damage to one hemisphere releases activity in the other hemisphere, a process they refer to as contralateral disinhibition. For example, negative thoughts and mood may be produced as a result of disinhibition to the left hemisphere, and crying and emotional distress may be the result of activation of the right.

Fox (1994) has proposed a model that takes into consideration these ideas and describes four possible consequences of left–right activation or inhibition. In this model, activation or inhibition of approach or withdrawal is mapped onto hemispheric activation/hypoactivation as shown in Table 3.1. This model extends the approach–withdrawal model presented earlier by considering regulative, as well as expressive, aspects of an individual's response to emotionally arousing events. Thus, the left-frontal region would be associated with the behavioral approach system and positive affect when activated, and the absence of both when not activated. Similarly, right-frontal activation would be associated with the behavioral inhibition system and fearful or anxious emotion, whereas lack of activation might be associated with inability to inhibit behavior or impulsivity. Although much research is needed to clarify these issues pertaining to the relationship between emotional expression and regulation and hemispheric activation, models that use the dichotomy "approach–withdrawal" may fare better than models that use the dichotomy "positive–negative" emotion. As we shall see in Chapter 4, the term *negative emotion* is inherently vague and confusing, and is especially problematic in its assumption of functional equivalence in the emotion systems of anger, fear, sadness, and disgust. The idea that different emotions may involve different brain systems is currently championed by one of the leading

Table 3.1 The Development of Emotion Regulation

Left Frontal Activation	Right Frontal Activation
Active approach	Active withdrawal
Positive affect	Negative affect
Exploration	Fear/anxiety
Sociability	
Left Frontal Hypoactivation	**Right Frontal Hypoactivation**
Absence of positive affect	Disinhibition of approach
	Impulsivity
Depression	Hyperactivity

Source: Fox (1994). Used by permission of SRCD.

neuroscientists investigating the neural basis of emotion, Joseph LeDoux.

LeDoux's Amygdala Theory of Fear

Like MacLean, Joseph LeDoux considers evolutionary theory as critical in leading scientists to understand the origins of emotion in the brain. However, unlike MacLean who viewed emotion as a unitary faculty of mind mediated by a single unified system within the brain, LeDoux believes that different emotions may involve different brain systems. Instead of a universal emotion system in the brain, LeDoux believes that it is more plausible to assume that different emotions are mediated by different brain systems, and that evolution acted upon each of these basic survival systems somewhat independently.

Historically, cognition was considered to be part of a trilogy of mind that also included emotion and motivation as equally important processes. The tendency of cognitive scientists to reduce these processes of the human mind to general cognitive information processing is reductionistic and inconsistent with recent formulations in the neurosciences regarding the relative autonomy of emotional processes. The analogy of the human brain to the information processing of a computer is certainly useful, but to understand human emotions it may be more useful to remember that it is only an analogy.

Rather than viewing the emotional brain as a general computer, LeDoux (1996), Panksepp, (1993), Plutchik (1980), and others believe that during the long course of its evolution, the brain evolved multiple behavioral-emotional systems, each with its own distinct structural and functional properties. From this perspective, because different emotions are involved in different adaptive tasks—seeking protection from the caregiver, defending against danger, securing a mate, and so on—each emotional system may be linked to specific brain systems that evolved for each specific purpose. This idea leads LeDoux to propose that scientists investigate one emotional system at a time, without assuming, for example, that the emotional network responsible for activating the organism's response to fear is the same system that activates one's romantic attachments.

The key to understanding this point of view is the idea that natural selection often leads to functional equivalence in evolved systems across diverse species that must successfully solve common problems if they are to survive. As a result, systems have been designed by natural selection for fear, anger, attachment, play, and sexuality that share common ground across diverse species of primates and mammals. This idea is very similar to MacLean's description of the triune brain, and consistent with MacLean's data that demonstrate functional equivalence across different species regarding the same behavioral display. LeDoux differs from MacLean in assuming that each basic emotional system is somewhat localized anatomically and mediated by separate neural systems. From a research standpoint, one would hypothesize that each system would respond differently to lesions and electrical and chemical stimulation.

Given the arsenal of techniques available to neuroscientists to understand how emotional functions are mediated by specific patterns of neural connections, the only other requirement for progress is selecting a well-defined, reliably measured emotion. Because many of the methods outlined in this chapter can be employed only with nonhuman subjects, the emotion selected should also be common to a diversity of species.

In his book, *The Emotional Brain,* LeDoux argues that the basic emotion of fear is the top candidate for neurological study:

> Fear conditioning is thus an excellent experimental technique for studying the control of fear or defense responses in the brain. It can be applied up and down the phyla. The stimuli involved can be specified and controlled, and the sensory system that processes the conditioned stimulus can be used as the starting point for tracing the pathways through the brain. The learning takes place very quickly and lasts indefinitely. Fear conditioning can be used to study how the brain processes the conditioned fear stimulus and controls defense responses that are coupled to them. It can also be used to examine the mechanisms through which emotional memories are established, stored, and retrieved, and, in humans, the mechanisms underlying conscious fear. (1996, p. 148)

Using a research strategy that combines the classical lesion method with modern neuroanatomical tracing techniques, LeDoux has developed a process model of the brain that demonstrates how a cognitive appraisal becomes transformed into an emotional response, with all the heart-pounding, bodily sensations that psychologists since James have ascribed to fear. The key to this transformation in the brain is the involvement of the **amygdala,** which LeDoux describes as the hub in the wheel of fear, as shown in Figure 3.6.

To illustrate LeDoux's theory of the role of the amygdala in the processing of fearful stimuli, let us consider a hunter walking alone in the Maine woods who is suddenly deafened by the blast of a shotgun fired at close range. Previous models of how the brain responded to such inputs routed the incoming information from the sensory thalamus up to the sensory cortex where

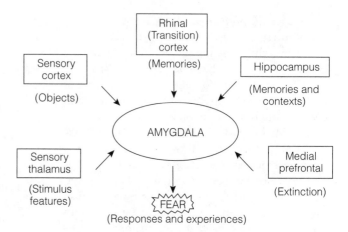

Figure 3.6 The amygdala plays a central role in the emotion process. Inputs from many sources with different levels of cognition may trigger an emotional response from the amygdala. Anatomical knowledge about which cortical areas project to the amygdala allow predictions about how those functions contribute to fear responses.

Source: LeDoux (1996). Reprinted with permission of Brockman, Inc.

the sound was consciously perceived. The cortex then sent signals to **subcortical** areas of the limbic system (including the amygdala) responsible for appraisal. After evaluating the emotional significance of the sound as dangerous, the limbic system sent a return message up to the cortex to activate the fear system in the ANS, which in turn produced the heart-pounding subjective feeling of fear.

By skillful application of the experimental techniques of lesions and tracing, LeDoux's research revealed that the brain can process the same auditory information via a shorter, more direct route that bypasses the cortex altogether. From an evolutionary vantage point, the direct route evolved first and remains the only pathway available in the lower vertebrates. With the evolution of the cortex, the older, more primitive processing system continued to function alongside the more complex system for millions of years, plenty of time to atrophy if it was not useful. But the direct thalamic pathway to the amygdala is two to three times faster than the thalamo-cortico-amygdala pathway. However, the increase in speed is offset by reduced cognitive processing that can be provided only by the cortex. According to LeDoux, this gain in processing time must occasionally provide substantial benefits that more than offset the loss of informa-

tion, since both pathways remain functional in the human brain where they converge in the lateral nucleus of the amygdala. (See Figure 3.7.)

Once the information arrives at the lateral nucleus of the amygdala via either route, it can be quickly transmitted to the central nucleus, which can release whatever level of defensive response the situation warrants. The response systems controlled by outputs from the amygdala central nucleus include ANS responses like blood pressure, endocrine responses that release stress hormones into the bloodstream, reflexes, and other behaviors. This double pathway may account for the common experience of sudden and extreme fright to a nondangerous stimuli that resembles a dangerous one, only to be followed seconds later by a second, slower, calmer response once the stimuli has been more fully evaluated. As shown in Figure 3.8, the frame-by-frame analysis captured by Eibl-Eibesfeldt's films dramatically illustrates this double reaction in a young German girl and in a Yanomamö adult male when confronted with a stimuli that "fools" the amygdala but not the cortex. Of course, as LeDoux argues, the retention of the double pathway in the human brain implies a functional significance to the faster processing system in our EEA. According to this logic, the price of false alarms (being startled into an aroused state when no real danger is

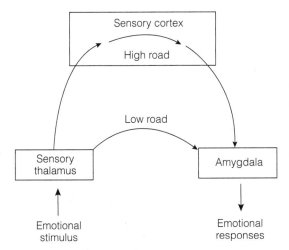

Figure 3.7 Two pathways to fear. LeDoux's research reveals a faster, subcortical path to the amygdala that has been retained in the human brain despite the evolution of the more cognitively sophisticated cortical route. The direct path allows for a rapid response to what appears to be a dangerous stimulus before we consciously process it. LeDoux believes that this direct path may control emotional reactions that we do not understand.

Source: LeDoux (1996). Reprinted with permission of Brockman, Inc.

present) is more than offset by the benefit of reacting quickly to real danger.

In concluding this section on the neural basis of emotion, it is useful to recall that any comprehensive model must necessarily include an equally detailed analysis of physiology and behavior. Evolutionary models must eventually connect brain processes to an analysis of CNS outputs at the level of physiological, expressive, and behavioral responses. This is because an evolutionary model presumes that the CNS is constructed according to consequences of these outputs for the organism.

PHYSIOLOGICAL ANALYSIS OF EMOTION

From the theories of Darwin and James to the present, psychologists have been interested in the **autonomic nervous system (ANS)** that controls the functioning of internal organs, such as the heart and the glands in the endocrine system that produce hormones. Since early times ANS changes have been thought to accompany or intensify emotional experiences. The term itself is actually a misnomer. Scientists once believed

this part of the nervous system was independent of the brain and spinal cord, thus the label *autonomic*. It is true that most of the activity of the ANS is automatic, in the sense that we are generally not conscious of its functioning. However, it is not the case that the ANS is independent of the CNS; instead, they are intimately linked.

The ANS is composed of two systems that are sometimes opposed and sometimes act in concert. The **sympathetic division** of the ANS consists of two chains of neurons found along both sides of the spinal cord. Its primary function is to ready the body to respond to emergencies such as "flight or fight." The **parasympathetic division** of the ANS is composed of neurons linking the spinal cord to the internal organs. Its function is to maintain the body's state in nonemergency situations. It does this by decreasing the heart rate during periods of relative inactivity, aiding in digestion, and so on. A comparison of the two systems is provided in Table 3.2.

Researchers interested in the relationship between the ANS and emotions have recorded various physiological changes such as the level of **cortisol** circulating in the blood or contained in saliva, and changes in the cardiac and vascular systems via indices such as **heart rate (HR),** **vagal tone,** galvanic skin response (GSR), blood

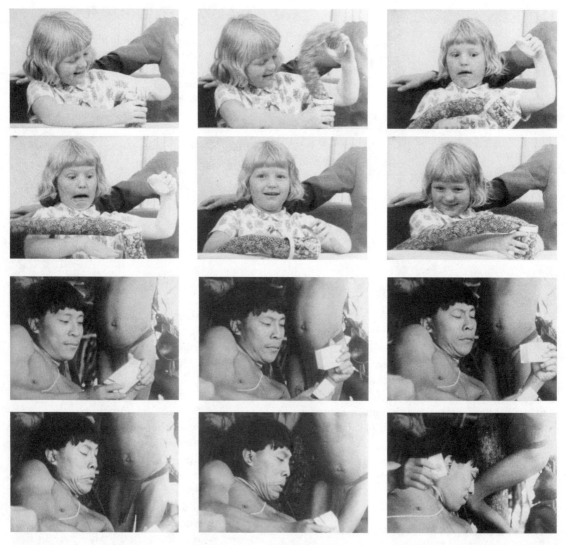

Figure 3.8 Fear reactions in a young German girl and adult Yanomamö male. Filming at 48 frames/second, Eibl-Eibesfeldt captures a double response to an unexpected event. Both subjects were given a box from which a cloth snake or cloth mouse jumped out when it was opened. The sequence of expressive reactions are nearly identical in these two subjects of different ages, gender, and cultural backgrounds. The first response is a classic fear reaction (notice the eye and mouth regions and the pulling back of the head) followed by a bemused expression mixed with smiling and embarrassment (for the German girl) when the slower cortical pathway allows them to complete their cognitive appraisal of the stimulus.

(Photos by I. Eibl-Eibesfeldt, 1989)

pressure, and respiration. This research has led to a clearer understanding of the relationship between emotion and physiology, and to the general view that the study of emotion must involve an analysis of both behavioral and physiological systems and their interrelation.

Table 3.2 A Comparison of the Sympathetic and Parasympathetic Divisions of the ANS

Sympathetic System (uses much energy)	Parasympathetic System (conserves energy)
Pupils open	Pupils constrict
Saliva decreases	Saliva flows
Pulse quickens	Pulse slows
Sweat increases	Sweat decreases
Stomach less active	Stomach churns
Epinephrine (adrenaline) secreted	

Heart Rate

The early position on the interrelation of behavioral and physiological systems was that the physiological response was a direct reflection of the degree of emotional arousal elicited by a particular stimulus. Researchers used a number of different emotional elicitors and interpreted increases in **heart rate** (HR) as a measure of the subject's arousal, and decreases or stable HR as indicating no arousal. This early view gave way to the idea that the physiological correlates of ANS activity are associated with specific psychological states rather than general arousal. Researchers such as Ax (1953), and later Ekman, Levenson, and Friesen (1983), attempted to distinguish basic emotions such as anger and fear on the basis of ANS responses. Graham and Clifton (1966) proposed that a sudden rise in HR reflects a defensive response and a decrease in HR indicates an orienting response. Campos, Emde, Gaensbauer, and Henderson (1975) substantiated this view in their work with infants, showing that infant HR increases with the approach of a stranger and departure of the mother, but decreases while the infant attends to a novel or interesting event. As research by neuroscientists like LeDoux indicates, such changes in the ANS are brought about by a complex process initiated in the brain and involving emotional networks that include the amygdala and hypothalamus, and often, but not always, the cortex.

A central problem in research that seeks to understand the links between specific emotions and their expressive and physiological components is the time course for changes in these various systems (Fox, 1994). Changes in facial expressions and brain electrical activity occur within milliseconds after presenting the emotional elicitor. However, most autonomic change is on the order of seconds, and some indices such as cortisol levels take place 10 to 15 minutes after the emotional elicitor. For this reason, it is not always possible to integrate different physiological indices within a single study. In the following sections we review two major types of ANS responses that have been related to emotion, vagal tone and cortisol. However, keep in mind that these two systems are not independent of one another, and neither is independent of the brain structures previously discussed.

Vagal Tone

Cardiac **vagal tone** is an index based on the time period between heartbeats, rather than heart rate which measures the number of heartbeats per minute. On a beat-to-beat level, vagal tone is measured using time–series analyses of the sequential time intervals between heartbeats. This more precise measure takes into consideration the rhythmic increase and decrease of heart rate with respiration. The term *vagal* refers to the tenth cranial nerve called the vagus. The vagus is a complex system of bidirectional neural pathways linking the brain stem to various bodily organs, such as the heart and the digestive system (Porges, Doussard-Roosevelt, & Maiti, 1994). Scientific interest in the vagus complex arose in Austria at the beginning of the twentieth century with the work of Eppinger and Hess (1910). At that time, vagal tone was viewed as a possible mechanism by which to explain problems in the regulation of autonomic function in patients suffering from neurotic symptoms. This early work laid the foundation for understanding the role of the vagal system in regulating physiological responses associated with emotional states.

The most current model of the role of the vagus nerve in the expression and regulation of emotion was developed by Stephen Porges and colleagues (Porges, 1992; Porges, Doussard-Roosevelt, & Maiti, 1994). As shown in Figure 3.9, the emotion process can originate in either the cortex, the amygdala, or as feedback from internal organs. From any origin, the nucleus ambiguus, once stimulated, triggers the vagus, which in turn regulates heart rate and intonation of vocalizations. As an illustration of this model, let us consider an example of emotional stress. A psychological stimulus, such as ruminating about an impending examination in a course that has already been failed, may stimulate the amygdala and lead to physiological changes associated with stress. This stressful condition could result in stomach pains that continue the emotion process by stimulating the tractus solitarius with feedback loops projecting to the cortical, subcortical, brain-stem, and autonomic responses associated with expression and regulation of the emotional state. With emotional circuits of this complexity, it is small wonder that early theorists debated whether the body or the brain was more central to an emotional experience. In a very real sense, they were all right.

When the organism is in a resting state, the ANS, through the vagus, maintains the body's homeostasis and enhances the growth and recovery of the internal organs. However, in response to sensory, cognitive, or visceral challenges, the ANS activates the metabolism of the organism to meet the challenge. Depending upon the intensity of these challenges, the CNS regulates the strength and duration of ANS response systems. In mammals, the right side of the brain stem mediates the processes of homeostasis and physiological reactivity. High vagal tone resulting from stronger input from the vagus nerve is related to metabolic increases associated with exercise or strong emotional arousal accompanying fight–flight demands. Three aspects of the basic behavioral systems of approach and withdrawal that are hypothesized to be associated with vagal tone are (1) behavioral reactivity, (2) facial expressivity, and (3) emotion regulation.

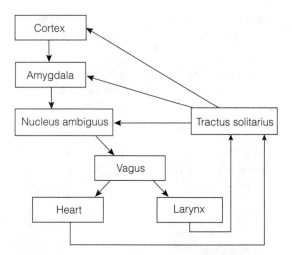

Figure 3.9 The vagal circuit of emotion regulation. This schematic diagram depicts the circuit by which the CNS and ANS interact during emotional reactions. Inputs originating from the brain affect the vagus, which in turn influences the heart and larynx, producing emotional reactions that may be relayed by the tractus solitarius to the cortex, completing the circuit.

Source: Porges, Doussard-Roosevelt, and Maiti (1994). Reprinted by permission of SRCD.

A number of recent studies using infants have supported the hypothesis of vagal tone as an index of behavioral reactivity. For example, high vagal tone in neonates was found to be correlated with greater heart-rate acceleration in response to circumcision (Porter, Porges, & Marshall, 1988), and greater reactivity and irritability to stimuli assessed with the Neonatal Behavioral Assessment Scale (Brazelton, 1984). Six-month-old infants with high vagal tone looked longer at novel stimuli and exhibited more heart-rate reactivity to it (Linnemeyer & Porges, 1986). These and other studies consistently show that neonates, infants, children, and adults with high vagal tone have an appropriate range of autonomic and behavioral responses to environmental stimulation.

Facial expressions of emotions may be related to vagal tone because of the proximity of the facial nerve to the vagal system. Indeed the facial nerve is often included as part of the vagus complex.

Only a few studies have been conducted to examine this hypothesis. Higher resting heart-rate variability has been linked to greater expressiveness in newborns, and longer expressions of interest (Field, Woodson, Greenberg, & Cohen, 1982; Fox & Gelles, 1984). In addition, 5-month-old infants with higher vagal tone were found to display greater interest and joy toward strangers (Stifter, Fox, & Porges, 1989). These findings are complicated by other studies that show that neonates with high vagal tone are more irritable and appear to be less able to soothe themselves, a condition that may change dramatically over the first three months of life, presumably because of sensitive caregiving. In any case, our current level of knowledge does not permit any firm conclusions regarding the relationship between vagal tone and self-regulation of emotion.

The research program of Porges and colleagues advances our conceptualization of the physiological aspects of emotion in four important ways: It (1) offers a noninvasive, reliable, and precise index of vagal tone; (2) stresses the importance of the vagal system in the physiology of emotional processes; (3) provides a possible mechanism for explaining individual differences in emotional reactivity with respect to brain damage, drug-induced dysfunction, and learned dysfunction; and (4) provides a mechanism by which to explain the effects of various emotion regulation practices in infants and adults, such as nonnutritive sucking (a baby's pacifier), massage, exercise, yoga, and different cognitive strategies (Porges, Doussard-Roosevelt, & Maiti, 1994).

Cortisol

Cortisol is the primary stress hormone produced by the **hypothalamic-pituitary-adrenocortical (HPA) system.** This system is a **neuroendocrine system** that is regulated by outputs from the amygdala to the hypothalamus, which in turn regulates the production and release of stress hormones into the bloodstream. The production of cortisol varies rhythmically during 24-hour day–night cycles, referred to as the **circadian rhythm.** Inputs from the limbic system modulate circadian rhythm according to the timing of salient events such as naps, meals, and exposure to light. In adults who follow a typical day/night schedule, cortisol production is accelerated during the last few hours of sleep, leading to high levels in the early morning that typically decline sharply for the first few hours after peak and more gradually throughout the remainder of the cycle. This circadian rhythm provides for greater energy in the morning hours and stimulates the appetite for carbohydrates. In human newborns, the rhythm emerges at about 3 months and becomes well established at about 2 years (Price, Close, & Fielding, 1983). The circadian production of cortisol is the physiological mechanism that is responsible for the common experience of "jet lag" that occurs when one travels across six or more time zones or shifts from the day to the night shift. It takes almost two weeks to completely reorganize the timing of the circadian rhythm following a 12-hour shift in the sleep/wake cycle (Stansbury & Gunnar, 1994).

Knowledge concerning the circadian rhythm is important for distinguishing basal levels of cortisol from elevated levels that are produced as part of the HPA system's biological response to stress. Three distinct pathways are involved in this stress response. First, biochemicals in the bloodstream can directly stimulate the pituitary and hypothalamus. Second, visceral and sensory stimulation, including pain, can affect the hypothalamus through brain-stem pathways. Third, psychological stimuli can affect the hypothalamus via routes from the cerebral cortex and limbic structures. The amygdala appears to be instrumental in activating the stress response, while the hippocampus appears to terminate it, allowing for a return to basal levels (de Kloet, 1991; LeDoux, 1996; Smuts & Levine, 1977). According to LeDoux (1996), the stress hormone flows through the bloodstream into the brain where it binds to various receptors, including the amygdala and hippocampus. This provides a feedback loop that serves to regulate the production and release of the stress hormone to match the demands of the stressful situation, as shown in Figure 3.10.

The HPA system evolved to facilitate the organism's response to stress arising from interaction with the environment. An adaptive biological response to stress involves the increased production of cortisol, which begins 10 to 15 minutes after the onset of a stressful stimulus, peaks at about 20 to 30 minutes, remains elevated during the stressful experience, and gradually declines to basal levels after termination of the stress response. The adrenocortical system mobilizes the organism for action against the stressor, regulates other stress-sensitive systems in the body such as the natural opiate system and the immune system, and influences brain mechanisms responsible for learning, memory, and emotions (Selye, 1950; Stansbury & Gunnar, 1994). In the short-term, increases in stress hormones raise the organism's threshold for pain and provide an increase in energy and concentration, but long-term effects (after several days of artificially high stimulation) appear to reverse these effects and may lead to depressed affect. Some researchers interpret this two-phase sequence as initially providing hormonal support for heightened behavioral and emotional responses, while later facilitating the organism's withdrawal and recovery from the stressful experience.

To illustrate the time course of an HPA stress response, consider the following example. An individual is driving home with friends at midnight (when basal cortisol levels are low), on a winter night under icy conditions, and is involved in a serious highway accident. Within a few minutes after the accident, increased levels of cortisol could facilitate an adaptive response that might involve rescuing oneself and fellow passengers, applying first aid and taking emergency medical actions to ward off shock, and running a mile back to a gas station to call for help. Later in the hospital, the individual begins to feel the pain of an injury that was sustained at impact, fatigue, and an inability to concentrate while being questioned regarding the event. Still later the individual falls into a deep sleep until noon the

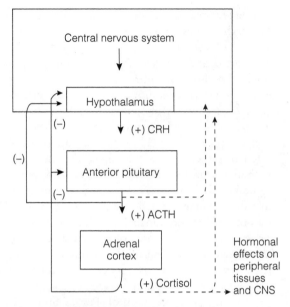

Figure 3.10 The hypothalmic-pituitary-adrenocortical (HPA) system. This diagram represents feedforward and feedback loops (solid lines) and physiological effects (dotted lines) in normal stress reactions for children and adults.

Source: Adapted from Stansbury and Gunnar (1994). Reprinted with permission of SRCD.

following day. Underlying the body's sequence of responses to these events is the hormonal output of the adrenocortical system.

Understandably, research on the HPA system in humans is severely constricted by ethical concerns. Typically, experimental techniques involving mild stressors are insufficient to produce elevations in cortisol, though other psychophysiological systems may be responsive (for example, HR). For this reason, many researchers have turned to naturally occurring stressors that may be studied in order to understand the role of the HPA system. Naturalistic studies with adults show that work stress and rigorous military training are associated with cortisol elevation and self-reports of negative emotions, including impatience, irritation, fear, and anxiety (Frankenhaeuser, 1980; Ursin, Baade, & Levine, 1978).

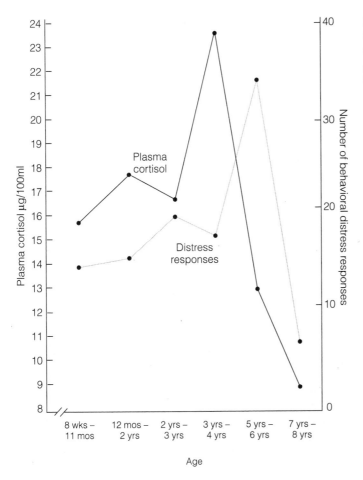

Figure 3.11 A cross-sectional analysis of observed distress and plasma cortisol in children with PKU during venipuncture.

Source: Gunnar, Marvinney, Isensee, and Fisch (1994). Reprinted with permission of SRCD.

Researchers like Megan Gunnar and colleagues have been exploring changes in cortisol level that accompany infants' and children's responses to naturally occurring stressors. Three hypotheses have been proposed to account for the different relationships observed between emotional expression/regulation, changes in cortisol level, and various stressors. The first hypothesis is that stressors that produce negative affect will also produce elevations in basal cortisol. This hypothesis is supported by data showing that neonatal crying in response to circumcision and heel-stick blood sampling is associated with increased plasma cortisol (Stansbury & Gunnar, 1994). However, this pattern does not always

hold. In human infants, monkey infants, and adults, the HPA stress response shows rapid habituation to repeated exposure to the same psychological stressor. This capacity makes adaptive sense. However, behavioral and negative affective responses to the same stressor do not habituate so quickly, undoing the association between negative affective displays and cortisol level.

These results led researchers to propose a second hypothesis in which the novelty, discrepancy, or incongruity of the stimulus is responsible for increased cortisol. Although this hypothesis is consistent with the habituation findings, other data appear to contradict it. Sometimes the repeated exposure to stressors is linked to increases in cortisol. Cross-sectional research in children from infancy to 8 years of age indicates that we cannot always expect a simple relation between negative emotional expression and cortisol level. One study was conducted with children with PKU (phenylketonuria) from whom regular blood samples were drawn as part of the treatment process (Gunnar, Marvinney, Isensee, & Fisch, 1989). The data presented in Figure 3.11 reveal that young preschoolers show high levels of crying but low levels of cortisol, older preschoolers show the reverse, and still older children show low levels of crying and cortisol. The authors interpret this complex pattern of results in terms of the children's knowledge of display rules and ability to generate emotional control strategies. Children who voiced the display rule of not crying when receiving their shots, but who could not yet generate emotion regulation strategies, showed low levels of crying but high levels of cortisol. Older children who showed low levels of both responses were able to verbalize the display rule and generate strategies to enact it. Cortisol levels were elevated for children who were uncertain about their ability to refrain from crying.

These results led to the formulation of a third hypothesis that proposes that cortisol production may be linked with uncertainty about how to control the stressful event and/or one's emotional reaction to it (Stansbury & Gunnar, 1994). As more research is conducted regarding the links between emotional expression/regulation and activation of the HPA stress response, we are discovering more complexity in the HPA system than was initially expected.

SUMMARY

In this chapter we introduced the neurological and physiological bases of emotion. Neuroscientists use a variety of techniques to identify the brain mechanisms by which we selectively attend, process, and evaluate sensory stimulation, and assign to it emotional significance. Historically, laboratory work with animals was important

in this area because of the functional similarities of vertebrate brains and because artificial stimulation can reproduce the chain of events that occurs due to natural stimulation. If a particular set of neurons in the brain is stimulated and a certain type of behavior follows, then neuroscientists assume that those neurons are the part of the brain that controls that behavior. Based on laboratory research, we know that the brain communicates on the basis of chemical and electrical signals transmitted from neurons in one area of the brain to another.

When sufficiently stimulated, a neuron will release a wave of electrical charge, or action potential, down the output axon where it branches off into many axon terminals. When the action potential reaches a terminal, it causes a chemical, called a neurotransmitter, to be released. The neurotransmitter flows across the synapse (the space between the axon terminal of one neuron and the dendrites of its neighbor) to the dendrites of surrounding neurons where it contributes to the release of electrical energy, and so on throughout an area of the brain. In this manner, both electrical and chemical stimulation form the basis for communication between nerve cells.

Over the past decade there has been an explosive growth in the use of brain imaging techniques such as positron emission topography (PET scan), magnetic resonance imaging (MRI), and magnetoencephalography (MEG). These techniques give neuroscientists the opportunity to study the human brain at work by identifying those brain structures that are activated while subjects perform various tasks that call on specific abilities. Viewing computer images of the living brain at work, activating specific areas of the brain through artificial stimulation, and deactivating areas by surgical lesions remain the key tools for understanding brain function.

These improvements in methodology have led to theoretical advances in understanding the neurological basis of emotion. As a product of a long evolutionary history, the brain appears to be modular in its adaptive design, composed of a hierarchy of three major developments that are radically different in chemistry and function and that, in an evolutionary sense, are eons apart. These three steps in the evolution of the human brain correspond to phylogenetic adaptations common to reptiles, early mammals, and late mammals.

The physical structure in the brain thought by MacLean to be responsible for regulating the evolving behavioral programs related to maternal care, infant attachment, vocal signaling, and play is the limbic system. With the emergence of these new behavioral systems, the limbic system evolved in mammals as the brain's primary emotional and motivational system. This portion of the brain is closely connected with the hypothalamus, which in turn controls the ANS. Based on both organizational structure and clinical findings, MacLean asserts that two phylogenetically older modules, the striatal region and limbic system, lack any capacity for verbal communication with those areas of the neocortex that are responsible for speech.

Rather than viewing the emotional brain as a general computer, evolutionary psychologists believe that during the long course of its evolution, the brain evolved multiple behavioral-emotional systems, each with its own distinct structural and functional properties. From this perspective, because different emotions are involved in different adaptive tasks—seeking protection from the caregiver, defending against danger, securing a mate, and so on—each emotional system may be linked to specific brain systems that evolved for each specific purpose.

By skillful application of the experimental techniques of lesions and tracing, LeDoux's research reveals that the brain can process the same sensory information via two routes, the thalamo-cortico-amygdala pathway, and a shorter, more direct route that bypasses the cortex altogether and is two or three times faster. From an evolutionary vantage point, the direct route evolved first and remains the only pathway available in the lower vertebrates. With the evolution of the cortex, the older, more primitive processing system continues to function alongside the more complex system.

At the level of physiology, scientists have been equally active in exploring the relationship between emotion and autonomic nervous activity, such as heart rate and the production of stress hormones. The ANS is composed of two systems that are sometimes opposed and sometimes act in concert. The sympathetic division consists of two chains of neurons found along both sides of the spinal cord. Its primary function is to ready the body to respond to emergencies such as "flight or fight." The parasympathetic division is composed of neurons linking the spinal cord to the internal organs. Its function is to maintain the body's state in nonemergency situations.

When the organism is in a resting state, the ANS, through the vagus, maintains the body's homeostasis and enhances the growth and recovery of the internal organs. However, in response to sensory, cognitive, or visceral challenges, the ANS activates the metabolism of the organism to meet the challenge. Depending upon the intensity of these challenges, the CNS regulates the strength and duration of ANS response systems. High vagal tone resulting from stronger input from the vagus nerve is related to metabolic increases associated with exercise or strong emotional arousal accompanying fight–flight demands.

Hormonal systems like the hypothalamic-pituitary-adrenocortical (HPA) system evolved to facilitate the organism's response to stress arising from interaction with the environment. An adaptive biological response to stress involves activity of the pituitary gland or other glands located in the body, which are controlled by outputs from the hypothalamus. Once activated, the pituitary gland secretes stress hormones that stimulate the production and release of cortisol that circulates in the bloodstream to reach the specific organs that respond to its presence. For this reason, hormones usually require more time to have an impact on the body than neurotransmitters. Cortisol production begins 10 to 15 minutes after the onset of a stressful stimulus, peaks at about 20 to 30 minutes, remains elevated during the stressful experience, and gradually declines to basal levels after termination of the stress response. Developmental researchers are currently interested in physiological systems as a possible basis for individual differences in emotional functioning.

FURTHER READING

Fox, N. A. (Ed.) (1994). The development of emotion regulation: Biological and behavioral considerations. *Monographs of the Society for Research in Child Development, 59*(2/3, Serial No. 240), 152–166.

This is a useful introduction to contemporary developmental research in the physiology of emotion regulation.

LeDoux, J. E. (1996). *The emotional brain: The mysterious underpinnings of emotional life.* New York: Simon & Schuster.

This book is a fascinating and accessible account of how the brain processes incoming stimuli and evaluates its emotional significance.

4

Psychological Perspectives

He discloses the basic character of science as the eternal attempt to go beyond what is regarded scientifically accessible at any specific time. To proceed beyond the limitations of a given level of knowledge the researcher, as a rule, has to break down methodological taboos which condemn as "unscientific" or "illogical" the very methods which later on prove to be basic for the next major progress.

KURT LEWIN (1949)

The scientific study of emotion within psychology has a curious history, but one which I believe is illuminated by Lewin's insightful comment concerning the dynamics of scientific progress. Many philosophers, artists, and early psychological theorists like James and Freud assumed a central role of emotions in human affairs. However, beginning with the rise of radical behaviorism within mainstream American psychology, the topic of emotion was no longer considered to be suitable for scientific inquiry. This has been referred to as the first revolution in American psychology. In a nutshell, the radical behaviorists, led by Watson, Skinner, and others, decided that it was time to lock all the fuzzy concepts relating to thinking and feeling into a "black box," and concentrate instead on overt behavior. According to Skinner (1953), idle speculations about inner dispositions of persons as mediators between stimulus–response (S-R) connections are scientifically unproductive. Whatever strategic advantage this may have had, its restrictive attitude left little room for the traditional faculties of mind (cognition, motivation, and emotion) and led to the description by Deese (1985) of Skinner's behaviorism as "the abolition of mind" (p. 31). It proved to be such a straightjacket on American psychology that it led directly to the second revolution.

By the 1960s dissatisfaction with the oversimplifications fostered by radical behaviorism led to the cognitive revolution. The first step in this movement was to open the S-R connection just enough to insert mental processes that mediate the individual's response to a given stimulus. In this new stimulus–organism–response (S-O-R) version of the theory, it was admitted that the organism's cognitive processing of a stimulus influences its response. But once the "black box" had been opened, it was difficult to put everything back in. It would not be long before American psychologists would make their way back to the original conception of mind and revive the banished concepts of motivation and emotion along with cognition.

By the 1980s the third revolution in American psychology was underway. At the beginning of the new millennium, the topic of emotion is visible everywhere in psychology, so much so that it is difficult to fully appreciate the icy grip that radical behaviorists had on the research agenda of American psychologists for so much of the twentieth century. It is instructive to reflect on the history of emotion research within psychology, if only to understand and avoid the pitfalls of belonging too much to any particular generation of scholars. Consider the famous prediction of Meyer (1933) regarding the future of psychology viewed in his day:

> Why introduce into science an unneeded term, such as emotion, when there are already scientific terms for everything we have to describe? . . . I predict: the "will" has virtually passed out of our scientific psychology today; the "emotion" is bound to do the same. In 1950 American psychologists will smile at both these terms as curiosities of the past. (p. 300)

This prediction was by no means as farfetched as it seems to us today. In the 1950s it did indeed seem to be becoming true. However, in the year 2000, if American psychologists were smiling, it was certainly not over the quaintness of the old-fashioned notions of motivation and emotion! Instead of dying out, during the 1980s and 1990s, we witnessed a renaissance in research on emotion, accompanied by a bewildering proliferation of emotion theories, each with its own particular

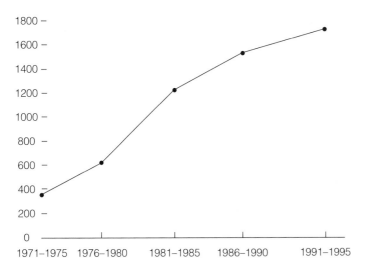

Figure 4.1 Rise in publications on emotions since 1970. The annual rate of publications on emotion listed in PSYCHLIT tripled during the 1970s and has been rising continuously since to approximately 2000 per year at the end of the century.

orientation and focus, each seeking to explain different aspects of emotion in relation to evolution, neurobiology, physiology, cognition, personality, development, culture, and psychopathology. To substantiate the presence of this third revolution in American psychology, I recently analyzed the references in the psychology literature that listed *emotion* as a key word. This process yielded an average of 1,728 references per year during the 1990s, compared to about 500 per year in the 1970s, and barely a trickle before that (see Figure 4.1).

In this chapter, the major psychological theories on emotion are presented. Three basic perspectives will be emphasized: (1) the psychodynamic tradition, (2) cognitive and cultural approaches, and (3) developmental theories. Although these perspectives are not mutually exclusive, they provide an effective means to organize some of the many diverse theoretical views on emotion within psychology. Since psychology stands midway between the natural sciences and the social sciences, these psychological theories of emotion are presented in parallel with, rather than in opposition to, the biological perspectives presented in the previous chapter. Before exploring them, we begin our discussion

with the basic question of what a theory of emotion ought to do.

GENERAL FUNCTIONS OF A SCIENTIFIC THEORY OF EMOTION

A scientific theory is an integrated set of statements that serve to define basic constructs, describe their interconnections, and relate these constructs to observable events. This last point has been a stumbling block for many of the earlier theories of emotions, but its resolution is absolutely critical for progress in emotion research. An observable event may be a facial expression, body posture or gesture, tone of voice, eye movement, heart rate, cortisol level, electrical activity in the brain—literally anything that can be detected by direct observation or other forms of scientific assessment. So a fundamental theoretical and methodological issue in building a science of emotions is how to deal with feelings, which by definition are subjective states. Scientists will probably always be divided regarding how to proceed on this issue. At one extreme, feelings are considered irrelevant to a science of emotions, and in any case, they are simply not observable and thus cannot be included as useful data. At the other end of the spectrum, researchers simply ask their subjects to report what they are feeling or even what they are likely to feel in certain hypothetical situations, and this constitutes their data. Most researchers fall somewhere in the middle between these two extremes, cognizant of the pitfalls of subjective data drawn from self-report, but wary of eliminating the subjective feeling aspect of emotion from our scientific methodology.

This debate is crucial for emotion research, because methodological choices determine the various data that become grist for the scientific mill. They are the facts that the theory is supposed to organize and explain. So a major function of a theory is to integrate within a single, coherent framework all the known facts regarding a phenomenon of interest. Because research on emotions is still relatively immature, an even more important function for a theory of emotion is to stimulate our thinking about the topic and open up and guide new research. A useful theory is one that is capable of generating logically consistent hypotheses concerning events that have not yet been observed. This heuristic function of generating testable hypotheses is critical to the scientific process of confirming or disconfirming predictions, which in turn feeds back upon the process of constructing more adequate theories.

A number of criteria may be used to judge the merits of a scientific theory, including its heuristic value, parsimony, coherence, relevance, and generality. The early theories of Darwin, Freud, Pavlov, Watson, James, Skinner, and others have demonstrated great **heuristic value,** that is, they each stimulated a great deal of research activity. These theories differ somewhat in terms of their parsimony and coherence. Darwin and Skinner get very high marks on these criteria because both theories are economical in the number of assumptions and postulates they set forth. **Parsimony** refers to the ability to formulate a few basic principles that will relate and explain a large number of facts. Such simplicity lends itself to coherence, or the degree of logic and internal consistency within the interrelated theoretical postulates and principles. Psychoanalytic theory gets lower marks on this criteria, because of the complexity and often vague quality of its many reformulations. It is especially problematic if its proponents cannot agree on how to assess basic constructs or cannot link constructs to observable events.

The relevance and breadth of a theory of emotion may be considered together to judge how adequate the theory addresses the diverse questions posed by emotion scholars. It is clear that the early theories were distinct in their focus on particular aspects of the emotion complex. Darwin was largely concerned with the expressive and behavioral component. James was interested in feelings, bodily sensations, and the physiological component. Pavlov, Watson, and Skinner were interested in stimulus–response connections and classical and instrumental conditioning. In stark contrast, Freud sought to empty the contents of the behaviorist "black box" and examine the subjective quality of complex human emotions. Throughout this book, we will adopt the attitude that all of these approaches have something important to contribute to our understanding of emotion, and we will integrate them wherever possible.

The more contemporary theories of emotion that will be examined in this chapter draw upon these pioneering theories and extend their ideas further. In many cases they seek to synthesize several existing theories in order to acquire more generality, and theoretical progress may be viewed in these terms. All things being equal, the more a theory encompasses—the more phenomena that it is capable of explaining—the better it is. If this greater generality is acquired without sacrificing parsimony and coherence, then it should gradually gain ascendance in the scientific community. We begin our discussion of modern psychological theories with Erik Erikson, a theorist who illustrates this very aspect of theoretical progress.

PSYCHODYNAMIC THEORIES

By the mid-twentieth century, many aspects of Freud's original theory had been extensively criticized and some ideas entirely discredited. Nevertheless, few psychological theorists have attracted as many followers or stirred up as much debate as Sigmund Freud. What other psychologist exerted as much influence on psychology and Western thought over the entire span of the twentieth century? Freud compelled us to consider the irrational, unconscious side of human nature unlike any thinker before or since. He also laid the groundwork for viewing adult personality within a developmental framework, insisting upon the special importance of early experience. Unlike any previous theorist of mental illness, Freud insisted that ideas and emotions can induce physical effects upon the body in the form of medical problems like hypertension and ulcers, as well as effects upon the mind that find expression in compulsive rituals and psychosomatic illnesses. Unlike many of his predecessors, Freud saw such pathology as explicable by science, and he was the first theorist who sought to explain both normal and abnormal behavior with the same laws. If his stage model of psychosexual development seems antiquated to us now, remember that psychoanalytic theory was the very first attempt to explain how personality developed and the intellectual ancestor of all existing **psychodynamic theories.**

Freud brought to our attention the role of strong emotions and emotional conflict as forces underlying our everyday behavior of which we may be unaware. In each of Freud's psychosexual stages, biological impulses seek expression and thereby inevitably involve the self in conflict with societal demands. One of his most enduring contributions was the idea that psychological **defense mechanisms** in healthy and unhealthy personalities function to protect the self from conscious awareness of unpleasant emotions, ideas, and memories. His daughter, Anna Freud, developed this idea further in her classic work entitled *The Ego and the Mechanisms of Defense* (A. Freud, 1936/1958), which was to influence a new generation of Freudian scholars, among them Erik Erikson.

Erikson's Psychosocial Theory

In 1950, with the publication of his major work *Childhood and Society,* Erikson significantly revised Freud's theory of personality development. However, it was not until the book's second edition thirteen years later that he truly emerged as a seminal theorist in his own right. Though the linkages between Erikson's **psychosocial theory** and Freud's earlier stages of psychosexual development are apparent, Erikson's views evolved beyond those of his predecessor in several crucial respects. Working from Freud's tripartite model of id, ego, and superego as the basis of personality, Erikson attaches relatively greater importance to the rational, adaptive side of human nature. This emphasis characterized most of the neo-Freudians of his era including that of his analyst, Anna Freud. They came to be known as ego psychologists because they attributed a central role to the ego or self in adapting to life's challenges. In general, their orientation was less deterministic and more optimistic than Freud's original vision, possibly because Freud based his theory largely on observations of his patients, a small sample of neurotic adult women living in Vienna around the turn of the century.

A key contribution of Erikson was to expand Freud's original model to accommodate a greater range of cultural variation, and by doing so, he rendered it more generalizable and less ethnocentric. These changes are readily apparent from comparing the stages in the two theories. For example, the second stage in Freud's theory is called the anal stage because he viewed the central conflict of the second and third year of life to be the persistent socialization demands associated with toilet training. Freud's developmental theory postulated that escalations of conflict around this issue would be more likely if the resolution of the previous oral stage had been unsuccessful. In the ensuing battle of wills between parent and toddler, the emotionally harsh practice of shaming or punishing the child could have a lasting impact on certain aspects of the individual's personality.

In developing his psychosocial model, Erikson retained Freud's central insights that certain emotional conflicts are universal according to a developmental timetable, that socialization experiences around these basic developmental tasks shape the individual's personality, and that the child's own developmental history becomes a potent force in influencing the resolution of subsequent crises (see Table 4.1). However, Erikson expanded the cultural context of Freud's theory by reformulating the nature of these developmental tasks. The resolution of the first task, **trust versus mistrust** (what Freud saw as the oral stage and what we would now describe as the establishment of a secure or insecure attachment), provides a basis for predicting the resolution of the next. Rather than the anal stage, the second stage for Erikson is the conflict of **autonomy versus shame and doubt.** Unlike Freud's focus on one specific context for a conflict of wills (toilet training), the issue is reformulated in more abstract terms dealing with the general problem of fostering a child's sense of emerging autonomy (I can do it myself!) while communicating clear expectations of culturally appropriate behavior and establishing firm limits on the toddler's inevitable rebellion. Freud's earlier view may still have limited validity as a specific case, but Erikson's reformation can be more readily applied across different cultural contexts.

In a sense this abstract quality is both the strength of Erikson's theory and its weakness. Because it is abstract, it does not elaborate on specific developmental processes or environmental influences associated with each life crisis in his eight stages. Notwithstanding, Erikson's theory remains highly influential today. As a general framework for understanding psychosocial development across the life span, it has no serious rival, except perhaps from the more detailed and explicit developmental theories that it has inspired. Several of these theories, notably

Sroufe's theory of early emotional development, will be presented later in this chapter, and we will revisit Erikson in our discussion of adolescence in Chapter 10.

Object Relations Theory

According to Freud's initial formulation (1895/1966), infant emotion is both passive and undifferentiated, and the infant's motives are characterized in terms of drive reduction. This view of the infant's emotional life has been strongly challenged by many developmental theorists including a group of British psychoanalysts who developed another neo-Freudian perspective known as "object relations theory" (Fairbairn, 1952; Horner, 1989, 1991; Mahler, Pine, & Bergman, 1975).

The primary concern of object relations theory is to explain how individuals develop in relation to the emotional interactions they have with the people around them (Hamilton, 1989). Unlike Freud's view that the adult personality is forged during the preschool years as a result of Oedipal conflict resolution, object relations theory emphasizes the infant's relationship to the mother during the first few years of life. Early affective transactions with the social environment are mentally stored in the form of representations of the self emotionally interacting with significant objects. Emotions are central to the construction of object relations which principally involve the sharing and communication of affect, and the specific quality of such affective exchanges implies a particular form of relatedness (Schore, 1994). The use of the term **object relations** is explained by Horner (1989):

> We use the term "object" rather than "mother" because the particular mental image is in part created by the child in accord with his or her limited mental capabilities, and with his or her own unique experience of the early caretaking environment. In a way, the child creates a metaphor or template for the significant other from his or her interpersonal

Table 4.1 Erikson's and Freud's Stages of Development

Approximate Age	Erikson's Stage or "Psychosocial" Crisis	Erikson's Viewpoint: Significant Events and Social Influences	Corresponding Freudian Stage
Birth to 1 year	Basic trust versus mistrust	Infants must learn to trust others to care for their basic needs. If caregivers are rejecting or inconsistent, the infant may view the world as a dangerous place filled with untrustworthy or unreliable people. The primary caregiver is the key social agent.	Oral
1 to 3 years	Autonomy versus shame and doubt	Children must learn to be "autonomous"—to feed and dress themselves, to look after their own hygiene, and so on. Failure to achieve this independence may force the child to doubt his or her own abilities and feel shameful. Parents are the key social agents.	Anal
3 to 6 years	Initiative versus guilt	Children attempt to act grown up and will try to accept responsibilities that are beyond their capacity to handle. They sometimes undertake goals or activities that conflict with those of parents and other family members, and these conflicts may make them feel guilty. Successful resolution of this crisis requires a balance: The child must retain a sense of initiative and yet learn not to impinge on the rights, privileges, or goals of others. The family is the key social agent.	Phallic
6 to 12 years	Industry versus inferiority	Children must master important social and academic skills. This is a period when the child compares him- or herself with peers. If sufficiently industrious, children acquire the social and academic skills to feel self-assured. Failure to acquire these important attributes leads to feelings of inferiority. Significant social agents are teachers and peers.	Latency
12 to 20 years	Identity versus role confusion	This is the crossroad between childhood and maturity. The adolescent grapples with the question "Who am I?" Adolescents must establish basic social and occupational identities, or they will remain confused about the roles they should play as adults. The key social agent is the society of peers.	Early genital (adolescence)
20 to 40 years (young adulthood)	Intimacy versus isolation	The primary task at this stage is to form strong friendships and to achieve a sense of love and companionship (or a shared identity) with another person. Feelings of loneliness or isolation are likely to result from an inability to form friendships or an intimate relationship. Key social agents are lovers, spouses, and close friends (of both sexes).	Genital
40 to 65 years (middle adulthood)	Generativity versus stagnation	At this stage, adults face the tasks of becoming productive in their work and raising their families or otherwise looking after the needs of young people. These standards of "generativity" are defined by one's culture. Those who are unable or unwilling to assume these responsibilities become stagnant and/or self-centered. Significant social agents are the spouse, children, and cultural norms.	Genital
Old age	Ego integrity versus despair	The older adult looks back at life, viewing it as either a meaningful, productive, and happy experience or a major disappointment full of unfulfilled promises and unrealized goals. One's life experiences, particularly social experiences, determine the outcome of this final life crisis.	Genital

Source: Copyright © 1977 by Lawrence Erlbaum Associates.

experiences. . . . Through its genetically endowed intrinsic creative capacities, its inborn intrinsic power, the infant creates an inner image of itself as well. "Object relations" refers to the dynamic interplay between the inner images of both self and other. (pp. 28–29)

The inner representations of salient social interactions constructed by the infant are not merely disembodied memories or ideas; they are imbued with great emotional energy as well. The essential developmental question posed by object relations theory is, what are the early events that account for the transformation of the relatively unformed infant to the relatively patterned adult? (Greenberg & Mitchell, 1983). This transformation of the self from a reflexive, physiological organism to a thinking, feeling human being is one of the profound mysteries that challenge a developmental science. In a few short years, the infant, who can maintain an organized state solely in the context of the regulation provided by the caregiver, emerges as a young child with the capacity for self-guided emotion regulation. This important developmental transformation will be discussed in subsequent chapters dealing with attachment theory, which is itself derived from object relations theory.

COGNITIVE AND CULTURAL APPROACHES

It has long been evident that biological approaches to the study of emotion must incorporate some form of cognitive processing in order to explain how certain stimuli acquire emotional meaning in a particular culture and to explain why individuals within a given culture can differ so dramatically in their emotional responses to the same stimuli. Beginning with Aristotle, an **appraisal** of the arousing stimuli has been viewed as central to the emotion process. The combination of cognitive appraisal with a

certain level of arousal became the hallmark of the cognitive theories of emotion that arose in psychology in the latter half of the twentieth century (Arnold; 1960; Lazarus, 1991; Mandler, 1975; Schachter & Singer, 1962). At one extreme, some of these theorists believed that emotions could be reduced to the cognitive interpretation of arousal. Others argued for a central, activating role for a cognitive appraisal process, but stopped short of defining emotion as a special kind of cognition. Our goal in presenting a succinct account of these different cognitive theories of emotion is not to equate emotion with cognition, but to highlight the diverse ways in which cognitive processing has been seen in relation to emotion.

An Appraisal Theory of Emotion

One of the first of the cognitive theories of emotion to become prominent within psychology was that of Magda Arnold (Arnold, 1960). Arnold's position, which closely resembles that of Aristotle (see Chapter 1), views the emotion process as a sequence of events that begins with the perception of the stimulus, immediately followed by an act of appraisal, which in turn activates the emotional response. She defines perception as the immediate, direct apprehension of the stimulus, and appraisal as a judgment of it as either good or bad. It is the appraisal of the stimulus in relation to the perceiver that triggers a feeling toward the object, person, or event that, in turn, produces a behavioral response of approach (if the object is judged to be likely to benefit the self) or avoidance (if the object is appraised as potentially harmful). Neutral stimuli are simply ignored.

In this theory, an emotional response is largely determined by the individual's memory of past experiences with the particular object, person, or event, or by his or her imagination of what is likely to transpire. Like Freud, Arnold (1960) views the appraisal process as direct, immediate, and intuitive rather than conscious, planful, and deliberate: "The sequence perception-appraisal-emotion is so closely knit that our everyday experience is never the strictly objective knowledge of a thing; it is always a knowing-and-liking, or a knowing-and-disliking" (p. 177).

Arnold extends Aristotle's view that emotion can in turn influence cognition, by noting that emotions can organize and bias later perceptions. This process can lead to situations in which the perception-appraisal of an object, person, or event can stabilize and generalize to a whole class of people, objects, or events. This aspect of Arnold's theory is important for understanding the automatic quality that characterizes the deeply felt emotional reactions of some to a whole group of people, based on their experience with one or several individuals.

Two-Factor Theory

Some theorists have challenged Arnold's view that "preferences require inferences" and have argued that affective processes can be independent of cognition (Zajonc, 1980), while others have adopted an even greater reliance on cognitive processing to explain emotion. In Schachter's **two-factor theory,** it is the cognitive appraisal of the general state of physiological arousal that determines which emotion is felt. These two factors, arousal and its interpretation, construct the emotion. In his view the stimulus (an object, person, or event) creates some physiological arousal in the perceiver. The resulting feeling state does not depend on the arousal that is experienced, but rather it depends on how the individual evaluates the context in which it occurs. The same general state of arousal is believed to be common to all emotions, and no clue can be gained from internal physiological cues as to which emotion is being experienced. Rather it is the "sizing up" of the social situation that determines whether one feels happiness, sadness, anxiety, or any other emotion. Someone who is aroused in a hostile situation becomes angry, but the same arousal in a friendly situation is experienced as happiness. The specific emotion feeling is created out of the individual's interpretation of how others are feeling in the situation in which the arousal occurs.

Consistent with this view, some research has demonstrated that the attributions people make concerning their physiological responses to a given stimulus will sometimes determine the specific emotional response. Some data supporting this view come from an experiment conducted by Schachter and Singer (1962). Arousal was induced in three experimental groups by epinephrine injections, while a fourth group received a placebo injection. Subjects were given accurate, misleading, or no information regarding the effects of the drug. They were then exposed to either an angry or euphoric model. The results indicated that subjects were more likely to imitate the model's mood and behavior if they had been provided no information or misinformation about the nature of their arousal. Subjects who were provided with accurate information about the effects of epinephrine were not influenced very much by any of the models. The subjects who received no information or misleading information were more likely to conform to the model than those subjects who received accurate information, but not more likely than the placebo group.

While Schachter and Singer's study partially supports Schacter's theory, subsequent researchers have not found any evidence supporting it (Marshall & Zimbardo, 1979; Maslach, 1978; Reisenzein, 1983). Schachter's theory originated during the cognitive revolution in American psychology, but from our present vantage point it overemphasizes the role of cognition at the expense of other factors. Two factors, while parsimonious, fail to adequately account for the complexity and diversity of human emotional experience. A contemporary of Schachter, Richard Lazarus (1991), has offered three cogent critiques:

First, it overemphasizes the social environment in the generation of an emotion at the expense of the motivation and thought characteristic of the reacting individual in a relationship with the environment. Second, it makes the cognitive mediation in the emotion process too much a matter of labeling and too little a matter of evaluation and judgment. . . . Third, the reasoning seems backward to me in that it doesn't help to explain why the emotion was aroused in the first place. (p. 19)

Another contemporary of Schachter, Sylvan Tomkins, was even less sympathetic to the idea that emotions are really cognitions in disguise. He offers the following blistering critique:

[I]n 1962 Schachter and Singer offered a new theory of emotions that quickly became a classic in social psychology. Studies in psychology often become classic under two conditions. They need to be believed, and they are not read. For over a decade, addressing a couple hundred or so professional audiences, I was confronted with the rhetorical question, "but didn't Schachter and Singer demonstrate that there are no discrete emotions?" I was somewhat surprised that, with one exception, none of these psychologists had in fact read the article. As a student of the psychology of knowledge, I had to ask myself why this theory needed to be believed. The paper itself was seriously flawed, both empirically and theoretically, and yet it was not seriously challenged by social psychologists until almost 20 years later, by Maslach [(1978)]. Empirically, it was an experiment without a statistically significant main effect, and the reported significant effects were small in size and not always in the predicted direction. Theoretically it was no more persuasive. Only the trained incapacity of professionals, combined with a bias in favor of the counterintuitive, could have permitted acceptance of the theory. Surely no one who has experienced joy at one time and rage at another time would suppose that these two radically different feelings were really the same except for different "inter-

pretations" placed on similar "arousals." Only a science which had come to radically discount conscious experience would have taken such an explanation seriously. It is as reasonable a possibility as a theory of pain and pleasure which argued that the difference between the pain of a toothache and the pleasure of an orgasm is not in the stimulation of different sensory receptors, but in the fact that since one experience occurs in a bedroom, the other in a dentist's office, one interprets the undifferentiated arousal state differently. (Tomkins, 1981, pp. 34–35)

Cognitive-Motivational-Relational Theory

Another social psychologist with a cognitive orientation has recently formulated an influential and comprehensive model of the emotion process. The emotion theory of Richard Lazarus grew out of his efforts to develop a cognitive approach to psychological stress and coping that focused on the phenomenological or subjective quality of stress. The appraisal process for Lazarus is viewed as highly subjective, dependent on the personal meaning of the eliciting event for the perceiver. For example, Lazarus (1966) demonstrated that subjects' emotional reactions to stressful films were partly dependent on their subjective appraisal of the meaning of the events portrayed. The meaning of the events was manipulated by exposing two experimental groups to the same film depicting tribal surgical practices. One showing was accompanied by a calm, factual narration, while the other group heard a more dramatic narrative emphasizing the painful aspects of the operation. In the latter condition, both physiological and self-report data indicated that viewers experienced more distress in reaction to the film. This research clearly demonstrates a role for cognitive processes by establishing that the appraisal of events as benign or threatening can affect the degree of emotional reaction to them.

As a result of these insights, research on psychological stress progressed from formulations that emphasized the objective environment toward subjective, transactional processes that stressed the highly personal meaning of the stressor in relation to the person's motivations or goals. During the 1970s and 1980s, Lazarus expanded his theory of psychological stress into a general theory of emotion. This entailed a wider consideration of the diverse emotional states that arise from our attempts to actively cope with an environment that can pose threats to our well-being, as well as offer benefits and opportunities.

Lazarus (1991) defines emotions as

complex, patterned, organismic reactions to how we think we are doing in our life-long efforts to survive and flourish and to achieve what we wish for ourselves. . . . When we react with an emotion, especially a strong one, every fiber of our being is likely to be engaged—our attention and thoughts, our needs and desires, and even our bodies. The reaction tells us that an important value or goal has been engaged and is being harmed, placed at risk, or advanced. . . . No other concept in psychology is as richly revealing of the way an individual relates to life. . . . (p. 7)

In Lazarus's **cognitive-motivational-relational theory,** *cognitive* refers to the appraisal process, *motivational* refers to the fact that events are appraised from the standpoint of a person's goals and desires, and the *relational* view combines the outer and inner, emphasizing the person's continuous negotiation with the physical and social world. This new theory of emotions, while quite complex, may be summarized in six major principles:

1. A *system principle* is necessary to integrate the various components of the emotion complex, including its antecedents, mediating processes, and outcomes. No single component is sufficient to explain the whole, and all component processes are interdependent.

2. and 3. Emotions simultaneously express responses to flux or change (*process principle*) and

stable emotional patterns within the individual (*structure principle*).

4. The *developmental principle* states that emotions undergo change according to a biosocial process, especially in the early years.

5. The *specificity principle* states that the emotion process is distinctive for each discrete emotion.

6. Finally, the key to his theory is the *relational meaning principle* that states that each discrete emotion is defined by a core relational meaning. The emotional meaning is constructed by the appraisal process according to the harms or benefits afforded by each person–environment relationship.

Because of the central importance of the relational meaning principle to Lazarus's theory, let us examine it in greater detail.

The idea that each emotion has at its core a unique relational meaning expresses Lazarus's view that most of us share an implicit or intuitive folk psychology of emotion, that is, we tend to agree about many of the themes associated with particular emotions, as presented in Table 4.2. Lazarus (1991) proposes that each of these core relational themes can be classified according to its pattern of six appraisal components: goal relevance, goal congruence or incongruence, type of ego involvement, harm or credit, coping potential, and future expectations. The person's appraisal of a situation according to these criteria determines the meaning of any given emotional state. A unique feature of his theory is the central role given to the coping process in the construction of meaning, a component retained from his earlier work on stress, appraisal, and coping (Lazarus & Folkman, 1984).

To further illustrate how Lazarus views the role of appraisal and coping in the emotion process, examine the flow chart depicted in Figure 4.2. In his model he highlights three main components: (1) antecedent variables, (2) mediating processes, and (3) outcomes. Beginning at the top of the flow chart, antecedent variables consist of stable personality traits and fluctuating situations.

Table 4.2 Core Relational Themes for Each Emotion

Anger	A demeaning offense against me and mine.
Anxiety	Facing uncertain, existential threat.
Fright	Facing an immediate, concrete, and overwhelming physical danger.
Guilt	Having transgressed a moral imperative.
Shame	Having failed to live up to an ego-ideal.
Sadness	Having experienced an irrevocable loss.
Envy	Wanting what someone else has.
Jealousy	Resenting a third party for loss or threat to another's affection.
Disgust	Taking in or being too close to an indigestible object or idea (metaphorically speaking).
Happiness	Making reasonable progress toward the realization of a goal.
Pride	Enhancement of one's ego-identity by taking credit for a valued object or achievement, either our own or that of someone or group with whom we identify.
Relief	A distressing goal-incongruent condition that has changed for the better or gone away.
Hope	Fearing the worst but yearning for better.
Love	Desiring or participating in affection, usually but not necessarily reciprocated.
Compassion	Being moved by another's suffering and wanting to help.

Source: (Lazarus, 1991). Used by permission of Oxford University Press.

These two factors interact to initiate the emotion process. For example, a challenging situation whose outcome is of vital importance will initiate a different emotion process depending on one's confidence level. The antecedent variables will impact the appraisal process and lead to an appraisal outcome that is composed of the immediate emotional responses (action tendencies, feelings or affect, and physiological responses). These short-term outcomes influence the coping process whose results feed back into the flow chart and influence the direction and intensity of the emotional response. Long-term outcomes are also considered in the model and consist of the ultimate effects that recurring patterns of emotional responses may have on a person's health and sense of well-being.

Social Constructivist Theories

Another approach to understanding emotions that emphasizes the importance of the cognitive appraisal process is the social constructivist perspective. As the name implies, the principal theme of a social constructivist approach is that emotions, like all other aspects of human experience, are social products. That is, emotions are based on cultural beliefs, rather than the biology of the organism. According to social constructivists, emotions and their expression can take any form depending upon socialization within the particular culture. This view of emotion is a relatively recent extension of a broader social constructivist movement that has its roots in the works of nineteenth-century sociologists like Marx and Durkeim, and social anthropologists like Mead. Within psychology, a social constructivist position has been influenced by the constructivist ideas of cognitive psychologists.

Because most scientists now regard the position that biological processes do not influence either the experience or expression of emotion as untenable, a "weaker" version of social constructionism has gained ascendancy and is now preferred over the "strong" view (Armon-Jones, 1986). Social construction theorists now hold positions that may be more or less antagonistic to biological perspectives. For example, contemporary theorists like Oatley

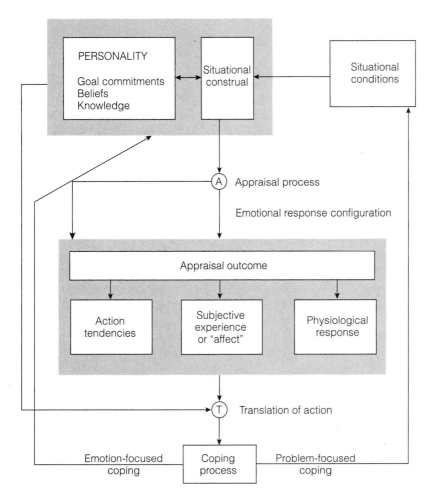

Figure 4.2 Lazarus's model of the cognitive-motivational-emotive system.

Source: Lazarus (1991). Used by permission of Oxford University Press.

(Oatley, 1993; Oatley & Johnson-Laird, 1987) and Cornelius (1996) adopt an integrative approach with important roles for biological and cultural processes in the construction of an emotion complex. Other social constructivists like Ortony and Turner (1990) or Averill (1980, 1985) adopt a more exclusionary attitude, as if culture and biology were somehow pitted against one another; if biology is viewed as important, then somehow culture is not, and vice versa.

James Averill, like his mentor Richard Lazarus, emphasized the importance of the appraisal process, but viewed this process as culturally determined, rejecting any firm link with biology. According to Averill's (1980) view, there is no necessary core to emotions, and no such thing as a basic emotion; rather, "there are an indefinite number of emotions. That is, societies can shape, mold, or construct as many different emotions as are functional with the social system" (p. 326). Averill (1980) defines an emotion as "a transitory social role (a socially constituted syndrome) that includes an individual's appraisal of the situation and that is interpreted as a passion rather than as an action" (p. 312). A central idea, shared by all social constructivists, is that the experience and expression of emotions are social roles that are learned through socialization within a given culture. Because there are culturally diverse emotion vocabularies, these theorists believe that there must be culturally diverse emotions as well (Harré, 1986).

Keith Oatley, another proponent of a social constructivist position within psychology, views emotions as a by-product of both biological and cultural processes (Oatley, 1993; Oatley & Johnson-Laird, 1987). In his view,

> a basic emotion occurs when the brain enters a particular mode of functioning on recognition of an event relevant to a goal, such as progress toward something one wants, a loss, a frustration, a conflict of goals—but conscious knowledge about what counts as something to want, as a loss, as a frustration, as a conflict, or about which of such events caused the emotion, to whom it is directed, and so forth, is added to the basic emotion mode. This knowledge can be largely culturally determined, and it emerges in the emotion terms used in a culture. (Oatley, 1993, p. 345)

In this regard Oatley's position is quite similar to that of Richard Lazarus outlined earlier. Central to both views is an emphasis on cognitive appraisal. For both Lazarus and Oatley, this is where culture meets biology in the emotion process. Unlike proponents of a "stronger" version of the constructivist position, Oatley views cognitive appraisals as reflecting both evolutionary pressures for adaptation, as well as cultural influences. The impact of culture is most apparent in the language used to imbue the emotion with a particular significance for the individual, a meaning that is generally shared with other members of the same cultural and linguistic group. This model incorporates the views of most comprehensive emotion theorists in combining a universal biological core of emotion that represents our common humanity, with a semantic component that is largely a product of social construction.

In order to analyze this semantic-linguistic component of emotion concepts common to English-speaking peoples, Zoltan Kovecses (1990) assembled various folk expressions regarding anger, such as "getting hot under the collar," "blind with rage," "red with anger," "shaking with anger," and "ready to explode." Kovecses sees such folk expressions and metaphors as a means to explore the structure and content of a culture's emotion concepts. For him, metaphors matter. If we think of anger as a fluid under pressure, as in "I've reached my boiling point," we may act in ways to safely release or vent the impending explosion or justify an outburst as essentially beyond our control. Alternatively, if anger is viewed as a dangerous opponent with which we are struggling, we might attempt to circumvent situations likely to give rise to anger.

Attribution Theory

Another group of social psychologists have formulated alternative cognitive theories of emotion that highlight a particular kind of cognitive appraisal known as causal attributions. The most well known is the attribution theory of Bernard Weiner (1985, 1986). Like social constructivists, attribution theorists are primarily interested in how people perceive their social world and how such perceptions influence their emotions. In Weiner's view, the emotion arises from the causal attribution that is made by the individual about some meaningful event. **Attributions** about causes of events can vary along three dimensions involving the locus of the cause as (1) internal or external, (2) stable or unstable, and (3) controllable or uncontrollable.

Weiner does not claim that all emotions are mediated by causal attributions. For example, love, hate, joy, fear, excitement, boredom, and disgust may have little to do with our perceptions of causality. However, a number of commonly occurring emotions that relate to one's social motivations have been extensively studied from an attributional perspective. The emotions of anger, gratitude, pity, pride, shame, and guilt all appear to be influenced in important ways by attributions about causality.

Weiner and Graham (1989) summarize the causal antecedents and behavioral consequences of these emotions in Table 4.3. Using this table, consider the impact of one's causal attributions given a negative, self-related outcome, such as

Table 4.3 Antecedents and Consequences of Some Affective Experiences

Outcome	Causal Antecedent	Affect	Action Tendency
Negative, self-relevant	Controllable by other	Anger	Retaliation against other
Negative, other-relevant	Controllable by other	Anger (irritation)	Retreat from other (neglect)
Positive, self-relevant	Controllable by other	Gratitude	Restitution; go toward other
Negative, self-relevant	Controllable by self	Guilt	Reproof; go toward task
Negative, other-relevant	Controllable by self	Guilt	Reproof and restitution; go toward other
Negative, other-relevant	Uncontrollable	Pity (sympathy)	Restitution; go toward other
Positive, self-relevant	Self	Self-esteem (pride)	Reward; go toward task
Negative, self-relevant	Self	Self-esteem decrease[a]	Retreat away from task
Negative, self-relevant	Uncontrollable by self	Shame (humiliation)	Recoil; go away from task

[a]There is not a single emotion label comparable to pride in success when the outcome is failure given an internal cause, irrespective of information about controllability.

Source: Weiner and Graham, 1989.

failure to achieve an important goal. If one attributes the cause to an intentional (controllable) action of another, the resulting emotion is likely to be anger, and one may seek some form of retaliation. This may serve an adaptive function by communicating the social message "do not do that again," which may ultimately restore or maintain social order (Trivers, 1971). However, if the same outcome was due to one's own neglect (controllable by self), the resulting emotion could be guilt or personal reproach. This emotion might be instrumental in achieving ultimate success by motivating one to try harder the next time.

Emotions associated with negative outcomes relevant to others are similarly influenced by one's attributions of causality. One may feel pity or sympathy in response to hearing that a close friend has been seriously crippled in a car crash, if the cause is perceived as uncontrollable (a blowout that causes the car to crash). But would the same emotional reaction occur upon hearing that your friend's car was run off the highway by a gang of drunks out for a joyride? Or if you had loaned your friend the car knowing that the brakes were defective? Not only are the answers to these questions intuitively obvious, they are also supported by systematic research.

For example, research has shown that students who state that they need to borrow class notes elicit annoyance if they are at the beach, but sympathy if they have serious eye problems (Reisenzein, 1983). In each case the emotional reaction is dependent on one's attribution of controllability in the person requesting assistance. For this reason charitable contributions may flow to those suffering from uncontrollable causes (famine, drought, natural catastrophes, crippling diseases) but only trickle toward those suffering from causes that are perceived to be under their own control (Weiner & Graham, 1989). Because of the intimate relation between cognitive factors and the self-conscious emotions of pride, shame, and guilt, we will consider Weiner's attributional model of emotion in more detail in Chapter 7.

DEVELOPMENTAL PERSPECTIVES

An Organizational Approach

By the 1980s the field of emotion research in developmental psychology was being rejuvenated by a new perspective on emotions. This change in the zeitgeist of emotion research was stimulated by innovations in systems theory and human ethology, particularly attachment research. A few years after these innovations took hold and began to enliven developmental research on emotion, Campos and Barrett (1984) provided this commentary:

> There is a new and very different perspective on emotions—what Emde (1980a, 1980b) and Sroufe (1979) are calling the "**organizational approach**" [emphasis added]—an approach based on systems theory, that emphasizes the role of emotions as regulators and determinants of both intrapersonal and interpersonal behaviors, as well as stressing the adaptive role of emotions. Current research is thus abandoning the prior tendency to merely measure or index a central neurophysiological or feeling state and is beginning to explore how a subject's feeling state or emotional behavior impacts the perceptions, thoughts, or behaviors of that person or others [(Charlesworth, 1982)]. (p. 233)

L. Alan Sroufe has recently updated his views with a comprehensive theoretical statement concerning the emergence of emotions in infancy and early childhood that draws upon the research of the intervening decade. In Sroufe's model, emotion is defined as "a subjective reaction to a salient event, characterized by physiological, experiential, and overt behavioral change" (Sroufe, 1996).

The main task of any model of the development of emotions is to specify what exactly develops, and how, when, and why. Sroufe begins by assuming that the principles underlying the development of emotions are the same as those underlying other aspects of development. Development is assumed to be unitary and lawful. The principle of unity implies that emotional development is interwoven with other domains of development. The principle of lawfulness assumes an underlying logic to the unfolding of

human emotions. Sroufe further assumes that discrete, psychologically based emotions do not appear until the emergence of consciousness—until the infant is capable of some basic distinction between the self and the outer world.

But if emotions do not exist at birth, where do they come from? Like Bridges (1932), Sroufe invokes the basic principle of differentiation to explain how more complex forms emerge out of successive transformations of earlier, more primitive structures. Unlike Bridges, Sroufe characterizes the neonates's emotional experience as bipolar, with an inborn capacity to express distress by reflexive crying, and contentment or pleasure via endogenous smiling. These reflexes, and others, represent physiological starting points or **prototypes** from which the primary, psychological emotions of infancy will emerge.

The general trajectory for any particular line of emotional development entails not only differentiation but also an increasingly important role for cognitive processes as the infant becomes more active in engaging the environment. In the first months of life, emotions evolve from passive, physiological prototypes to more active, psychologically based responses dependent upon an evaluation of the meaning of a given stimulus or event. In his **dynamic tension model,** Sroufe hypothesizes a dynamic threshold range for affective response in which tension is viewed as a natural by-product of actively engaging the environment. The critical feature of the tension model is that thresholds for inciting a given emotional response are not stationary but vary as a function of the meaning of an event in context. His model differs from earlier arousal models by distinguishing between physically produced arousal and arousal that has a psychological basis, dependent on the evaluation of meaning. For these reasons, the precursor stage falls midway between the physiological prototype and the truly psychological emotion.

To illustrate Sroufe's theory, consider the development of anger. The initial stage in the development of anger, defined as an "immediate, negative reaction directed at an obstacle to an intended act" (Sroufe, 1996, p. 63), may be seen in the first days of life in the reflexive flailing of the infant in response to restraining the head. Sroufe views this as the physiological prototype of anger, not anger itself. Following the newborn period, precursor emotions emerge that are no longer purely physiological, but begin to incorporate psychological components related to evaluating the content and meaning of a specific event. The precursor is not yet the equivalent of the mature emotion. Unlike an immediate emotional response, it is expressed only after a gradual building up of tension. It is also a more diffuse reaction than later responses, often involving the whole body, and it is based on a general rather than specific evaluation of the elicitor.

Empirical support for this three-stage developmental model of anger is provided by cross-sectional studies of infants' responses to physical restraint or removal of an object. These studies reveal developmental changes in the rapidity and specificity of infants' facial expression of anger. For example, Stenberg and Campos (1990) have observed negative facial and vocal expressions in 1-month-olds and found them to be delayed, gradual, and undifferentiated. Similar findings were obtained by Brazelton (1969), who observed a precursor of anger in the 2-month-old's response to failure to execute a well-established motor pattern. However, by the second half of the first year, the infant's expressions become clearer, more immediate, and specifically directed toward the elicitor, meeting the criteria of the mature emotion of anger. We will elaborate the normative aspect of Sroufe's theory of emotional development further by illustrating the dynamic tension model in detailed discussions of the ontogeny of smiling and laughter, and the development of fear, in Chapter 5.

Besides describing **normative development** or progressive changes for children in general, Sroufe's is one of the few theories of emotional development that also addresses the important question of how individuals differ in their emotional makeup and why. He argues that norma-

tive patterns of growth, and the emergence and consolidation of individual differences in emotional expression and regulation, be viewed as complementary parts of the whole of emotional development. Thus, individual differences are defined in terms of significant variations in normative processes.

One of the best examples of this complementarity between discovering normative patterns and defining individual differences will be seen in our discussion of attachment research. From an organizational perspective, an understanding of the developmental processes underlying the emergence of attachment to the caregiver is directly relevant to the analysis of individual differences in the infant's emotional development. Without a scientifically valid description of normative developmental changes, there would be no guide as to what phenomena require careful scrutiny in the assessment of individual differences. With no theoretical map indicating the important developmental milestones in the infant's emotional development, researchers could get lost in the description of differences in literally thousands of experimental tasks, but to what ultimate purpose?

Beginning with the theories of Freud and Erikson, developmental researchers have been refining their theoretical maps by conducting empirical studies, especially longitudinal studies that address questions concerning the continuity and discontinuity of emotional development over time. In Sroufe's model (shown in Table 4.4), physiological regulation, management of tension, and establishing an effective attachment are key developmental issues in the first year, while emotion regulation, gender identity, and developing peer friendships are viewed as central tasks during the preschool years. In Sroufe's longitudinal research, empirical assessments are guided by developmental theory to investigate the central issues of emotional development that provide markers for the individual's developmental status at a given age, and provide a basis for predicting their future adaptation. From his perspective, an understanding of emotional development also

Table 4.4 Sroufe's Issues in Emotional Development

Period	Age	Issue	Role for Caregiver
1	0–3 months	Physiological regulation (turning toward)	Smooth routines
2	3–6 months	Management of tension	Sensitive, cooperative interaction
3	6–12 months	Establishing an effective attachment relationship	Responsive availability
4	12–18 months	Exploration and mastery	Secure base
5	18–30 months	Individuation (autonomy)	Firm support
6	30–54 months	Management of impulses, sex-role identification, peer relations	Clear roles, values; flexible self-control
7	6–11 years	Consolidating self-concept, loyal friendships, effective same-gender peer group functioning, real-world competence	Monitoring, supporting activities, co-regulation
8	Adolescence	Personal identity, mixed-gender relationships, intimacy	Available resource, monitor the child's monitoring

Source: Sroufe (1996). Reprinted with the permission of Cambridge University Press.

serves as an important foundation for the study of developmental psychopathology.

Differential Emotion Theory

An alternative model to Sroufe's view that emotions become differentiated with maturation, cognitive development, and socialization is the position initially formulated by Tomkins (1962), and later refined by Izard (1978, 1991) and others, that has come to be known as **differential emotion theory** (DET). This theory, as the name implies, emphasizes discrete emotions in a manner similar to Sroufe's theory, rather than dimensions, as in the cognitive theories of Schachter (1966) and Mandler (1975). In contrast to differentiation theories, DET assumes emotional states are innate, present at birth in an already differentiated form, and eventually available to the organism as they are needed in the life cycle (Izard, 1991). According to Izard (1991), five key assumptions define DET:

(1) ten fundamental emotions constitute the principal motivational system for human beings;

(2) each fundamental emotion has particular organizing and motivational functions and unique experiential properties;

(3) fundamental emotions such as joy, sadness, anger, and shame lead to different inner experiences and have different effects on cognition and action;

(4) emotion processes interact with and exert influence on homeostatic, drive, perceptual, cognitive, and motor processes.

(5) In turn, homeostatic, drive, perceptual, cognitive, and motor processes influence emotions. (pp. 40–41)

Within DET, emotion is defined as a set of neural processes that lead to efferent processes and sometimes an observable expression, but always a subjective feeling or experience. As with most theorists, the term *emotion* refers to these three levels—neural, expressive, and experiential—as an integrated system. Following Tomkins (1962), Izard views emotions as central to personality development, social relationships, and human motivation, in the sense that they imbue human existence with meaning and significance. The eclectic mix of ideas underlying the views of Tomkins and Izard may also be seen as an integration of ideas derived from both Darwin and Freud. From Darwin, there is the idea that a certain core group of discrete emotions evolved in humans. These basic emotions are characterized by prewired, universal facial expressions and serves adaptive intrapersonal and interpersonal functions. From Freud, there is the notion that affect is central to personality development and human motivation. However, Tomkins discarded Freud's notion of affect as drive. As a result, DET views affective-cognitive structures not as representations of instinctual drives, but as structures created by the interaction of emotion and cognition (Izard, 1991).

Izard (1991, 1993) has argued that emotion expressions emerge during development as they become adaptive in the life of the infant, and particularly in infant–caregiver communications and relationships. This view is partially supported by the tight schedule of appearance of specific expressions in connection with the appropriate context observed across a wide range of studies. The timing of these appearances is attributed to the maturation of the nervous system, rather than experience or learning. Specific emotions may co-occur with the emergence of cognitive structures, but they are considered to be independent of them. While the discrete-systems approach emphasizes the "why" question concerning the specific functions of primary emotions as stressed by Darwin, DET provides less insight into the "how" question concerning ontogenetic processes underlying the emergence of these fundamental emotions.

According to DET, the causes of an emotional experience may be neural, affective, or cognitive. At the neural level, an emotional experience may be activated naturally by hormones and neurotransmitters, or artificially by drugs, or by facial expression and its sensory feedback. Affective activators include pain, fatigue, sexual activity, or another emotion. Cognitive activators involve anticipation, memory, appraisal, and attributional processes. The theory specifies that cognitions are distinct from and not necessary to emotion, that is, that emotions can sometimes occur independently of cognitive processes (Izard, 1991; Izard & Malatesta, 1987). Support for this assertion has recently been documented in neurological research on fear responses (LeDoux, 1996).

A Cognitive-Emotional Fugue

During the 1980s another theoretical account of emotional development was articulated by Lewis and Michalson (1983), who outlined a structural theory of emotion consisting of five major components: elicitors, receptors, states, expression, and experience. Emotional elicitors are the particular events, objects, people, thoughts, fantasies, and so on that instigate the emotional process as outlined in most of the emotion theories that we have examined. Lewis and Michalson use the term *receptor* to refer to the structures that mediate the relationship between the eliciting event and the person. Temperament, personality, and arousability may all be thought of as emotional receptors that mediate the precise impact of the elicitor and influence the individual's emotional response to it. These two components—elicitors and receptors—are similar to Lazarus's antecedents.

Emotional state refers to the neurological, physiological, and hormonal changes associated with a particular emotional response. Not all theories view emotions in terms of specific states that are inferred on the basis of bodily and facial expressions, though the term *expression* has been used since Darwin to refer to the outward manifestation of internal states. Cognitive theories, such as Schachter's, hold that general arousal and cognitive activity are sufficient to account for specific emotions. Biological theories view emotional states as discrete packages that include evolved connections between elicitors-receptors, internal physiological responses, and expressive behavior. For Lewis (1993a), emotional states are

> transient, patterned alterations in ongoing levels of neuropsychological and/or somatic activity. These alterations imply that there is a constant stream of change. It becomes difficult to imagine, therefore, being awake and not being in some emotional state or at some level of arousal. However, since there need not be any correspondence between the emotional state and emotional experience and expression,

there is no reason to assume that we are aware of the states that we are in. This does not mean that these states are not affecting our ongoing behavior—only that they are not apparent. (p. 225)

Emotional expressions are the observable changes in the face, tone of voice, body posture, and activity level that represent the best means of inferring the underlying emotional state. Of course, a major problem arises when the individual becomes skilled at masking emotional expression, and for this reason the relationship between state and expression remains vague. We will discuss this problem in more detail in subsequent chapters on early and middle childhood, which is when these skills emerge.

Lewis and Michalson (1983) define emotional experience as the subjective interpretation and evaluation of one's own emotional state and expression, as well as the social situation and reaction of others, and one's own beliefs. This component is therefore highly cognitive and depends on one's own attention to and awareness of the emotion process. Lewis (1993a) argues that attending to emotional signals is not automatic, and may not necessarily be conscious. Drawing upon Freud's concept of defense mechanisms, he offers the following example:

A man may be in an emotional state of anger. That is, proper measurement techniques would show a pattern of internal physiological responses indicative of anger. Moreover, this person may act toward those objects that or persons who have made him angry in a way suggesting that he is intentionally behaving in response to an internal state of anger. Nonetheless, the person may deny that he feels anger or is acting in an angry fashion. Within the therapeutic situation, this man might be shown that (1) he is angry, and (2) he is responding intentionally as a consequence of that anger. The therapeutic process may further reveal that unconscious processes are operating in a fashion

parallel to conscious ones. Defense mechanisms, for example, function at separate levels of awareness. Although awareness may not be at a conscious level, unconscious awareness may still exert powerful effects. (Lewis, 1993a, p. 227)

From a developmental perspective, all five components of Lewis and Michalson's model may be presumed to undergo developmental change as a function of maturation and socialization. In addition, the links between these components may change with age. To deal with this complexity, Lewis and Michalson proposed a stage theory to describe the emergence and development of human emotions in five periods marked by qualitative changes. The theory is focused on the self-system and incorporates aspects of Piaget's cognitive-developmental theory. In later writings, Lewis (1993a) elaborated this model to describe the emergence of emotions during the first three years. This latter theory is comparable to that developed by Sroufe (1979, 1996) presented earlier.

The first period (birth to 3 months) is characterized by an undifferentiated sense of self, as the infant is not yet able to fully distinguish between its own actions and the responses of others. Lewis assumes that at birth the child's emotions are bipolar, consisting of distress and pleasure, with interest as a somewhat intermediate state. In the second period (4 to 8 months), a rudimentary sense of oneself as distinct from others emerges, and with it concepts like goals and intentions. In this period, the basic emotions of joy, surprise, sadness, disgust, anger, and fear emerge. It is at this stage that an infant acquires a basic ego identity, and thus its goals may be seen as thwarted by another who then becomes the object of the infant's anger. Similarly, a pleasant exchange in which the infant's goals are realized might result in a joyful expression. Both emotions are distinguished from the earlier, less focused expressions of distress or contentment. The development of basic emotions will be the focus of Chapter 5.

The third period (9 to 12 months) involves the emergence of self-permanence, in which the sense of self is maintained across different contexts. The fourth period (12 to 18 months) is characterized by consolidation and further development as the toddler begins to grasp cultural rules and meanings. In the fifth period (18 to 22 months), self-referential behavior may be observed. Children at this age show that they recognize themselves in a mirror, photo, or video. This more elaborate categorical self allows for the expression of various self-conscious emotions such as embarrassment and empathy. Finally, the acquisition and retention of standards and rules, together with self-consciousness, ushers in the more complex emotions of pride, shame, and guilt. These developments will be the focus of Chapter 7 where data relevant to Lewis's theory of self-conscious emotions will be presented in greater detail.

A New Functionalism

Writing at about the same time as Lewis and Michalson, Campos and Barrett (1984) adopted a functionalist perspective in their theory of emotion in much the same sense as we saw with earlier biological theories emphasizing the adaptive function of emotion. According to their model, there are three essential characteristics of emotion. First, emotions function to regulate social and interpersonal behavior through their expressive components. Second, emotions regulate the flow of information and the determination of the response to it. Finally, basic emotions regulate behavior through an innate prewired communication process. If the type of functionalism they advocate is new to some psychologists, nevertheless it is

> already well established in biology, where the dependence of organisms for their existence on the presence of other organisms and the physical environment has repeatedly been demonstrated. . . . [T]he new relational approach in the social sciences extends the notion of open systems to a more complex level—that of all person-

environment interactions of significance to the person. (Campos et al., 1994, p. 300)

Campos and Barrett view emotional development as a complex process that reflects both continuity and discontinuity. They begin by postulating an invariant core of affective continuity across the life span. Each basic emotion (actually a "family" of closely related emotions) represents an invariant relationship between a type of goal and an appreciation of one's progress in relation to it. See Tables 4.5 and 4.6 for the types of goals and appreciations associated with different emotions. These goals may be genetically prewired (as is the goal of proximity to the attachment figure in infancy) or socially constructed (a teenager who wishes to own a car). Emotions are viewed as reactions to one's evaluation of the relationship between an event and one's goals. Goals certainly change with development; however, affective continuity refers to the unchanging relationship between goals and emotions. To illustrate their idea of affective continuity, Campos et al. provide the following example:

> [A]nger may be elicited in persons of any age: The neonate may show anger following the appreciation that a preadapted end state is blocked (e.g. impeding the baby's movement when it is exercising reflexive movements—cf. Stenberg, 1982); an 8-month-old may show anger when she anticipates that an event will impede progress toward a visible goal; a 2-year-old may be angered by the content of a verbal remark that may thwart progress toward a symbolic goal, like play; a 10-year-old may be angered by an insult; and so forth. Similar considerations apply to other fundamental emotions. (Campos, Barrett, Lamb, Goldsmith, & Sternberg, 1983, p. 818)

Of course, there are also important aspects of emotion that change with development. For Campos and Barrett, these changes include the relationship between emotional expression and

Table 4.5 Generalized Schema for Predicting Elicitation of Some Basic Emotions

Emotion	Goal	Appreciation	Action Tendency	Adaptive Function
Joy	Any *significant* objective	Goal is perceived or predicted to be attained	Approach, energizing	Reinforcement of successful strategy; facilitation of rehearsal of new skill; encouragement of response to new challenges; social message to initiate or continue interaction
Anger	Same as above	Perception of, or anticipation of, an obstacle to attainment of goal; perception of obstacle as not easily removable	Elimination (not just removal) of properties of an object that make it an obstacle	Restoration of progress toward a goal; effecting a change in behavior of a social other; in later development, revenge, retaliation
Sadness	Securing or maintaining an engagement with either an animate or an inanimate object	Perception of the goal as unattainable	Disengagement	Conservation of energy; eventual redirection of resources to other pursuits perceived to be more attainable; encouragement of nurturance from others
Fear	Maintenance of integrity of the self, including self-survival and later, self-esteem	Perception that the goal is not likely to be attained, *unless* protective action is taken	Flight, withdrawal	Survival; avoidance of pain; maintenance of self-esteem; alerting others to avoid the situation and/or help one
Interest	Engagement or involvement in a task or event	Perception that information is potentially relevant to *any* goal	Receptor orientation; processing of information	Extraction of information from environment; communication of willingness to enter into a relationship, consider figure action

Source: Campos and Barrett (1984). Used by permission of Cambridge University Press and the author.

emotional experience, coping responses to emotion, emotional complexity, and receptivity to the emotional expressions of others.

Emotional expression in the neonate appears to be poorly coordinated and may be mixed with contextually inappropriate components. For example, Stenberg and Campos (1983) found that neonates mix some nonanger facial expressions (eye closing and tongue protrusion) with classic anger expressions. Similarly, Camras has observed the same type of phenomenon repeatedly with her own infant for a variety of basic emotions (Camras, 1992). These qualities are probably due to the baby's neurological immaturity, and within a short time expressions are likely to become more congruent with a particular emotional state. However, in later infancy and childhood, emotional states and their expression are

Table 4.6 Generalized Schema for Predicting Elicitation of More Complex Emotions

Emotion	Goal	Appreciation	Action Tendency	Adaptive Function
Shame	Maintenance of others' respect and affection; preservation of self-esteem	Perception of loss of another's respect/affection; perception that others have observed one doing something bad	Like those of sadness, anger (at self), and fear	Maintenance of social standards
Guilt	Meeting one's own internalized standards	Anticipation of punishment because one has not lived up to an internalized standard	Like those of sadness and anger	Encouragement of moral behavior
Envy	Obtaining a desired object	Perception that an object cannot be had because another has it and one's deficits prevent oneself from attaining the object	Like those of sadness and anger	Motivation of achievement to obtain similar goods
Depression	Having the respect and affection of *both* others and oneself	Perception of lack of love or respect from both others and oneself; perception of lack of possibility of attaining any very significant goal	Like sadness and anger (at self)	Elicitation of affection and nurturance from others

Source: Campos and Barrett (1984). Used by permission of Cambridge University Press and the author.

subjected to socialization pressures that lead to dissociations between them. As Ekman and Friesen (1982, 1986) have shown, display rules are learned in every culture that influence the relationship between felt emotion and its expression.

The development of an increased capacity to cope with emotion alters its visible intensity and the infant's subjective experience. Campos and Barrett illustrate this type of change in the infant's motor development, which allows the infant to regulate tension by controlling distance to a stranger. Similarly, Gunnar (1980) has shown that the infant's coping skills may serve to transform potentially aversive feelings into pleasurable ones by exerting control over the environment.

All theorists agree that emotional complexity increases with development. Many theorists view this outcome as the result of increasingly sophisticated cognitions. We shall discuss the joint impact of cognitive growth and socialization in terms of the acquisition of rules and standards underlying the emergence of the self-conscious emotions of pride, shame, and guilt in Chapter 7.

Finally, the ability to read or infer emotional states from the expressions of others certainly increases with age. The ability to recognize familiar faces and read emotional expressions emerges during the first six months. Finer understanding of another's emotional state, dependent on contextual cues, emerges later. Understanding that someone may simultaneously be feeling two different emotions at the same time requires still further development. Much of this progress may be related to cognitive change. However, no matter how complex the level of cognitive processing involved in these aspects of emotional development, Campos and Barrett insist that the basic appreciation of how events are related to one's goals forms the affective core that allows direct comparison between the infant's experience and that of the adult.

COMPARING AND INTEGRATING PERSPECTIVES

In this chapter we have attempted a partial survey of some of the most important historical and contemporary psychological theories of emotion. Some of these theories are expressly designed to deal with just one dimension of emotion, while others offer a more comprehensive view. At this point you may be wondering, *why so many theories?* First of all, let me reassure you that I will not be adding my own to the list. Probably the last thing this emergent field of study needs at this point is another theory of emotion. Indeed, given the many diverse theories already available, what is a reasonable attitude to adopt by a student of emotion? Should these theories be regarded as a diversity of products offered to consumers of theories in a free marketplace? Is psychology just a bunch of theories and you can pick the one you like the best? Obviously, this is not my recommendation.

My rationale for presenting such a diversity of perspectives on emotion stems from my conviction that each major perspective presented has unique and essential elements of a biosocial perspective on emotions and their development. The student's task, and it is a challenging one, is to integrate these different perspectives into a coherent whole, not simply collect a bunch of facts, figures, and opinions.

From biology we retain the idea that emotions evolved, and that basic human emotions share some similarities with the emotional repertoire of primates in general, and chimpanzees in particular. We also retain the view that emotions evolved because they serve vital functions in promoting the adaptation of the individual throughout the life span. These diverse functions may be classed into two broad categories: (1) internal regulation, and (2) social communication. We also retain the view that physical and chemical structures evolved to facilitate emotions in action, particularly in relation to important goals of our species. The structures of the brain, both cortical and subcortical, are critical to the experience of emotion, as are the structures in the body that regulate the ANS, heart rate, and hormonal systems designed by evolution to prepare the body to respond to various life challenges and emergencies throughout the life span. Emotions are a central part of these motivational systems.

From psychology we retain the view that emotions are a central part of one's interpersonal life. Within psychology we have emphasized three basic perspectives on emotion: (1) the psychodynamic tradition, (2) cognitive and cultural approaches, and (3) developmental theories. These approaches were presented as overlapping rather than mutually exclusive, yet they are grouped according to theoretical emphasis. Psychodynamic approaches, such as Erikson's stage theory and object relations theory, view emotional life in relational terms. That is, emotions are viewed as central to interpersonal goals and concerns. These theories are forerunners of contemporary developmental theories, especially attachment theory, which will be dealt with at length in Chapter 6. Like attachment theory, they emphasize the importance of early experience with primary caregivers as the cornerstone of future relationships, personality, and emotional competence. And they view the growth of personality in terms of integration versus dissociation. They also tend to deal fearlessly with constructs that are particularly challenging from the standpoint of assessment, but for which some progress has been achieved.

The second set of psychological theories of emotion are drawn from social psychology and propose, in different ways, that cognition and culture are essential determinants of our emotional experience. Most of these theories are united by the view that cognitive appraisal of an event, an event of particular relevance to one's goals, is central to the unfolding of the emotional process. They differ in terms of how much and how successfully they have incorporated more basic neurological and physiological processes into their models. They also differ with respect to the incorporation of ideas of evolutionary theorists regarding the ultimate function and core universal expressions of basic emotions. Social constructivists tend to view such an approach as negating the preeminent role of culture in determining one's emotions. Many social constructivists are generally antithetical to a Darwinian worldview, but cognitive-motivational-relational theorists incorporate functionalist thinking in a central way. Other cognitive theories, such as attribution theory, aim to contribute specifically to our understanding of the special role of causal attributions to the experience of some of our emotional responses, particularly the experience of pride, shame, guilt, and anger. Some theorists, and Lazarus in particular, strive to integrate a wide range of ideas into a single comprehensive framework for understanding the entire range of our emotional experience. Thus, theories differ greatly regarding their generality, though each of them has proven to have great heuristic value.

Developmental theories all emphasize the idea that emotions increase in complexity over the life span, and some provide detailed accounts of the relative contribution of cognitive advances, maturation, and socialization to the unfolding of emotions in a normative sense, and the development of individual differences in socioemotional competence. Developmental theories differ with respect to the role of cognitive factors, with Izard being the least oriented to a cognitive approach, whereas the views of Sroufe, Lewis, and Campos all share an emphasis on cognitive development as a key to understanding the emergence of both basic and self-conscious emotions in infancy and early childhood. All of these theories are functionalist in a very real sense, and most accept a general Darwinian approach to the study of emotional expression and adaptive function, though Izard's DET is perhaps the most orthodox in this regard. Campos labels his approach a new functionalism, but mostly what is new is what is missing, namely, the view that one's goals are generally tied to adaptational issues in the biological sense. Sroufe's organizational approach is sophisticated with respect to integrating a developmentalist view of goals with biologically based structures

and functions, although its focus is limited to early development. All of these theories share Lazarus's emphasis on goal relevance as a key determinant of emotion. As developmental theories, they add an emphasis on the changing nature of the individual's goals over the life span.

Given our developmental orientation, we shall prioritize the discussion of emotional growth in terms of both normative advances and the origins and course of individual differences in emotional functioning for the remainder of the book. These broad topics are presented in separate chapters for infancy and early childhood, and combined within the chapters on middle childhood and adolescence. This reflects the relatively greater amount of research on emotion in the early years of life, where both cross-sectional studies on normative development and longitudinal research on individual differences have been major areas for researchers for many years. Research on current topics like emotion regulation in later childhood and adolescence is both more recent and less extensive.

Within each developmental period, I have attempted to introduce and rework a number of common questions and themes relating to how emotions are expressed, how they are regulated, and how they are recognized and understood. All of these aspects of emotion undergo profound developmental change. In terms of understanding the mechanisms of these patterns of normative emotional growth, I have tried to maintain a holistic approach by consistently relating these changes to cognitive and social development, illustrating the interpenetration of all three aspects in the whole child.

These same aspects of emotional development form the core of the chapters on the origins and significance of individual differences. Just as individuals in different developmental periods differ in their expression, regulation, and understanding of emotions, so too do individuals of the same age differ. Longitudinal studies are irreplacable sources of information on how individuals come to differ so dramatically in their emotional makeup. Throughout the book I argue that such differences arise as the result of complex transactions with inputs from the child's own genotype interwoven with socialization influences. In particular, the child's close relations with family and peers are emphasized, as well as influences from the broader sociocultural milieu.

SUMMARY

A brief sketch of the history of twentieth-century American psychology was presented, noting three major revolutions in the focus of theory and research: (1) the rise of radical behaviorism; (2) the cognitive revolution; and (3) the emotion revolution. Theories of emotion, like scientific theories in general, may be judged according to several criteria including *parsimony, coherence, relevance, heuristic value,* and *generality.* A major challenge for a scientific theory of emotion is to generate meaningful constructs that can be related to observable events, and thus provide a means for corrective empirical feedback essential to the scientific enterprise.

Three major types of emotion theories within psychology were reviewed. Psychodynamic theories influenced by Freud's psychoanalytic theory emerged in the mid-twentieth century, including Erikson's psychosocial theory and object relations theory. Both theories retained from Freud a central role for emotion in personality and a developmental perspective emphasizing the importance of early experience with the caregiver. Erikson's theory modified Freud's psychosexual stage theory in three important ways. First, he expanded the theory beyond adolescence to encompass the entire life span. Second, he softened its deterministic character, emphasizing the rational, adaptive side of human nature. Finally, he placed Freud's theory into a wider cultural perspective by providing a more abstract, less ethnocentric view of development.

Object relations theorists also revised Freud's views chiefly by according a more active role to the individual and by shifting the most critical period for personality development from early childhood to infancy. They emphasized that the actual experiences of the infant, rather than fantasies, are the main source for the child's representational model of close relationships. The term object relations was created to emphasize that infant representations of the self and other are not well differentiated and that the awareness of a distinct self emerges out of the affective transactions with the primary caregiver.

Some social psychology theories were formulated to explain adult emotional functioning, and theorists like Arnold and Schachter viewed emotions as highly dependent on cognition. Schachter's two-factor theory held that emotions are constructed by the individual's cognitive interpretation of arousal in a social context. The same undifferentiated state of arousal is assumed to underlie all emotions, which are experienced differently because of the different interpretations that are made of the arousal.

Other social psychologists, like Lazarus and Tomkins, strongly challenged this reduction of emotional experience to different types of cognitive interpretations. Lazarus proposed a more comprehensive cognitive-motivational-relational theory which assumed that emotions are complex processes with many components. The component processes are viewed as interdependent, but no single component is sufficient to explain the emotion. Lazarus summarizes his model in terms of five major principles pertaining to (1) systems, (2) process-structure, (3) development, (4) specificity, and (5) relational meaning. The central idea is that each emotion is defined by a core relational meaning constructed by one's evaluation of any given situation as furthering or opposing one's goals.

Also rooted in cognitive constructionism are the social construction theories that view the experience and expression of emotions as social roles that are learned through socialization within a given culture. The impact of culture is most apparent in the language used to imbue the emotion with a particular significance for the individual, a meaning that is generally shared with other members of the same cultural and linguistic group. Some social construction theorists integrate a universal biological core of emotion with a semantic component that is largely a product of social construction.

Another recent theory from social psychology emphasizes a specific type of cognition in relation to emotion, the attribution of causality. According to Weiner's model, attributions about causes vary along three dimensions: (1) internal versus external; (2) stable versus unstable; and (3) controllable versus uncontrollable. In Weiner's view, some emotions may have little relation to such attributions, while other emotions involving social motives are strongly related to causal attributions. These emotions are anger, gratitude, pity, pride, shame, and guilt.

In developmental psychology, cognition is also seen as a major influence on emotional processes, and emotional development in infancy and childhood is often viewed as intimately related to cognitive development. This tendency is particularly evident in the theories of Sroufe and Lewis, both of whom describe the emergence of emotions as a process of differentiation that is propelled by maturation, cognitive development, and socialization. In Sroufe's organizational approach, this normative course of emotional growth provides a basis for studying individual differences in emotional functioning. Development is seen as progressing through a number of critical life tasks, and the strategy of prospective-longitudinal research is used to investigate the coherence of the individual's emotional development over time.

Izard's differential emotion theory (DET) was strongly influenced by Tomkin's neo-Darwinian theory of affect that preceded it. From Darwin, there is the idea that a core group of discrete emotions evolved in humans, characterized by universal facial expressions and adaptive intrapersonal and interpersonal functions. In contrast to differentiation theories, DET assumes emotional states to be present at birth in an already differentiated form, and eventually available to the organism as they are needed in the life cycle. Ten fundamental and unique emotions constitute the principal motivational system for human beings, each having different effects on cognition and action.

Lewis and Michalson developed a structural theory of emotion consisting of five major components: elicitors, receptors, states, expression, and experience. Each of these components is presumed to undergo developmental change as a function of maturation and socialization. In addition, the links between these components may change with age. Lewis and Michalson proposed a stage theory to describe emotional development in five periods marked by qualitative changes. Their theory is focused on the self-system and incorporates aspects of cognitive-developmental theory. Developmental changes in the infant's self-awareness, together with the acquisition of cultural standards and rules, underlie the emergence of the self-conscious emotions of pride, shame, guilt, and empathy, to be taken up in Chapter 7.

Campos and Barrett propose a functionalist theory of emotion similar to that of Lazarus. Emotions are viewed as reactions to one's evaluation of the relationship between an event and one's goals. Campos and Barrett view emotional development as a complex process that reflects both continuity and discontinuity. They begin by postulating an invariant core of affective continuity across the life span. Each basic emotion family represents an invariant relationship between a type of goal and an appreciation of one's progress toward it. These goals may be genetically prewired, especially in infancy, or socially constructed. With development, one's goals may change, but the relationship between goals and emotions remains essentially the same.

FURTHER READING

Campos, J., Mumme, D., Kermoian, R., & Campos, R. (1994). A functionalist perspective on the nature of emotion. In N. Fox (Ed.), The development of emotion regulation: Biological and behavioral considerations. *Monographs of the Society for Research in Child Development, 59*(2/3, Serial No. 240).

This is a succinct statement defining a functionalist perspective from one of its leading proponents.

Erikson, E. H. (1963). *Childhood and society* (2d ed.). New York: Norton.

This Pulitzer prize winning classic is best known for its influential framework for conceptualizing the stages of growth in the development of personality.

Izard, C. E. (1991). *The psychology of emotions.* New York: Plenum Press.

This is an excellent reference book on the form and function of discrete emotions from a biosocial perspective.

Lazarus, R. S. (1991). *Emotion and adaptation.* Oxford: Oxford University Press.

This comprehensive account of emotional life from a functionalist perspective emphasizes emotion in relation to the pursuit of one's goals.

5

The Emergence of Emotions in Infancy

What emerges derives in a logical, though complex way from what was present before as a precursor. The "emergent" is qualitatively different from the precursor and at a new level of complexity; yet the precursor serves as a prototype for the emergent, embodying an important core essence of that which is to come.

SROUFE (1996)

Figure 5.1 Emotional competence in infancy. The young infant is surprisingly competent in both expression of emotion and reading of emotional expressions. From an early age, infants can alter their behavior depending upon their parents' emotional cues.

(Photo by LaFreniere)

One afternoon after work I decided to drop by and visit a friend who was at home on maternity leave with her 10-month-old daughter. I rang the doorbell and was greeted at the door by my friend who was holding little Katy. Katy blinked rapidly as the door opened and she found herself face-to-face with a stranger. Her jaw dropped and eyebrows raised as she looked at me inquisitively for just a second before turning to face her mother who was smiling broadly as she greeted me. A second later Katy turned her face back to mine and smiled broadly at me as I entered.

Our understanding of the emotional life of infants has increased dramatically over the past several decades, chiefly on the basis of systematic observation and experimentation. An everyday observation like that just presented provides plenty of food for thought on such questions as the emergence of emotions in the first year, their relation to cognitive and social development, and whether facial expressions reveal the presence of a given emotion. During the encounter with Katy and her mother, I reasoned that Katy was quite surprised to see a person suddenly standing at the door, though the wind and light from the door's opening may have elicited a blinking reflex. Unlike her mother, who knew what to expect at the sound of the doorbell, Sarah had no such foreknowledge. I interpreted her facial expression as a mixture of surprise, even startle, followed by an inquiring gaze into my eyes. When I saw her turn briefly to her mother then back to me with a completely altered expression, I reasoned that in the face of ambiguity, she looked to her mother for cues for how to deal with such a sudden turn of events. Her mother "explained" everything in an instant with her warm smile and greeting. As a result Katy was completely relaxed and interested in my visit, being capable of understanding the nonverbal cues being presented to her. Within a few minutes, her mother was able to transfer her to me, and we proceeded to have quite an amicable "conversation," though for Katy it was entirely nonverbal.

In this chapter we will examine both naturalistic and experimental research on emotional development during infancy. Two broad issues concern us: (1) How do human emotions develop? and (2) How do they organize development? First we will review research that pertains to general or normative patterns of growth, and then in the following chapter, we will discuss questions concerning the origin and significance of individual differences in the expression and regulation of emotion. Our story begins at birth with the neonate.

At birth the infant is already expressive, but can we call such expressions emotions? We observe crying and distress, as well as interest and smiles, from the first days of life. Of course, the infant has been alive for about nine months already, and much development has taken place. Indeed, it is now possible to observe facial expressions and other behaviors prior to birth. In the not too distant past, some psychologists considered the newborn as a "tabula rasa," a blank slate upon which the multiple influences of the environment would eventually write the destiny of the child. One prominent psychologist emphasized what once seemed certain and obvious to nearly everybody, that the infant was completely helpless and incompetent in dealing with all the diverse and novel stimulations that surrounded it. For William James (1890), infancy was a state of "blooming, buzzing confusion," and this is partly true. In the earlier example, Katy had not yet learned to associate the sound of the doorbell with the arrival of someone at the front door and seemed confused by my sudden and unpredictable appearance before her. However, scientists who study infants are now virtually unanimous in their appreciation of how organized and competent the human infant really is during the first year. In this section we will explore the idea that the infant comes into life equipped by nature to deal with a broad, but not infinite, range of possible encounters.

THE NEWBORN'S PREADAPTATIONS FOR EMOTIONAL COMMUNICATION

A modern developmental perspective recognizes the inherent capacities of the newborn to engage the social world, to respond to it, and to learn from experiences with it. This view that the infant is somehow prepared or preadapted to begin life is based upon a wide array of evidence. We will examine, in turn, the inborn capacities and preferences human infants exhibit in visual and auditory perception, their capacity for reflexive or automatic responses to various stimuli, and their ability to learn from their experience and accommodate to their environment.

Visual Capacities and Preferences

Infants are born with a visual system that is still in the process of developing. At two weeks, an infant's visual acuity is still rudimentary, and has been estimated to be the equivalent of an adult with 20/300 vision. Even after six months, infants are still only capable of focusing on objects near at hand. Though their visual acuity is moving closer to adult vision, it is still only about 20/100 (Banks & Salapatek, 1983). The optimal range for infant visual acuity is about 7 to 15 inches, the same distance most caregivers hold their heads from the infant when interacting face-to-face (Haynes, White, & Held, 1965).

Research on infant visual perception, using duration of visual attention, systematic recording of eye movements, electrical activity in the brain in response to visual stimuli, and other techniques, has demonstrated a number of significant capacities and preferences. From very early in life infants orient to movement, to curved rather than straight lines, to light/dark contrasts, and to a moderate degree of complexity, all features possessed by a human face (Banks & Salapatek, 1983; Haith, 1966). Caregivers who lean over their baby smiling, nodding, and cooing to capture and hold the infant's attention provide quite naturally just the sort of visual stimulation that attracts infants.

Since newborns are unable to detect fine-grained patterns in complex stimuli, they prefer stimuli with bolder, sharper contrasts that present detectable patterns. As infants begin to resolve finer details, they shift their preference to the

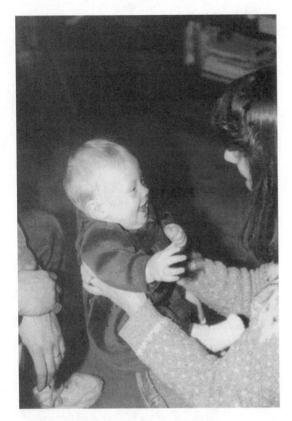

Figure 5.2 The optimal range for face-to-face interaction with the young infant is about 7 to 15 inches. This enables the infant to readily explore and respond to the parent's facial expressions. Parents seem to provide this distance naturally, probably because their infant has shaped this behavior by being more responsive to them at close range. From birth onward, learning and socialization between parent and infant is bidirectional, with each partner shaping the other's behavior.

(Photo by LaFreniere)

more detailed pattern, a principle known as contrast sensitivity (Banks & Salapatek, 1981). Infants also develop more complex scanning patterns in the first few months. For example, when presented with drawings of the human face, 1-month-olds do not look as long as 2-month-old babies. They also do not look at the face in the same manner. The younger infants are more likely to concentrate their gaze on a single element, such as the hairline or beard, and limit their exploration to the outer edges of the face. As contrast sensitivity and scanning ability improve, older infants explore internal features by moving their eyes around the figure, pausing to look at each element, particularly the eyes (Maurer & Salapatek, 1976).

Infants' tendency to scan all the elements in a pattern is directly applied to their perception of human faces. Young infants study complex stimuli longer than simpler ones, and by 2 to 3 months, infants show a preference for a facial pattern over the same elements scrambled in another configuration. In a study comparing 3-month-old and 6-week-old infants, the older infants looked longer at a face than at the same pattern reversed, but showed no such preference when shown an abstract pattern and its negative (Dannemiller & Stephens, 1988).

Recognizing Faces These capacities and preferences lead to a remarkable development at 3 months. At this stage the infant is beginning to organize the various elements into a distinct pattern or schema for the human face that may be recognized. At this age infants can recognize their mother's face in a photograph, and they prefer to look at her rather than a stranger (Barrera & Maurer, 1981a). If the mother's face as a schema is not assimilated, because the mother's bearded brother has taken her place at the crib, the infant may become quite distressed.

Soon after 3 months, infants can remember and distinguish between faces of different strangers and they show preferences for more attractive faces (Langlois, Roggman, Casey, Ritter, Reisser-Danner, & Jenkins, 1987). A preference for physically attractive faces was once presumed to be a learned cultural stereotype, but these data have led to a reexamination of this position. Although it is clear that infants show preferences for the same kind of faces adults find attractive long before socialization practices could have

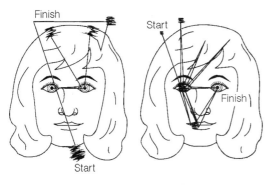

Finish

Start

Start

Finish

1 month old   2 months old

Figure 5.3 The infant's visual exploration of the face. At 1 month, infants scan the outer edges of the face, but by 2 months they seem to have discovered the eyes as the window on the soul. Two-month-olds look at the face longer and concentrate their gaze on the internal features, particularly the eyes.

Source: Maurer and Salapatek (1976). Reprinted by permission of SRCD.

produced a culturally specific standard, it is unclear what specific characteristics influence infants' choices. It may be that infants prefer attractive faces because they contain more of the individual features that infants prefer, such as high contrast, contours, curves, and vertical symmetry. Or it could be that babies are attracted to average faces and look longest at stimuli that come closest to the prototypical face. Whatever the explanation, babies are clearly predisposed to attend to human faces because of the important functional significance of face-to-face interaction for later socioaffective development.

Recognizing Facial Expressions As infants' visual acuity improves and they gain experience with human faces in social interaction, they begin to make finer and finer discriminations of facial affect. A number of convergent findings from experimental work suggest that infants develop the capacity to discriminate between different facial expressions at about 3 months (Haviland & Lelwica, 1987; Nelson, 1987; Nelson & de Haan, 1997). At this age, infants can discriminate happy and sad faces from surprised faces (Younge-Browne, Rosenfeld, & Horowitz, 1977), smiles from frowns (Barrera & Maurer, 1981b), and smiling faces that vary in intensity (Kuchuk, Vibbert, & Bornstein, 1986). By 4 months infants are capable of discriminating joyful faces from angry or neutral faces

(LaBarbera, Izard, Vietze, & Parisi, 1976), and by 5 months they are beginning to make discriminations among sad, fearful, and angry expressions (Schwartz, Izard, & Ansul, 1985) based on vocalizations and facial expressions.

By the second half of the first year, infants are able to perceive emotional expressions as organized wholes. They can distinguish mild and intense expressions of different emotions (Ludemann & Nelson, 1988), and they respond to happy or surprised expressions differently than sad or fearful faces, even if these emotions are expressed in slightly varying ways by different people (Ludemann, 1991). Infants also begin to rely upon facial expressions as an important indicator of how to respond emotionally to an uncertain situation or event. In the example at the beginning of this chapter, baby Katy used her mother's expression as a social reference to guide her response to an ambiguous stimulus, me. If her mother had responded with a fearful expression, it is highly probable that Katy too would have shown fear.

Social referencing is one of the first clear examples of emotion regulation. Like other examples throughout the first year, it occurs in a dyadic context. As early as 10 weeks, infants begin to respond meaningfully to their mother's facial expressions (Haviland & Lelwica, 1987), and by 10 months, infants rely on these emotional cues to decide how to respond to a wide

Figure 5.4 Testing pattern preferences in young infants. Infants look longer at the complex stimuli (a and b), but at 2 months they do not yet show a preference for the facelike figure over the scrambled face.

Source: Adapted from Frantz (1961).

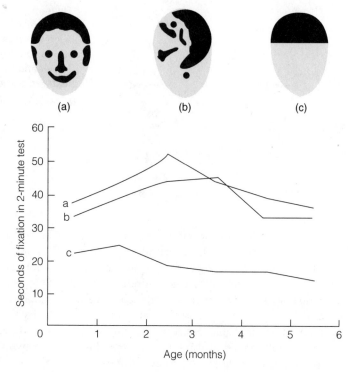

variety of events for which they lack experience. For example, Feinman and Lewis (1983) demonstrated that 10-month-olds can more readily overcome their typical wariness of an intruding stranger if their mothers show positive behavior toward the stranger.

Similarly, maternal facial expressions serve to regulate the coping behavior of infants to other interesting, but frightening, objects. Klinnert (1984) exposed 12- to 18-month-olds to three unfamiliar toys—a model of a human head, a dinosaur, and a remote-controlled spider, instructing the mothers to look alternately from the toy to the infant while expressing joy, fear, or a neutral attitude. Infants guided their behavior according to their mother's expression, retreating toward her when she showed fear, but approaching the toy when she was happy. In a modification of the visual cliff experiment, all 1-year-olds avoided the deeper side when their mothers

posed a fearful expression, but 74 percent of the infants crossed the cliff when their mothers expressed happiness (Sorce, Emde, Campos, & Klinnert, 1985). Because the face carries the most information, by 14 months infants use it more than any other cue (Walden & Ogan, 1988). Clearly these advances in the recognition and understanding of facial expressions play a central role in the development of early relationships. Just consider how your social life would be affected if you could not recognize faces of familiar people or interpret the meaning of different facial expressions!

Auditory Capacities and Preferences

Of course, an infant is not just drawn to the visual stimulation of the adult caregiver, but is also drawn to the caregiver via other sensory channels critical to infant care, communication, and socialization. In much the same way that infants are preadapted to respond to the visual characteristics of the human face, they also show a similar predisposition to the sound of human speech. The frequency, intensity, and structure presented by typical human speech patterns present a very attractive auditory cue to the infant (Papousek, Papousek, & Bornstein, 1985).

A number of conclusions can be drawn from research on infants' auditory capacities and preferences. Using measures of eye blinks, changes in heart rate, and changes in the brain's electrical activity, research has demonstrated that infants are capable of detecting sounds as slight as 10 dB as early as the second week, but respond more reliably to sounds of 60 dB, about the sound level of the average speaking voice (Aslin, 1987). They can hear higher frequencies than adults, and prefer frequencies between 500 and 900 Hz. As with visual stimuli, infants are more attracted to complex sounds and will attend to them longer than simple, pure tones. These capacities and preferences correspond quite closely to the pitch range of human voices, including the soft, high-pitched voice used by many caregivers when interacting with an infant. In addition, neonates show a differential sensitivity to the maternal voice and quickly learn to distinguish it from other female voices, though it is likely that some of this learning occurred prior to birth (DeCasper & Fifer, 1980; DeCasper & Spence, 1986). All of this evidence is consistent with the notion that infants are preadapted for later social, emotional, and linguistic development.

Another similarity between infants' capacity in the visual channel and that in the auditory channel concerns their innate coordination between sensory inputs and their head movements. Just as infants can orient toward a moving object, so too can they orient in the direction of a voice and look directly at the person who is speaking, even if the infant is too far away to bring the face into precise focus (Muir & Clifton, 1985).

Figure 5.5 Face-to-face social interaction between grandfather and 6-month-old infant

(Photo by LaFreniere)

Consider a typical morning breakfast shared between a baby boy and his mother in the first months of life. The mother may lean in close to the infant, speaking his name softly and carrying on a one-sided conversation full of modulations in cadence and pitch, as she prepares to feed the infant. Because of this close proximity, all of the infant's senses are directed toward her. The infant takes in not only the visual and auditory cues she provides, but also the smells, tastes, and touch of the mother during feeding. The infant's ability to detect sweetness, similar to that of the mother's milk, helps account for the early development of a general preference for sweet substances in humans (Engen, Lipsitt, & Peck, 1974). Experiments by Harlow and colleagues with rhesus monkeys, presented later in this chapter, have demonstrated the critical importance of touch for attachment in primate infants. Taken as a whole, there is little doubt that the human infant is predisposed to respond positively to the sort of stimulation naturally provided by human caregivers across diverse cultures.

Most developmental psychologists interpret these and other findings as evidence that human infants (like other infants within the mammalian order) are biologically programmed to orient to the stimulation typically afforded them by adult caregivers. As we will see in our discussion of attachment processes in the next chapter, the establishment of close bonds with caregivers is too vital for the infant's survival to be left entirely to the vicissitudes of chance.

Reflexes

In addition to the infant's built-in capacities for sensing and orienting to social stimulation, the infant possesses a wide range of reflexes. A **reflex** is a congenitally organized stimulus–response connection that is automatically released when the infant encounters the appropriate stimulation. Ethologists speak of "releasing" behaviors, since the behaviors themselves are, in a sense, already present. When the sign stimuli come along, the behaviors are emitted without the benefit of prior learning. Of course, learning will play an important role in shaping many of these early appearing reflexes into adaptive, cognitively mediated responses.

Human reflexes represent a storehouse of *phylogenetic adaptations* that have been retained because they provided some advantage or function for the infant's survival during our evolutionary past. Reflexes are the starting point of behavioral development in that they give direction to the process and provide something for development and learning to act upon. There is an automatic, involuntary quality to reflexive

behavior, in much the same sense as a "knee-jerk response." Many of the reflexes that are critical for infant care and socialization will be transformed during the first months of life into voluntary behavior guided by the infant's motivation and cognition. For example, two especially important reflexes for establishing social communication, crying and smiling, provide a biological foundation for the development of positive and negative emotions. Other reflexes that may have once been important, but serve no current function, disappear shortly after birth. For example, in arboreal primates, the Moro reflex may have been important for clinging to the mother as she moved about. If an infant suddenly lost support, the reflex would cause the infant to embrace the mother and, along with the grasping reflex, enable the infant to regain its hold on the mother's body (Kessen, 1965). The Moro reflex simply disappears in the first few months of life, whereas the grasping reflex becomes increasingly voluntary and will be functional in many different contexts.

Scientists are still learning about human infants' surprising capacities for adapting to their environment, but it is now firmly established that many preadaptations enable infants to organize and respond to sensory input and influence the caregiver long before the development of intentionality and the experience of true emotions. Rather than being born as a blank slate on which the environment will write the destiny of the individual, it is clear that crucial biological preadaptions in the form of perceptual capacities and preferences, as well as reflexive responses, allow the infant to actively engage the environment into which he or she is born from the very beginning of life. In the next section we will trace the development of infant action in the realm of emotional expressions from their starting point as biological refelexes to the cognitively mediated affective responses that become possible during the first year of life.

SIX BASIC EMOTIONS OF INFANCY

Six emotional systems have received a great deal of attention by developmental researchers since Darwin's seminal contribution (1872/1965). Positive emotions like joy/happiness and surprise/interest have been investigated in thousands of studies, as have negative emotions like anger, sadness/distress, disgust, and fear. The criteria for inclusion on this short list of basic emotions may vary somewhat among modern researchers. Some contemporary investigators differentiate two lines of emotional development, an infantile nonverbal affect system and a verbal-conceptual system, that are localized in separate hemispheres in the brain (Gazzaniga, 1985; Krystal, 1978). Evidence is now available that indicates that the right hemisphere mediates arousal due to pleasure and pain and certain biologically primitive emotions associated with these sensations (Schore, 1994; Semenza, Pasini, Zettin, Tonin, & Portolan, 1986). According to a leading proponent of the concept of **basic emotions,** Ekman (1992), nine criteria must be met in order for the emotion to be considered "basic": (1) universal expression, (2) quick onset, (3) comparable expressions in other animals, (4) an emotion-specific physiology, (5) universal antecedent events, (6) coherence in response systems, (7) brief duration, (8) automatic appraisal mechanism, and (9) unbidden occurrence.

Although researchers differ somewhat in regard to what constitutes a basic emotion (could it be otherwise?) and some may even question the value of such a classification scheme (Ortony, Clore, & Collins, 1988), nevertheless, these six emotions are mentioned by Darwin and nearly every investigator since that time, as shown in Table 5.1. They are presumed to be basic to all humans because they share a number of common characteristics (Ekman, 1971, 1989). First, they are rooted in our ancient evolutionary heritage, make their appearance early in infancy, and arise quickly and automatically in the course of interaction with the environment. Second, they are characterized by universal facial expressions that are remarkably constant and recognized across different cultures as indicating the presence of a particular emotion. Third, these expressions are considered to be hardwired into the neural circuitry linking the brain to the facial muscular system, are correlated with distinct autonomic system activity, and may show subcortical conditioning. Although learning will eventually play a critical role in how, when, and where the individual expresses a basic emotion, no social learning appears to be necessary to their initial production or reception.

The smile, startle, cry, and expression of disgust that researchers commonly report in newborns are phylogenetic adaptations and represent the prototypes necessary for the emergence of the primary affective systems in infancy. The task of a student of developmental psychology is to describe how each affective system emerges from earlier precursors and the process by which it is transformed and reorganized over the life course. For a student of evolutionary biology, the task is to determine how these basic emotions are related to adaptive biological, motivational, and social processes that have functional significance for the organism. We shall discuss these various aspects—phylogenesis, universality, ontogenesis, and function—for each of the basic emotion systems.

Positive Emotions

Joy/Happiness The smile is a very influential social signal even when no communication is intended by the sender. The earliest smiles to appear in the neonate have been labeled **endogenous smiles** (Spitz, Emde, & Metcalf, 1970; Wolff, 1963) because these smiles are spontaneous or reflexive, seem to depend on the infant's internal state, and typically occur during **REM (rapid eye movement) sleep.** These

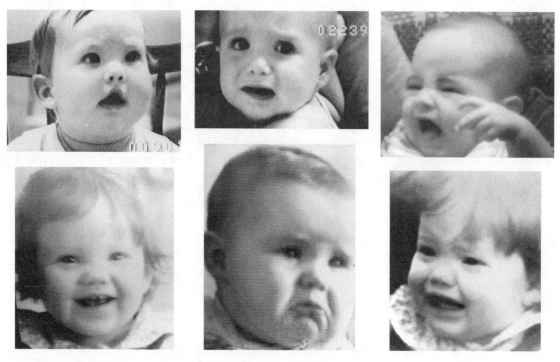

Figure 5.6 Basic emotions in infancy. Young infants around the world display a small number of species-typical facial expressions that are readily recognized as emotional signals by caregivers.

(Photos by Carroll E. Izard, University of Delaware)

Table 5.1 Basic Emotions of Early Infancy According to Different Theorists

Theorist	Joy	Surprise (Interest)	Anger	Fear	Sadness	Disgust
Darwin (1872/1965)	x	x	x	x	x	x
McDougall (1926)	x	x	x	x		x
Bridges (1932)	x		x	x	x	x
Tomkins (1962, 1963)	x	x	x	x		x
Plutchik (1980)	x	x	x	x	x	x
Izard (1991)	x	x	x	x	?	x
Ekman (1992)	x	x	x	x	x	x
Campos and Barrett (1984)	x	x	x	x	x	
Oatley and Johnson-Laird (1987)	x		x	x	x	x

first smiles, which involve simply turning up the corners of the mouth, do not occur when the infant is awake and alert, but only when the infant is asleep, most often in periods characterized by low levels of cortical activity (Emde & Koenig, 1969). The endogenous smile occurs more frequently in premature infants, and among all infants declines in frequency over the first three months (Emde, McCartney, & Harmon, 1971; Spitz et al., 1970). This decline is associated with the development and functioning of the cortex, which does not appear to be implicated in the production of endogenous smiles, since they have been observed in a microcephalic infant without a functioning cortex (Harmon & Emde, 1972).

According to Sroufe (1996), endogenous smiles are due to fluctuations in CNS arousal, with the smile ocurring during the drop below a hypothetical threshold of arousal as the infant relaxes following a momentary excitation of the CNS (see Figure 5.7). Light stimulation of the newborn during sleep, but not when awake, will produce a smile five to eight seconds after the stimulation. Shaking a rattle or gently shaking the sleeping infant will tend to produce a series of little smiles. If the infant is startled, causing arousal levels to spike, sleep smiles will not occur for some time. These findings are interpreted by Sroufe as indicating that the endogenous smile is produced during the relaxation phase of excitation–relaxation cycles as the infant's arousal drops below a threshold.

The first waking smiles of the infant appear to be very similar to endogenous smiles. They are produced by the same type of mild stimulation, and they still involve the action of a single muscle. At about 1 month, infants move to the phase of exogenous smiles, in which smiling occurs in response to a wide range of external stimulation while the infant is awake and alert. Alert smiles involve the action of multiple muscles and include the crinkling of the eyes as the mouth is pulled into a grin. Known as **Duchenne smiles** after the French scientist who first described them, these broad smiles are readily identified by adults as expressions of happiness (Ekman, Friesen, & Davidson, 1990; Emde, Izard, Huebner, Sorce, & Klinnert, 1985).

Infants may smile in response to a wide variety of stimulation, including vigorous tactile stimulation, interesting sights, and social stimuli such as faces and high-pitched voices. Gradually these smiles become less dependent on organismic state with less of a latency following stimulation. In his detailed observations, Wolff (1963) reported that patty-cake becomes a highly effective stimulus at 4 weeks, and at 5 weeks visual stimuli (nodding head and masked faces) become effective, as the voice begins to wane in its effectiveness. Spitz et al. (1970) showed that the emergence of smiling to a still face at about 2 months points to a new organization in which the infant's expression is less reflexive and more responsive. This is accompanied by decreases in endogenous smiles and important developments in the cortex as indexed by EEG and sleep patterns.

From the standpoint of infant cognitive development, this achievement is important because it indicates the presence of a true visual schema. Sroufe (1979, 1996) views this stage to be a midpoint between the reflexive, physiological prototype of the endogenous smile and the first true social smiles that clearly indicate immediate joy at the arrival of the caregiver. Smiles at this stage are intermediate because they no longer depend entirely on external stimulation, but may also occur as a function of the infant's active engagement of the stimulus. **Recognitory assimilation** (Kagan, 1971; Piaget, 1952) reflects an emerging cognitive component that is fundamentally different from the earlier excitation–relaxation cycle produced by stimulation. According to Piaget (1952, 1962), recognitory assimilation involves both an affective and a cognitive component. When the infant is presented with a stimulus such as the stationary face, there is strong effort leading to assimilation of the schema, followed by tension release and smiling. If there is no successful assimilation, the infant may turn away or cry.

The evidence supporting the involvement of cognition in infant smiling at about 2 to 3 months is extensive. Infants who show delayed cognitive development, such as institutionalized infants (Gewirtz, 1965) and infants with Down's syndrome (Cicchetti & Beeghly, 1990), also show

Figure 5.7 Hypothetical threshold of arousal. The newborn's smiles during sleep are related to fluctuations in CNS activity. Smiles may occur spontaneously (see part a) when the infant's depth of sleep changes. Following a startle it takes some time before the excitation falls below the arousal threshold (straight line) and the smile recurs. As shown in part b, sleep smiles may also occur in response to mild stimulation such as shaking a rattle.

Source: Sroufe (1996). Reprinted by permission of the Cambridge University Press.

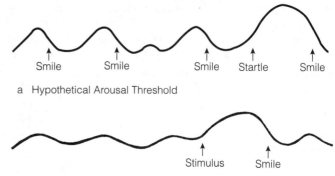

delays of several weeks in their responsiveness to a stationary face. In addition, there is a dynamic quality to effective stimuli that suggests the importance of novelty or challenge involved in recognitory assimilation. Since effortful assimilation is central, stimuli that are effective at an early age lose this potency over time. For example, a stationary face no longer reliably elicits a smile after age 3 to 5 months (Ahrens, 1954; Gewirtz, 1965; Spitz et al., 1970). The cognitive involvement of the infant may also be shown in a repeated measures experiment, in which infants smile at the stimulus for several trials but return to neutral looking after a series of presentations. With these repeated exposures, there is no longer any effort required to assimilate the schema. However, if a novel or discrepant aspect, such as a masked face, is introduced, there is renewed smiling followed again by a decline with repetition (Kagan, 1971; Sroufe & Wunsch, 1972). Finally, older infants smile more readily to the same novel stimulus than younger infants, indicating more rapid accommodation (Zelazo, 1972). In summary, smiles produced by recognitory assimilation represent a new phase of active, cognitive engagement of the infant that is not present earlier.

With the emergence of cognitive factors in infant smiling, the first truly social smiles appear. As the infant becomes increasingly involved in rudimentary social interaction, the content and

meaning of an event become more reliable clues to the emotional reaction than the amount of external stimulation. This is illustrated by changes in the infant's response to social stimuli during the first year. As we have seen, the schema of a human face evokes a broad grin from infants between 6 and 8 weeks. By 3 months infants begin to show a preference for familiar faces, and by 4 or 5 months infants smile in response to their caregiver's voice or face. At this point the smile is no longer elicited by a stranger regardless of context, and the silent stranger's face will begin to elicit a wary look from the infant. The appraisal process has led to a very different emotional response than that of the 2-month-old. That affect and cognition are intimately linked is perhaps best illustrated by the use of affective responses to demonstrate advances in infant cognition (Charlesworth, 1969; Cicchetti Hesse, 1983; Piaget, 1952; Shultz & Zigler, 1970; Sroufe & Wunsch, 1972; Zelazo & Komer, 1971).

As the smile becomes firmly embedded in the infant's behavioral repertoire, its functional significance becomes clearer. Even before the smile becomes a truly social act, its presence has a special significance for the caregiver, who is likely to interpret it as a sign of affection and joy. The infant's smile to the face suggests recognition of the caregiver and enhances the parent's interest and affection for the child. For example, mothers reported feeling good when shown photographs of an infant's positive expressions, and they stated that they would talk, play, and interact more with the infant as a result (Huebner & Izard, 1988). At 2 months smiles are easily elicited by a variety of social stimulation, providing reinforcement of caregiving to parents. By 3 months infants begin to smile selectively to their caregivers, further shaping the caregivers' behavior (Camras, Malatesta, & Izard, 1991), and infants smile more in response to the smiles and vocalizations of their mothers than equally responsive, but unfamiliar, female adults (Wahler, 1967). As the infant enters the phase of attachment in the making, the smile is used to greet the arrival of the mother and to engage her in play. The most important social functions of the smile include eliciting approaches and positive responses from others and promoting interaction essential to the development of mother–infant attachment (Ainsworth, 1963, 1977; Bowlby, 1969/1982). The smile also functions to promote mastery by shaping social partners to provide novel stimulation. Smiling during effortful play releases tension and allows the infant to stay engaged as well as encourages caregivers to continue the stimulation (Sroufe, 1996). Finally, the smile is one of the infant's expressive behaviors, along with gaze aversion, that mediates the intensity of face-to-face interaction, essential to the development of reciprocity (Field & Fogel, 1982; Tronick, 1989).

Laughter too plays an important role in promoting mother–infant interaction. Sroufe and Wunsch (1972) provided the earliest data on the development of laughter, which may first be elicited reliably at about 4 months. Using mothers as their research assistants, Sroufe and Wunsch carried out what must have been one of the funniest longitudinal studies of infants ever conducted. From the age of 4 to 12 months, they investigated the amount of laughter elicited by tactile (bouncing on knee, blowing hair, kissing the baby's stomach), auditory

(lip popping, "Aaah" sounds, whinnying and speaking in a falsetto voice), social ("I'm gonna get you!," playing tug, peek-a-boo), and visual (penguin walk, sucking baby bottle, human masks) stimulation. Figure 5.8 shows the results. As with the development of smiling, clear age trends reveal that the elicitors of laughter begin with intrusive tactile and auditory stimulation and shift to social and more subtle visual stimulation after 6 months.

Sroufe (1996) interprets these data as supporting his tension modulation model in which a dynamic threshold range for affective response is hypothesized. Tension is viewed as a natural byproduct of actively engaging the environment. The critical feature of the tension model is that thresholds for inciting a given emotional response are not stationary but vary as a function of the meaning of an event in context, which changes with age. Sroufe's model differs from earlier arousal models by distinguishing between physically produced arousal and arousal that has a psychological basis, dependent on the evaluation of the meaning of an event.

Interest and Surprise Few authors do not draw some distinction between interest and surprise. The purpose of presenting them together in this section is to draw attention to the epistemic quality of both rather than merge them as constructs. Interest may be discerned in the facial expression and behavior of infants in the first weeks of life and is tremendously important as a motivational state to support learning and cognitive development in infancy and throughout life (Izard, 1991). In contrast, surprise is both dependent on and facilitative of cognitive development, and is not observable until the infant has developed the cognitive capacity to formulate an expectation, sometime between 5 and 7 months (Charlesworth, 1969).

The facial expressions of both interest and surprise convey the impression of someone who is rapidly drawn to and greatly absorbed in a particular object or event. The classic expression of

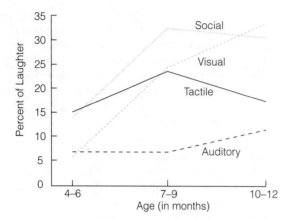

Figure 5.8 The development of laughter. Laughter of infants in the first year of life in response to four different classes of stimuli.

Source: Sroufe and Wunsch (1972). Reprinted with permission of SRCD.

surprise was described by Darwin as a sudden opening of the eyes and mouth widely while raising the eyebrows and freezing all other behavior, which he saw as functioning to enhance perception of the novel event. The expression of interest is a bit different. According to Izard (1991), "interest may be signaled by a movement in one region of the face—lifted brows, brows drawn medially (together but neither raised nor sharply lowered), visual tracking, softly opened mouth, or pursed lips. Any of these movements either on their own or in any combination may signal interest." Both expressions are relatively brief in duration, and both may be only partially expressed in the face. Several investigators have noted that the full facial expression of surprise occurs infrequently in situations likely to elicit the emotion. For example, Charlesworth & Kreutzer (1973) reported that the classic expression noted by Darwin occurs about 3 to 7 percent of the time, and this percentage changes little from infancy to the sixth grade. Other investigators (Hiatt, Campos, & Emde, 1979; Vaughn & Sroufe, 1979) have reported similar findings using the "vanishing object" paradigm and several other surprising events for infants between 8 and 17 months.

If surprise and interest are only sometimes accompanied by a distinctive facial expression, it appears that they are more regularly associated with distinctive physiological responses. In one study, researchers videotaped the facial expressions of infants and monitored their heart rate while they were viewing a human face or facelike objects (Langsdorf, Izard, Rayias, & Hembree, 1983). Infants showed greater interest expression and HR deceleration in response to the human face than an inanimate object with similar stimulus properties. Earlier research on the **orienting reflex** (an involuntary behavioral and physiological response to a sudden, novel, or unexpected event) summarized by Charlesworth (1969) demonstrated a wide range of instrumental responses. These included (1) heightened sensitivity of the sense organs, (2) a directing of sense receptors toward stimuli, (3) rapid inhibition of ongoing behaviors, (4) a change in EEG, (5) vasoconstriction in the limbs, (6) vasodilation in the head, (7) GSR, (8) a change in respiration rate, and (9) a change in HR.

The orienting reflex may be viewed as a physiological prototype of interest in a sense similar to that described by Sroufe. In a comparative sense, the orienting response is widespread in mammals where it serves a critical function of alerting the organism and organizing an adaptive response to potentially dangerous aspects of the environment. In the human newborn, the orienting reflex serves multiple functions. For example, if an infant's cheek is brushed by the nipple, the infant will reflexively respond by orienting the mouth toward the source of stimulation (rooting reflex). Other infant orienting reflexes are activated by sights and sounds. According to Tomkins (1962), these orienting reflexes underlie and support sustained interest to important stimuli, such as the caregiver's face and voice.

Interest, as an emotion, must be distinguished from the orienting reflex, which cannot be activated without external sensory stimulation. Interest, which is increasingly directed and regulated through cognitive mechanisms, can eventually be activated and sustained by mental images alone. This dynamic, psychological quality of interest is fundamentally different than the reflexive orientation that is essentially controlled by the stimulus rather than the infant, though these distinctions may be less apparent in the first few months of life.

In a similar sense, surprise is closely related to its prototype, the startle reflex, such that some investigators confuse the two responses. However, as with all prototypes, the startle may be elicited as an involuntary physiological response, with no psychological component. The startle reflex is a rapid, defensive reaction to an "unexpected" event that is often intense, as in the example of a pistol shot close to the individual's head. Surprise, which may or may not be accompanied by a similar facial expression, is a cognitively mediated response to the "misexpected" (Charlesworth, 1969). As a result of distinct elicitors and morphology of the expression, surprise and startle are quite distinguishable in character and form and effectively illustrate the distinction between a reflex and an emotion (Ekman, Friesen, & Simons, 1985).

In a series of ingenious studies, Charlesworth used a trapdoor in the baby's high chair to cause the sudden disappearance of an object of the infant's attention. If the alert infant were to look closely at an object, track its movement, and reach for it as it approached, we would all agree that the infant would be showing interest in the object. If the same object suddenly vanished through a trapdoor and the infant remained expressionless and showed no search behavior for the object, we would probably conclude that the infant had not acquired object permanence, or the understanding that objects continue to exist even when they disappear from our sight. We adults take this concept for granted, but it is not until about 5 or 6 months that infants respond to the vanished object paradigm with a surprised expression and begin to look for it. Charlesworth infers a fundamental cognitive advance (acquisition of object permanence) on the basis of these affective and behavioral cues. Like interest, the emotion of surprise may be considered as an important epistemic emotion because of its function of activating and sustaining curiosity, exploratory behavior, and discovery.

Negative Emotions

Since Darwin, four negative emotions have been viewed as primary: fear, distress or sadness, anger, and disgust. In this section we shall summarize research dealing with the early development, expression, and regulation of these negative affective systems. Throughout this discussion we shall consider comparative data from animal research alongside data from human infants. Negative emotions are often experienced as disruptive and unpleasant, but we shall also explore the idea that these emotions serve adaptive functions within a biodevelopmental model. Finally, we shall consider the role of maturation, cognitive development, observational learning, and conditioning.

Carroll Izard and colleagues regard the infant's facial expression as the basis for inferring the presence of an emotion. Infants are seen as ideal subjects for observational research because they are not likely to mask or inhibit emotional expression as a result of learned cultural display rules. Following Darwin's methodological and theoretical example, these researchers have developed sophisticated systems for coding observations of emotional expression (see Figure 5.9).

Anger In a longitudinal study, Izard and colleagues videotaped 25 infants at 2, 4, 6, and 18 months of age during a series of routine medical injections required for the diptheria-pertussis-tetanus immunization (Izard, Hembree, & Huebner, 1987). At 2 months and throughout the first 6 months, all the infants responded with physical distress signals including facial expressions of pain-distress and strident crying. The strength of this response would appear to channel all the infant's energies into a cry for help. During

Happiness

Fear

Figure 5.9 Can you identify the infant's emotional expression? The MAX (Maximally Discriminative Facial Movement) System is widely used by researchers for classifying infants' emotional expressions. Facial muscle movements are carefully rated to determine their correspondence with basic feeling states. For example, cheeks raised and corners of the mouth pulled back and up signal happiness (a). Eyebrows raised, eyes widened, and mouth opened with corners pulled back straight denote fear (b).

Source: Figures from *The Maximally Discriminative Facial Movement Coding System,* by C. Izard. Copyright © 1983 University of Delaware. Reprinted by permission.

the period from 2 to 7 months, 90 percent of the infants showed a clear, full-faced anger expression following the pain-distress expression. The anger expression was fleeting and secondary to the pain-distress. One year later, as 19-month-olds, these same infants responded to the fourth and last inoculation with anger. In contrast to their response in early infancy, these toddlers showed short-lived physical distress, and 100 percent showed an anger expression that was dominant for a relatively long period of time. Izard (1991) interpreted these developmental changes in the following manner:

> The young infant is incapable of defending himself against such stimulation, so the baby channels all his energy into the physical distress expression, an all-out plea for help. This is the most natural and adaptive thing for the relatively helpless and defenseless young infant to do. However, as the child becomes capable of warding off painful stimulation or participating in his own defense, channeling all of his energies into a plea for help would not be maximally adaptive. Our study showed that as the baby matures, his expressive behavior changes. The all consuming physical distress expression gives way to the anger expression. The anger expression is more adaptive in the face of unanticipated painful stimulation because anger mobilizes energy that can be used for protection and defense. . . . [E]ventually the child has to learn not only how to regulate or inhibit anger but how to harness anger-mobilized energy in instrumental acts of self-defense when situations call for it (p. 246)

As Izard and others have shown, there is little doubt that infants show a variety of basic facial expressions, similar or identical to universally recognized adult expressions, but can we infer the presence of an emotion on this basis? As we saw with smiling during REM sleep, most researchers do not believe that facial expression alone is sufficient for inferring an emotional state.

Many infancy researchers agree that the initial starting point for the development of the negative affects is a state of undifferentiated distress (Bridges, 1932; Camras, 1992; Lewis, 1993a; Matias & Cohn, 1993; Oster, Hegley, & Nagel, 1992; Sroufe, 1979, 1996). In an interesting contemporary counterpart to Darwin's observational study of his infant son, Linda Camras observed and videotaped her daughter Justine's emotional expressions during the first three months of life.

She observed considerable overlap in the elicitors of the four negative emotions, as well as alternating patterns of sad, angry, and pain-distress expressions during single episodes of crying. From detailed observations of Justine's emotional expression in context, Camras provides a number of examples of elicitors that appear to be mismatched with expression. For example, Justine showed a fear expression when she was protesting being fed, distress-pain in response to the removal of her pacifier, and sadness in response to a distasteful vitamin. In Camras's (1992) view, Izard was correct in his identification of basic and universal human emotions, but wrong in assuming that facial expressions in infants are necessarily "automatic read-outs of emotion." Instead, she proposes that expressions of sadness may first appear as muted, less intense expressions of distress, with pain and anger reflecting more intense levels of the same general state.

Sroufe (1979, 1996) views negative emotions as **emergent** systems in the same sense that we saw earlier in his description of the development of joy. According to this model, physiological prototypes of the mature emotion exist at birth in the form of reflexes. The initial stage in the development of anger, defined as an "immediate, negative reaction directed at an obstacle to an intended act," may be seen in the first days of life in the reflexive flailing of the infant in response to restraining the head. Sroufe views this as the physiological prototype of anger, not anger itself. Following the newborn period, precursor emotions emerge that are no longer purely physiological, but are beginning to incorporate psychological components related to evaluating the content and meaning of a specific event. The precursor is not yet the equivalent of the mature emotion. Rather than an immediate response, it is expressed only after a gradual building up of tension. It is also a more diffuse reaction than later responses, often involving the whole body, and it is based on a general rather than specific evaluation of the content and meaning of the elicitor.

Brazelton (1969) observed a precursor of anger in the infant's response to the failure to execute a well-established motor pattern at about 2 months. He offers the following description:

> The force behind this integration can be aroused in a baby of this age by leaving him with a toy that he cannot pull into him. He is left with vision and fingers. He will play happily this way for a period. Then, his frustration builds up as he strains to get his mouth on it. He ends up by screaming furiously when he cannot examine it all over with his mouth and hands, as well as his eyes. (p. 131)

Lewis, Allessandri, and Sullivan (1990) also reported that displays of anger and fussiness occur at 2 months in response to the extinction of a learned contingency. Infants learned to pull on a string attached to their arm to turn on a short period of music. Infants as young as 2 months learned the contingency and expressed pleasure as a result of their mastery of it. However, when the contingency was removed, the infants expressed anger as a result of the violation of expectancy and loss of control of the situation. This would be a common elicitor of anger at any age. For example, if you learned to routinely save your thesis text onto your hard drive but, in following the same procedure as always, lost it, you can imagine your own emotional response to this violation of expectancy and loss of control.

An angry response, as opposed to a sad response, may be adaptive if it promotes instrumental goals. In the paradigm just described, infants who responded to extinction of the contingency with anger were also more likely to relearn the contingency. In contrast, infants who displayed just sadness showed the least interest and joy during the relearning phase of the experiment. In this example, it appears that anger can energize and prepare the organism for sustained and persistent effort. Lewis et al. (1992) suggest that these early individual differences may be precursors of mastery or learned helplessness orientations.

Cross-sectional studies of infants' responses to physical restraint or removal of an object reveal developmental changes in facial expressions. Stenberg and Campos (1990) observed negative facial and vocal expressions in 1-month-olds and found them to be delayed, gradual, and undifferentiated responses, in much the same manner as Sroufe's concept of a precursor. However, in 4- and 7-month-olds, the expressions are clearer, more immediate, and directed toward the elicitor, meeting the criteria of a mature angry response.

Since Aristotle and Darwin, anger has been associated with the cognitive capacity of means–end thinking. The definition used by many theorists of anger as an emotional response to enable the organism to overcome an obstacle implies that the organism has some knowledge of the necessary means to achieve a goal. Although anger may be seen as maladaptive, it also can be seen as serving a variety of adaptive functions. First and foremost, anger supplies the organism with a surplus of energy necessary for sustained goal-directed activity. This may be illustrated in the infant's response to a violation of a learned contingency, as in the Lewis et al. study cited earlier. A more dramatic example would be the response to unprovoked aggression or victimization. Anger, as opposed to sadness, would be the emotion best suited to mobilize and sustain a long and difficult course of action. However, dysregulated anger can also lead to maladaptive responses, so we can see that adaptation or competence is not inherent in the emotion itself, but rather in the coordination of emotion, cognition, and behavior. Ultimately, only the behavior of the organism can promote or undermine its adaptation, and thoughts and feelings that do not lead to expressive or instrumental behavior do not count in the biological game of adaptation. In subsequent chapters we shall continue to illustrate the positive functions of the negative emotions, as well as instances in which these emotions do not promote adaptation.

Sadness The study of sadness, in contrast to discrete emotions such as anger and fear, has been remarkably neglected, perhaps because it has characteristics that have more in common with a mood or emotional state. Developmental and clinical psychologists have focused a great deal of attention on depression and grief as emotional states experienced in response to loss (Bowlby, 1960, 1980), but relatively few studies have focused on the more common and normative experience of sadness. The most extensive literature on sadness in infancy involves the study of the infant's response to separation from the mother or maternal unresponsiveness, and this would appear to be the first elicitor of sadness in the life of the child, occurring at approximately 3 months according to some observers (Lewis, 1993a). At this age the infant has become tuned to the caregiver's emotional expressions, and the expressions of both partners function to regulate the interaction between them. As Darwin (1872/1965) observed, "Movements of expression in the face and body . . . serve as the first means of communication between the mother and her infant" (p. 364).

In an ingenious experimental study of the signal value of maternal expression for the 3-month-old, Cohn and Tronick (1983) observed how infants would respond to mothers who showed no expression in face-to-face interaction. In the "depressed" condition, mothers were instructed to direct their gaze at the infant, but remain expressionless by speaking in a flat monotone, with their face neutral, minimizing movement and avoiding contact with their infant. This was contrasted with a three-minute normal condition, in which mothers displayed their natural expressions. Infant responses to this puzzling pattern of stimulation were videotaped and coded using a sophisticated analysis of conditional probabilities of the infant's changes in behavior and emotional state. As shown in Figure 5.10, infants responded to their expressionless mothers by becoming increasingly disorganized and distressed. Expressions of positive affect and play declined when they went unreciprocated, and were replaced by wariness and protest. In contrast, during the normal condition these same

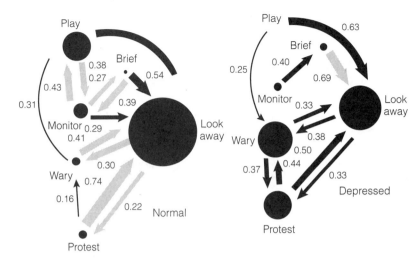

Figure 5.10 Infant state transitions under two conditions. These diagrams represent the responses of infants when their mothers were in the normal condition (left) and when they were simulating depression (right). Proportion of time in each state is represented by circle size, arrow thickness represents conditional probabilities, and gray arrows indicate statistically significant conditional probabilities, $p < .05$.

Source: Cohn and Tronick (1983). Reprinted with permission of the SRCD.

infants cycled merrily through play and positive expressions while maintaining eye contact with their mothers. These data dramatically illustrate the supportive role of affective expression to social interaction in early infancy, a theme to which we shall return in our discussion of later developmental periods and other types of social interaction involving peers.

In a second study using the "still face" paradigm with infants and mothers who were truly depressed, a different pattern of results was obtained (Field, 1984). For these depressed mothers and their infants, the behavior and affective expression remained unchanged across the spontaneous and still face conditions, although nondepressed dyads reacted in much the same manner as in the Cohn and Tronick study. Tiffany Field believes that infants of depressed mothers grow accustomed to their mother's interactional style and thus do not become agitated in the "still face" condition, as do the infants of nondepressed mothers. Depressed mothers in videotaped laboratory interaction with their infants spontaneously spent less time touching, talking, and looking at their infants, and their affective expression was less positive and more negative than that of nondepressed mothers (Cohn, Matias, Tronick,

Connell, & Lyons-Ruth, 1986; Field, 1984). Reciprocally, infants of depressed mothers vocalized less and matched the lower activity level and more negative affective style of their mothers. They also showed more gaze aversion and protest behavior and looked more weary than infants of nondepressed mothers.

In a replication study conducted with older infants (9 months) and their mothers, Termine and Izard (1988) found that simulated maternal expressions of sadness in face-to-face interaction increased sad and angry expressions of the infants and decreased their level of exploration and play. As in the previous studies, these effects of sadness and depressed affect have profound implications, and researchers have concentrated much attention on studying the potential effects of maternal depression on the infant.

Field (1994) recently reviewed the research in this area and concluded that the infant's depressed style of interacting can often generalize to social interactions with nondepressed adults, a result predicted by transactional models of depression such as that of Emde, Harmon, and Good (1986). In this model, depressive or sad feeling states in the infant resonate in the new person with whom they are interacting:

We may respond to children's depressive feelings with depressive feelings of our own and then react in various ways to that. We may feel sad or even helpless but then, recognizing those feelings, respond with understanding, availability, and caring. In contrast, we may restrict our feelings, pull back, and remove ourselves from such painful transactions. Either way, a depressed child will resonate with the other's response, and the interactive process will continue at a new level. (Emde et al., 1986, p. 136)

The infant's response to separation has also received considerable scrutiny by researchers following the publication of John Bowlby's landmark trilogy on attachment, separation, and loss (1969, 1973, 1980). Accumulating data from primate (including human) studies indicate that separation from the mother is associated with changes in the infant's level of activity, heart rate, play, and affect similar to those we have just noted in response to experimentally induced sadness. The widespread use of Ainsworth's "strange situation" involving two 3-minute separations from the caregiver confirms this normative response to brief separation in infants between 9 and 18 months. However, the negative emotions produced as a consequence of separation include much more than sadness, and may be mixed with fear, anxiety, and anger at this age. The mixture and alternation of negative emotions appears to be a common occurrence across a variety of situations involving aversive stimulation or undesirable behavior on the part of others.

Ethologists view these infant responses as functionally significant in terms of their signal value as well as the regulation of internal state. Facial, vocal, and other nonverbal displays of sadness often elicit caregiving from others. The protest and crying of infants to separation typically result in their caregiver's return, followed by soothing and attention, and the communicative function of these displays is self-evident.

Depressed activity and withdrawal may also serve an adaptive function if protest has been unsuccessful in bringing about the caregiver's return. A primate infant in the wild that is separated from its mother and alone is extremely vulnerable. The depressed activity level and withdrawal may allow the infant to recover from agitation that is costly in terms of energy depletion. Another cost of continued crying and screaming may result from drawing unwanted attention from potential threats in the environment that would be increased as a result of continued activity and exploration. It may be that natural selection has equipped the infant with a conditional strategy that first calls for a vigorous attempt to reestablish the care and protection of the parent or another member of the social unit. Should this fail, a second strategy is enacted, calling for depressed levels of activity and withdrawal, that serves to reduce energy depletion and the probability of harm until help is forthcoming.

Although sadness may be elicited in situations that may also elicit anger (separation, failure in achieving a goal, pain), it is clearly distinct in its physiological effects. Functional theorists, such as Tomkins (1963) and Izard (1991), have noted the unique function of sadness in depressing cognitive and motor systems, in direct contrast to the mobilizing and energizing effects of anger. Tomkins (1963) has advanced another possible adaptive function of sadness. In his view, the slowing down of cognitive processes as a result of sadness may lead to a deeper reflection and more careful search for the causes underlying this troubling emotional state that will ultimately promote adaptation.

Averill (1968) has speculated on yet another possible function of sadness, particularly in relation to the response to loss of a loved one. Averill proposes that in the course of human evolution, grief, by strengthening social bonds within a community, increased the group's chances of survival. Shared sadness over the loss of a family member may strengthen and renew supportive relationships within an extended family.

Although plausible, such speculation concerning the functional significance of mourning remains difficult to support empirically.

Finally, sadness is certainly not always adaptive. In a factor analysis of behavior and emotional expression, we found that sadness in young children is closely associated with fatigue and depressed levels of exploration, play, positive affect, and social interaction (LaFreniere, Dumas, Capuano, & Dubeau, 1992). Because exploration and play are the central activities of infants and children that promote competence in both social and cognitive domains, their absence for prolonged periods and the resulting lack of attention and acceptance from peers must be viewed in terms of maladaptation. Thus the study of prolonged sadness and depressed feelings merges with the study of depression as a clinical syndrome.

Disgust The expression of disgust was first described by Darwin (1872/1965) who had the occasion to observe it in different cultures throughout his voyage on the Beagle, as well as in his own children in early infancy. He defined disgust as a sensation arising in reference to "something revolting, primarily in relation to the sense of taste, as actually perceived or vividly imagined; and secondarily to anything which causes a similar feeling, through the sense of smell, touch and even of eyesight" (p. 253). Darwin considered it an evolved response because of its early onset and universal expression, as well as its presumed function in motivating the individual to reject food that may be contaminated. He noted in his diary the following episode:

> I never saw disgust more plainly expressed than on the face of one of my infants at the age of five months, when, for the first time, some cold water, and again a month afterwards, when a piece of ripe cherry was put into his mouth. This was shown by the lips and whole mouth assuming a shape which allowed the contents to run or fall quickly out; the tongue being like-

wise protruded. These movements were accompanied by a little shudder. It was all the more comical, as I doubt whether the child felt real disgust—the eyes and forehead expressing much surprise and consternation. (Darwin, 1872/1965, p. 260)

The latter remark is interesting because of the distinction Darwin draws between the clear expression of the emotion and the emotion itself. This distinction is echoed by some contemporary researchers who consider the expression of disgust in the newborn to be a reflexive response (for example, Sroufe, 1996), while others believe the expression to be innately connected to the emotion feeling (for example, Izard, 1991).

In any case, disgust is considered to be one of the earliest emotions to evolve from a primitive avoidance mechanism. The response may occur with minimal cortical involvement being based in the archaic olfactory brain that served the chemical sense of taste and smell (Schore, 1994). The disgust response may be elicited by putting a tiny amount of bitter substance on the tongue of a newborn, including infants without functional cerebral hemispheres due to disease or birth defects (Izard, 1991). Steiner (1979, cited from Izard, 1991) concludes that these brainstem-mediated disgust expressions are accompanied by feeling states that motivate the expressive behavior that results in the rejection of the bitter substance. This type of data has led Izard to the view that expressions and feelings are innately connected.

Fear The topic of fear has received a great deal of attention from neuroscientists, ethologists, behaviorists, and cognitive-developmental psychologists. A long-standing debate concerns the role of hereditary and environmental factors, whether there exist innate, species-specific fears or whether fear is a learned phenomenon. The "answer" of course is yes, and yes! In this section we shall discuss which stimuli seem to arouse innate fears in humans, what innate behavioral systems seem to be connected to fear, and to what extent an individual's predisposition to be anxious or fearful is inherited or learned. We shall also be concerned with describing the ontogeny of fear as it relates to maturation and cognitive development, since the appraisal process is closely connected to the fear response. Finally, the role of classical and instrumental conditioning and observational learning in the development of fear responses will be emphasized.

In his excellent summary of the early literature on the psychology of fear, Gray (1971) begins the nature/nurture debate with J. B. Watson's classic work *Behaviorism* (1924/1970). Watson proposed that there are three innate stimuli for fear (pain, sudden loss of support, loud noise) and that all other elicitors of fear are produced by classical conditioning. Watson's view that classical conditioning is a key mechanism that accounts for the diversity of fears acquired by an individual over the course of a lifetime is well founded, and many experiments have demonstrated that a wide range of behavioral responses associated with fear can be classically conditioned (Gray, 1971). However, unlike Darwin, who emphasized that the behavior of different species was adapted to particular environments through natural selection, Watson apparently viewed all species as equal. Accordingly, one statement regarding innate fears applied equally to all species, and results from one species applied equally to all. Gray countered this tendency, which pervaded behaviorist thought for half of the twentieth century, with evolutionary logic, insisting that there is no more reason why the same innate behavioral mechanisms should evolve in all species, than morphological or physiological mechanisms. Consequently, an ethologist would hardly be surprised to find that a diverse array of stimuli naturally elicit fear and that these may be quite different in different species.

According to Gray, Watson's theory of fear, while parsimonious, was too simplistic. Instead of limiting the list of unconditioned fear stimuli to three, Gray proposed five general principles to account for all fear stimuli: intensity, novelty, evolutionary dangers, social stimuli, and conditioned stimuli. Pain and loud noise are examples of intense stimuli, though animals respond in a variety of ways to pain, including anger-aggression as well as fear-avoidance. Novel objects and persons may also give rise to fear, though as we shall see later, in humans, temperament, maturation, cognitive development, context, and learning all affect the probability that fear is expressed in response to novel stimulation.

Researchers who observe infant behavior in the first month or two of life are generally in agreement that no specific fear reaction is present at birth. Rather, infants become distressed for a variety of reasons and cry as a response to pain, discomfort, hunger, and other unpleasant experiences. John Bowlby (1969) considered that infant fears are caused by a combination of biology and experience and that infants would more readily respond with fear to events or situations that provided the infant with "natural clues to danger." Bowlby listed only four such clues: pain, being left alone, sudden changes in stimulation, and rapid approach. Gray has expanded the list of the potential stimuli that might have an evolutionary basis to include fear of strangers; separation anxiety and fear of being alone; fear of open places, heights, falling, or loss of support; fear of the dark; and fear of snakes or spiders. We shall discuss those infant fears that have received the most attention from researchers: stranger distress, separation anxiety, fear of heights, and fear of impending collision.

Stranger Anxiety **Stranger anxiety** was originally described by Rene Spitz as an emotion that suddenly appears in all infants at about 8 months. However, we now understand that this emotion is foreshadowed by behaviors that occur at an earlier period of development. At about 4 or 5 months, infants show a distress response to a strange face. At this age, if a stranger stares in silence at an infant, the infant will often return the look and after about 30 seconds begin to cry. Bronson (1972) has termed this distress reaction

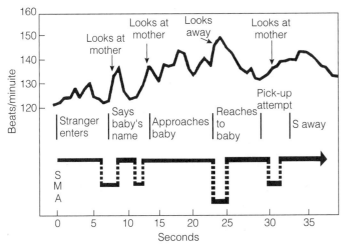

Figure 5.11 Heart rate and visual regard as a stranger approaches. These behavioral and physiological responses were recorded from a 10-month-old male infant rated "wary" at reach and pickup during a standard stranger approach sequence. The letter S denotes looks at stranger; A denotes looks away; M denotes looks to mother.

Source: Sroufe (1996). Reprinted by permission of SRCD.

to a stranger's sober face "wariness," and interprets the emotional distress as a reaction to the failure to assimilate the unfamiliar face to a more familiar schema.

A few months later, infants react negatively and immediately to strangers, especially if approached suddenly or picked up by the stranger. This negative reaction, which can be readily elicited in most infants between 7 and 12 months, has been called stranger distress or stranger anxiety. Unlike the gradual response arising from failure to assimilate, stranger anxiety is an immediate reaction to an appraisal of a situation as threatening. This is supported by the observation that infants show even greater distress over the second instance of intrusion by a stranger, a finding that is compatible with the infant's capacity for appraisal and incompatible with the notion of a failure to assimilate a novel event. If the latter was the instigating cause, the infant should be less frightened by the second approach.

The context and qualitative aspects of the stranger's approach are also critical. If the stranger approaches slowly when the caregiver is accessible, smiling and speaking softly, offering a toy, the infant will often show interest or joy, and distress is unlikely. Finally, the degree of distress shown by an infant to the silent intrusion of the stranger

varies greatly from baby to baby, a finding that many believe is rooted in the genetic temperament of the infant (Kagan, Keasley, & Zelazo, 1978).

While context and cognition play important roles in determining stranger anxiety, there is nevertheless evidence suggesting a universally precise timetable for the emergence of stranger anxiety across different cultures, including Uganda (Ainsworth, 1963), Hopi Indian (Dennis, 1940), and the United States (Sroufe, 1977). A genetic basis has also been shown by twin research, with identical twins showing more similar onset of stranger distress than fraternal twins (Plomin & DeFries, 1985). It would appear that the emergence of this fear response in the second half of the first year is associated with physiological maturation, as well as cognitive development. Both EEG and heart rate patterns in human infants show a major developmental shift at this time in response to the presentation of threatening stimuli (Emde, Gaensbauer, & Harmon, 1976).

Comparative physiological and observational data of a variety of other species support a biological basis for the development of the fear response. Observations of the development of stranger distress in human infants have shown a resemblance to the fear of strangers observed in 4-month-old chimpanzee infants by Hebb in his classic 1946 study "On the Nature of Fear." Hebb argued that this fear emerged at 4 months not as a result of learning, but as a result of perceptual and cognitive maturation. That this fear of strangers is innate is demonstrated by animals reared in the laboratory. That it is dependent on cognitive development is demonstrated by another of Hebb's experiments. Two groups of chimpanzees were reared under two different conditions. One group was provided with normal visual experiences, including seeing other chimps, while the other group was blindfolded. When exposed to a plaster replica of a chimpanzee head, the first group showed extreme fear, while the blindfolded group showed mild curiosity. Hebb reasoned that the group with normal visual experiences had learned a schema for a chimpanzee that included head, torso, arms, and legs. Confronted by a replica of a head alone, familiar but incomplete, the chimps became extremely upset. It appears that the discrepancy between the familiar and the partially familiar causes the fear response.

This violation of expectancies is similarly implicated in the maturation of the human response to strangers. Until the schema of the caregiver is well established, no fear of strangers is evident in human infants. Other primate data also suggest a biological timetable regulating the onset of social fears. For example, Sackett (1966) found fear responses at about 3 months in isolation-reared rhesus monkeys when they were presented with a picture of an adult with a threatening expression, but not when neutral pictures of infant or adult monkeys were shown.

Separation Anxiety Like stranger distress, **separation anxiety** also emerges according to a developmental timetable during the second half year in human infants. We have noted the changes in the infant's emotional life that reflect advancing physiological and cognitive maturation in the first half year. By 8 or 10 months, infants become increasingly active in their relationship with the caregiver as well as increasingly mobile. With this new mobility the infant expands the capacity for eager exploration of the outer world, returning to the caregiver as a "secure base" (Ainsworth, 1967; Sander, 1975). At just this time separation anxiety begins to peak, possibly as a result of the infant's new preoccupation with the presence and location of the caregiver. Not only is the infant concerned with remaining connected as he or she moves about, but this concern can shift to real distress if the caregiver is the one who decides to move away!

As illustrated in Figure 5.12, infants from cultures as diverse as Kalahari bushmen, Israeli kibbutzim, and Guatemalan Indian display similar patterns in their response to maternal separation that peak at the end of the first year and remain elevated for variable lengths of time (Kagan, Kearsley, & Zelazo, 1978). Cultural practices also appear to have an impact on separation anxiety. Infants who remain in constant contact with their mothers may show an earlier onset of separation anxiety (Ainsworth, 1967), and possibly more intense and longer periods of reactivity. For example, Japanese infants who were tested in Ainsworth's "strange situation" showed more intense reactions to the separation, presumably as a result of cultural norms prescribing constant contact between mother and infant for the first several years of life (Miyake, Chen, & Campos, 1985).

Although the onset of stranger anxiety is precisely timed, it is less clear when this behavior disappears. For example, it is not unusual for toddlers and preschoolers to show intense separation anxiety when they are dropped off at day care, especially during the first week or two. Their distress may actually be a mixture of separation anxiety and stranger anxiety. Typically, children will gradually accept the new situation and, though they may show intense distress when the parent leaves, tend to settle eventually and become engaged in the many interesting people and activities that surround them, as illustrated by the photos in Figure 5.13.

Fear of Heights Fear of heights in infants has been studied primarily by using a "visual cliff," which

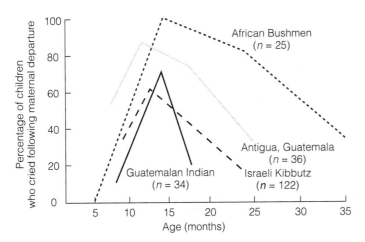

Figure 5.12 Infant separation anxiety in different cultures. These graphs show the percentage of infants in different cultures who cried during a brief separation from their mothers. This distress response appears to peak in human infants at about one year.

Source: Kagan et al. (1980).

consists of a Plexiglas-covered floor with two distinct levels, one shallow and the other several feet deep. The different depths are visually cued by covering the floor with a checkerboard pattern. In a series of experiments, Campos and colleagues (Bertenthal, Campos, & Barrett, 1984; Campos, et al., 1978) outlined a developmental progression from perception of and heightened attention to the deep side at 5 months, to the onset of a fear response at about 9 months. Because of the convergence of the behavioral and physiological data, these studies are particularly convincing regarding the onset of fear. Five-month-olds looked more often at the deep side and showed HR deceleration and no signs of negative affect. Heart rate deceleration has been shown by Lacey (1967) to accompany orienting and attending to new information, and may be assumed to be a sign of interest. In contrast, 9-month-olds showed sharp HR acceleration to the deep side that many refused to cross, and some began to cry. Other data also show that infants as young as 5 months are capable of perceiving depth (Fox, Aslin, Shea, & Dumais, 1980), but this capacity alone is not sufficient for the onset of fear.

According to Campos, several weeks of crawling experience appears to account for the emergence of fear of heights, since this fear emerges at a relatively constant period after crawling begins, rather than a fixed chronological age. Most infants learn to crawl at varying ages between 7 and 11 months, and they show fear of the visual cliff at various ages, but only after they have been crawling for about three weeks (Bertenthal, Campos, & Barrett, 1984). Learning to fear heights is not based on experiences of falling, nor would such trial-and-error learning make sense from an evolutionary perspective. Rather, it appears that this fear, like the fear of strangers and separation from the attachment figure, is programmed into human infants as a consequence of natural selection and requires only normal physiological and cognitive maturation to appear.

Fear of Collision Another fear that appears to have a biological basis is the fear of an impending collision. Research on "looming" stimuli has been meticulously designed to isolate visual information from other stimuli such as noise or wind, both of which can trigger reflexive responses. In a series of experiments using a shadow-casting apparatus, Yonas, Cleaves, and Pettersen (1978) provided infants only visual cues of an impending collision in the form of an exponentially expanding dot that appeared to rush toward them until it covered their entire field of vision. Research on newborns consistently demonstrates the presence of reflexive blinking, but anticipatory defensive reactions, HR accelerations, and other signs of fear do not appear until 8 or 9 months in normal

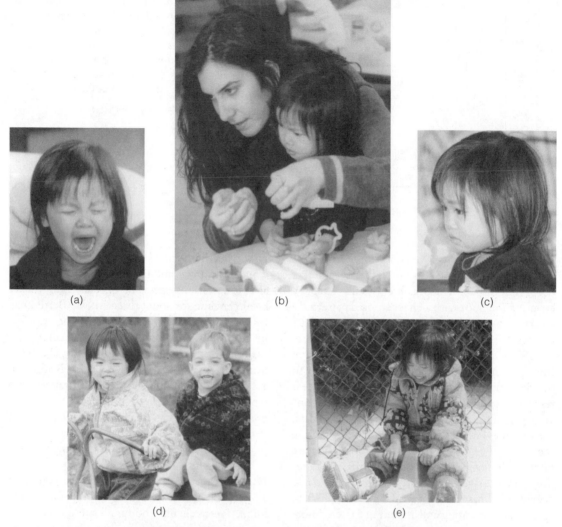

Figure 5.13 Separation protest and its resolution. These photos of a 3-year-old girl were taken on a typical morning at our laboratory preschool early in the semester. Initially, she vigorously protested separation from her mother (a, 8:15) and was comforted by a familiar teacher's aide (b, 8:20). This allowed her to partially recover (c, 8:26), but she needed more time to fully regain her composure. This was shown in her social interactions with the teacher (8:30), then with a friendly peer (8:42). Two hours later she was engaged in a high level of excited activity on the playground and was reluctant to leave for home (d and e).

(Photos by LaFreniere)

infants and in the second year for Down syndrome infants (Cicchetti & Beeghly, 1990; Yonas, 1981). Once again, the instinctive defensive response of the infant requires maturation before it appears in the second half year of life, and no evidence suggests that the timetable for the emergence of this fear is determined by specific learning experiences with colliding objects.

Lessons from the Study of Fear

The study of fear in infancy is instructive regarding a number of basic issues in the study of emotional development. Infancy researchers, like ethologists working with animals, must rely on observable events rather than verbal reports. Researchers who address questions regarding the ontogeny of fear must, by necessity, confront methodological questions pertaining to the expression of fear. What are the specific criteria that allow one to infer that fear, as opposed to general distress, sadness, or anger, is being expressed?

Bowlby and Charlesworth have listed a number of observable fear indicators involving expressive and motor behaviors. Bowlby (1973) offers the following, not as an exhaustive list, but as a start: "wary watching combined with inhibition of action, a frightened facial expression accompanied perhaps by trembling or crying, cowering, hiding, running away, and also seeking contact with someone and perhaps clinging to him or her" (p. 88). Charlesworth (1974) includes "momentary arresting or slowing of ongoing behaviors or prolonged freezing, heightened vigilance or awareness, stimulus-distance maintaining or expanding behavior, serious or fearful facial expressions . . ." (p. 263). He goes on to note that fear may be followed by withdrawal, flight, wary exploration, or even smiling or laughing. As a consequence of attending to observational methods, facial expressions have become the most reliable and unambiguous indicators of fear in infants and children, and advances have been made in understanding physiological and behavioral precursors to fear and the connections between them.

Comparative analyses have also played a prominent role and have led to an increased understanding of the fear system and its functional significance across many species including primates. These data indicate that fear reactions emerge precipitously across species according to comparable developmental timetables (Columbo, 1982), and that the onset of specific fear responses and fearful mood is accompanied by brain maturational changes involving the integration of corticolimbic systems and developments in the parasympathetic system (Schore, 1994). As discussed in Chapter 2, LeDoux (1996) considers the emotion of fear to be the most amenable to investigating the neural basis of emotion.

The study of fear underscores the critical link between affect and cognition. Discrepancy theories originating in the work of Hebb (1946) and Piaget (1952) provide an account of the steps in the epigenesis of this primary affective system in infancy and demonstrate its dependence on perceptual and cognitive development. Later work demonstrates the emergence of the psychological emotion of fear based solely on the cognitive appraisal of threat in the environment. The importance of context and meaning has been clearly shown in the work of Kagan, Sroufe, and others to be the hallmark of the mature fear response, as distinct from the undifferentiated, physiologically based distress of early infancy.

The study of fear allows for an integration with other lines of development in the physical and motor spheres and illustrates the active role of the infant in bringing about the conditions for the experience of separation anxiety and fear of heights, which both become functional very soon after the infant learns to crawl. Such convergent lines of development illustrate the biological unity of development and suggest the functional significance of the timetable itself.

The study of fear requires a balanced treatment of the role of hereditary and environmental factors in promoting the adaptation of the organism. In everyday life, many fears can be acquired without direct negative experience through observational learning. The primate infant, by virtue of its extended period of care and protection, can learn to regulate its behavior by observing others, particularly the caregiver. As we shall see in the next chapter, attachment theorists have studied how the presence of the caregiver provides a secure base for the infant's confident exploration of the environment. If something threatening should occur, the infant's attention will be directed to the caregiver's face. Should the caregiver express fear in relation to an event, a fear response can be classically conditioned to that event after a single trial. Evolution is better served by constructing an organism capable of evaluation and observational learning than by constructing hundreds of specific reflexes for the myriad potentially dangerous events facing a primate.

This illustrates the superiority of an open program over a closed program for promoting flexible adaptation to a wide range of environmental stimulation (Mayr, 1982). According to Mayr, a closed program is based on a genotype that does not allow appreciable modifications during the process of development, whereas an open program allows for additional input and modification based on learning and experience throughout the life span. A closed program can be highly adaptive in short-lived species facing relatively constant life challenges, a mosquito for instance. In contrast, an open program would be much more adaptive in long-lived species facing a high level of diverse and variable life challenges. The altricial status of humans provides an extended period that enables each generation to learn the many variable characteristics of life-relevant stimuli required for successful adaptation. Mayr goes on to point out that the invariant stimuli are typically associated with the morphological and behavioral characteristics of conspecifics.

As Charlesworth (1982) has argued, one important constant in human adaptation is the facial displays and signals of other humans. These may be sufficiently small in number, sufficiently stereotyped, and sufficiently important to allow for evolution to construct recognitory programs that are relatively closed. Thus, while emotion expression and regulation may eventually incorporate a high degree of learned behavior, basic emotions, such as fear, regulate behavior through closed, prewired, genetic programs that control their production and reception. A great deal of evidence now supports the Darwinian viewpoint that such processes are innate. As Campos and Barrett (1984) have stated, "no social learning appears necessary either for the *reception* of facial and gestural signals, or for the *production* of such" (p. 229).

Mineka's studies of observational learning in the development of fear of snakes in rhesus monkeys serve to illustrate the interaction of innate and learned components in the production of adaptive fear responses. In the wild, monkeys show a strong fear of snakes that generalizes to objects that even resemble snakes. Better to err on the side of caution. This fear is so strong and so universal in the wild that early observers, such as Hebb, were inclined to believe that it was innate. Indeed, Hebb (1946) found that a painted wax replica of a coiled snake elicited fear (hair erection and screaming) in 21 out of 30 chimpanzees tested, and was second in potency to all stimuli, surpassed only by a skull of a chimpanzee with a movable jaw controlled by a string. Since the chimpanzees that had been born and bred in Hebb's laboratory were just as likely to show snake fear as the others, Hebb concluded that the fear was innate.

This question was reopened forty years later when Mineka and colleagues compared wild-reared and laboratory-reared monkeys and found that the laboratory-reared monkeys did not show fear of snakes (Mineka, Davidson, Cook, & Keir, 1984). It is interesting to note that the wild-reared monkeys had been captured and imported from India 24 years prior to the study. Yet they all maintained a strong fear of snakes, despite having had no experience with them for nearly a quarter of a century! This too could have led the investigators to conclude that this was an innate fear. Instead, Mineka and colleagues paired a wild-reared monkey with a laboratory-reared monkey in order to demonstrate how quickly and permanently fear of snakes could be conditioned. In the test situation, laboratory-reared monkeys showed no differences in their responses to a live boa constrictor, snakelike objects, and neutral objects that were placed in a Plexiglas box and moved toward them. But when the laboratory-reared monkeys were exposed to the fearful reactions of the wild-reared monkeys, they quickly learned to fear the snake and snakelike objects. From the standpoint of classical conditioning, it may be that the expression of fear was the unconditioned stimulus and the snake was the conditioned stimulus.

In summary, the role of learning is interwoven in subtle and complex ways with genetic predispositions to provide for the safety of the primate infant. Clearly, for an organism to adapt to a complex environment of opportunities and dangers, a dynamic balance must be struck between its intrepid exploration of the novel, and a measured response to threat ranging from cautious wariness to terror and rapid flight. Moreover, these responses cannot be acquired over long periods of time through trial-and-error or gradual shaping. The individual who cannot escape the predator or who falls off a real cliff will be eliminated from the breeding population. One evolutionary solution to this **adaptive problem** is to provide the infant offspring with reflexes that quickly mature into adaptive responses and to hardwire into the neural circuitry of the organism certain innate fears. The fears of being alone, heights, and impending collisions appear to fit this category.

Another functional solution is to equip the young with the capacity to acquire a fear response to a given stimuli on a single trial, and with no direct experience of it. Clearly, one experience with a poisonous snake or spider, or an aggressive conspecific, will also eliminate the individual. Natural selection would strongly favor individuals capable of using the parent as a source of information from which to quickly learn what to approach and what to avoid. This solution provides for rapid acquisition of the fear response, as well as the capacity for flexible modulation or regulation of the emotion, and the behavioral response, according to contextual cues. The use of the parent as a secure base from which to explore the novel or unfamiliar is clearly a hallmark of primate socialization and will be taken up in the next chapter.

SUMMARY

We began our treatment of emotional development with the basic question of how human emotions develop and how they organize development. In this chapter, we reviewed research that pertains to general or normative patterns of growth. First we examined the inherent capacities of the newborn to engage the social world. Research was described that demonstrates newborns' (1) capacities and preferences in visual and auditory perception, (2) capacity for reflexive responses to various stimuli, and (3) ability to learn from their experience and accommodate to their environment. Together this extensive evidence leads contemporary developmental theorists to believe that newborns are preadapted for emotional communication with their caregivers.

Biosocial theorists view the complement of human reflexes as a kind of storehouse of phylogenetic behavioral adaptations that have been retained because they provided some advantage or function for the infant's survival during our evolutionary past. They provide a starting point for the individual's emotional development by giving direction to the process and providing something for development and learning to act upon. Thus, the smile, startle, cry, and expression of disgust that researchers commonly report in newborns represent the physiological prototypes necessary for the emergence of the primary affective systems in infancy.

Infants begin to discriminate between different facial expressions at about 3 months, and by 5 months they are beginning to make discriminations among negative expressions like sad, fearful, and angry expressions. By the second half of the first year, infants are able to perceive emotional expressions as organized wholes. They can distinguish mild and intense expressions of different emotions, and they respond to happy or surprised expressions differently than to sad or fearful faces, even if these emotions are expressed in slightly varying ways by different people.

Infants also begin to rely upon facial expressions as an important indicator of how to respond emotionally to an uncertain situation or event. Social referencing is one of the first clear examples of emotion regulation. Like other examples throughout the first year, it occurs in a dyadic context. As early as 10 months, infants rely on these emotional cues to decide how to respond to a wide variety of events for which they lack experience.

Six basic emotions were extensively reviewed, including joy/happiness, surprise/interest, anger, sadness/distress, disgust, and fear. According to Ekman, nine criteria must be met for an emotion to be considered "basic": (1) universal expression, (2) quick onset, (3) comparable expressions in other animals, (4) an emotion-specific physiology, (5) universal antecedent events, (6) coherence in response systems, (7) brief duration, (8) automatic appraisal mechanism, and (9) unbidden occurrence.

These six emotions are presumed to be species-typical emotions because they are shared by humans everywhere and because they exhibit a number of common characteristics. They are rooted in our primate evolutionary heritage, and they make their appearance early in infancy, arising automatically in the course of interaction with the environment. Moreover, they are characterized by universal facial expressions that are remarkably constant and recognized across different cultures as indicating the presence of a particular emotion. Finally, these expressions are considered to be hardwired into the neural circuitry linking the brain to the facial muscular system, are correlated with distinct autonomic system activity, and may show subcortical conditioning.

Throughout the chapter the related themes of development and adaptation were emphasized in relation to these six basic emotional systems. The development of each basic emotion system as it emerges from earlier physiological prototypes and the process by which it is transformed and reor-ganized during infancy were discussed. Understanding emotional development in infancy requires an appreciation of the unity of development, particularly the reciprocal influence of cognition and affect. Finally, evidence was reviewed in support of the view that basic emotions are related to adaptive biological, motivational, and social processes that have functional significance for the organism.

FURTHER READING

Camras, L. A. (1992). Expressive development and basic emotions. *Cognition and Emotion, 6,* 269–283.

An interesting case study of expressive development is provided as the author documents the emergence of facial expressions of emotions in her infant daughter.

Kopp, C. (1989). Regulation of distress and negative emotions: A developmental view. *Developmental Psychology, 25,* 343–354.

This is an influential statement on how infants and toddlers learn to deal with negative emotions and acquire self-control.

Malatesta, C. Z., Culver, C., Tesman, J. R., & Shepard, B. (1989). The development of emotion expression during the first two years of life. *Monographs of the Society for Research in Child Development, 54*(1–2, Serial No. 219).

This is a detailed study of how emotional expressions develop during infancy.

Sroufe, L. A. (1996). *Emotional development: The organization of emotional life in the early years.* Cambridge: Cambridge University Press.

A comprehensive account of early emotional development, this book integrates a strong research tradition on normative development with more recent research on individual differences in emotion regulation.

6

Individual Differences
in Emotional Development
in Infancy

This girl exhibited a striking degree of amenability, sociality and good nature as early as the age of nine months. . . . She is now five years of age, and in spite of a varied experience in boarding homes and institutions she has not lost these characteristics. . . . It can be predicted with much certainty that she will retain her present emotional equipment when she is an adolescent and an adult. But more than this cannot be predicted in the field of personality. For whether she becomes a delinquent, and she is potentially one, will depend upon her subsequent training, conditioning, and supervision. She is potentially, also, a willing helpful, productive worker. Environment retains a critical role even though heredity sets metes and bounds.

ARNOLD GESELL (1928)

As scientific research on the origins of individual differences was just getting underway, Gesell expressed the dominant philosophical view in Western society that personality characteristics are visible early and endure throughout life, despite the many obvious changes in behavior that occur with maturation, learning, and development. Gesell's expectations regarding this young girl also anticipated contemporary views of developmental psychologists: that different outcomes can be reached from the same starting point and that similar outcomes can be reached via different pathways. Although biology always plays a role in determining these outcomes, it is not destiny.

In this chapter, it is argued that children differ widely in their emotional makeup and that these differences arise as the result of complex transactions with inputs from the child's own genotype interwoven with environmental influences from conception onward. **Cross-sectional** studies can demonstrate *how* children in different developmental periods differ in their expression, regulation, and understanding of emotions. **Longitudinal** studies can tell us *why* children of the same age differ in their emotional makeup. Two major research literatures, temperament and attachment studies, provide a framework for considering the nature and nur-

ture of these individual differences during infancy. First, we review research on infant temperament as a basis for stable and heritable emotional dispositions. Second, the infant's first relationships within the family will be examined as a basis for the emergence of stable individual differences in socioemotional competence. Finally, we examine the relationship between these important constructs and the influence of cultural context for understanding infant emotional development.

TEMPERAMENT: ADVANCES IN THEORY AND RESEARCH

Temperament refers to individual differences in behavior and emotionality, such as activity level, attentiveness, adaptability, and mood, that appear early in life and are assumed to be inborn **traits** of the infant. These traits are generally measured as continuous dimensions that are expected to have a high degree of stability over time and across situations, and a biological basis, both in terms of neurophysiological underpinnings and heritability. Although theorists differ in their definition of temperament, in general they all agree that it represents the biological contribution to personality.

It is often said that parents become believers in temperament upon the birth of their second child. Although the parents may attribute the characteristics of the firstborn to the manner in which the child was socialized, sometimes the same techniques and strategies that worked well with the firstborn are not as effective with the second child. The early appearance of differences between siblings in activity level, soothability, or intensity of expression inevitably gives rise to new interpretations about the source of such differences. Grandparents, friends, and neighbors too may comment about differences between siblings, especially if the firstborn enjoyed robust social interaction with a wide variety of partners, while the secondborn is more reserved in contact with new people. Although it is abundantly clear that great differences exist between infants at an early age, it has not been a simple matter for researchers to agree on the key dimensions of infant temperament, or how they are best measured. In this section, we shall examine different conceptual and methodological approaches to this fascinating problem, as well as the evidence pertaining to the stability, neurophysiology, and heritability of temperament.

Roots of Temperament Research

The earliest roots of the concept of temperament can be found in the ideas of the Greeks and Romans who believed that an individual's personality was formed by different mixtures of four cardinal humors—melancholic, sanguine, phlegmatic, and choleric. The use of the term in English dates back to early nineteenth-century authors like Byron, who wished to convey the idea of inborn dispositions, as in the phrase "he has a nasty/pleasant temperament."

Modern temperament research has important historical foundations in developmental and clinical psychology, as well as behavioral genetics and comparative psychology (Rothbart & Bates, 1998). Early developmental psychologists, like Gesell (cited in Kessen, 1965) and Shirley (1933), provided some informal observations of early individual differences in personality that they believed endured over the life span. Behavioral geneticists and comparative psychologists were also interested in biologically based individual differences and have investigated characteristics like reactivity, fearfulness, and basic approach and withdrawal systems, both within and across species (Schneirla, 1959). Biologically oriented clinicians were interested in how predispositions to respond to seemingly low levels of stimulation with high reactivity affected personality development. In *The Roots of Individuality,* Escalona (1968) developed the idea that children experience events differently because of inborn differences in their nervous systems. One child may squeal with delight while being bounced on Grandpa's knee, while another child heads for mother's skirts when he enters the room, having experienced such "torture" previously. This active construction of the meaning of events by the infant became an important foundation for both temperament and attachment research.

The pioneers of contemporary research on temperament were the psychiatrists Alexander Thomas and Stella Chess, who in 1956 initiated the **New York Longitudinal Study** (NYLS) (Thomas, Chess, Birch, Hertzig, & Korn, 1963). In this research program, 141 children were studied during infancy and followed up with assessments that extended into adulthood. These researchers relied upon parents' descriptions of infant behavior that were elicited by asking the parents specific questions regarding the behavior of the child in specific contexts, such as "What does your child do during bathtime?" Initially, a small sample of 22 parents was extensively interviewed when their infants were between 3 and 6 months of age. Each behavior and the context in which it occurred was recorded on separate sheets of paper, which were then inductively sorted by Birch into nine sets and eventually labeled as the nine NYLS dimensions. Subsequently, Michael Rutter suggested the term *temperament* to Thomas and Chess, which they adopted to describe their study (Rothbart & Bates, 1998). These nine different dimensions were clustered together into three basic types of temperament— easy, difficult, and slow-to-warm-up, as shown in Table 6.1.

A child with an **easy temperament** (40 percent) is generally cheerful, quickly establishes regular routines, and adapts easily to new experiences.

A child with a **difficult temperament** (10 percent) tends to react negatively and intensely, has irregular daily routines, and is slow to accept new experiences.

A child with a **slow-to-warm-up temperament** (15 percent) reacts somewhat negatively, but not intensely, has a low activity level, and adjusts slowly to new experiences.

Figure 6.1 Stella Chess, one of the pioneers of temperament research.

(Photo from AP/Wide World Photos)

Approximately 35 percent of the sample was not classifiable into this scheme and instead displayed a unique mix of the same characteristics.

A number of other models of temperament, typically with fewer than nine dimensions, have been devised since this initial formulation. These simpler, more parsimonious models were responding in various ways to the problem of overlap among the nine dimensions formulated by Birch. For example, Mary Rothbart's model (1981) retains some of the initial dimensions of Thomas and Chess (for example, activity level) while reducing the number of dimensions to six and minimizing the overlap or associations between the dimensions. Rothbart's model also provides greater emphasis on emotional expression by including categories pertaining to inter-

est, happiness, fear, and distress. These distinctions correspond to four basic emotions that emerge in the first few months, as discussed in the previous chapter. Besides differentiating positive and negative emotions, it is critical to differentiate distress into two basic types reflecting fear and anger.

Personality psychologist Arnold Buss and behavior geneticist Robert Plomin have suggested another model of temperament composed of only four different components that are considered to be heritable, stable personality traits. Their first model was labeled EASI (an acronym for emotionality, activity, sociability, and impulsivity), though they later reduced their model to just three factors: activity, emotionality, and sociability (Buss & Plomin, 1984). Activity level appears to be approximately the same in all three models and refers to the general tempo and vigor of movement. Sociability refers to the tendency to prefer others' company to being alone. Emotionality refers to the tendency to become distressed and reflects arousal thresholds in an individual's sympathetic nervous system. Buss and Plomin (1984) view the distinction between "easy" and "difficult" as rooted in the infant's emotionality but do not have a clear differentiation between the negative emotions of fearfulness/inhibition and irritability/anger. See Table 6.2 for a comparison of these three well-known models of temperament.

Despite the proliferation of different temperament measures, most researchers agree that these scales measure about five or six dimensions, including the emotional moods of joy, fear, and anger, and activity, persistence of attention or interest, and rhythmicity or how predictable the baby is (Rothbart & Mauro, 1990).

Some temperament researchers prefer a taxonomic approach and seek to classify infants into a few basic types according to their position along each of these various dimensions. Some critics of temperament research view such parsimony as reductionistic. For example, the global concept of sociability may mask important qualitative distinctions (Eisenberg, 1992). Shy children feel tense around other people and become inhibited

Table 6.1 Chess and Thomas's Dimensions and the Basic Clusters of Temperament

This table identifies those dimensions that were critical in spotting a basic cluster of temperament and the level of responsiveness for each critical feature. A blank space indicates that the dimension was not strongly related to a basic cluster of temperament.

TEMPERAMENT DIMENSION	DESCRIPTION	TEMPERAMENT CLUSTER		
		Easy Child	Difficult Child	Slow-to-Warm-Up Child
Rhythmicity	Regularity of eating, sleeping, toileting	Regular	Irregular	
Activity level	Degree of energy movement		High	Low
Approach-withdrawal	Ease of approaching new people and situations	Positive	Negative	Negative
Adaptability	Ease of tolerating change in routine plans	Positive	Negative	Negative
Sensory threshold	Amount of stimulation required for responding			
Predominant quality of mood	Degree of positive or negative affect	Positive	Negative	
Intensity of mood expression	Degree of affect when pleased, displeased, happy, sad	Low to moderate	High	Low
Distractibility/attention span/persistence	Ease of being distracted			

Table 6.2 Three Models of Temperament

Thomas and Chess	Rothbart	Buss and Plomin
1. Activity	1. Activity	1. Activity
2. Rhythmicity	2. Smiling and laughter	2. Emotionality
3. Approach-withdrawal	3. Fear	3. Sociability
4. Adaptability	4. Soothability	
5. Intensity	5. Distress to limitation	
6. Threshold	6. Undisturbed persistence	
7. Mood		
8. Distractibility		
9. Persistence of attention		

and awkward in their presence, while other children labeled as **introverted** simply prefer to spend more time alone, but not as a result of fear or tension. An individual may be highly sociable and affiliative but without being **extroverted,** defined as the tendency to seek social interaction as a source of stimulation rather than any true interest in others.

There is no one solution to the problem of conceptualizing temperament, and researchers typically sort themselves into two basic types: "lumpers," or those who prefer broad, global, and inclusive categories, and "splitters," who prefer to make as many distinctions as possible. From the standpoint of research, it is often important to tailor such taxonomic issues to the broader purposes of one's study. In the earliest wave of longitudinal research on temperament, three basic categories (easy, difficult, and slow-to-warm-up) appeared to provide the most pragmatic basis for asking the question of how the child's temperament influenced social and personality development. In the next section, we shall lay the groundwork for addressing the fundamental question of genetic influences on emotional development by examining the methods used to assess temperament.

Assessment Issues

The earliest studies of infant temperament relied upon parental ratings, and temperament is still often assessed through interviews or questionnaires given to parents. Although such methods are convenient for researchers and parents should be the most knowledgeable informants regarding their infant, these methods have been criticized for several reasons. First, these studies were capable of demonstrating only minimal correspondence between parental ratings and observational data (Siefer, Sameroff, Barrett, & Krafchuk, 1994). Second, maternal ratings of temperament were more strongly related to maternal personality than observations of infant behavior (Bates, 1987; Vaughn, Bradley, Joffe, Seifer, & Barglow, 1987). For example, mothers who rated themselves high in anxiety and depression also rated their babies as more difficult (Mebert, 1991). In one study, mothers rated their infant's temperament prior to birth, even before the unborn infant was moving in the uterus (Zeanah, Keener, Thomas, & Viera-Baher, 1987). These maternal "expectations" were correlated with maternal ratings of the infant months after birth, suggesting that expectations of the parent play some role in shaping parental ratings of actual behavior.

Leading temperament researchers have recently summarized four potential explanations for the well-established connection between parental personality ratings and infant temperament (Goldsmith, Losoya, Bradshaw, & Campos, 1994). First, parental personality may bias ratings of infant temperament, thus inflating the associa-

tions between the two variables. Second, these similarities may be due to direct genetic transmission of personality traits from parent to infant. Third, parental personality partly determines the relationship context for the infant's personality development. Finally, the infant's temperament may influence parental personality. From a transactional perspective, it is likely that all of these potential sources of influence are operating during the child's development. Transactional models will be dealt more extensively at the end of this chapter and again in Chapter 8.

Recently, some temperament researchers have proposed that parental reports should be abandoned because of persistent problems of bias and inaccuracy associated with them (Kagan, 1994). Other temperament researchers strongly disagree, arguing that parents have a privileged vantage point from which to observe their child in a wide variety of situations, especially relatively infrequent behaviors that are nevertheless critical to some dimensions of temperament. These researchers have attempted to reduce potential sources of bias in parental ratings by formulating more objective items and by combining parental ratings with those of other observers and laboratory tests (Matheny, 1989; Rothbart, 1989).

Recently, Goldsmith and Rothbart (1991) have developed an assessment tool that employs systematic observations under standardized laboratory situations. These situations are designed to elicit characteristic responses from the infant to a variety of novel stimuli and situations. We shall discuss a similar strategy employed by Kagan and colleagues for assessing behavioral inhibition in young children in Chapter 8.

Another potential solution to the problem of assessing temperament lies in the development of psychophysiological measures, which are not hampered by the subjectivity and bias of parental ratings. This makes theoretical sense because of the genetic basis of temperament. According to Zuckerman (1995), the child does not inherit personality per se, but rather "chemical templates that produce and regulate proteins involved in building the structure of nervous systems and the neurotransmitters, enzymes, and hormones that regulate them. . . . How do these differences in biological traits shape our choices in life from the manifold possibilities provided by environments?" (pp. 331–332). Because genes exert their influence on the development of physical structures, neurological and physiological measures may provide markers for differences in temperament that may be observed at the behavioral level. Recent research suggests that this is a promising new direction, though it is too early to draw definite conclusions. Candidates for physiological markers of temperament include vagal tone and cortisol indices, which were introduced in Chapter 3.

Consistency and Stability

A fundamental problem for current temperament researchers is the search for coherent links in individual behavior across different situations and over significant periods of time. Because of the early reliance on parental reports, with their attendant problems of bias and "halo" effects, initial studies of stability are probably inflated, reflecting stable attributions in the parent at least as much as stability in infant behavior. As a result, little evidence is currently available demonstrating stability in temperament in the first year of life, although a few studies do report modest levels of stability (Korner, Hutchinson, Koperski, Kraemer, & Schneider, 1981; Worobey & Lewis, 1989). The situation improves after the first year with modest year-to-year correlations of approximately .20 reported by testers on the Infant Behavior Record from age 1 to age 4 (Plomin, McClearn, Pedersen, Nesselroade, & Bergeman, 1988).

More impressive findings have been reported by a number of investigators on the frequency of positive and negative emotions, which appear to become moderately stable by one year (Emde et al., 1992; Rothbart, 1989). In a longitudinal study of 130 twin subjects at 12, 18, 24, and 30 months, Matheny (1989) reported moderate to high correlations using three different assessments of emotionality/fearfulness. As with most longitudinal studies, correlations were higher between adjacent periods. In addition, parental ratings showed the most stability, while laboratory observations were more stable than testers' ratings.

The measure of vagal tone developed by Porges (1986) provides a feasible answer to the search for a physiological marker of temperament in infancy because it is noninvasive, shows moderate stability, and is related to more traditional indices of infant temperament. High vagal tone in early infancy has been found to be associated with irritability, distress, soothability, and higher cortisol levels during and after a heelstick procedure (Gunnar, Porter, Wolf, Rigatuso, & Larson, 1995; Huffman, Bryan, del Carmen, Pedersen, & Porges, 1992; Porges et al., 1994). Longitudinal research has shown that higher newborn vagal tone predicted maternal ratings of infant behavior at 5 months, specifically low frustration tolerance and behavioral inhibition. However, the newborn measure of vagal tone did not predict vagal tone at 5 months, a problem that has plagued parental ratings as well (Stifter & Fox, 1990). However, Porges and Doussard-Roosevelt (in press) have recently demonstrated stability of vagal tone in infants after 9 months.

The consistent lack of demonstrable stability in the first year of life raises serious concerns for understanding the congenital effects of temperament on later emotional and personality development. Traditionally, temperament has been defined explicitly in terms of the assumptions of stability and heritability (Buss & Plomin, 1975). Recently, some researchers have no longer insisted on stability as a defining criteria of temperament, noting that despite the lack of stability over time, genetically related individuals show strong similarities in their change (Rothbart & Bates, 1998). The results of research in behavioral genetics appear to play a crucial role in maintaining the viability of the scientific construct of temperament.

Heritability

Evidence for genetic effects on temperament, its **heritability,** derives from two principal sources, **twin studies** and adoption studies. In general,

Figure 6.2 Identical twins share 100 percent of their genes.

(Photo by LaFreniere)

Table 6.3 Percentage of Genetic Relatedness in Different Relations

Relationship	Percent Relatedness
Identical twins	100
Fraternal twins Full brothers or sisters Parent/child	50
Half brothers or sisters Grandparent/grandchild Aunt or uncle/niece or nephew	25
First cousins	12.5
Second cousins	6.25

adoption studies that have attempted to demonstrate links between the temperament of parents and their biological and adopted children have demonstrated only minimal heritability. Twin studies are generally viewed as more conclusive. According to scientists like Bouchard (1997) and Segal (1998), twin studies provide an important window on the direct influence of genes on whole organisms and will continue to complement studies in molecular genetics.

How does the study of twins inform us about genetic influences? The logic begins by recalling that **monozygotic** or **identical twins** have the same genotype. They share 100 percent of their genes, unlike **dizygotic** or **fraternal twins** who share only half their genotype. (See Table 6.3 for the percentage of genes shared in different types of kin relations.) One of the most informative research designs would contain a sample of monozygotic twins reared together (MZT), unrelated individuals reared together (URT), and monozygotic twins reared apart (MTA) (see Figure 6.3). Of course, the latter group is hard to find in sufficient numbers, and as a result, relevant data can be obtained by just a few research centers specializing in twin studies. Much more

research is available comparing identical and fraternal twins.

Figure 6.3 illustrates the correlation between MZAs (represented by the circles) for a given trait (represented by the boxes). Any similarity between such identical twins is assumed to be genetic in origin and can be quantified as the sum of the multiplication of the terms of each path that connect the trait. This value represents the broad heritability of the trait (Bouchard, 1997).

Similar logic applies to unrelated individuals reared together (URT), though it is the inverse of the MZA design. These correlations represent the influence of shared environmental factors. Finally, in the MZT design, the correlation confounds genetic and environmental influences. This means that the difference between the MZT and MZA correlations provides another estimate for the shared environmental influence.

In the Minnesota Study of Twins Reared Apart (MISTRA), a large sample of identical and fraternal twins was recruited as each twin pair came to light in the English-speaking world (Bouchard, Lykken, McGue, Segal, & Tellegen, 1990). The MISTRA researchers have demonstrated that the similarities observed between these twins on a wide array of measures including personality cannot be explained by factors like age of separation, amount of contact, and measurable characteristics of the families. As shown in Table 6.4, the mean broad **heritability coefficient** for personality was found to be .41.

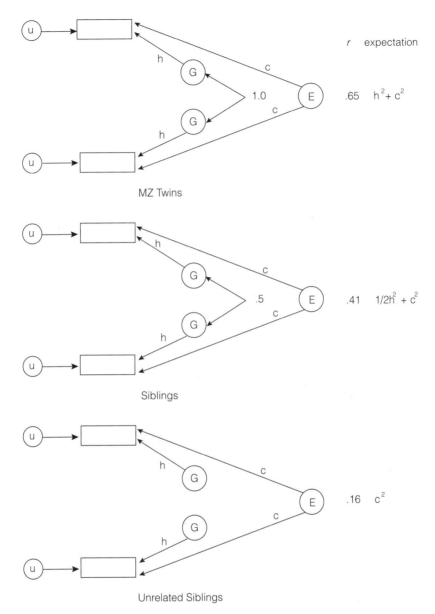

r expectation

.65 $h^2 + c^2$

MZ Twins

.41 $1/2h^2 + c^2$

Siblings

.16 c^2

Unrelated Siblings

Figure 6.3 The phenotypic resemblance of identical twins, and related and adopted siblings.

Source: D.C. Rowe (1994). Reprinted by permission of Guilford Press.

Most behavior genetic studies rely on model-fitting research designs that use equations outlining the expected correlations of different kinship groups in order that relatives of different types can be combined in a single analysis. The discrepancies between the expected and observed correlations provide a basis for testing the model's "goodness of fit." The inclusion of many different types of kinship groups allows for more rigorous model fitting to the many

Table 6.4 Intraclass Correlations for MZA, DZA, MZT, and DZT Twins and Model-Fitting Results for Multidimensional Personality Questionnaire Big Five Markers

Trait	TWIN TYPE				PROPORTION OF VARIANCE			
	MZA (59)	DZA (47)	MZT (522)	DZT (408)	Additive Genetic	Nonadditive Genetic	Common Environment	Broad Heritability
Extroversion	.41	−.03	.54	.19	.09	.29	.15	.38
Neuroticism	.49	.44	.48	.19	.41	.09	.00	.50
Conscientiousness	.54	.07	.54	.29	.29	.13	.13	.42
Agreeableness	.24	.09	.39	.11	.05	.25	.09	.30
Openness	.57	.27	.43	.14	.29	.15	.00	.44
Mean	.45	.17	.48	.18	.23	.18	.07	.41

Source: Data compiled from Bouchard (1996).

different correlations that are observed. This type of analysis yields estimates of heritability and shared environmental effects. In practice, all such heritability estimates of temperament may vary depending upon (1) assessment technique (parental ratings versus observation), (2) which dimension of temperament is being assessed, (3) what developmental period is being examined, and (4) the assumptions of the model used to generate the estimates.

Table 6.5 displays comparisons of correlations based upon parental ratings of Rothbart's six dimensions of temperament for identical and fraternal twins based on data from studies by Goldsmith and colleagues. The first column of the table shows the **concordance** between parental reports for monozygotic (MZ) and dizygotic (DZ) twins. The degree of the genetic influence is reflected by the difference in the two concordance estimates between MZ and DZ twins. Across the six scales of the Infant Behavior Questionnaire, concordances are substantially higher for activity level and the two negative affect scales, but more equivocal for positive scales. This suggests that negative emotionality may have a greater genetic basis than positive mood.

The MacArthur Longitudinal Twin Study (Emde et al., 1992) also supports this conclusion. Results from this study, which assessed 200 iden-

tical and fraternal twin pairs at 14 months, are presented in Table 6.6.

The data indicate much greater variability in the estimates of genetic heritability of infant temperament and emotion than do comparable data on older subjects. Similar to previous findings, this research indicates that the tendency to express negative emotions is highly heritable, but only for parental reports, and only when uncorrected estimates are used. In contrast, positive emotionality did not show significant heritability for either parental report or observational measures. This is because both MZ and DZ twins were rated as highly similar, especially by parents. Remember that the key to showing genetic heritability lies in the *differences* in concordances between MZ and DZ twins. Notice, for example, that the high heritability estimate for empathy (.89) derives primarily from the lack of any concordance between DZ twins (−.03), rather than exceptionally high concordances between MZ twin pairs (.42). Because a negative correlation between DZ twins violates the model's assumptions, the second, more conservative estimate of .36 is probably more accurate than the uncorrected estimate (.89). Another important finding, is the modest, but significant, genetic loadings for behavioral inhibition and shyness, further establishing the viability of these measures as temperament constructs.

Table 6.5 Twin Similarity for Rothbart's Infant Behavior Questionnaire (IBQ)

IBQ Scales	Identical R	Fraternal R
Activity level	.69	.35
Fear	.67	.43
Distress to limitations	.71	.29
Smiling and laughter	.72	.66
Soothability	.69	.71
Duration of orienting	.76	.57

NOTE: Rs are means from Goldsmith (1978, 1986), Goldsmith and Campos (1986), and Goldsmith, Jaco, and Elliott (1986).

Table 6.6 Twin Correlations and Heritability Estimates for Infant Temperament and Emotion

Measure	MZ	DZ	h²	h²
Temperament				
Observational				
Inhibition	.57**	.26**	.62**	.56**
Shyness	.70**	.45**	.49*	
Parental report				
CCTI-Emotional	.35**	−.02**	.72**	.28**
CCTI-Shyness	.38**	−.03	.82**	.28**
Emotion				
Observational				
Positive	.53**	.37**	.33	
Negative	.11	.06	.10	
Overall mood	.19**	.02	.34	.16
Empathy PC	.42**	−.03	.89**	.36**
Frustration PC	.26**	.19	.15	
Parental report				
Positive	.84**	.82**	.05	
Negative	.71**	.39*	.68**	

*p < .05
**p < .01

Source: Plomin et al. (1993).

Measurement error in assessments of infant temperament necessitates that conclusions be drawn from many different studies using different samples and different methods, rather than the results of any single study. Taken together, twin studies tend to support three broad patterns in the database. First, there is moderate heritability shown when parental reports are used (Buss & Plomin, 1984), but only minimal evidence for heritability when using observational measures of temperament (Emde et al., 1992; Goldsmith & Campos, 1986; Matheny, 1989). Second, heritability estimates are consistently higher for indices of negative emotionality (defined variously as behavioral inhibition, shyness, fear, or distress) than positive mood (Emde et al., 1992; Goldsmith, 1993). Third, heritability estimates in one developmental period do not necessarily generalize to other ages. For example, Reise (1990) found no evidence for heritability for any temperamental dimensions in neonates, including such behaviors as irritability, soothability, and activity level, though these traits show at least some genetic influence at the end of the first year. It is instructive to compare the concordances for infant temperament and personality with similar measures for intelligence. As seen in Table 6.7, concordances are considerably higher for intelligence than for personality, which are in turn higher than those for infant temperament.

Recent analyses reveal a clear increase in heritability estimates in IQ with age (Finkel, Pedersen, McGue, & McClearn, 1995; McGue, Bouchard, Iacono, & Lykken, 1993). It is reasonable to speculate that the similar gap between infant temperament and childhood and adult personality is produced, at least in part, by increased measurement error in early infancy. Further research using more refined indices of infant temperament is needed to clarify this question. Twin studies will no doubt continue to play a prominent role.

In summary, infant temperament has not been easy to research, and assessment issues figure prominently in various controversies regarding the stability of infant temperament and the role of constitutional factors in socioemotional development. Some temperament researchers believe that emotional development may not be comprehensible without considering the infant's characteristics within a broader relational context (Bates, 1980).

Table 6.7 Kinship Correlations for Temperament, Personality, and Intelligence

Kinship Pair	Temperament in Infancy	Personality in Childhood and Adulthood	Intelligence
Identical twins reared together	.36	.52	.86
Fraternal twins reared together	.18	.25	.60
Biological siblings reared together	.18	.20	.47
Nonbiological siblings (adopted-natural pairings)	−.03	.05	.34

NOTE: Correlations are averages across a variety of temperament and personality characteristics.

Sources: Braungart et al. (1992) and Emde et al. (1992) for temperament at 1 year of age; Nichols (1978) and Plomin, Chipuer, & Loehlin (1990) for personality in childhood and adulthood; and Bouchard & McGue (1981) for intelligence.

Temperamental traits do not override contextual influences in organizing the infant's behavior (Goldsmith, 1993), and more and more researchers are turning to transactional models in their attempts to determine the origin of individual differences in emotional expression and regulation.

Temperament and Emotion

The tendency to express certain emotions and the capacity for self-regulation have emerged as important qualities of temperament in recent years (Bridges & Grolnick, 1995; Goldsmith & Alansky, 1987; Rothbart & Bates, 1998), though the concepts of emotion and temperament were linked in the early writings of personality theorists such as Gordon Allport. Allport (1937) viewed temperament as synonymous with an individual's characteristic emotional expression. He provided an early definition of temperament as

> the characteristic phenomena of an individual's emotional nature, including his susceptibility to emotional stimulation, his customary strength and speed of response, the quality of his prevailing mood, these phenomena being regarded as dependent upon constitutional make-up and, therefore largely hereditary. (Allport, 1961, as cited in Rothbart & Bates, 1998, p. 34)

Contemporary personality theorists like Malesta subscribe to a similar view of tempera-

mental traits as "emotional biases" (Malatesta, 1990). Goldsmith (1989) and Mehrabian (1991) also define temperament primarily in terms of individual differences in the likelihood of experiencing and expressing basic emotions. In this approach, emotionality may be manifested in brief states, in somewhat longer moods, or as stable traits that characterize an individual's emotional expression over significant periods of the life span. The key properties of such a trait perspective are cross-situational consistency and temporal stability. It is clear that infants differ in important ways regarding their characteristic expression of emotions or emotionality, and twin studies demonstrate that some aspects of the infant's emotionality are inherited. But heritability explains only a portion of the infant's emotional behavior, leaving an important role for the environment. In the next section, we examine a model that stresses the importance of infants' early social relationships for their emotional development in infancy and beyond.

FOUNDATIONS OF ATTACHMENT THEORY AND RESEARCH

We begin this section with a review of three key theoretical and methodological contributions that led directly to an explosion of research on attachment in the mid-1970s that still shows no sign of abating. In the concluding section we review some of this recent research, emphasizing the longitudinal study of the origins and course of attachment during infancy.

Rene Spitz

Trained in Vienna under Freud, Rene Spitz was the first psychoanalytic investigator who actually observed infants. Like Darwin, and later Piaget, Freud was convinced that the only means for obtaining reliable information about early development was through direct observation of infants. Fortunately Spitz took him quite literally on this point and began a series of studies investigating emotional development in infancy during a period when psychologists all but dismissed both the topic of emotion and the method of naturalistic observation.

Spitz ignored this dismal climate and began recording 16-mm films of affective communication in 1935 as a means of conveying his ideas to students. He used a technique he called "screen analysis" to slow down the speed from 24 to 8 frames per second to illustrate the points he wanted to make regarding expression. The methodological innovations of Spitz were prototypic of today's increasingly complex video technology for decoding the often subtle and brief affective expressions that characterize face-to-face interaction. Spitz's film archives remain available today at the University of Colorado, School of Medicine, as vivid documentation of the emotional traumata and profound deterioration suffered by infants separated from their mothers and reared within the impersonal gray walls of institutions created for their welfare. One of his methods was to walk through the hospital holding all the babies to get a direct perception of their emotional responsiveness. His subsequent description of the "affect hunger" of these infants and their general "failure to thrive" was instrumental in alerting professionals and the public to the joint impact of an impoverished social and physical environment, and the absence of any consistent caregiver.

Although Spitz is best remembered for his work on institutional effects on infants, he also formulated one of the most sophisticated theories of infant emotional development of his era. Based on detailed observations, Spitz (1965) formulated an epigenetic theory involving three major developmental reorganizations. His concept of "developmental organizers" refers to critical turning points that are marked by specific changes in the infant's emotional responses and reflective of fundamental transformations in the psychological life of the infant. Spitz theorized that the converging lines of development and the precise timetable for the developmental reorganizations parallel maturational changes in the CNS (Spitz, Emde, & Metcalf, 1970).

The first reorganization is signaled by the advance of social smiling in which the infant demonstrates a new awareness of the surround and a basic differentiation between self and other. For Spitz, this new awareness at about 3 months marks the onset of true emotional responsiveness as distinguished from the reflexive smiling of the newborn. At this stage the infant can find pleasure in familiar contact as well as disappointment when the contact is broken. At the physiological level, basic changes in REM occur and it becomes restricted to sleep states, which become more differentiated at this time. A variety of other psychophysiological changes occur at this time including changes in the EEG and the disappearance of some reflexes.

In the second half of the first year, the second reorganization is signaled by the onset of stranger anxiety in which the stranger's unfamiliar face cannot be assimilated to the familiar schema of the caregiver. In large part this negative emotional reaction to strangers stems from the cognitive advances involved in the development of object permanence and the capacity for recognition and recall, as well as motivational advances reflected in the beginnings of intentional movement and manipulation of objects. At the physiological level, maturational changes in the limbic system regulating emotional reactivity are prominent. The hippocampus rapidly increases to its adult size, and a dense network of interconnections between the limbic system and the frontal cortical system are established (Schore, 1994).

Influenced by Spitz's ideas, Bowlby (1951), Robertson (1952), and Schaffer and Callender (1959) studied the emotional reactions of infants to brief hospitalization. Consistent with Spitz's theory of a developmental reorganization in the second half of the first year, they found that the experience of hospitalization was much more disruptive for older infants than infants younger than 7 months. The younger infants seemed to have little difficulty in accepting the changes and the unfamiliar hospital staff, and their return home was equally smooth. Older infants showed a dramatically different pattern of adjustment to the same event. These infants were wary and negative toward the hospital staff, remained fretful and perturbed throughout much of their stay, and had problems readjusting when they returned home. In particular these infants displayed a high degree of insecurity in their relation to their mothers. The films and descriptive work of Spitz, Robertson, Schaffer, and other early investigators were pivotal in shaping a new theory of socioemotional development that would become one of the most influential theories in the latter half of twentieth century psychology. This new theoretical synthesis would be realized by the British analyst John Bowlby.

John Bowlby

Historically attachment theory was developed by John Bowlby as a variant of object relations theory, itself a variant of Freud's theory that the infant's tie to the mother is the cornerstone of the adult personality. Although it is true that Bowlby's theory is sometimes referred to as an ethological theory of attachment, Bowlby was not an ethologist, but rather a psychoanalytically trained clinician who integrated a number of theoretical approaches and research paradigms, including systems the-

ory, evolutionary theory, and object relations theory, in formulating modern attachment theory. Hereafter, we shall refer to this theoretical integration simply as attachment theory.

Prior to the general acceptance of Bowlby's attachment theory, psychologists conceptualized attachment as a drive or reinforced-based trait, similar to dependency. Assessment was merely a matter of indexing certain behaviors. Thus, a child was thought to be too attached if crying and clingy behavior were high in frequency. Similarly, as crying and clinging diminished over time, children became less attached to their parents. Ultimately, such thinking led psychologists to conclude that attachment was untenable as an individual difference construct because *frequency counts* of attachment were neither stable over time nor consistent across different situations (Masters & Wellman, 1974).

Theoretically, in both early psychoanalytic and behaviorist approaches, attachment was viewed as a secondary drive, derived from primary drives like hunger. The infant eventually became attached to the mother because she supplied food, and thus became the object of the infant's attachment through association with feeding and the reduction of other primary needs. In contrast, Bowlby considered the attachment process to be a primary, innate behavioral system that evolved in primates through natural selection.

Abundant evidence now supports this view, and traditional learning theory models of attachment as drive reduction were refuted in a classic series of studies by Harry Harlow and colleagues during the 1950s and 1960s (Harlow & Harlow, 1966; Harlow & Zimmerman, 1959). Using an ingenious paradigm involving surrogate "mothers," Harlow was the first to put the notion that attachment to the mother forms as a result of feeding to an empirical test. In one study, Harlow separated infant rhesus monkeys from their mothers at birth, then reared them with two surrogate mothers, one made of stiff wire equipped with a bottle for feeding, the other covered with soft terry cloth, but without the bottle (see Figure 6.4). If an infant monkey became attached by associating the mother with food, we would expect to see attachment behaviors exhibited toward the wire surrogate with the bottle. Instead the infant monkeys all showed a clear preference for the soft, cuddly surrogate without the bottle, spending most of their time (when not feeding) clinging to it and leaping into its "lap" when frightened or distressed. Although feeding may be an important context for the development of the mother–child bond in nature, contact comfort is clearly more central than feeding per se.

Drawing upon dynamic systems theory (von Bertalanfly, 1968) and classic ethology (Lorenz, 1935; Tinbergen, 1951), Bowlby reformulated the concept of attachment as a dyadic, behavioral system distinct from earlier models. He framed his model using the technical language of **cybernetics,** the scientific study of methods of control and communication common to organisms and certain machines, like computers. Because emotion constructs were outcast in the scientific community of his era, Bowlby initiated a discussion of emotional attachments modeled after a control system that operates in terms of set goals, feedback loops, goal correction, and function. Accordingly, the attachment system would be activated automatically when the infant's dynamic threshold for threat in the environment was surpassed and would remain operative until proximity with the caregiver was reestablished. The set goal of the attachment system was thus defined as proximity to the caregiver. As an evolved system, attachment was viewed as a product of natural selection, selected for its effect on the individual's survival and reproductive success in the environment in which our species evolved. Thus the function that Bowlby initially ascribed to the attachment system was infant survival. As we shall see, both the set goal and function were to be reevaluated and redefined in more emotional terms as attachment theory gathered scientific momentum.

As a developmental system, the infant's repertoire of attachment behaviors is seen as gradually unfolding in the context of interaction

Figure 6.4 The wire and cloth surrogate mothers used in Harlow's experiments.

(Photo from Harlow Primate Lab, University of Wisconsin)

with the caregiver according to a relatively fixed timetable. As discussed previously, the primate infant is preadapted to engage the caregiver with innate behaviors such as looking, smiling, crying, and clinging. In time, other behaviors such as "following" and "signaling" emerge with the same set goal of maintaining proximity to the caregiver. In this view, it is no longer necessary to invoke secondary drive concepts to explain these developments. Neither is it necessary for the adult to teach or model such behaviors for them to appear in the infant's repertoire. Rather, the interactive presence of the caregiver provides a sufficient context for the species-typical attachment behaviors to emerge and to become organized into a dynamic system. As we shall see later, learning may provide an essential context for this organization by shaping individual differences in the specific qualities of this dyadic, behavioral system.

In Bowlby's (1988) own words, the principal propositions of his general theory are the following:

> (a) that emotionally significant bonds between individuals have basic survival functions and therefore a primary status;
>
> (b) that they can be understood by postulating cybernetic systems, situated within the central nervous system of each partner, which have the effect of maintaining proximity or ready accessibility of each partner to the other;
>
> (c) that in order for the systems to operate efficiently each partner builds in his mind working models of self and of other, of the patterns of interaction that have developed between them;
>
> (d) that present knowledge requires that a theory of developmental pathways should replace theories that invoke specific phases of development in which it is postulated a person may become fixated and/or to which he may regress. (p. 162)

The development of the attachment relationship must be distinguished from the emergence of attachment behaviors. According to an organizational perspective of attachment (Sroufe & Waters, 1977a), various behaviors may serve the function of attachment, but no particular behavior is exclusively an attachment behavior. Smiling, crying, or proximity-seeking are common infant behaviors and may be employed in a variety of contexts, serving a variety of functions in each different context. They may be expressed in relation to strangers or even objects in the infant's presence. This is why frequency counts of these behaviors can never index attachment. Rather, attachment refers to the organization of these behaviors with respect to the specific caregiver and the overall context. The history of the infant's relationship to the caregiver, as well as the emerging cognitive and emotional capacities of the infant, provides the context for the development of this vital bond.

Bowlby characterized this development in four stages:

1. *Preattachment: Phase of indiscriminate sociability* (birth to 6 weeks). The key observation in this phase is the lack of differential responsiveness to the primary caregiver. The infant responds positively to a variety of cues regardless of the person providing them. Though there is some evidence that infants may recognize their mother's smell and voice, they do not yet demonstrate a clear preference for her over others.

2. *Attachment in the making: Phase of discriminating sociability* (2–7 months). In this phase (similar to Spitz's first reorganization), infants can readily distinguish the mother from other adults and typically respond to her differently than a stranger. They may smile and vocalize more readily in her presence and quickly settle in her arms when distressed. During this phase the infant begins to learn the natural contingencies of this special relationship and develop expectations about how the caregiver will respond to various signals. Without any notion of object permanence, the infant does not protest separation during this phase.

3. *Clear-cut attachment: Proximity-seeking phase* (7–24 months). With the onset of stranger anxiety (recognized by Spitz as the second developmental organizer), the infant has entered the phase of true attachment. The hallmark of this phase is the infant's general tendency to explore from the secure base provided by the mother or primary caregiver and to return to her for contact and comfort if threatened or distressed. Separation is actively protested if the infant is on unfamiliar ground.

4. *Goal-corrected partnership: Phase of reciprocal relationship* (after 2 years). As the infant moves into toddlerhood around 18 months, the separation protests and proximity-seeking that once characterized the infant's behavior in relation to the attachment figure are on the wane. Toddlers enter a new phase in their

(a)　　　　　　　　　　　(b)

(c)

Figure 6.5 Attachment in the making. In the first year, infant emotion is especially labile, and can rapidly fluctuate from joy to extreme distress and back to joy again. The caregiver's pattern of response to the infant's signals of distress is a key to understanding the quality of the attachment relationship at this stage. In these photos, baby Sarah swings happily one moment (a), but suddenly erupts into real distress the next (b). This signal elicits prompt attention from the mother, who effectively soothes the infant (c). The entire sequence lasted just two minutes.

(Photos by LaFreniere)

relationship with the caregiver referred to by Bowlby as a **goal-corrected partnership** because each partner is able to represent the goals of the other. This phase is characterized by negotiation, give-and-take, and the emergence of a new kind of reciprocity. Parents often intuitively recognize that this new desire for autonomy of their 2-year-old also reflects a continued dependence on them for many years to come.

As with most stage theories of development, infants are thought to proceed through the different stages in an invariant sequence, though the timing may be slightly different between infants. In his initial cybernetic model, Bowlby stressed proximity-seeking as the set goal of attachment, discarding drive reduction and with it more viable motivational and affective components. Later theorists argued that "felt security" is a more appropriate set goal of the system because it reinstates the central role of affect in mediating

adaptive behavior (Sroufe & Waters, 1977a), which Bowlby clearly alluded to by describing attachment as an affective bond within his larger theoretical framework. With later development, the older infant can make use of multiple strategies to maintain a sense of security and will require proximity less and less, even as the attachment relationship to the caregiver deepens. By explicitly incorporating an emotional-motivational component into the behavioral system, it becomes a more viable model for describing the dynamic stability of this important relationship beyond the period of infancy.

Bowlby was interviewed by a reporter after the completion of his trilogy in 1980. He characterized his contribution with typical modesty in the following way:

Look back thirty years, and there were four theoretical paradigms that were totally distinct from each other—psychoanalysis, learning theory, cognitive psychology,

Figure 6.6 Pioneers of attachment research John Bowlby and Mary Ainsworth.

(Photo by Erik Hesse)

and ethology—[t]here was no conversation between any of these four fields, and they each had a different set of assumptions. . . . One of the things I've been concerned about is to try to develop some sort of theoretical framework that does justice to the contributions that each has made, so that there could be interchange and communication, and data drawn from different fields. I think that's a useful thing to have attempted. (Dinnage, 1980, cited from Karen, 1994, p.60)

In the next section we shall review the growing body of empirical studies of attachment that Bowlby's theory inspired, particularly the origin and developmental course of secure and insecure mother–infant attachment relations.

Mary Ainsworth

The first and most important test for Bowlby's theory of attachment was conducted by Mary Ainsworth in a series of naturalistic and laboratory studies. Ainsworth's early thinking was influenced by "security theory," formulated by her thesis advisor, William Blatz, who proposed that a secure dependency on parents in childhood lays the foundation for a mature dependency in rela-

tion to peers and, later, one's mate. After her doctoral training at the University of Toronto, Ainsworth became involved in attachment research at London's Tavistock Clinic under the direction of John Bowlby. During this time she was not much swayed by Bowlby's ethological explanations, having already become convinced that attachment and dependency are best explained by principles of drive theory.

Her first independent research opportunity arose a short time later while living in Uganda. She intended to study weaning practices in Gandan mothers because she had heard that they weaned their children by sending them off to stay with their grandparents. When she found out that such separations were no longer practiced, she turned her attention to the attachment behaviors described by Bowlby. Much to her surprise, the experience of observing 28 Gandan mothers and their infants in their everyday environment convinced her entirely of the essential validity of Bowlby's ethological model. She observed that the typical Gandan infant formed a specific attachment to the mother, used her to explore the surrounding environment, and protested separation by crying or attempting to follow her. The different stages of their attachment appeared to unfold according to the sequence outlined in

Bowlby's model, though Ainsworth remained alert to observations that did not seem to fit his theory. Indeed, her attention to individual differences in the attachment relations she observed in Uganda formed the basis of her extremely important contribution to attachment research.

Ainsworth's first scheme for classifying attachment patterns is presented in *Infancy in Uganda* (1967) and describes a threefold taxonomy including secure, insecure, and unattached types based on the apparent strength and security of the attachment relation. Later Ainsworth became convinced that all infants become attached but that some show little felt security and others attempt to conceal their need for their mothers. The empirical process exerted its own inevitable press on theory development. Taking Bowlby's cue that differences in attachment security reflect differences in quality of caregiving, Ainsworth conducted extensive exploratory analyses on the factors associated with security of attachment, but came away from this initial study convinced that more formal research would be needed to draw firm conclusions regarding this important question.

In 1962 Ainsworth returned to this task in her now classic Baltimore longitudinal study of mother–infant attachment. Again she relied upon extensive naturalistic observation of relatively few subjects. Regular 4-hour home visits were made to observe 26 families beginning a few weeks after delivery, and continued at 3-week intervals until about 54 weeks. Consistent with the traditions of ethological field work, Ainsworth believed that only extensive naturalistic observation could provide a broad enough, and fine enough, net to capture the details of the attachment process as it was played out in each unique setting. From this inductive approach involving about 72 hours of observation in each home, together with the cross-cultural observations in Uganda, Ainsworth was able to document an ethogram of the typical attachment behaviors shown by the Gandan and American infants (see Table 6.8).

With this descriptive base, Ainsworth was then in a position to develop a laboratory procedure to assess attachment patterns. The impetus for developing such a procedure was provided in part by her failure to observe the secure base phenomenon in the American babies, as she did with the Gandan babies. Ainsworth reasoned that the American infants were comfortable with the familiar routines of the mother coming and going inside the home and that she would need to place the infant and mother in a less familiar environment in order to elicit the secure base behavior.

The breakthrough came during a half-hour flash of inspiration during which Ainsworth worked out the essential details of what has become known as the **strange situation** (Karen, 1994). The goal of the procedure was to provide a novel environment that would arouse the infant's motivation to explore while at the same time arouse a certain degree of security seeking. Separation in such an unfamiliar setting would also be likely to activate the attachment system and allow for a direct test of its functioning. The validation of the procedure and its scoring method was grounded in the naturalistic observation of exploration, crying, and proximity-seeking in the home.

The strange situation paradigm consists of eight episodes that can be construed as involving mild, but cumulative, stress for the 1-year-old American infant. Table 6.9 presents the eight episodes and the attachment behaviors that can typically be observed. Figure 6.7 presents the observed frequency of infant crying in episodes 2 through 7 of the strange situation, attesting to its cumulative stress on the infant. The peaks of crying occur during the separation in episodes 4 and 6. Episode 7, in which the stranger, not the mother, returns to comfort the infant, is the second most stressful episode according to this behavioral index.

No single behavior can be used to assess the quality of the infant's attachment to the caregiver. By itself, crying in response to separation merely

Table 6.8 Ainsworth's (1967) List of Attachment Behaviors

1. Differential crying (i.e., with mother as compared with others)
2. Differential smiling
3. Differential vocalization
4. Crying when the mother leaves
5. Following the mother
6. Visual motor orientation toward the mother
7. Greeting through smiling, crowing, and general excitement
8. Lifting arms in greeting the mother
9. Clapping hands in greeting the mother
10. Scrambling over the mother
11. Burying the face in the mother's lap
12. Approach to the mother through locomotion
13. Embracing, hugging, kissing the mother (not seen in Gandan infants but observed frequently in infants in Western societies)
14. Exploration away from the mother as a secure base
15. Flight to the mother as a haven of safety
16. Clinging to the mother

Source: Oatley and Jenkins (1996).

Table 6.9 Episodes in the Strange Situation

1.	Experimenter introduces parent and baby to playroom and then leaves.	
2.	Parent is seated while baby plays with toys.	Parent as a secure base
3.	Stranger enters, is seated, and talks to parent.	Reaction to unfamiliar adult
4.	Parent leaves room. Stranger responds to baby and offers comfort if upset.	Separation anxiety
5.	Parent returns, greets baby, and if necessary offers comfort. Stranger leaves room.	Reaction to reunion
6.	Parent leaves room.	Separation anxiety
7.	Stranger enters room and offers comfort.	Ability to be soothed by stranger
8.	Parent returns, greets baby, if necessary offers comfort, and tries to reinterest baby in toys.	Reaction to reunion

NOTE: Episode 1 lasts about 30 seconds; the remaining episodes each last about 3 minutes. Separation episodes are cut short if the baby becomes very upset. Reunion episodes are extended if the baby needs more time to calm down and return to play.

Source: Ainsworth et al. (1978).

shows that the attachment system has been activated, as would the other behaviors listed in Table 6.6. Infants could differ in the amount and intensity of crying as a function of many factors including age, temperament, and transitory contextual factors like illness. In her second book, *Patterns of* *Attachment: A Psychological Study of the Strange Situation* (Ainsworth, Blehar, Waters, & Wall, 1978), Ainsworth and colleagues describe the behavior-in-context criteria for scoring attachment in the strange situation. The key to assessing the quality of attachment lies in detecting the organization or

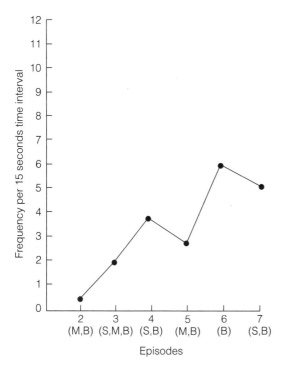

Figure 6.7 Ainsworth's strange situation is one of increasing stress for the infant. The frequency of crying in different episodes of the strange situation.

Key: M = mother peresent, B = baby present, S = stranger present.

Source: Ainsworth, Blehar, Waters, and Wall (1978). Reprinted by permission of SRCD.

pattern of the infant's responses to the changing context, particularly the infant's response to the caregiver upon reunion in episodes 5 and 8. See Table 6.10 for an abstraction of the criteria adapted from this source.

Without question Ainsworth's strange situation paradigm provided the key for moving attachment theory out of the armchair of theoretical speculation and into the crucible of empirical debate. It is supremely ironic that Ainsworth has been criticized for relying on an artificial laboratory procedure to assess the quality of the infant's attachment to the mother. No one before Ainsworth, and no one since, has ever invested anything like the 72 hours of home

observation per infant–mother pair, to say nothing of the earlier years invested in observing attachment patterns in the everyday life of Gandan mothers and children. Looking back at the phenomenal interest the scientific community has accorded her laboratory procedure, Ainsworth commented, "The fact that the Strange Situation was not in the home environment, that it was in the lab, really helped. . . . I only did it as an adjunct to my naturalistic research, but it was the thing that everyone could accept somehow. It was so *demonstrable*" (Karen, 1994, p. 163).

CONTEMPORARY RESEARCH ON ATTACHMENT

Basic Patterns of Attachment

Using the strange situation procedure, three basic patterns of attachment were described by Ainsworth, and a fourth type has recently been added by one of her most influential students, Mary Main (Main & Solomon, 1990). Using Ainsworth's original taxonomy, researchers in the United States and elsewhere have observed a securely attached pattern in approximately 65 percent of all infants. Two distinct types of anxious patterns were originally described by Ainsworth, resistant attachment (about 15 to 20 percent) and avoidant attachment (about 10 to 15 percent), though these percentages vary in different cultures. Finally, a fourth type, disorganized attachment, has been observed by some investigators, though it is observed in less than 10 percent of all infants.

Secure Attachment These infants show an optimal balance between exploration and play and the desire to remain near their caregiver in the unfamiliar laboratory context. They typically separate readily from the caregiver but remain friendly toward her, and to the stranger as well. They may be upset during the

Table 6.10 Four Patterns of Attachment

Anxious-Avoidant Attachment
- A.   Independent exploration
  - 1.   Readily separates to explore during preseparation
  - 2.   Little affective sharing
  - 3.   Affiliative to stranger, when caregiver absent (little preference)
- B.   Active avoidance upon reunion
  - 1.   Turning away, looking away, moving away, ignoring
  - 2.   May mix avoidance with proximity
  - 3.   Avoidance more extreme on second reunion
  - 4.   No avoidance of stranger

Secure Attachment
- A.   Caregiver is a secure base for exploration
  - 1.   Readily separates to explore toys
  - 2.   Affective sharing of play
  - 3.   Affiliative to stranger to caregiver's presence
  - 4.   Readily comforted when distressed (promoting a return to play)
- B.   Active in seeking contract or interaction upon reunion
  - 1.   If distressed
    - (a) Immediately seeks and maintains contact
    - (b) Contact is effective in terminating distress
  - 2.   If not distressed
    - (a) Active greeting behavior (happy to see caregiver)
    - (b) Strong initiation of interaction

Anxious-Resistant Attachment
- A.   Poverty of exploration
  - 1.   Difficulty separating to explore, may need contact even prior to separation
  - 2.   Wary of novel situations and people
- B.   Difficulty settling upon reunion
  - 1.   May mix contact seeking with contact resistance (hitting, kicking, squirming, rejecting toys)
  - 2.   May simply continue to cry and fuss
  - 3.   May show striking passivity

Disorganized-Disoriented Attachment
- A.   Child shows signs of disorganization
  - 1.   Cries for parent at door, then moves away when it opens
  - 2.   Approaches parent with head averted
- B.   Child shows signs of disorientation
  - 1.   Displays odd, frozen postures
  - 2.   Maintains dazed facial expression
  - 3.   Stares vacantly at caregiver

Sources: Adapted from Ainsworth, Blehar, Waters, and Wall (1978); Main and Cassidy (1988).

separation episodes, but their contact with the caregiver upon reunion provides effective relief from this distress. Upon settling, they once again become engaged in play. Infants who show little distress during separation show that they are pleased by greeting their mothers upon their return and engaging them in social interaction by smiling and sharing discoveries with them.

Resistant Attachment This pattern is characterized by emotional ambivalence and physical resistance to the mother. These infants are typically reluctant to separate from the mother and are quick to show anxiety and distress in the unfamiliar setting. Their general wary attitude extends to the stranger and they become highly distressed by the separation, which is not surprising given their need for contact prior to it. The key behavioral criterion is the difficulty these infants have settling in the reunion episodes with the mother. The classification is also referred to as anxious-ambivalent because of the anger expressed by these infants toward their mother at the same moment that they are expressing their need for contact and comforting. They often mix contact seeking with active resistance, squirming, fussing, and even striking out at their mothers when they are upset.

Avoidant attachment As the label suggests, the key behavioral criterion in this pattern is the active avoidance of the mother when the infant is upset. These infants readily separate from their mothers to explore and may be more friendly toward the stranger than their own mother. Unlike securely attached infants, they show little preference for the caregiver and little affective sharing when playing. Their emotional distance from the caregiver becomes more evident following separation. Some infants may begin to seek proximity upon reunion, then suddenly break off the intended movement and turn away. The avoidance of the mother is typically more pronounced following the second separation. These approach–avoidance conflicts sometimes result in displaced behaviors, behaviors that appear out of sequence and have no apparent function. Ethologists interpret such behavior as resulting from the activation of two conflicting motivational systems.

Disorganized Attachment The fourth category reflects a variety of confused and contradictory behaviors on the part of the infant. For example, during reunion with the parent, the infant might look away while being held by the mother or approach her with a blank or even depressed look. Many of these babies convey a dazed or disoriented facial expression. Others may exhibit confusing patterns, such as crying unexpectedly after having settled or displaying odd, frozen postures.

Determinants of Attachment Security

Bowlby theorized that the interactive history between the infant and the caregiver is the major determinant of the quality of attachment observed at one year. In his view, the infant will come to form an expectation concerning the availability and responsiveness of the caregiver based on the repeated cycles of distress signals and responses throughout the first year of life. Bowlby referred to these cognitive representations of the self and other that infants construct from their interactions with their caregiver as an **internal working model.** The infant's internal working model of the relationship is thought to be revealed in the infant's behavior toward the caregiver in the strange situation.

Ainsworth was the first to provide empirical support for Bowlby's ideas. Ainsworth's method uses systematic changes of salient aspects of the immediate mother–child context to study transactional patterns in a situation of increasing stress for the infant. From this perspective, active avoidance of the caregiver, or a mixture of approach and resistant behaviors by the infant while under stress, interferes with the contact and comfort typically afforded by attachment figures. Apparently dysfunctional behaviors like actively resisting the caregiver's efforts to comfort or lashing out in anger at the caregiver are interpreted as a response formulated by the child that reflects a history of inconsistent, chaotic care. Similarly, the infant's active avoidance of the caregiver while stressed reflects an internal working model of the caregiver as someone who is often emotionally unavailable. It is the observation that infants are particularly avoidant when they are in distress that led attachment researchers to view this behavior pattern as a defensive response by the infant to a difficult situation, rather than a precocious sign of independence. In this sense, the history and quality of the relationship itself may be discerned from a careful analysis of infant behavior in relation to changes in context, particularly the separation and reunion episodes with the caregiver.

Ainsworth rated maternal sensitivity toward the infant at several points over the first year and found that when caregivers had been rated high on sensitivity, their attachment relationship with their infants was more likely to be classified as secure. In contrast, caregivers who were rejecting of their infants' desire for contact and comfort were more likely to have anxious attachments with their infants (Ainsworth et al., 1978; Blehar, Lieberman, & Ainsworth, 1977). Ainsworth's basic findings relating quality of care to quality of attachment have been widely replicated (Bates, Maslin, & Frankel, 1985; Belsky & Isabella, 1988; Egeland & Farber, 1984; Isabella & Belsky, 1991; and so on). In each study, Ainsworth's sensitivity scale was related to attachment assessments at one year. The link between caregiver rejection and avoidant attachment has also been replicated in several studies (Grossman, Grossman, Spranger, Suess, & Unzer, 1985; Isabella, 1993).

Various studies have generally shown that emotional availability and other aspects of emotional communication are related to security of attachment (Tronick, 1989, 1990). For example, infants whose mothers are depressed are often found to be insecurely attached (Egeland & Sroufe, 1981) and may be depressed themselves (Lyons-Ruth, Connell, Grunebaum, & Botein, 1990), though not all infants of depressed parents will develop insecure attachments. It is the quality of caregiving, not the depression per se, that is predictive of attachment.

As would be expected, when caregiving is extremely insensitive, as in the case of child abuse

and neglect, major disruptions to the infant–caregiver attachment are observed. Among maltreated infants, the rates of all three patterns of insecure attachment are high, and as many as 90 percent of maltreated infants form insecure attachments (Crittenden, 1988; Lyons-Ruth et al., 1991), especially the disorganized pattern (Carlson, Cicchetti, Barnett, & Braunwald, 1989).

Temperament and Attachment

Factors such as infant temperament and other infant characteristics may also be related to attachment behaviors. Attachment researchers generally agree that the infant's temperamental traits are visible during the strange situation. For example, babies with difficult temperaments are predictably more upset by the separation from the caregiver. A number of studies demonstrate this. Using both parental reports as well as measures of cortisol reactivity to stress, researchers have found that temperament predicts the amount of crying during separation, but not reunion episodes (Gunnar, Mangelsdorf, Larson, & Herstgaard, 1989; Vaughn, Lefever, Seifer, & Barglow, 1989). In his analysis of the alternating sequences of separations and reunions in the strange situation, Thompson (1990) noted that temperament seems to determine what infants require from their caregivers upon reunion. Similarly, an infant who has been recently ill or atypically stressed may require more contact on reunion before settling. However, being upset by separation from the caregiver is not the same as being insecurely attached. In fact, most attachment researchers like Bowlby, Ainsworth, Sroufe, and their numerous students who are now also leading researchers in the field (Bretherton, Cassidy, Crittendon, Lieberman, Main, Vaughn, Waters, and so on) have consistently argued that attachment status and temperament are largely independent. (For example, see Cassidy, 1994, or Sroufe, 1996.) According to Sroufe (1996), there are two main reasons for this:

First, they represent different levels of analysis. Assessments of attachment are at the level of the organization of behavior. Thus, it is not how much an infant cries and squirms, but in what context and sequenced with what other behavior and in what manner that are critical. (Infants who cry a great deal during separation, even early in reunions, and who squirm mightily with the stranger are still judged to be securely attached if they are comforted by caregiver contact and return to play.) Second, . . . securely attached infants (and anxiously attached infants) show great differences of behavioral style, from slow to arouse and noncuddly (B1) to slow to warm up and easily aroused (B4). (p. 188)

According to this conceptualization, measures of infant temperament, while clearly related to some behaviors observed in the strange situation, are not expected to be related to attachment quality, unless difficult temperament is combined with unresponsive caregiving. Longitudinal studies that provide repeated measurements of infant temperament, maternal caregiving, and infant attachment status are most relevant to this important debate. The empirical literature extensively documents that the quality of maternal caregiving, not the infant's inborn temperamental dispositions, consistently predicts the quality of infant–mother attachment (Ainsworth et al., 1978; Bates et al., 1985; Belsky, Rovine, & Taylor, 1984; Blehar, Lieberman, & Ainsworth, 1977; Egeland & Farber, 1984; Vaughn et al., 1989). In summary, research has demonstrated consistent links between parental reports of infants' proneness to distress and observed distress in the strange situation, but not between temperament ratings and attachment security.

If parental ratings of temperament are not directly related to attachment security, infant characteristics nevertheless exert an important indirect influence whenever they affect the quality of caregiving the infant receives (Calkins & Fox, 1992). For example, newborns with neurological problems were not more likely to be classified as insecurely attached, except when this factor was combined with low levels of social and emotional support for caregivers (Crockenberg, 1981). Similarly, infant proneness to distress was not predictive of anxious attachment, except in combination with high levels of maternal controllingness (Mangelsdorf, Gunnar, Kestenbaum, Lang, & Andreas, 1991). Because of the complex nature of the relationship between neonatal irritability, caregiving responsiveness, and eventual attachment status in mid-infancy, researchers are likely to persist in their efforts to clarify the transactional nature of this important milestone in emotional development. The recent work of van den Boom provides a glimpse into the immediate future of research in this area.

In their longitudinal study, van den Boom (1991, 1994) and colleagues have taken a closer look at the early emotional development of infants who are at risk for developing insecure attachment (highly irritable infants born to low SES mothers). Dutch infants who were assessed as highly irritable at 10 and 15 days using Brazelton's Neonatal Behavioral Assessment Scale (NBAS) were more likely to be classified as insecurely attached (especially avoidant) to their mothers at one year than nonirritable infants drawn from the same low SES sample. These irritable infants were also judged by their mothers as more difficult at 6 and 12 months using traditional parental ratings of temperament. These same mothers were found to be minimally responsive to the relatively few positive expressions of their infants. Mothers of future avoidant infants tended to ignore infant crying for relatively long periods and were more distant in their soothing attempts. Mothers of future resistant babies were inconsistent in their responses, showing a mixture of effective soothing and ineffective attempts at distraction that often increased the infant's distress. These findings can be viewed in terms of child effects on maternal behavior (prolonged infant irritability suppresses maternal sensitivity) and maternal caregiving effects on type of attachment classification.

However, as van den Boom (1994) cautions, few data exist examining neonatal irritability over time, and these data do not appear to show consistent results. Consistent with van den Boom's results, some earlier studies show that mothers do tend to withdraw from difficult infants (Peters-Martin & Wachs, 1984), while other researchers report the opposite (Bates, Olson, Pettit, & Bayles, 1982). It may be that the presumed lower levels of support and higher levels of life stress that characterize mothers living in isolation or poverty provide the key for understanding these complex dynamics. Summarizing the data on temperament effects on attachment, Rothbart and Bates (1998) conclude that research has not yet demonstrated that inherited temperament can have a direct effect on attachment security without the mediation of caregiving.

To the extent that attachment security is not rooted in the infant's biology, but rather shaped by the caregiving environment, researchers should be able to demonstrate that (1) attachment security can change during infancy, (2) these changes are meaningfully related to corresponding changes in the caregiving environment, and (3) interventions that are successful in improving caregiver sensitivity and responsiveness also increase infant–caregiver attachment security. Several studies reveal how malleable early infant–mother attachment is under changing life circumstances. Researchers observed that when mothers experienced changes in their level of stress that influenced the quality of their caregiving, the quality of their attachment to their infant also changed. Such changes reflect coherence in the attachment relationship which may improve if life circumstances for the caregiver improve, or worsen under conditions of increasing stress for the caregiver (Thompson & Lamb, 1984; Vaughn, Egeland, Waters, & Sroufe, 1979). These empirical findings, together with the earlier research by Ainsworth and others showing links between early caregiving and later attachment security, provide an important foundation for the development of early interventions aimed at promoting sensitive caregiving and a secure attachment relationship.

In summary, infant characteristics such as temperament may interact with caregiving abilities and other environmental factors to increase or decrease the risk of insecure attachment. This is quite different than asserting that infant temperament is the basis of attachment or that caregiving and temperament play an equal role in determining attachment. Further insight regarding this issue may be gained by comparing the attachment status of infants in relation to both their mothers and fathers. If the infant's temperament determines attachment status, researchers should find the same basic pattern of attachment regardless of which parent is present during the strange situation. In contrast, if temperament does not determine the quality of attachment, then infants could show differences in their attachment to their mother and father, if the parents differ in their sensitivity of care.

Attachment to Fathers

A number of studies have established that infants sometimes show a different pattern of attachment with their mothers and fathers (Cox, Owen, Henderson, & Margand, 1992; Fox, Kimmerly, & Shafer, 1991). In one study that examined this question, Main and Weston (1981) found that about half the infants they studied formed a different pattern of attachment with each parent. In order to determine the father's contribution to the infant's social development, they compared the social responsiveness of infants who were securely attached to one parent only with that of infants who were securely attached to both or insecurely attached to both. Not surprisingly, infants who were securely attached to both parents were the most socially responsive. Importantly, infants who were securely attached to one parent only (whether father or mother) were more social than infants without a secure attachment relationship.

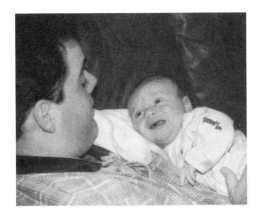

Figure 6.8 Attachment to fathers. The same caregiving qualities that promote secure mother–infant bonds apply equally to fathers.

(Photos by LaFreniere)

Historically, the vast majority of research on parent–infant relationships has involved mothers, so much so that in 1975 Michael Lamb described fathers as "the forgotten contributors to child development." Although this situation is gradually changing, it remains true that most research on attachment has focused on the infant's tie to the mother, probably because fathers spend less time interacting with their babies than mothers do (Parke, 1981). Nevertheless, the same caregiving qualities that promote secure mother–infant bonds apply equally well to fathers. If the father engages in sensitive caregiving and becomes the object of his baby's affection, he too will begin to serve as a secure base for his infant (Hwang, 1986).

In American families, fathers tend to become increasingly involved with their infants over the first year of life. However, they may not be doing the same things with their infant as mothers do. Typically, mothers devote more time to physical care—holding, soothing, and feeding their baby—whereas fathers are more likely to engage their baby in playful physical stimulation (Lamb, 1986; MacDonald & Parke, 1984). Considering these different styles, it is not surprising that most infants prefer their mothers when distressed and look to their fathers for play.

Early Intervention
Based on Attachment Theory

In the preface to his last book, Bowlby (1988) wrote: "It is a little unexpected that, whereas attachment theory was formulated by a clinician for use in the diagnosis and treatment of emotionally disturbed patients and families, its usage hitherto has been mainly to promote research in developmental psychology" (p. ix). Now, after his death, attachment researchers have introduced experimental designs involving therapeutic interventions to learn whether, and to what extent, early patterns of attachment can be modified (Erickson, Korfmacher, & Egeland, 1992; Jacobson & Frye, 1991; Lieberman, Weston, & Pawl, 1991). These studies provide experimental evidence in support of external factors influencing quality of attachment consistent with earlier nonexperimental designs. For example, based on Crockenberg's (1981) correlational study linking maternal social support to quality of attachment, Jacobson and Frye (1991) reported experimental evidence that increased social support during the first postpartum year can positively influence attachment at 14 months. Lieberman et al. (1991), using a similar design, provided evidence that a one-year program involving infant–parent therapy based on attachment theory can enhance maternal empathy and sensibility to the child's developmental needs and affective experience.

Van den Boom (1994) recently conducted an intervention on a sample of 50 high-risk mother–infant dyads selected on the basis of infant irritability. In a series of just three 2-hour home visits, mothers were taught to be more sensitive and responsive to their infants' cues. The intervention emphasized reading infant signals, prompt and effective soothing, and positive interaction when the infant was not distressed. Results indicated positive effects for the mother, the infant, and their relationship. Outcome assessments revealed greater maternal responsiveness and stimulation; increased sociability, self-soothing, and exploration by the infant; and a better chance for the pair to establish a secure attachment relationship. In summary, a recent analysis of 12 attachment-based interventions by van Ijzendoorn, Juffer, and Duyvesteyn (1995) demonstrated that behaviorally oriented, short-term interventions are consistently effective in increasing parental sensitivity and, to a lesser extent, in improving children's attachment security.

Attachment and Culture

Attachment theorists propose that infant attachment behavior and complementary caregiving behavior have a species-characteristic genetic basis (Bowlby, 1969). As a result, one expects evidence for a certain degree of universality in attachment processes across diverse human societies. However, because any particular attachment relationship is always embedded in a larger family or cultural system, one also expects variation in attachment relations to arise owing to differences in caregiving both within and across different cultures. The earliest empirical work from this theoretical perspective (Ainsworth, 1977) provides a two-point cultural comparison between Baltimore and Uganda samples and reveals much similarity between these groups in the development of infant attachment behavior, in the distinction between secure and anxious patterns of attachment, and in relations between maternal attitudes and behavior and attachment patterns. However, cross-cultural differences were also found for several important aspects of infant behavior relating to separation anxiety, fear of strangers, and the use of the mother as a secure base from which to explore (Ainsworth, 1977).

This early evidence of cross-cultural variation necessarily qualifies the use of Ainsworth's strange situation as a diagnostic tool for assessing differences in infant–mother attachment across cultures. The strange situation is widely regarded as the most valid means of standardizing attachment assessment, despite both criticism (Lamb, Thompson, Gardner, Charnov, & Estes, 1984) and the construction of alternative methods, such as the Q-sort instrument (Waters & Deane, 1985).

From the standpoint of an ethological/control systems model, the attachment–exploration balance and the secure base phenomenon remain the central defining features of an attachment relation. According to Waters and Deane (1985), the validity of any attachment measure depends upon:

1. referencing attachment, exploratory, and secure base behavior;

2. recognizing contextual influences on behavior;

3. assessing relationships among affect, cognition, and behavior;

4. assessing nonquantitative developmental change; and

5. assessing stability despite underlying behavioral change.

In addition, the general process of construct validation cannot take place in a theoretical vacuum, but requires a nomological network that specifies the relation between the construct and observable events as well as between the construct and other theoretical constructs. This network must be sufficiently clear and empirically falsifiable in order to validate any particular measure of a construct (Cronbach & Meehl, 1955). Because of the primacy of the strange situation in the ongoing process of validating the attachment construct, other techniques must initially be validated against it, in terms of both directly relating the two measures, as well as examining similarities and differences in the range of their external correlates. The process of construct validation leads to considerable complexity in cross-cultural research where specific denotative and connotative meanings attached to objects, events, and behaviors may vary from one group to the next (Irvine & Carroll, 1980). Since this problem is endemic to all cross-cultural comparisons, it is instructive to turn to that discipline for further methodological discussion.

Berry (1980) has suggested that cross-cultural construct validation requires evidence for three distinct types of **equivalence:** (1) functional, (2) conceptual, and (3) metric. The first two are considered to be necessary preconditions for comparison, while the latter can be established only after data have been collected and analyzed. *Functional equivalence* exists when behavioral units or behavioral systems serve the same function across comparison groups. As seen in Chapter 2, ethologists make the further distinction between functional unity owing to a common phylogenetic origin (homology) and similarities arising from convergent, but independent, evolution (analogy). The ethological view of attachment assumes the former with respect to the attachment system. Questions arise, however, concerning the immediate function or set goal of the attachment system. Bowlby initially proposed that proximity is the set goal, though most developmentalists now regard "felt security" as a more valid, more comprehensive characterization of the purposive orientation of infants in reference to their caregivers, especially during the second year when visual contact with the caregiver can substitute for proximity or physical contact (Sroufe & Waters, 1977a). In either case it is important to note that measurement must be

congruent with attachment theory. Thus, any valid measurement must be achieved by assessing success or failure with reference to the set goal, rather than mere indices of behavioral output.

A second precondition for making cross-cultural comparisons is *conceptual equivalence,* which refers to the similarity in the meaning of research materials, procedures, and situations across comparison groups. This is a classic distinction for anthropological fieldworkers, who since Durkheim and Malinowksi have insisted that "social facts are functions of the social system of which they are a part; therefore they cannot be understood when they are detached" (Durkheim, 1912/1960, p. 133). In a sense, this perspective is intrinsic to attachment research, which has long recognized the importance of contextual influences for determining the meaning of behavior (Sroufe, 1979, 1996). Thus, no radical readjustments are required as long as the cultural context is considered in addition to the relational context.

A recent summary of attachment research using the strange situation in different cultures may be used to illustrate these issues of functional and conceptual equivalence (van Ijzendoorn & Kroonenberg, 1988). As shown in Table 6.11, the distribution of attachment types in U.S. samples (N = 1230) and that in samples from other countries (N = 760) are identical. But this general comparison may mask important divergences. For example, anxious patterns of attachment in German, Japanese, and Israeli samples appear to be substantially different from American norms, though the sample sizes in these countries are far too limited to serve as a basis for national norms. Nevertheless, such data are provocative—interesting from the standpoint of understanding the source of these differences, and problematic if the basic assumption of conceptual equivalence is not met. In other words, these differences in attachment classification could arise from sampling error, a lack of conceptual equivalence in the assessment procedure, or genuine cultural differences in early child-rearing patterns. For example, conceptual equivalence would be violated if

Table 6.11 Distribution of Attachment Types (Percentages) Across Various Samples

Samples	Attachment Type (%)		
	A	B	C
Germany (FRG) (3 samples, N = 136)	35	57	8
Great Britain (1 sample, N = 72)	22	75	3
Netherlands (4 samples, N = 251)	26	67	6
Sweden (1 sample, N = 51)	22	74	4
Israel (2 samples, N = 118)	7	64	29
Japan (2 samples, N = 96)	5	68	27
China (1 sample, N = 36)	25	50	25
USA (18 samples, N = 1230)	21	65	14
Total (32 samples, N = 1990)	21	65	14

Source: Van Ijzendoorn & Kroonenberg. Reprinted by permission of SRCD.

infants and/or mothers from other cultures experience the strange situation differently from their American counterparts, despite the most stringent attempts to standardize the procedure.

In their study of Japanese mother–infant dyads, Miyake, Chen, and Campos (1985) reported that 37 percent of all subjects were classified as anxious/resistant in the strange situation while none were classified as anxious/avoidant, a marked difference from American norms. In some respects the behavior of this group of infants was quite similar to resistant infants in American samples; they cried a great deal at separation and were unable to settle upon reunion. However, when interpreted within the cultural context of traditional Japanese society where mothers rarely leave their infants alone for even a few minutes during the first year, and never in a strange setting, this result becomes more comprehensible. Moreover, Sroufe (1985) comments that Japanese investigators, in their zeal to duplicate precisely Ainsworth's procedure, allowed very stressful separations to continue for the required three-minute interval, rather than cutting them short, as is the practice among American investigators. As a result of these cultural differences in caregiving and procedural differences in the test situation, it is doubtful that the average level of stress that was experienced by

the Japanese infants was comparable to that experienced by American infants.

Interpreting infant behavior within a cultural context does not require postulating difficult Japanese temperaments. Indeed, such an interpretation counters previous characterizations of Oriental infants as more placid and composed than American infants (Freedman, 1974). This issue may be resolved by studying a group of Japanese mothers who exhibit child-rearing styles similar to American norms. Recent data on this question confirm the primacy of child-rearing practices as the principal source of variation in the classification of infants in the strange situation (Durette, Otaki, & Richards, 1983).

Another instructive example from the cross-cultural literature is provided by a series of studies in Germany. Grossman, Grossman, Huber, and Wartner (1981) reported a markedly higher incidence of avoidant patterns of attachment in a North German sample, while data from a South German sample were congruent with American norms (Grossman, Grossman, Spangler, Suess, & Unzer, 1985). Rather than implicating North German temperament, the Grossmans suggest that culture-specific child-rearing attitudes and practices were responsible for a higher proportion of avoidant patterns of attachment in the North

German sample. These mothers emphasize training toward obedience and independence before the end of the first year, in advance of the middle-class South German and American norms. In behavioral terms, mothers in the North German sample tended to respond to attachment behaviors such as crying by diverting or scolding their infants, rather than offering solace and close bodily contact. As a result, mean levels of sensitivity at 10 months were lower and less variable than corresponding measures at 2 or 6 months. Moreover, only the earlier measures of sensitivity predicted quality of attachment at 12 months. Viewed as a natural experiment, these results support Bowlby and Ainsworth's central hypothesis that quality of attachment is dependent upon maternal sensitivity.

The possibility of finding different antecedents or consequences of attachment in different cultures raises the issue of metric equivalence. *Metric equivalence* implies consistent statistical relationships among dependent variables as well as stable patterns of covariation among independent and dependent variables (Berry, 1980). Although the hypothesis that maternal sensitivity predicts quality of attachment has been supported by studies in several cultures, metric equivalence has yet to be demonstrated for the diverse array of consequences associated with attachment in American studies.

Apart from the problems of equivalence already mentioned, several other problems inherent in American studies involving the strange situation may be exacerbated in cross-cultural research. These problems include the narrow age range in which the procedure is valid, difficulties in standardizing scoring, maintaining rapport with subjects unfamiliar with test procedures across repeated assessments, and analytic limitations due to taxonomic methods that severely limit the number of A, C, and D classifications in an average sample (LaFreniere, 1985). Understanding attachment from an emic perspective (that is, within a specific culture's framework) provides a necessary counterpoint to an imposed etic (that is, an assumed universal, sometimes merely an articulate

expression of a culture-specific ideology) (LeVine, 1982; LeVine, et al., 1994). For attachment theory, this implies an important function for cross-cultural research in distinguishing what is species-specific from what is culture-specific in attachment relations in infancy and their role in subsequent development.

SUMMARY

From the first year of life onward children exhibit striking differences in their emotional responses to similar events and situations. Developmental psychologists believe that these differences in their emotional makeup arise as the result of complex transactions with genetic and environmental inputs interwoven from conception onward. Longitudinal research that combines repeated measures from multiple sources provides invaluable information on the factors that contribute to these individual differences. Such research in the past 30 years has been dominated by two distinct models of infant emotional development, emphasizing either inborn genetic traits or primary social relationships as the cornerstone of emotional development. Throughout this book we emphasize that a biosocial perspective must take into consideration both the nature and nurture of emotional development. Our discussion of the origin and significance of individual differences in the expression and regulation of emotions in infancy highlights these transacting influences.

Thomas, Chess, and Birch provided the impetus for contemporary research on infant temperament in the famous New York Longitudinal Study. They formulated a typology of infants as easy, difficult, or slow-to-warm-up based on nine dimensions derived from parental reports. Research has progressed a great deal from early work that relied exclusively on parental ratings, though the concept of temperament has remained highly similar over this period. Today, infant temperament generally includes assessments of three aspects of the infant's emotional responsiveness—joyfulness, fearfulness, and irritability—as well as activity level, persistence, and rhythmicity as basic dimensions.

Despite strong evidence for genetic influences on various aspects of infant temperament, problems remain in the demonstration of stability over time, especially in the first year of life. To resolve such problems, some researchers are now attempting to index infant temperament using psychophysiological approaches involving measures of vagal tone and cortisol measures. Other researchers are investigating laboratory measures of behavioral inhibition to novelty and advocate abandoning parental reports because of intractable problems of bias and contamination. However, most temperament researchers continue to refine parental ratings and advocate their use as part of a battery of assessments that includes other sources of information.

A second research tradition, emphasizing the importance of the infant's primary relationships as a context for emotional development, has also flourished over the past 30 years. Initiated by such pioneers as Bowlby and Ainsworth, attachment theory has broadened its influence in psychology well beyond the period of infancy. Bowlby developed an ethological model of attachment incorporating ideas from ethology, primatology, object relations theory, and systems theory. This theoretical work was complemented by methodological and empirical advances by Ainsworth, Main, Sroufe, Waters, and others. In this chapter, research during infancy based upon Ainsworth's original strange situation paradigm was described. A number of important findings have become established in the attachment literature on the basis of careful replication.

First, patterns of infant attachment to the mother have been shown to be stable in middle-class samples from 12 to 18 months, with the secure pattern the most prevalent. Second, a number of studies have shown that attachment quality at this age is related to maternal responsiveness and sensitivity, but not directly related to infant temperament. Third, infant characteristics like difficult temperament or neurological problems have been shown to indirectly influence attachment security if they affect the quality of caregiving. These effects appear to be more likely in caregiving environments that are stressful with low levels of support. Fourth, changing patterns of attachment reflect coherence. If life circumstances for the caregiver improve or deteriorate, corresponding changes in attachment security may be observed. Fifth, the infant's attachment relationships may be different for fathers and mothers if caregiving sensitivity is different between the two parents. Sixth, preventive interventions in the first year of life have demonstrated that it is possible to modify both parental sensitivity and responsiveness to infant signals and the quality of the attachment relationship. Finally, cross-cultural research on attachment has begun to investigate how cultural influences modify this basic primate adaptation to fit the ecology in which the infant and caregiver are immersed. More research will be necessary to distinguish what is species-specific from what is culture-specific in attachment relations in infancy and their role in subsequent development.

FURTHER READING

Ainsworth, M. B. S., Blehar, M., Waters, E., & Wall, S. (1978). *Patterns of attachment*. Hillsdale, NJ: Erlbaum.

This publication is an account of Ainsworth's pioneering methodological and empirical contribution to attachment research.

Bowlby, J. (1969). *Attachment and loss: Vol. I. Attachment.* New York: Basic Books.

Bowlby, J. (1973). *Attachment and loss: Vol. II. Separation, anxiety, and anger.* New York: Basic Books.

Bowlby, J. (1980). *Attachment and loss: Vol. III. Loss.* New York: Basic Books.

Bowlby's trilogy ranks as one of the classics of developmental psychology and is still required reading for advanced students of attachment.

Rothbart, M. K., & Bates, J. E. (1998). Temperament. In W. Damon (Series Ed.) & N. Eisenberg (Vol. Ed.), *Handbook of child psychology: Vol. 3. Social, emotional, and personality development* (5th ed.). New York: Wiley.

This is an up-to-date and authoritative review of research on temperament.

Scarr, S., & McCartney, K. (1983). How people make their own environments: A theory of genotype-environment effects. *Child Development, 54,* 425–435.

This article provides a lucid account of the nature–nurture problem and articulates a useful resolution to this false dichotomy.

Sroufe, L. A., & Waters, E. (1977). Attachment as an organizational construct. *Child Development, 48,* 1184–1199.

This groundbreaking defense of attachment as a scientific construct led to a new era of thinking and research on relationships and emotions in developmental psychology.

7

The Expanding Emotional World
of Early Childhood

*We can cause laughing by tickling
the skin, weeping or frowning by a blow,
trembling from the fear of pain, and so forth;
but we cannot cause a blush . . . by any physical
means—that is by acting on the body. It is the
mind which must be affected.*

DARWIN (1872/1965)

DEVELOPMENT OF SELF-CONSCIOUS EMOTIONS

Since Darwin, a fundamental distinction has been drawn between emotions that appear early in infancy and emotions that make their appearance later in development, depend on complex cognitive processes, and may be uniquely human. In contrast to the expressions linked to basic emotions, for which there are clear parallels in the animal world, Darwin (1872/1965) viewed the self-consciousness of a blush as "the most peculiar and human of all expressions." Although Darwin clearly intended his book on emotional expression to support his theory of evolution, he was unconvinced of any legitimate parallel to blushing in the animal world, stating that "it would require an overwhelming amount of evidence to make us believe that any animal could blush" (p. 309). To date none has been forthcoming.

Darwin believed that the essential element in the mental states that induce blushing, including shyness, shame, embarrassment, modesty, and guilt, was a heightened attention to the self. Despite the lack of any comparative evidence, Darwin believed that these emotions also evolved, and the creationist thought of his day provided some important insights into the development of this aspect of his theory. Darwin (1872/1965) quotes Sir C. Bell who believed that blushing "is a provision for expression, as may be inferred from the colour extending only to the surface of the face, neck, and breast, the parts most exposed. It is not acquired, it is from the beginning." He also cites Dr. Burgess who believed that blushing was designed by the Creator in "order that the soul might have sovereign power of displaying in the cheeks the various internal emotions of the moral feelings; so as to serve as a check on ourselves, and as a sign to others, that we were violating rules which ought to be held sacred" (p. 336). Darwin incorporated the latter observation in his view that these emotions reflect an evaluation of the self in relation to a standard. He invoked his principle of association to explain the evolution of a response that originated in relation to physical appearance in the eyes of others to self-consciousness in relation to moral conduct. "It is not the simple act of reflecting on our own appearance, but the thinking what others think of us, which excites a blush" (p. 325).

Self-conscious emotions are currently enjoying much renewed interest among contemporary researchers. The **self-conscious emotions** that we shall discuss in this chapter include embarrassment, envy, empathy, pride, shame, and guilt. Echoing Darwin, these emotions are generally seen as arising from the development of self-awareness and the acquisition of rules and standards. The first of these cognitive prerequisites, **self-awareness,** emerges in humans during the transition from infancy to toddlerhood. Research by Amsterdam (1972), based on the mirror self-recognition paradigm developed by Gallup (1977) for studying chimpanzees, revealed that most human infants recognize themselves in a mirror by the age of 22 months. During the first year infants will respond with interest and excitement to their own image in the mirror and may attempt to touch the baby they see there. Late in the second year, there is a dawning awareness of just who that "other" baby really is. This can demonstrated by unobtrusively smearing a dab of rouge on the forehead or nose of the toddler who must clearly reach to touch the rouge on his or her face rather than the face in the mirror in order to pass the **rouge test.** Some precocious infants even name themselves delightedly when admiring their image in the mirror, providing further evidence of a categorical self-concept as well as a healthy ego!

(a)

(b)

(c)

Figure 7.1 Reflections in the mirror: (a) In the first year, infants show a great deal of interest in their reflection in a mirror. (b) Toward the end of the second year, infants demonstrate that they recognize themselves in a mirror by touching their own forehead when they see a dab of rouge on their reflected image. (c) Chimpanzees show this same pattern of development.

(Photos by: (a) LaFreniere, (b) Ann Dowie, (c) Frans de Waal, 1996)

Subsequent research has shown that embarrassment and empathy emerge in relation to the development of self-referential behavior (Lewis, Sullivan, Stanger, & Weiss, 1989). Lewis argues that embarrassment, unlike shame, requires only self-consciousness, but not self-evaluation. In his theory of emotional development, pride, shame, and guilt become apparent at about 3 years, and are preceded by the development of the capacity to evaluate one's behavior against a standard (see Figure 7.2). Most investigators agree that children are able to judge their behavior in relation to a performance standard after 2 years. Should children fail to meet this standard, they are likely to experience shame; should they succeed, they are likely to feel pride (Lewis, 1993b).

Even before 2 years, toddlers react to social demands with an understanding that certain activities are forbidden (Kochanska, 1993; Kopp, 1989), but these reactions do not reveal a distinct awareness that a specific standard or rule has been violated. Rather, it seems that toddlers at this age are responding to parental negative affect and disapproval (Emde, 1992). As many authors have noted, the full internalization of parental rules, societal values, and the development of individual moral principles involves socialization processes that are played out over the first twenty years of

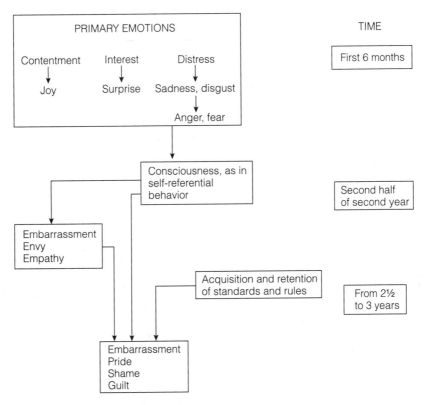

Figure 7.2 Development of emotions over the first three years of life.

Source: Lewis (1993a). Used by permission of the Guilford Press.

life, not just the first two. Still, the beginnings of this socialization are apparent in the first attempts of the toddler at self-regulation.

In this chapter we shall focus our discussion on the emergence of the self-conscious emotions in early childhood, and show how these developments in the affective domain are related to developments in the cognitive and social realms. It is important to keep in mind that although cognitive advances provide the basis for the emergence of the self-conscious emotions, the intensity these emotions assume, and whether they exert a healthy or pathogenic effect on development, depends upon the quality of the interpersonal context in which the toddler is socialized, particularly the attachment relations. As with our discussion of the basic

emotions in infancy, we shall attempt to chart the developmental course of self-conscious emotions as far as they are known at the present time. Because of the limited research base, we shall concentrate our discussion on the emotions of pride, shame, guilt, and empathy.

Pride and Shame

Despite the early descriptive work of Darwin (1872/1965) and the historically important role of shame and guilt in the psychoanalytic tradition (Freud, 1923/1961), and later in Erikson's (1963) psychosocial theory, these emotional states have received only sporadic empirical attention until quite recently. Lewis (1993b) suggests several reasons for this neglect. One possible reason has to do with the difficulty of inferring the presence of these emotions. As Darwin indicated, there is no widely recognized species-specific facial expression of shame, nor is there any universal elicitor, at least not in the sense that we have seen with the basic emotions. Instead, Darwin notes that blushing, gaze aversion, hanging the head, shrinking and closing of the body, and turning away as if to hide oneself from view are the most central expressive cues. But since blushing may be associated with other emotional states besides shame, it is less useful as a behavioral criteria. His account of this expression is still unsurpassed in its exacting description and forms the basis for current research on shame. Contemporary investigators use a similar array of facial, bodily, and postural cues in conjunction with contextual cues that are thought to be likely to induce shame, such as failing an easy task or accidentally damaging a prized object (Barrett, Zahn-Waxler, & Cole, 1993; Geppert, 1986; Lewis et al., 1992; Reissland, 1994; Stipek, Recchia, & McClintic, 1992).

There is not yet a consensus on the developmental course that best accounts for the emergence of the self-conscious emotions. Some researchers see embarrassment as a precursor to shame, with the latter emerging in the toddler period at the same time as pride and guilt (Lewis, 1993b). Other theorists view shame as a global precursor to the more specifically focused emotion of guilt (Sroufe, 1996). In Sroufe's theory, guilt and pride are not fully developed until the preschool period, though each is seen as arising from a prototype representing a diminution (shame) or swelling (positive self-evaluation) of the self. According to Sroufe, feelings of shame and positive self-evaluation require only a rudimentary sense of being bad or good, primarily as a reaction to the caregiver's blame or praise. They are global feeling states that often transcend the boundaries of a specific act and do not entail an exact appreciation of what one has done. In contrast, the more cognitively and socially sophisticated preschooler has acquired a more distinct identity and is capable of reacting to the achieve-

ment or violation of internalized standards, rather than just external praise or blame. It is this more differentiated and separate sense of self and the internalization of one's own standards that allow these emotions to be experienced in private, as well as public, situations.

Many examples of the expression of pride in one's own sense of self, or in specific accomplishments, may be observed by watching young children in a wide range of contexts. In the photos in Figure 7.3, a 5-year-old displays various emotions during the course of a swimming lesson. After entering the water at the deep end with some trepidation, we see expressions of effortful concentration while swimming with a flotation device. After discarding the floats, some anxiety and tension are expressed regarding the outcome ("I could drown here if somebody doesn't rescue me quick!"). Instead the lesson is successfully concluded, and the boy reacts with traces of relief and an afterglow of pride and joy that is expressed in both a universal expression (Duchenne smile) and a culture-specific signal (thumbs up).

Contemporary research on the development of pride and shame is beginning to make some headway regarding the conceptual and methodological issues that previously limited empirical work in this area. Earlier theorizing was guided largely by clinical observation and insight in naturalistic contexts, in which the strong and disorienting affect associated with shame and humiliation was present. In contrast, the use of experimental techniques to elicit pride or shame in relation to task performance or competitive outcomes is by ethical imperatives, not designed to elicit highly arousing negative states, a limitation that should be kept in mind when interpreting the results. Nevertheless, a number of interesting developmental findings have emerged from these experimental studies.

Geppert and Gartmann (1983) observed the facial expressions and postural reactions of children aged 18 to 42 months in tasks in which the experimenters manipulated the children's success or failure. Behaviors associated with success included smiling, head up and chin out (the "plus

(a)

(b)

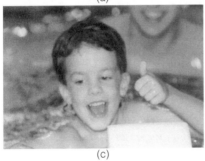

(c)

(d)

Figure 7.3 A 5-year-old displays various emotions during a swimming lesson: (a) effortful concentration between the floats; (b) anxiety and tension without the floats; (c) pride and joy expressed in culture-specific form and (d) universal form.

(Photos by LaFreniere)

face" described by Zivin [1977] in relation to success), and erect posture, while antithetical behaviors (Darwin, 1872/1965) were found following failure (frowning, gaze aversion, head hung, trunk forward and down). Similarly, Heckhausen (1984) reported that success for preschoolers resulted in an open posture while failure was associated with a closed posture. Heckhausen distinguishes the child's joy or delight in producing an intended outcome, which may be observed in infancy, from self-reflective pride. In his view, the latter emotion does not emerge until after 3 years, as indexed in the child's approval seeking from the experimenter and clear negative reactions to losing a competition. Heckhausen has argued that a concept of personal competence is a prerequisite to pride, in addition to the capacity to compare one's performance to a standard.

In a series of cross-sectional studies designed to explore similar developmental issues, Stipek and colleagues reported evidence for systematic age-related changes in young children's experience of pride and shame (Stipek et al., 1992). For example, in laboratory tasks involving success or

failure, the percentage of children who displayed a frown after failing the task increased from 10 percent to nearly 50 percent from age 2 to 4 years, as shown in Figure 7.4. Sex differences were also found for this behavior, with preschool girls significantly more likely to frown or pout after failure than boys (Stipek et al., 1992).

A similar age trend was reported for displays of positive emotion. At all ages tested, children were more likely to smile after winning than after finishing a race (but losing). However, smiling after winning was more likely than smiling after finishing only after 32 months. As with frowning after failure, smiling after winning increased dramatically from age 2 to 4 years, rising from 25 percent to nearly 80 percent over that span (see Figure 7.5).

Stipek (1995) posits a three-stage model of the early development of these self-evaluative emotions. In the first stage, toddlers younger than 22 months show no evidence of "having reflected upon the effect that their achievement might have on another individual's reactions toward them" (p. 248). Specifically, they do not look to the experimenter after success or call

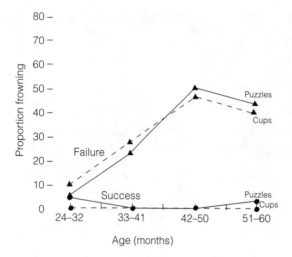

Figure 7.4 Percentage of children displaying frown in success and failure conditions

Source: Stipek, Recchia, and McClintic (1992). Used by permission of the SRCD.

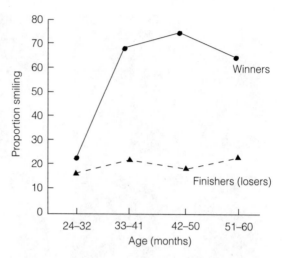

Figure 7.5 Percentage of children displaying smile in winning and losing conditions

Source: Stipek, Recchia, and McClintic (1992). Used by permission of the SRCD.

their mother's attention to achieving success. In the second stage, children begin to exhibit these two behaviors in about half the trials, suggesting that they have become aware of achieving a socially valued outcome. Similarly, children's social avoidance behaviors following failure suggest that they wish to avoid an anticipated negative reaction by the adult. However, neither behavior pattern provides any evidence for an internalized standard. Stipek's criteria for inferring an internalized standard are negative facial expressions following failure, which were not observed until over a year after the manifestation of atttention-seeking and avoidant reactions.

In our research on children's responses to success and failure, we examined preschool boys' ability to regulate negative affect in order to achieve cooperation with a peer (Janosz & LaFreniere, 1991). To experimentally induce mild negative affect, we controlled the outcome of a competition in a manner similar to that used in the research by Geppert and Gartmann (1983) and Heckhausen (1984) described earlier. Each session began with a short competition. Boys were instructed that the first one who completed

his jigsaw puzzle would be rewarded a prize. The boys typically competed enthusiastically. Success in the competition was characterized by broad smiling, plus faces, and triumphant looks at the partner with occasional boasting, while losing the competition was followed by looking down or away, frowning, slumping posture, and occasional whining or complaining.

In the subsequent cooperative task, which involved sharing an attractive toy, typically some form of turn-taking prevailed, with each child employing the toy for a brief period. However, great variation in the degree of cooperation, conflict, and competition was observed. Affective synchrony following the competition strongly predicted the subsequent degree of cooperation and conflict in the second task. Socially competent children were typically able to reconcile the asymmetry produced by unequal outcomes to the competition and engage in more cooperation and less competition and conflict than children who were less competent. In the "winner's role," they often showed affective perspective-taking to soften the impact of their partner's losing the competition. This ability to moderate prideful display has also been observed by Reissland and Harris (1991), who reported that 5-year-olds soften their display of pride and pleasure in winning competitions with their younger siblings. In contrast to socially competent preschoolers, preschoolers with a history of problem behavior showed considerably more tension and less synchrony in their interaction with each other. Those who lost the initial competition withdrew, while those who won became oppressive, and cooperation was virtually absent (Janosz & LaFreniere, 1991).

These observations of children's expressive behavior following success and failure, or winning and losing, demonstrate that a number of related behaviors may be associated with each outcome. Behaviors following success may reflect either pride or joy in mastery, while different behaviors following failure or losing may reflect shame, frustration, or anger. Rather than inferring the presence of an internalized standard from the presence of negative facial affect following failure, we would simply infer that a meaningful goal has been blocked. We also view such a context as an excellent means for assessing individual differences. Some children responded with initial, but short-lived, disappointment and thoroughly enjoy themselves in cooperative play during the second task. However, children rated by their preschool teachers as angry-aggressive tended to respond to failure with sharp frustration and have great difficulty regulating this emotion. Anxious-withdrawn children in the same circumstances often responded with passivity, dejection, and resignation. It is likely that stable individual differences in personality and attributional styles lead to such differences in children's emotional responses. In this chapter we are primarily concerned with describing age-related changes in children's emotions. The parallel topic of individual differences in their emotional development shall be addressed in depth in Chapter 8.

Guilt

Defined as an emotional response to a keen sense of having violated one's own internalized stan-

dards, guilt is most likely absent until the preschool period when children show clear evidence of the internalization of moral standards. The transition from the toddler phase to the preschool period (3 to 5 years) is characterized by rapid increases in self-control that are manifested by the preschooler in many ways. The oppositional tantrums of the so-called "terrible-two's" give way to a more reasonable mode of conflict resolution. With parents, preschoolers are developing the capacity for negotiation, and direct defiance and noncompliance show a marked decline between the ages of 2 and 5 (Kuczynski & Kochanska, 1990). With peers, preschoolers show a rapid decline in instrumental aggression (Goodenough, 1931) and a rise in empathic, prosocial behavior. These changes in social behavior are directly related to parallel developments in the child's cognition and understanding and regulation of emotion. Preschoolers are better equipped to direct and monitor their own behavior (Kopp, Krakow, & Vaughn, 1983) and begin to show a capacity to inhibit behaviors that were previously not under their control (Luria, 1980). While toddlers may be redirected by a parent or teacher away from a source of frustration, preschoolers have learned to incorporate this practice and can often redirect themselves to alternative activities when their initial choice is blocked.

Cognitive theorists have described these developments in terms of **scaffolding** (Bruner, 1975), which refers to the actions of parents and teachers that provide a framework around the young child's actions that stretches the limits of their competence into a new **zone of proximal development** (Vygotsky, 1978). This concept refers to children's ability to engage in more advanced behaviors in the context of external structure and support, the "scaffolds," provided by the caregiver. In this manner, caregiver-guided self-regulation gives rise to more effective and autonomous self-regulation. Vygotsky (1978) has summarized this aspect of development by stating, "Every function in the child's cultural development appears twice: first, on the social level, and later, on the individual level; first between people (interpsychologically), and then inside the child (intrapsychologically)" (p. 57).

Research on the internalization of parental values and moral standards has a long history in psychology. The classic psychoanalytic view of the development of guilt was formulated by Freud (1930/1961), which we can only briefly summarize here. According to Freud, guilt is dependent upon the formation of the superego, or conscience, which represents the internalized voice of parental authority. Guilt is viewed as a by-product of the conflict between the superego, the ego (self), and the id, the repository of instinctual impulses. Guilt is expressed by the self as a need for punishment. The ego's role is to find safe and appropriate ways for gratifying biological impulses, which are often in conflict with society's demands. Freud's theory was revolutionary in its day and represents the first attempt at formulating a developmental theory of the emergence of the self and the origins of personality, as a means of treating emotional problems in adulthood. The legacy of Freud is especially apparent in the research of the 1950s and 1960s, which emphasized the processes by which children internalize moral standards, particularly with regard to acts of wrongdoing. Much of this early research focused on topics like resistance to temptation, response to prohibition, and other aspects of guilt as a violation of internalized standards (Hoffman, 1970).

While Freud, and later researchers influenced by his theory, viewed the superego as forming with the resolution of the Oedipal conflict at about 5 years, more recent research indicates that much internalization takes place in the early preschool years (Zahn-Waxler & Kochanska, 1990; Zahn-Waxler & Robinson, 1995). Researchers have demonstrated that delay of gratification and compliance to prohibition are possible in the parents' absence in young preschoolers (Kopp et al., 1983). Preschool children often refuse to violate the parents' prohibitions and may seek to repair the relationship (and reduce guilt) by confessing to the parents if violations do occur (Emde &

Buchsbaum, 1990). Even young preschoolers engage in attempts to make reparations to peers after aggressive outbursts, and experimental work confirms that reparative behaviors are commonly directed to caregivers after mishaps (Cole, Barrett, & Zahn-Waxler, 1992). In this latter study, researchers arranged for children to be involved in mishaps, such as accidentally hitting their mother's finger with a hammer or breaking a valued object, and then coded the children's reactions from videotape. Tapes were coded for emotional expressions, including joy, anger, sadness, and tension/worry blends, as well as behavioral reparation attempts. No systematic relationships between reparation and emotional expression were found.

One might ask why emotional expressions of guilt were not directly coded, but what does the expression of guilt look like? No less an observer than Charles Darwin (1872/1965) described a guilty expression following a misdeed in his 2 1/2-year-old son as "an unnatural brightness in the eyes and an odd affected manner, *impossible to describe*" (p. 262, italics added). Modern researchers confirm that guilt does not appear to have a specific facial expression, though like shame, guilt may be accompanied by gaze aversion. Given the lack of a clearly differentiated expressive component, most researchers have chosen to assess guilt indirectly with measures of reparation or confession, rather than facial expression.

Because of the ambiguities in the expression of guilt and shame and their conceptual similarities, it is interesting to summarize their relation to one another, and how they are alike and different. Table 7.1 summarizes characteristics of each emotion in terms of eliciting conditions; age of onset; expressive, physiological, behavioral, and experiential components; and possible functions. It is important to state, however, that not all theorists agree with the consensual view formulated here.

For example, theorists differ widely in how they depict the interrelationship of these two emotion systems. Freud viewed them both as

Table 7.1 A Comparison of the Characteristics of Shame and Guilt

Dimensions	Shame	Guilt
Elicitor	External standards	Internal standards
Expression		
Vocal	Narrow, lax thin voice	Narrow, tense full voice
Physiological	Low HR, blushing	High HR, irregular breathing
Behavioral	Avoidance	Reparation
Signal function	Deference, submission	Contrition, positive intention

arising after the resolution of the Oedipal conflict, but associated guilt with the control of aggression and shame with the control of sexual impulses. Freud described guiltlike reactions involving social anxiety (fear of loss of love) as preceding guilt, which he viewed as fear of punishment. Later psychosocial theorists like Erikson used the term *shame* to denote the social anxiety associated with fear of loss of love, and thus began to view shame as preceding guilt developmentally (Erikson, 1963). Although contemporary psychoanalytic theorists like Schore (1991, 1994) differ substantially from earlier positions, there is still widespread agreement that shame occurs at an earlier age than guilt. Some theorists view shame as a developmental precursor to guilt in that shame appears earlier and requires only a global appreciation of the self as bad in the eyes of the caregiver, unlike guilt which involves a more specific focus (Nathanson, 1987; Sroufe, 1996). Lewis (1993a) also makes this distinction between shame and guilt, but views them as both emerging at the same point in development. Finally, one theorist (Barrett, 1991) has abandoned any cognitive prerequisites to emotions such as shame or guilt and even the conception of emotions as wholes that emerge at particular points in development. Such are the vagaries that stem from the study of a phenomenom with no clear behavioral referent.

Empathy

Not all researchers include empathy in the class of self-conscious emotions. It is clearly a social emo-

tion, since in its mature form it implies that the child has learned to distinguish between self and other and to recognize another's emotional state. Before these abilities emerge, there is a clear precursor of empathy that may be observed early in infancy. Hoffman (1979, 1984), who was one of the first theorists to formulate a developmental theory of empathy, believes that the empathic arousal in the newborn based on motor mimicry is a characteristically human response that is rooted in our primate heritage. Hoffman has observed that newborns tend to cry as a response to the cries of other babies, a phenomenon that may be more characteristic of females than males. He views this contagion of negative affect as a precursor to empathy in the same manner as previously discussed by Sroufe. This form of primitive empathic distress is experienced through very basic arousal modes, and is involuntary and global. As a precursor, it does not yet qualify as a truly empathic response to distress in another, yet it already embodies something of the emotional essence of the later, more mature form. This emotional contagion of newborns is the first of Hoffman's three stages in the development of empathy.

In the second stage, advances in self-awareness lead to the ability to more clearly differentiate between self and other. In the second year of life, the young toddler may react to another infant's distress by purposeful helping behaviors that are egocentric, such as comforting the other infant with the toddler's own favorite toy. The toddler can clearly distinguish between another and one's own distress, yet does not show the

174

Figure 7.6 Expressions of empathy in primates and children

(Photo above left by Frans de Waal, 1996; engravings and photo below left by I. Eibl-Eibesfeldt, 1989)

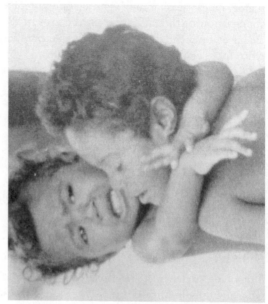

same role-taking skills that become evident in the early preschool years. In one example, reported by Zahn-Waxler and Radke-Yarrow (1990), a 21-month-old boy comforted his mother's simulated sadness by offering her a hand puppet and hugging her. As we observed in our discussion of attachment theory, the infant's primary relationships provide a vital context for understanding and responding to the partner's expressions of emotions.

In Hoffman's third stage, the young preschooler is developing the capacity for perspective-taking and becomes more aware that another's feelings may differ from one's own and that these feelings are based on the other's needs, which may be different than one's own. As one bright preschooler patiently explained to me when I questioned him about why another younger child was crying at our laboratory preschool, "Cuz he probly thinks his mother might not come back. He doesn't know she's really coming back in just a little bit." This insight may have been the product of a very good memory, as this child exhibited the same pattern of separation anxiety when he first arrived at our school!

Although our knowledge of the developmental course of empathy is limited by methodological difficulties (see the review by Lennon & Eisenberg, 1987), several studies that have investigated systematic age changes provide empirical support for Hoffman's developmental theory and also extend it in new directions. In two longitudinal studies (Radke-Yarrow & Zahn-Waxler, 1984; Zahn-Waxler, Radke-Yarrow, Wagner, & Chapman, 1992), researchers asked mothers to record their young child's responses to naturally occurring and simulated distress. At one year, most children attempted to comfort the other with physical contact (hugging or patting) regardless of the cause of the distress. These early responses may actually provide comfort to both the helper and the person in distress. This early form of empathy is interpreted as evolving out of the vicarious distress characteristic of early infancy. In the second year, these early helping behaviors become more differentiated and include

helping, sharing, sympathizing, and comforting the person in distress. Children's prosocial responses were observed to increase dramatically between 18 and 24 months, as did their empathic concern and active exploration for the cause of the distress. During the same period, children's vicarious distress decreased. (See Figure 7.7.)

This distinction between vicariously experienced personal distress and sympathetic concern is important for several reasons. Eisenberg, Fabes, and colleagues (Eisenberg & Fabes, 1992; Eisenberg et al., 1988; Fabes, Eisenberg, & Eisenbud, 1993) distinguish between personal distress and sympathetic concern on the basis of psychophysiological, facial, and vocalic expressions. Personal distress shares some of the characteristics associated with fear, including heart rate acceleration, whereas sympathetic concern is associated with heart rate deceleration. Whether a child reacts to another's misfortune with distress or concern may be important in determining whether the child actually attempts to help someone in distress.

These researchers report that sympathetic concern (which may include sadness) is linked with prosocial behavior, whereas personal distress is not, for preschool and school-age children. Zahn-Waxler, Radke-Yarrow, and colleagues (1992) report similar associations at age 2, indicating that poorly modulated emotional arousal that remains focused on the self may actually interfere with prosocial action. According to Eisenberg and colleagues (1988), children's heart rate and facial expression predicted children's attempts to help another in distress, whereas self-reported feelings of empathy did not. These data probably indicate that children's self-reports of empathy are unreliable rather than indicating that children's feelings are unrelated to their actual behavior.

However, the relationship between the child's emotional arousal and prosocial behavior may be quite complex. Eisenberg and Fabes (1992) proposed that an optimal level of arousal will most likely lead to sympathetic concern and prosocial behavior. Too little arousal is not expected to provide sufficient motivation, whereas too high

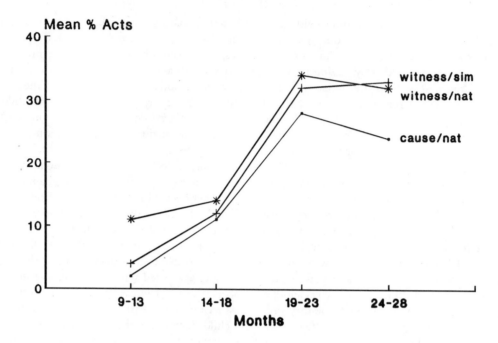

Figure 7.7 Age changes in children's prosocial and reparative behaviors

Source: Zahn-Waxler and Radke-Yarrow (1982).

arousal may lead the child to experience distress and to avoid its source. In their view, the key to responding helpfully to another's distress is the child's ability to modulate his or her emotional reaction to enable the child to focus attention on the person in distress rather than on his or her own distress. This ability to modulate one's level of emotional arousal entails neurophysiological regulation, attentional control, cognitive appraisal, and coping skills. We will continue our discussion of children's abilities to regulate their emotional arousal later in this chapter.

PRESCHOOLERS' UNDERSTANDING OF EMOTIONAL EXPERIENCE

In addition to the emergence of self-conscious emotions of pride, shame, guilt, and empathy, cognitive growth during the period of early childhood supports a number of other significant advances in emotional functioning. With the development of linguistic skills, preschoolers reveal a new understanding of their emotional experiences as well as those of others. These increases in the child's awareness and understanding of emotion have been investigated by a number of researchers in terms of recognizing and labeling emotional expressions, talking about emotions, and understanding their causes and consequences.

Emotion Recognition

Without question human infants and children are remarkably precocious in their practical understanding of emotion. As reviewed in Chapter 5, infants as young as 3 months are able to discriminate different expressions of emotions. During the first year of life, infants respond to the meaning of specific emotional expressions and understand that the parent's emotional expression can convey useful information. This understanding is revealed by studies of social referencing, in which infants use the emotional expression of the mother to vicariously evaluate a novel or ambiguous situation (Klinnert, Campos, Sorce, Emde, & Svejda, 1983).

During the toddler and preschool years, children become increasingly sophisticated in their abilities to identify emotional expressions. A number of studies have investigated the young child's ability to recognize and label spontaneous and posed facial expressions of different basic emotions, often using still photographs as experimental stimuli. For example, Odom and Lemond (1972) found that preschoolers can successfully distinguish the facial expressions associated with happiness, anger, sadness, and fear by asking the children to match photographs of posed facial expressions to different photos of the same emotion or to a related emotional situation. Some emotions may be easier for children to recognize and label than others. Several studies have shown that preschoolers are best able to recognize spontaneous and posed facial expressions of happiness, and they are better at recognizing facial expressions of sadness than anger (Felleman, Barden, Carlson, Rosenberg, & Masters, 1983; Harrigan, 1984). Similarly, when asked to imitate various facial expressions, preschoolers were better at matching their posed face to photographs of happiness than to fearful or angry expressions. In general, children's performance at decoding facial expressions of emotions in these experimental contexts tends to become progressively more accurate from early to middle childhood (Harrigan, 1984; Odom & Lemond, 1972; Zuckerman & Przewuzman, 1979).

Other studies have examined children's decoding accuracy with respect to different channnels, by asking children to identify and label different basic emotions based on information presented through the face, voice, or both channnels together. These studies have generally shown that children are better at recognizing the emotion when more information is presented (Stifter & Fox, 1987). Relatively few studies have investigated children's ability to recognize different basic emotions based upon the voice alone. As with recognition of facial expressions, decoding accuracy of the vocal-verbal channel tends to improve with age. In contrast with recognition of facial affect, several studies of vocal-verbal communication of affect show that anger is more accurately perceived than other emotions, while sadness appears to be more difficult to recognize from the voice. A similar pattern of emotion recognition from the voice channel is apparent in older children and adults (Scherer, 1986, 1989).

In addition to these advances in the recognition and labeling of basic emotional expressions, preschool children reveal an increased understanding of emotional experience. During this period children increase the amount and complexity of verbal commentary about their feelings (Bretherton, Fritz, Zahn-Waxler, & Ridgeway, 1986; Dunn, Bretherton, & Munn, 1987). They show dramatic advances in their ability to explain their feelings and to persuade others to comfort or attend to their feelings. As Daniel Stern (1985) has commented, "With language, infants for the first time can share their personal experience of the world with others, including 'being with' others in intimacy, isolation, loneliness, fear, awe and love" (p. 182).

Language and Emotion

During the toddler and preschool years, children are learning to talk about their emotions in much the same manner that they are learning to talk about a host of other things that interest them and excite their curiosity. Researchers have investigated the development of emotion language by examining receptive and productive vocabulary (Ridgeway, Waters, & Kuczaj, 1985), analyzing the emotional content of mother–child speech while viewing photographs of infant emotional expressions (Denham, Cook, & Zoller, 1992) or while reading together (Denham & Auerbach, 1995), and by recording children's spontaneous talk about emotions in naturalistic contexts (Bretherton, Fritz, Zahn-Waxler, & Ridgeway,

1986; Dunn, Bretherton, & Munn, 1987; Dunn & Brown, 1991).

Most children begin to use emotion words as early as 18 months. According to Bretherton et al. (1986), between the ages of 18 and 36 months children learn to (1) label the emotions of self and other, (2) refer to past as well as future emotions, and (3) discuss the antecedents and consequences of emotions. In a cross-sectional study from 18 months to 6 years of age, Ridgeway et al. (1985) recorded the percentages of children who could comprehend (reception) and use (production) various words related to internal states. In general, they noted that reception precedes production. For example, the majority of 18-month-olds understood such words as *happy* and *sad,* but only 50 percent used the word *happy* and just 7 percent used the word *sad.*

A favorite activity for many preschool children is reading a book with a parent, baby-sitter, or preschool teacher, and many popular children's books portray emotionally laden events. Denham and Auerbach (1995) capitalized on this naturalistic context to examine talk about emotions that included labeling an emotional state and interpreting the causes and consequences of it. Other naturalistic contexts such as solitary fantasy play with dolls, stuffed animals, and so on or sociodramatic play with peers provide a window on how the young child understands emotional experience. By the preschool years, children can label a wide range of feeling states in themselves and others, and show a rudimentary understanding of many typical emotional experiences, as well as the ability to predict emotional reactions (Saarni, Mumme, & Campos, 1998).

Emphasizing a functionalist perspective, researchers like Inge Bretherton and Judy Dunn have examined children's spontaneous talk about emotions in naturalistic contexts. Table 7.2 displays a sample of a 2-year-old's talk about emotions. From a functionalist perspective, these statements are viewed in terms of what the child is trying to accomplish. Many of the statements reflect the child's desire to influence another person's behavior. For example, the second observation is an attempt to stop parents from quarreling, and in the third observation, the child is telling the mother how to attend to another child who is crying. Such statements are typical of 2-year-olds. Such comments by 2-year-olds are by no means rare. In one study, 87 percent of children aged 2 verbalized concern, reassurance, or sympathy in relation to another's distress.

Naturalistic observations by Judy Dunn and colleagues (Brown & Dunn, 1991; Dunn, Bretherton, & Munn, 1987; Dunn & Brown, 1991) also confirm the interpersonal function of the young child's speech about emotions. In their longitudinal study of toddlers from 18 to 24 months, they recorded conversations in the home with mother and siblings and found that talk about the causes of emotions increased dramatically in this time span. Their findings that mothers play a central role in these conversations suggest that adults provide important information about the emotional experiences of the child and others by clarifying, elaborating, and interpreting the meaning of emotional displays. Reciprocally, children can probe for more information by asking questions about emotional events or by providing commentary about their own emotional reactions or those of others.

Preschoolers' questions and commentary about emotional events can also reveal what they find difficult to comprehend. Here is an example of such an exchange between a 4-year-old girl and her preschool teacher. Her teacher has just told a story about how her friends threw a surprise party for her birthday.

Teacher: I was so surprised that I cried!

Cathy: Why did you cry? Were you sad?

Teacher: No, I was happy.

Cathy: Did you get hurt?

Teacher: No, but sometimes when you are really happy you cry too.

Cathy: Oh. *(said with a puzzled look)*

Fathers, too, participate in their preschool child's emotional experiences. An anthropologist, Melvin Konner (1991), described (and

Table 7.2 Causal Statements by 24- to 30-Month-Olds in Their Conversational Context

Statement	Context
"I love Mommy, I want to hold Mommy."	Mother had just scolded child.
"No not angry. Not nice."	Parents are quarreling.
"Baby crying. Kiss. Make it better."	To mother, in store where child noticed other child crying.
"Hurt. Sorry. Sorry. Grandpa, hurt him."	To mother, about incident 2 weeks earlier when child accidentally hit grandfather's head.
"Daddy didn't kiss me good-bye. Didn't give Daddy kiss good-bye."	Father had scolded child at dinner on the previous evening and sent her to bed. In the morning she cried by the door.
Answer: "Daddy angry, I cry in crib."	Mother asked her why.
"I hurt your hair. Please don't cry."	To child victim, after being scolded for hair-pulling.
"Mommy you went away. I was sad."	After being left at preschool, and mother was asked to return.

Source: Adapted from Bretherton, Fritz, Zahn-Waxler, and Ridgeway, 1986.

commented on) three episodes in which his 3-year-old daughter expressed her emotional concerns:

> After falling and briefly crying, Sarah controls her sobs and says, "I hurt my knee and I also fell my shoe off." (She has cried already, babylike, adaptive, announcing the crisis and summoning help for the pain. But then, she feels, she must suppress the sobs and give the details to her father; this is no animal cry, but a shared human experience, hung in the air between two people in a vessel of simple words. She uses words and, as my mother used to say, she gets her troubles off her chest.)
>
> Papa are you listen-to-ing me . . . listening to me? (. . . [S]he catches me in one of my lapses of attention—it's a hazard of having an egghead for a father—and properly calls me on it, with a question I couldn't have asked at her age. She identifies here another central fact of childhood: There is no point in telling your woes (or your joys for that matter) to someone who isn't listening—"listen-to-ing" may be the better word—doesn't just mean sitting there; it's active. The words are a way of touching across a little

expanse of space; if the child is lucky, they will always be that, with someone, for a lifetime.)

> At a live performance in English of the opera *Hansel and Gretel,* Sarah is very frightened, actually shaking as she sits on her mother's lap, watching the witch. . . . At last she asks, "Is this a movie, or is this real?" (The play focuses all the terror a three-year-old can see in the grown-up world. She is on her mother's lap, and her brother and sister have tried to calm her, without success. Finally she asks the question, aiming to get an answer that will help her draw a firm line between imagination and reality—a line that her siblings, at eight and eleven, readily draw for themselves.) (pp. 156–158)

Although young preschoolers talk more often with parents and teachers than with peers, they do show an increased awareness of the emotional states of other children and link these emotions to their beliefs and desires. Preschool children will often attend to a crying child in a preschool setting, taking in as much of the situation as they can. Their knowledge about the event that led to the emotional display may be tapped by asking them to explain what happened. Using this

Table 7.3 Emotional Speech by 4- to 5-Year-Old Boys and Girls

Girls or Boys?	Girls or Boys?
Child was swinging stuffed elephant by its tail and teacher asked, "Is that a happy elephant?" Child answered, "No, it's not happy. He feels mad and bad! He doesn't like it when I swing him by his tail. This is what I do when he tries to eat people."	"Grown-ups don't cry. Except my mom. Once she cried because I had an itch under my arm and it itched so I had to itch it and she cried."
"George is hiding because he's scared he's to be in trouble."	"Ali's crying because he's sad and wants his Dad."
	"I love my brother, he's a good baby."
"He took the swing—I hate him."	"When I'm happy I love to sing that song. Will you sing it with me?"
"I am very mad. They ruined my sand castle I was making."	"I'm sad, I think Mei-Lee doesn't like me anymore because she won't play with me."
"I don't know what got into me, I was just feeling bad, but I'm better now."	She is hurting my feelings."
"I would be very scared if someone tied me up at the playground."	"People give each other hugs and kisses when they love each other."

naturalistic approach, Fabes, Eisenberg, Nyman, and Michealieu (1991) asked preschoolers who witnessed, but were themselves uninvolved in, spontaneous emotional displays to describe the emotion and what caused it. The preschoolers showed great interest in negative emotions and intense emotions of any kind. In their explanations of these emotions, the children often took into account beliefs, desires, and goals of the other person in explaining the other's behavior. We shall examine children's understanding of internal states in greater detail in Chapter 9.

For three weeks, undergraduate students at the University of Maine used a naturalistic approach to record spontaneous speech about emotion in three preschool groups. They recorded 92 examples over this period; 77 percent of these were from preschool girls, suggesting that girls may be more predisposed than boys to talk about emotion at this age. Such a hypothesis would need to be confirmed by more systematic research, but it is generally consistent with our current understanding of gender differences in this area. Further analysis of these data suggests that there may be qualitative differences between girls and boys as well. Table 7.3 presents a representative sample of emotion speech organized in

two blocks by gender. After reading these examples, see if you can guess the gender of the children who voiced these emotional concerns.

Developmental psychologists believe that talking about internal feeling states is important because it is related to the child's emerging ability to coordinate emotion with cognition and behavior in resolving challenging social situations. This function of emotion speech has begun to receive more research attention in recent years as investigators explore both intrapersonal and interpersonal dimensions of children's ability to regulate or manage their emotional experience.

THE DEVELOPMENT OF EMOTION REGULATION

The child's emerging capacity to monitor and control emotions is clearly tied to advances in language and cognition. This illustrates one of this book's central themes, that the nature of emotion calls for an integrative approach. It may be possible to discuss cognitive development without explicit reference to emotion, but the study of emotional development must be understood in relation to social, cognitive, and linguistic advances.

Besides the emergence of the self-conscious emotions, and advances in their understanding of emotion noted earlier, preschoolers manifest a number of other important changes in their emotional development. The popular conception of the "terrible two's" reflects an understanding that toddlerhood is marked by the child's willfulness and inability to deal with frustration arising from parental demands and restrictions. Fortunately for parents this phase gives way to a new more relaxed modus operandi for most children as they enter their preschool years. Researchers note a gradual decline in anger, frustration, defiance, and tantrum behavior over this period (Goodenough, 1931; Kuczynski & Kochanska, 1990). At the same time, children are learning to direct and monitor their own behavior (Kopp et al., 1983), to resist temptations and inhibit behaviors (Luria, 1980), to express their internal feeling states in words (Bretherton et al., 1986), and to use language and affect to persuade others to meet their emotional needs and goals (Dunn & Brown, 1991).

Together these changes may be understood as evidence for growth in emotion regulation. Although this term is used differently by different investigators, **emotion regulation** generally refers to the processes by which children monitor and control their emotional states and the expression of these states to adapt to different social situations or demands. In this sense it reflects both maturational changes and specific socialization effects that may vary within and between cultures. According to Thompson (1994), "emotion regulation consists of the extrinsic and intrinsic processes responsible for monitoring, evaluating, and modifying emotional reactions, especially their intensive and temporal features, to accomplish one's goals" (p. 27). Biological researchers like Porges have raised the question of what exactly is being regulated when we use this term. In Thompson's view, regulation is being used to encompass a range of interrelated processes, involving neurological activation, physiological arousal, cognitive evaluation, attentional processes,

and expressive and behavioral components. In this book we use the term in this broad and inclusive sense to refer to all these aspects of the emotion process—to both the amplification and inhibition of emotion, and to the monitoring and control of internal arousal, as well as expressive behaviors.

Personality theorists have long recognized the importance of the individual's ability to remain organized in situations of high emotional arousal. For example, Block and Block (1980) formulated the constructs of ego control and ego resiliency as the cornerstone of their theory of personality development. **Ego control** refers to the child's developing capacity to manage strong feelings, impulses, wishes, or desires, while **ego resiliency** refers to the flexibility of such emotion management. Longitudinal studies by the Blocks, as well as the Minnesota Longitudinal Study, provide empirical support that these abilities have their roots in early socialization experiences, take form in early childhood, and remain relatively stable from age 3 to adolescence and adulthood (Block & Block, 1980; Sroufe, 1983, 1996).

Early Forms of Regulation

Based on their longitudinal studies, these researchers are convinced that socialization experiences make a critical contribution to the child's growth in emotional regulation. Many developmental theorists, including attachment researchers, view this as a continuous process that begins at birth with the establishment of smooth routines between caregiver and infant to regulate physiological tension and distress and provide soothing and pleasant stimulation (Trevarthen, 1984; Tronick, 1990). Here the "regulation" is being provided by the sensitive caregiver by matching behaviors to the infant's state and capacity for stimulation (Sroufe, 1979, 1996). Infant cries stimulate the parents' ingenuity to find effective means to alleviate their infants' distress by cooing, caressing, feeding, rocking, and later by distracting their infants with a toy. These tactics may be thought of as **caregiver-guided regulation,** which is viewed as the first stage in a progression toward self-regulation by numerous developmental theorists.

For example, Kopp (1982, 1989) notes that both psychodynamic approaches and Russian theories (Luria, 1980; Vygotsky, 1978) share the view of a progression from external to internal regulation, stressing affective-motivational aspects of the infant–parent relationship, and verbal communication in parent–child interactions, respectively. In Sroufe's (1996) organizational perspective, caregiver-guided regulation of tension during the first half year gives way to "guided self-regulation" in the second year and increasingly internalized controls during the preschool years. In this view, regulation is conceived of as a series of qualitative reorganizations involving biological and behavioral systems, and maturational and socialization forces, with each new stage of development building upon and incorporating elements from the previous stage. Thus, failure at an early stage has implications for the resolution of subsequent stages.

When applied to the development of emotion regulation, maturational factors involve changes in CNS functioning, self-awareness, and cognitive and representational skills. Socialization forces include parental reactions to affective displays during interaction and parent–child talk about emotions. Based on an organizational perspective, Cicchetti and colleagues perceive two major trends as children approach and resolve basic developmental tasks involving the regulation of tension and establishment of primary emotional attachments:

First, emotion regulation becomes more complex and abstract. During this period, affect moves from being reflexive and guided by physiological discomfort to being reflective and guided by one's working models of attachment figures, the self, and the environment. When this occurs, the child's affect becomes less susceptible to environmental influences and increasingly controlled by his or her understanding of personal experiences.

Second, as the child develops, his or her emotion regulation differentiates. The internal, experiential components of affect become divorced from the outward expressions of affect, allowing for the adoption of specific affect regulatory strategies consistent with the qualities of the child's environment. (Cicchetti, Ganiban, & Barnett, 1991, p. 39)

In this model, increasing self-reliance in the management of negative affect arising from distress is emphasized. In the first stage, the infant relies upon the caregiver to interpret and respond to reflexive signals of distress in order to regain stability. In the second stage, more specific forms of affective expressions mediate interaction with the caregiver and the infant begins to assume some control over the management of tension, though much of this is guided by the caregiver. The third stage of clearly established attachment with the caregiver represents a new reorganization. Affective, cognitive, and behavioral systems function to ensure that proximity to the caregiver is maintained and that security needs are met. There is a new mutuality to the relationship in which the parent and the infant have expectations for each other based upon their relationship history. At this stage the infant is capable of mental representations of this history and forms a "working model" of the relationship. This working model lays the groundwork for the emergence of the self-system in the fourth stage.

We will return to the themes of emotion understanding and regulation in our discussion of individual differences in emotional functioning in the next chapter. In the remaining sections of this chapter, we turn our attention to the growth of social and emotional competence in early childhood and to an exploration of gender differences in emotional functioning.

Emotion Regulation and Social Competence

Researchers have consistently noted a gradual rise in social competence during the preschool years as children acquire greater cognitive and emotional maturity and self-control and a corresponding decline in angry outbursts and aggressive behavior. One of the first researchers to document these age trends was Florence Goodenough who questioned mothers regarding these behaviors in a study conducted over 65 years ago. Goodenough (1931) described a developmental trend in which the expression of anger and aggression peaked at age 2 and steadily declined during the preschool years, though it remained more common in boys than girls.

These age trends and gender differences in preschoolers' emotions and social behaviors were recently replicated on an extensive sample using teachers as informants. Over 300 preschool teachers in the United States, Canada, France, Spain, and Latin America completed the Social Competence and Behavior Evaluation (SCBE), a rating scale developed to assess patterns of social competence, emotion regulation and expression, and adjustment difficulties (Dumas, Martinez, & LaFreniere, 1998; LaFreniere & Dumas, 1995, 1996; LaFreniere, Dumas, Capuano, & Dubeau, 1992). The database consists of eight distinct samples, with data collected from preschool teachers using the English, French, or Spanish versions of the SCBE. Principal components analyses clearly identified three factors in all samples representing social competence, anger-aggression, and anxiety-withdrawal. A basic division between two broad types of emotional/behavioral disorders has been extensively verified in childhood and adolescence (Achenbach & Edelbrock, 1981, 1986; Peterson, 1961; Quay, 1979, 1983), and more recently has been shown to characterize emotional problems in preschoolers as well (Achenbach et al., 1987; LaFreniere et al., 1992, 1995).

From the standpoint of parents, teachers, clinicians, and the children themselves, the most readily apparent type of adjustment problem to the preschool classroom involves an inability to tolerate frustration, regulate anger, and control aggressive behavior. This type of problem is referred to as conduct disorder, externalizing behavioral problem, or undercontrolled behavior, depending upon the theoretical orientation of the investigator. A second basic type also has a long history of systematic investigation and is referred to variously as affective disorder, internalizing behavioral problem, or overcontrolled behavior. Children who illustrate this second type of problem often withdraw from social contact in the face of distress or high levels of emotional arousal and may inhibit behavioral and emotional expression when aroused.

The anger-aggression scale of the SCBE may be considered as a preschool equivalent of previous broadband syndromes labeled variously as conduct disorder or externalizing symptoms. The items on this scale describe angry, aggressive, selfish, and oppositional behaviors. Emotion regulation and affective expression were shown to be as central as aggressive behavior to this scale. Indeed, the item with the highest factor loading in all samples was "irritable, gets mad easily," and poor frustration tolerance and defiance were among the other high loadings. Children with extreme scores on this scale tend to express their negative emotions in ways that hurt or at least disturb others. They function poorly in social situations, where they require almost constant supervision, often to protect others from their outbursts. The angry-aggressive group was found to be the most interactive with peers, but also the most rejected, results that correspond precisely with theoretical expectations, since aggression is a well-known behavioral correlate of peer rejection across a wide age span (Asher & Dodge, 1986; Coie, Dodge, & Kupersmidt, 1990; LaFreniere & Sroufe, 1985).

The anxiety-withdrawal scale of the SCBE is composed of items describing anxious, depressed, isolated, and overly dependent behavior. The emotional items on this scale describe a child who is often sad, worried, timid, afraid, and who rarely smiles or laughs during play with peers. It is similar to previous broadband indices labeled as affective disorder or internalizing symptoms, though somatic complaints, eating and sleeping irregularities, and similar problems were not included in the item list because of the preschool context of the evaluation. In previous validation research, the anxious-withdrawn group was observed to be significantly less interactive than all other groups, though not necessarily neglected or rejected by their peers. However, anxious-withdrawn preschoolers spent much of their time in activities on the periphery of group life, such as onlooking and parallel play, and were also prone to be alone and unoccupied. In keeping with the pattern of affective and behavioral signs of maladjustment, children with extreme scores on this scale are seen by their teachers as sad, depressed, tired, and worried, as well as isolated. They show little interest in the activities in which their peers typically delight. These children tend to have poor self-concepts and to show high levels of immaturity, as they often seek adult attention in situations that do not require it, and find it difficult to perform tasks within their capabilities without regular assurance, giving up easily where others would persist.

The social competence scale of the SCBE taps a broad range of behaviors designed to assess the positive qualities of the child's adaptation, rather than specific behavioral competencies. As a developmental construct, social competence refers to behaviors that indicate a well-adjusted, flexible, emotionally mature, and generally prosocial pattern of social adaptation (Waters & Sroufe, 1983). The emotional items on this scale emphasize emotion regulation, including the child's ability to remain calm during conflict, show pride and pleasure in his or her own accomplishments, accept compromises cheerfully, and demonstrate empathic awareness of other children's needs and goals. Not surprisingly, the socially competent group received the most positive nominations and the least negative nominations from peers, and was highest in sociometric status (LaFreniere & Dumas, 1996). Because of its qualitative dimension, sociometric status is one of the most robust correlates of teacher ratings of social competence in preschoolers. Our research has consistently shown that socially competent preschoolers score high on assessments of ego resiliency, show cooperation and affective perspective-taking with peers, express high levels of positive affect and relatively low levels of negative affect during peer interaction, are popular with their peers, and are appreciated by their teachers (Janosz & LaFreniere, 1991; LaFreniere & Charlesworth, 1983; LaFreniere & Sroufe, 1985; Sroufe, Schork, Motti, Lawroski, & LaFreniere, 1984).

Given the extensive and diverse samples of children evaluated using the SCBE, these data are particularly robust with respect to age and gender differences (see Figure 7.8). Developmental trends toward a gradual increase in social competence for boys and girls are clearly evident in all samples. Children aged 5 and 6 are more able to take the perspective of another child into account and more likely to settle disputes through negotiation rather than aggression. They also show more attention, nurturance and assistance to younger peers, and are more willing to cooperate with the teacher and help out with everyday tasks. All of these changes in social behavior reflect underlying affective and cognitive advances.

Similarly, as shown in Figure 7.9, angry and aggressive behaviors showed a clear decline across this age range. Instrumental aggression is one aspect of behavior that decreases as children learn negotiation and emotion regulation skills. With each advancing year, preschoolers show less frequent displays of temper tantrums, defiance, and frustration over not getting their way. They appear to be better able to tolerate frustration and control their anger, and may verbalize their displeasure rather whine, yell, or scream. Despite using teachers, rather than parents, as informants, these results appear to be very similar to those found by Goodenough over 65 years ago.

In contrast to these dramatic age changes, anxious-withdrawn behavior appears to show more subtle age changes, with girls and boys showing a modest, though significant, decline in these behaviors over the preschool years (see Figure 7.10).

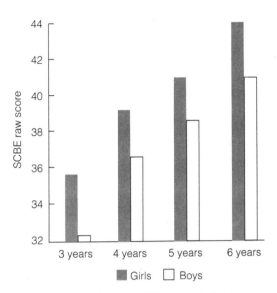

Figure 7.8 Age and gender differences in the Social Competence SCBE scale.

Source: LaFreniere and Dumas (1996).

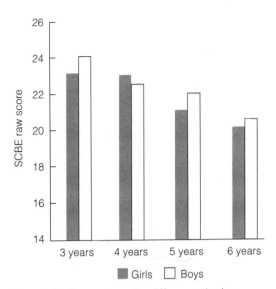

Figure 7.10 Age and gender differences in the anxiety-withdrawal SCBE scale.

Source: LaFreniere and Dumas (1996).

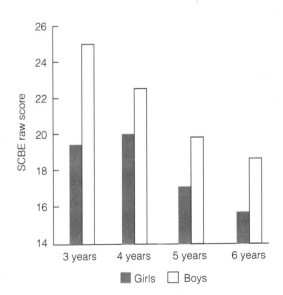

Figure 7.9 Age and gender differences in the anger-aggression SCBE scale.

Source: LaFreniere and Dumas (1996).

In agreement with much previous data was the evidence of significant sex differences. Boys were consistently rated substantially higher on measures of anger-aggression and lower on social competence than girls, though no sample showed any sex difference in anxiety-withdrawal. Taken together these results would appear to indicate that boys are, on the whole, not as well adapted to the preschool environment as girls, at least from the teacher's standpoint. It should be noted that over 95 percent of the teachers, from the several hundred programs that provided these data, were female, a proportion that is representative of pre-school programs in North America. This may be important in terms of a female bias in the ratings of the children's behavior and/or in the construction of a classroom environment that may be more suitable to girls than boys. Alternatively, other socialization factors from parents or peers, or underlying genetic differences between males and females, may account for these differences. These issues will be discussed briefly in the next section.

SEX DIFFERENCES IN EMOTIONS AND PEER RELATIONS

Many psychologists believe that both biology and socialization, particularly gene–environment interactions, are likely sources for behavioral differences between girls and boys. Although there is ample evidence for the influence of sex steroid hormones on the emotional states of adult men and women, much less information is available on infants and children. One of the few studies that examined this question was the Stanford longitudinal study conducted by Maccoby, Jacklin, and their associates (Marcus, Maccoby, Jacklin, & Doering, 1985). In this study, mothers filled out diaries on their child's emotional state throughout 24-hour periods during the first two years of life. These maternal reports were analyzed with respect to five sex steroid hormones (testosterone, andostenedione, estrone, estradiol, and progesterone) assayed from each child's umbilical cord blood. The influence of sex hormones on emotional mood was dependent on the sex of the child. The authors found that boys were more often reported by their mothers to be happy/excited and girls as quiet/calm, with no sex differences for irritability and negative moods. Individual scores for happy/excited and quiet/calm moods were found to be quite stable. The authors conclude that these differences are due to the *organizing* effects of sex hormones during prenatal development. As we shall discuss in Chapter 10, the *activating* effect of sex hormones is not present until puberty, the biological event that signals the onset of adolescence. Throughout early and middle childhood, the levels of circulating hormones do not differ much, if at all, between the sexes, and as a result, biosocial theories predict fewer biologically based sex differences during this period than after puberty (Geary, 1998).

There are, however, several well-documented exceptions to this prediction. The clearest evidence for direct influence of sex hormones on behavior in humans (and nonhuman primates) may be found in research on sex differences in play during early childhood (Collaer & Hines, 1995). In preindustrial and industrial societies, a general pattern of results emerges showing sex differences in rough-and-tumble play favoring boys and play parenting favoring girls. For example, in an American sample of preschoolers, DiPietro (1981) found that boys engaged in rough-and-tumble play involving playful pushing, shoving, hitting, tripping, wrestling, and so on four to five times as often as girls. Moreover, prenatal exposure to higher levels of androgen in girls is related to increased physical competition and play (Geary, 1998). Cross-cultural research indicates that although the magnitude of these sex differences varies across cultures, the direction of the differences is constant (Eibl-Eibesfeldt, 1989; Maccoby, 1988; Whiting & Edwards, 1988). For example, Whiting and Edwards (1988) studied social development in Guatemala, India, Japan, Kenya, Liberia, Mexico, Peru, the Phillipines, and the United States. They concluded that two sex differences were common across these diverse cultures: girls were found to be more nurturant than boys, and boys engaged in more dominance behavior than girls. As we discussed in Chapter 2, these same differences are found in different species of nonhuman primates, such as rhesus macaques. And most importantly, they are predictable from parental investment theory.

The details of the behavioral ecologies of boys and girls are important to understand because of the role of peers in the socialization of gender differences in emotional expression and emotion regulation. Universally, children begin to sort themselves into sex-segregated enclaves beginning at about 3 years, which also marks the emergence of **gender identity,** or the recognition by the child of his or her own gender as an enduring quality of the self. Prior to establishing sex-segregated play groups, girls and boys begin to develop sex differences in toy preferences. Toddlers show distinct sex differences in toy choices before they have established a stable gender identity or can accurately label toys as "boy

Figure 7.11 Rough-and-tumble play is more common among boys than girls.

(Photos by LaFreniere)

things" or "girl things" (Blakemore, LaRue, & Olejnik, 1979; Fagot, Leinbach, & Hagan, 1986). As early as 14 months girls are selecting dolls and soft toys while boys are choosing trucks and cars (Caldera et al., 1989; Smith & Daglish, 1977). To the extent that preferences for certain types of toys and activities are distinct between girls and boys, they may begin to associate more often with same-sex peers on the basis of these similarities.

One study that addressed the origin of same-sex preferences found that by 2 years of age, girls are already beginning to prefer same-sex peers while boys do not show a similar preference until age 3 (LaFreniere, Strayer, & Gauthier, 1984). These data, derived from extensive observations of peer play in 15 different children's groups, may possibly reflect avoidance of boys by girls, rather than preference for same-sex peers. This reasoning is based on a wide array of observational and experimental evidence in the nature and quality of play in groups of girls and boys, as well as negative sociometric nominations of boys by girls. Whatever the underlying causes of gender segregation during the preschool years, as same-sex play becomes increasingly evident, a number of differences emerge between the sexes.

According to Hartup (1989), sex differences in social and emotional behavior and peer relationships in childhood should not be dismissed

lightly, as male and female "cultures" appear to differ in many ways. Researchers have generally found that boys are more physically active, engage in more risk-taking and rough-and-tumble play, and exhibit more anger and aggression toward peers than girls (Benenson, 1996; Christophersen, 1989; DiPietro, 1981; Eaton & Yu, 1989; Ginsburg & Miller, 1982; Humpreys & Smith, 1987; Maccoby & Jacklin, 1974; MacDonald, 1987; Marcus, Maccoby, Jacklin, & Doehring, 1985; Money & Ehrhardt, 1972; Parke & Slaby, 1983; Strayer & Strayer, 1976; Tieger, 1980). From the point of view of most young girls, these sex-typed behaviors are all good reasons to avoid groups of boys. In addition, boys tend to play in larger groups (Eder & Hallinan, 1978), occupy more space, control more resources (Charlesworth & LaFreniere, 1983), and are more likely to do all of these things away from adult supervision than are girls (Carpenter, Huston, & Holt, 1986). In contrast, girls engage in more dyadic play than boys (Benenson, 1993) and prefer the company of their mostly female preschool teachers more than do boys, although one study found that girls' preference to remain nearer to adults was evident only when boys were present (Greeno, 1989).

In laboratory studies with the adults absent, investigators have consistently found that boys are not very responsive to verbal prohibitions and requests that are directed to them by girls (or by other boys), and boys use these strategies to obtain resources much less than girls in both same- and mixed-sex groups. The picture that emerges from a combination of naturalistic and experimental studies is one of limited but systematic sexual dimorphism in social behavior and emotional expression that is well established by early childhood and increases thereafter. These sex differences in children's social and expressive behavior are apparent if one compares the behavior of girls and boys in mixed-sex groupings (Charlesworth & LaFreniere, 1983; Jacklin & Maccoby, 1978; LaFreniere & Charlesworth, 1987; Powlishta & Maccoby, 1990), or if one compares the behavior of groups of girls with that of groups of boys (Charlesworth & Dzur, 1987; Jacklin & Maccoby, 1978).

If early sex-segregated play reflects girls' avoidance of boys, by the end of the preschool years, preference for same-sex peers is transformed into clear avoidance of crossing the gender divide for both boys and girls. Not only do preschoolers prefer to spend more time in the company of same-sex friends, they also express the belief that their own sex is better than the other (Kuhn, Nash, & Brucken, 1978). This belief is present as soon as gender identity is established and appears to increase throughout childhood (Serbin, Powlishta, & Gulko, 1993). Similarly, segregation between the sexes increases throughout early childhood. By age 4 the ratio of same-sex to opposite-sex peer play has increased to 3:1, and by age six it has climbed to more than 10:1 (Maccoby, 1988). The preference for same-sex peers is also reflected in children's affiliations and friendship choices. Several naturalistic studies of preschoolers' stable friendship relations have found that 90 to 95 percent of "strong associates" or close friendships are formed between same-sex peers (Hinde, Titmus, Easton, & Tamplin, 1985; LaFreniere & Charlesworth, 1983). Similarly, sociometric studies reveal that girls and boys rate members of their own sex as more liked in preschool and kindergarten and show increasing sex bias in their sociometric choices throughout middle childhood

(Denham & McKinley, 1993; Hayden-Thomson, Rubin, & Hymel, 1987). As researchers attend to the details of activities of peers, particularly in naturalistic settings with little adult supervision, the types of play and emotional experiences associated with the activities appear to differ substantially between girls and boys, and peers themselves may be contributing substantially to the development and maintenance of these differences. We shall continue our discussion of gender differences in friendships, group dynamics, and emotional experiences in our discussion of adolescent peer relations in Chapter 10.

SUMMARY

In this chapter we reviewed research on the emergence of self-conscious emotions; the growth of competence in emotion recognition, understanding, and regulation; and the development of gender differences related to children's emotional experience. Echoing Darwin, self-conscious emotions are generally seen as arising from the development of two cognitive abilities: self-awareness and the acquisition of rules and standards. The first of these cognitive prerequisites, self-awareness, emerges in humans during the transition from infancy to toddlerhood, whereas the second is acquired more gradually through socialization.

Self-conscious emotions have received only sporadic empirical attention until quite recently. One possible reason has to do with the difficulty of inferring the presence of these emotions. For example, there is no widely recognized species-specific facial expression of shame, nor is there any universal elicitor, at least not in the sense that we have seen with the basic emotions. Instead, blushing, gaze aversion, hanging the head, shrinking and closing of the body, and turning away as if to hide oneself from view are the most central expressive cues.

There is not yet a consensus on the developmental course that best accounts for the emergence of the self-conscious emotions. Some researchers see embarrassment as a precursor to shame, while others view shame as a global precursor to the more specifically focused emotion of guilt. In Sroufe's theory, guilt and pride are not fully developed until the preschool period, though each is seen as arising from a prototype representing a diminution (shame) or swelling (positive self-evaluation) of the self. Such feelings in the toddler require only a rudimentary sense of being bad or good, primarily as a reaction to the caregiver's blame or praise. In contrast, the preschooler has a concept of personal competence and is capable of reacting to the achievement or violation of internalized standards, rather than just external praise or blame.

Guilt is also defined as an emotional response to a keen sense of having violated one's own internalized standards, and thus may occur in private. Researchers have demonstrated that delay of gratification and compliance to prohibition are possible in the parents' absence in young preschoolers. Preschool children often refuse to violate the parents' prohibitions and may seek to repair the relationship (and reduce guilt) by confessing to the parents if violations do occur. Moreover, they engage in attempts to make reparations to peers after aggressive outbursts.

Not all researchers include empathy in the class of self-conscious emotions. It is clearly a social emotion, since in its mature form it implies that the child has learned to distinguish between self and other and to recognize another's emotional state. Before these abilities emerge, there is a clear precursor of empathy that may be observed early in the empathic arousal of the newborn to other babies' cries, a phenomenon that may be more characteristic of females than males. Hoffman views this contagion of negative affect as a precursor to empathy because it is experienced through very basic arousal modes, and is involuntary and global. In a second stage, advances in self-awareness lead to the ability to more clearly differentiate between self and other and the onset of an egocentric form of empathy. By the third stage, the young preschooler is developing the capacity for perspective-taking and

becomes more aware that another's feelings may differ from one's own and that these feelings are based on the other's needs, which may be different than one's own.

Eisenberg, Fabes, and colleagues distinguish between personal distress and sympathetic concern on the basis of psychophysiological, facial, and vocalic expressions. Personal distress shares some of the characteristics associated with fear, including heart rate acceleration, whereas sympathetic concern is associated with heart rate deceleration. These researchers report that sympathetic concern (which may include sadness) is linked with prosocial behavior, whereas personal distress is not. They propose that an optimal level of arousal will most likely lead to sympathetic concern and prosocial behavior. Too little arousal is not expected to provide sufficient motivation, whereas too high arousal may lead the child to experience distress and to avoid its source. In their view, the key to responding helpfully to another's distress is the child's ability to modulate his or her emotional reaction to enable the child to focus attention on the person in distress rather than on his or her own distress.

In addition to the emergence of self-conscious emotions, cognitive growth during the period of early childhood supports a number of other significant advances in emotional functioning. With the development of linguistic skills, preschoolers reveal a new understanding of their emotional experiences as well as those of others. These increases in the child's awareness and understanding of emotion were discussed in terms of the child's ability to recognize and label emotional expressions, to talk about emotions, and to understand their causes and consequences. Many developmental psychologists believe that talking about internal feeling states is important because it is related to do the child's emerging ability to coordinate emotion with cognition and behavior in resolving challenging social situations.

Other changes that take place during the preschool years signal advances in emotion regulation. Emotion regulation generally refers to the processes by which children monitor and control their emotional states and the expression of these states to adapt to different social situations or demands. Preschoolers show a gradual decline in anger, frustration, defiance, and tantrum behavior and a rise in social competence and prosocial behavior. During the preschool years, children learn to direct and monitor their own behavior, to resist temptations and inhibit behaviors, and to use language and affect to persuade others to meet their emotional needs and goals.

Age and gender differences in preschool children's emotion regulation and social competence reflect these various advances, particularly the ability to regulate emotions during social interaction with peers. Gender differences in the emotional experiences of girls and boys are substantial and are consistent with evolutionary models, with boys exhibiting more anger and aggression than girls, and girls exhibiting more nurturance and empathy than boys. During the preschool years both sexes prefer the company of same-sex peers and spend increasingly more time in sex-segregated play groups. Socialization within these somewhat separate cultures of boys' and girls' peer groups appears to contribute significantly to later gender differences in social and emotional behavior.

FURTHER READING

Eisenberg, N. (1992). *The caring child*. Cambridge, MA: Harvard University Press.

This book provides a comprehensive account of research on empathy and its development from one of the leading researchers on the topic.

Lewis, M. (1993). Self-conscious emotions: Embarrassment, pride, shame, and guilt. In M. Lewis & J. Haviland (Eds.), *The handbook of emotions* (pp. 563–573). New York: Guilford.

This chapter provides a useful overview and introduction to the early development of self-conscious emotions.

Tangney, J., & Fischer, K. (Eds.). (1995). *Self-conscious emotions: The psychology of shame, guilt, embarrassment, and pride*. New York: Guilford.

This is an up-to-date reference book on a rapidly emerging area of research dealing with self-conscious emotions.

8

Individual Differences
in Emotional Styles
in Early Childhood

Biological Influences

Temperament Framework

Evolutionary Framework

   Five-Factor Model of Personality

   Gene–Environment Interaction

**Environmental Influences:
The Role of Parents**

Attachment Framework

   Emotional Challenges
   of the Toddler Period

   Preschool Adaptation

Social Learning Framework

Attributional Framework

Integrating Perspectives

**Environmental Influences:
The Role of Peers**

Function of Peer Interaction in Primates

Preschool Peer Relations

   Naturalistic Observation

   Analog Situations

   Peer Sociometrics

The Role of Affect in Peer Competence

There is in every child at every stage a new miracle of vigorous unfolding, which constitutes a new hope and a new responsibility for all. Such is the sense and the pervading quality of initiative. The criteria for all these senses and qualities is the same: a crisis, more or less beset with fumbling and fear, is resolved, in that the child suddenly seems to "grow together" both in his person and in his body. He appears "more himself," more loving, relaxed and brighter in his judgment, more activated and activating. He is in free possession of a surplus of energy which permits him to forget failures quickly and to approach what seems desirable (even if it also seems uncertain and even dangerous) with undiminished and more accurate direction.

Initiative adds to autonomy the quality of undertaking, planning and "attacking" a task for the sake of being active and on the move, where before self-will, more often than not, inspired acts of defiance or, at any rate, protested independence.

ERIK ERIKSON (1963)

The preschool classroom is an ideal vantage point for observing the child's emerging personality in action. A striking feature of free play in the classroom or playground is the tremendous diversity in the patterns of social interaction and emotional expression among children of the same age range. Consider the first day of school at a typical laboratory preschool at a university. One child comes bursting through the door while her father hurries to catch up. She is eager to enter the classroom and runs immediately to an attractive set of toys in the middle of the room. As the children continue to arrive, she becomes the center of a high level of social activity, greeting her friends with excitement and invitations to join in her play. A second child arrives at the threshold of the classroom holding her mother's hand and looking about anxiously at all the commotion. With her mother's reassurance she is able to move to a quiet part of the classroom and begin playing with legos arranged on a tabletop. She does not appear to be greatly absorbed in the play, but glances about the room to observe what else is happening, while continually monitoring her mother's position. As her mother signals her intention to depart, the child rushes toward her and bursts into tears.

Systematic observation reveals that preschoolers bring to the new experience of the classroom distinct personalities and characteristic patterns of emotionality. These individual differences in emotional styles are apparent to teachers and other observers from the very first day in the preschool and can be assessed via a variety of observational methods, teacher rating scales, and other indirect methods. In this chapter we shall describe these characteristic patterns of emotionality and explore the wide range of answers to the basic question: What makes these children so different from one another?

In the first section on biological influences, we explore longitudinal studies of one aspect of temperament, behavioral inhibition, and examine its stability and different manifestations across time and in different settings. Next, an evolutionary account of personality differences is presented that postulates that gene complexes evolved to construct different types of personalities in order to serve adaptive functions. Different types of evidence from comparative, genetic, neurological, developmental, and cross-cultural research in support of an evolutionary psychology of personality are reviewed. Finally, we examine transactional models and illustrate how gene–environment interactions can account for individual differences in children's social, emotional, and personality development in early childhood.

The second section on environmental influences explores three theoretical approaches concerning the role of parents in the child's emotional development: (1) attachment theory emphasizing primary relationships as the principal context of development for toddlers and preschoolers; (2) social learning theory emphasizing parents as socializing agents, and the role of reinforcement, punishment, and modeling on behavior and

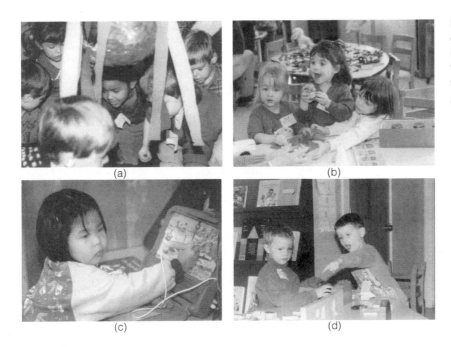

(a)

(b)

(c)

(d)

Figure 8.1 Preschoolers exhibit striking individual differences from the first day of school.

(Photos by LaFreniere)

development; and (3) attributional models that examine the effects of parents' causal attributions of child behavior on affective expression and socialization.

The final section on the role of peers emphasizes a multitheoretical approach as well. Ethologists, social learning theorists, and cognitive-developmental psychologists have all emphasized the function of peers in promoting competent behavior, by providing unique experiences that promote affective development through vigorous play, facilitate the regulation of aggressive behavior by the establishment of dominance hierarchies and modes of conflict resolution, stimulate perspective-taking and social problem-solving skills, and contribute to the acquisition of culturally defined social skills, emotional display rules, and gender roles. In this section we shall emphasize the methods used by researchers to describe how children differ in the emotional qualities of their peer relations, as well as discuss the processes of peer socialization that may contribute to these differences.

BIOLOGICAL INFLUENCES

Temperament Framework

Although the early work of Thomas, Chess, and others conceptualized temperament in terms of dimensions, more recent work, such as that of Jerome Kagan and his associates, has adopted a typological approach. In their longitudinal study focusing on the developmental and biological aspects of one particular aspect of temperament, **behavioral inhibition,** Kagan's group outlined a new approach to the study of temperament. In contrast with earlier studies that relied on parental reports of different dimensions of the child's functioning, Kagan chose to rely upon systematic observation of children's behavior to investigate individual patterns of behavior and physiology that could be categorized into two distinct types representing about half of the population (Kagan, Reznick, & Gibbons, 1989; Kagan, Reznick, & Snidman, 1986, 1988).

The first type, behaviorally inhibited children, comprise between 15 and 20 percent of the population and show characteristic patterns of fearful responses to novelty and uncertainty and varying degrees of sympathetic arousal. In contrast, the second type of uninhibited children eagerly engage new people and objects in unfamiliar environments and do not show sympathetic arousal. This type is more common with estimates as high as 25 to 40 percent. The basic research strategy has been to identify children at either extreme of this dimension and reassess them at different ages in order to understand how variable or stable these patterns of behavior are over time and across different situations.

In the initial study, 117 twenty-one-month-old children were observed in unfamiliar situations with unfamiliar people. Some of the children ($n = 28$) were consistently quiet, vigilant, restrained, and avoidant in response to the unfamiliar and were labeled behaviorally inhibited. These children remained near their mothers and avoided interacting with the unfamiliar adult for long periods. They were also distinguished by retreating from unfamiliar objects and by low levels of play and vocalization. Another group ($n = 30$) was not observed to exhibit these behaviors consistently across two different occasions (Kagan, Reznick, Snidman, Gibbons, & Johnson, 1988).

These same children were assessed again at age 4 (43 children), 5 1/2 (46 children), and 8 1/2 years (41 children) in order to investigate the stability of inhibited and uninhibited behavior. In general, moderate stability was found across the preschool age range, though Kagan noted less consistency between 5 1/2 and 8 1/2 years of age. At age 4, as in the initial testing, there was a significant association between inhibited behavior and high heart rate while solving a challenging problem (Garcia-Coll, Kagan, & Reznick, 1984). At 5 1/2 years, inhibited children were less talkative and less interactive in three different social settings involving an adult, an unfamiliar child of the same age and sex, and the child's school setting (Reznick et al., 1986). Kagan notes that different situations seem to reveal behavioral inhibition more readily than others, depending upon the child's age. At age 4, meeting an unfamiliar child for the first time with both mothers present provides a sensitive barometer of behavioral inhibition, but less so as the child matures. By age 5 and 6, behavior with an unfamiliar adult in a testing situation is a better marker of inhibited behavior, and at 7 years a large group of unfamiliar children provides a sensitive assessment.

In Kagan's view, it is not reasonable to expect that differences in temperament be expressed as stable behaviors regardless of context. Rather, temperament is viewed as an inborn pattern of behavior and physiology that is moderately stable for some individuals in certain specifiable contexts. In general, it would appear that the characteristic emotional tone of the child becomes notably more stable during the toddler/preschool period than during infancy. Both positive and negative affective expression become relatively more stable at this time (Bates, 1989; Rothbart, 1989). Of course, in demonstrating that a given behavior pattern is moderately stable in the preschool years, there is no logical basis for identifying the source of the stability as either nature or nurture. The genetic contribution to such stability in behavioral inhibition can only be addressed by behavior genetic studies. As seen in Chapter 5, twin studies reveal a genetic basis for inhibited behavior and shyness (Emde et al., 1992), though they also suggest an important role for environmental factors. Because behavioral genetics research on temperament clearly indicates the presence of genes operating on the development of neural and neurochemical structures, psychobiological models of inherited temperament and personality traits must consider the evolutionary basis and adaptive significance of these individual differences. In the next section we review evolutionary models of personality as species-typical systems that serve adaptive functions.

Evolutionary Framework

Personality theorists like Eysenck (1967), Gray (1982), and Panksepp (1982, 1998) have developed models linking personality with basic neurological systems of approach, affiliation and reward seeking, and avoidance and inhibition. Other personality theorists like Buss (1995), MacDonald (1998), and Plutchik (1980, 1991) have developed evolutionary perspectives of personality that address the question of why genetically determined personality traits exist in the first place. According to an **adaptationist approach,** gene complexes would have evolved to construct different types of personalities only if important adaptive functions were served in the human environment of evolutionary adaptedness.

Five-Factor Model of Personality Three types of evidence have been presented in previous chapters that provide qualified support for an evolutionary psychology of personality. First, comparative research has shown evidence for similar systems in animals that serve clear adaptive functions (see Chapter 2). Second, neurological research has shown evidence for a structural basis of these systems in the brain (see Chapter 2). Third, developmental research indicates the presence of recognizable precursors of the "Big Five" personality traits in infancy (see Chapter 5).

The term *Big Five* refers to the view that the major dimensions of personality can be accounted for by just five factors, referred to as the **five-factor model** (FFM). Most of the well-known personality inventories, including Cattell's, Eysenck's, and the MMPI, can be reduced through factor analysis to five major factors or a subset of the these factors. The Big Five personality dimensions are usually named for one end of the continuum they represent:

1. *Extroverted:* gregarious, sociable, dominant, adventurous

2. *Agreeable:* affectionate, warm, kind, friendly

3. *Conscientious:* organized, planful, reliable

4. *Stable:* calm, worry free, stable

5. *Open:* original, insightful, inventive, wide-ranging interests

Several important research findings concerning these five personality traits concern us here, particularly (1) the link between infant temperament and personality, (2) the cross-cultural universality of the FFM, and (3) the heritability of FFM personality traits. Four of the five factors have been linked with temperament dimensions, suggesting significant conceptual overlap between temperament and personality. Temperament research in early childhood yields a number of factors that map directly onto the FFM dimensions of extroversion, agreeableness, emotional stability, and conscientiousness. These results appear to be robust in the sense that though different temperament questionnaires yielded different factors, they were consistently linked with the FFM dimensions (Rothbart & Bates, 1998).

As more studies are conducted using the FFM, there is increasing evidence of its universality across different cultures, though more data are required to make this assertion. The five-factor structure has been replicated in many different linguistic groups using a variety of different instruments over the past 50 years (Rothbart & Bates, 1998; Rowe, 1994). Together, the early appearance of temperamental traits linked to the FFM, and the apparent universality of the FFM across many different cultures, suggest an evolutionary basis for individual variation in temperament and personality.

In addition, several personality systems identified by the FFM are thought to be sex-differentiated, reflecting asymmetries in reproductive strategies of males and females. Evolutionary psychologists propose that gender differences in personality systems may be understood as evolved affective-motivational systems that represent a range of alternative strategies for attaining universal human goals related to enhancing survival and reproduction (Buss, 1996; Daly & Wilson, 1978; MacDonald, 1998). **Parental investment theory** predicts that males will generally pursue relatively high-risk strategies compared to females, and thus will be higher in **behavioral approach systems** (BAS) (dominance/sensation seeking, risk-taking, impulsivity) and lower on **behavioral inhibition systems** (BIS) (fear, wariness, caution, safety seeking) (MacDonald, 1998). Consequently, one contribution to the study of individual differences in emotion and personality may be early gender differentiation in patterns of approach and avoidance behavior.

Ethologists report different patterns of sex differences in different species, but the pattern of sex differences is by no means arbitrary. In general, sex-typical patterns of courtship and mating are highly dimorphic across species and adaptively related to species-typical reproductive strategies and parental division of labor. Neurological and behavioral propensities of the two sexes begin to diverge during the embryonic stage of development due to the organizing influence of gonadal hormones. These developments depend upon further environmental support and the later activating influence of sex hormones at puberty before the mature adult behaviors emerge (Daly & Wilson, 1978; Geary, 1998).

Primates vary considerably in their social ecologies, reproductive strategies, and degree of sexual dimorphism. Even within a species, subspecies may differ as a function of regional ecological constraints and opportunities (Kummer, 1971). In general the life histories of females and males in any given species are quite different. With these points in mind, let us examine typical sex differences in one species that has received much scientific attention, rhesus monkeys.

Sex differences among rhesus monkeys are typically relative rather than absolute, with some overlap between the sexes. For example, compared to male age-mates, young females spend considerably more time in the presence of adult females, and at sexual maturity they remain with their mothers, sisters, aunts, and daughters for the rest of their lives. Female rhesus monkeys show considerably more interest in young infants and engage in allo parenting, or play parenting, throughout their juvenile years much more than males (Geary, 1998; Pryce, 1995). The functional significance of this type of play is apparent in primates, as research in many species shows that the chances of survival of the monkey's firstborn offspring are two to more than four times higher for mothers with previous experience in early infant care. Finally, daughters are socialized differently by their mothers. For example, female rhesus monkeys hold their daughters closer and show more concern if they should wander, compared to male offspring (Lindburg, 1971, and Mitchell & Brandt, 1972, as cited in Hinde, 1974).

In contrast, rhesus mothers will more often direct displays of anger toward a male offspring, and males are weaned at an earlier age. Young male rhesus monkeys spend more time in the company of peers, often without the mother close by; engage in high-energy games of chasing and play fighting; and leave their natal troop at sexual maturity. From an evolutionary standpoint, these aggressive displays are costly, since they involve a high expenditure of energy and risk of injury. Although females do not shun this rough-and-tumble play entirely, they participate rarely and with less energy. As adults, male rhesus monkeys engage in more aggression than females, who generally avoid aggression and direct competition (de Waal, 1996).

Monkey infants of both sexes begin to prefer the company of same-sex peers at an early age, and among juveniles, sex segregation is the rule (Rosenblum, Coe, & Bromley, 1975). Although differential maternal and peer socialization of male and female monkeys certainly supports the divergence in behaviors between the sexes, longitudinal research of isolated rhesus monkeys also demonstrates sex differences in behavior (Harlow & Harlow, 1962, 1965; Sackett, 1970).

Developmental research in humans has also produced a wealth of evidence that is generally consistent with predictions derived from parental investment theory. Research relevant to the BAS or the FFM trait of extroversion has consistently demonstrated that compared with girls, boys are more physically active from an early age (Eaton & Yu, 1989; Marcus, Maccoby, Jacklin, & Doehring, 1985; Money & Ehrhardt, 1972; Parke & Slaby, 1983); more assertive (Parke & Slaby, 1983); more aggressive, competitive, and dominant with peers

(LaFreniere et al., 1983, 1992; Maccoby & Jacklin, 1974, 1980; Strayer & Strayer, 1976); and more oppositional with adults (LaFreniere et al., 1992). Boys are also more likely to take physical risks (Christophersen, 1989; Ginsburg & Miller, 1982) and to engage in more rough-and-tumble play (DiPietro, 1981; Humphreys & Smith, 1987) and more high-energy sociodramatic play involving guns and superheroes (Huston, 1983, 1987; Paley, 1984).

In contrast, research on the BIS and the FFM trait of agreeableness has shown that preschool girls are more compliant to parents and teachers, and rated by them as more socially competent (LaFreniere et al., 1992; Maccoby, 1988). Girls rate themselves as more fearful, timid, nurturant, and empathic than boys (Lennon & Eisenberg, 1987; Maccoby, 1988), and girls tend to show more interest in and are more responsive toward infants than are boys (Blakemore, 1981, 1993; Reid, Tate, & Berman, 1989). Parental ratings indicate that when sex differences are found in fearfulness and timidity, parents rate girls as more fearful than boys (Buss & Plomin, 1975; Maccoby & Jacklin, 1974), and girls are more cautious in situations involving risks, as already noted. All data derived from indirect sources must be interpreted cautiously and wherever possible validated against direct observation, since the gender biases of the raters (parents, teachers, or children) cannot be ruled out. For example, unlike ratings, observational data do not show systematic sex differences in empathy and prosocial behavior, and in some situations boys or men are more likely to offer assistance than girls or women (Eagly & Crowley, 1986; Fabes, Eisenberg, & Miller, 1990).

It is also apparent that when systematic differences between the sexes are well documented, as in the list of differences just presented, in most cases it remains true that boys and girls are more alike than different. In other words, mean differences between girls and boys on some trait or behavior mask the fact that there is generally more variation within gender than between gender groups. However, when scientists examine the extreme tips of the normal distributions of the two sexes for various traits, it is often the case that extreme groups are heavily skewed by gender. For example, sex differences in aggression have been extensively documented and are consistently found despite differences in method and sampling. A meta-analysis of laboratory studies using highly artificial measures of aggression with poor ecological validity nevertheless revealed a clear asymmetry, but gender alone accounted for only 5 percent of the total individual variation in the measures (Hyde, 1984). Perhaps gender is not so important after all. However, in the United States, 80 percent of all children diagnosed with conduct disorder are boys (Richman, Stevenson, & Graham, 1982; Rutter & Garmezy, 1983), 85 percent of all violent crimes by adolescents are perpetrated by boys, and over 90 percent of all murders are committed by men (FBI crime reports, 1997). Measures derived from real-life data rather than indirect psychological tests certainly do not lead one to conclude that gender is trivial or irrelevant to understanding how individuals differ. Nevertheless, an astonishing number of psychologists ignore real-world indices like FBI murder rates in favor of statistics based on hypothetical indices of aggression that lack any demonstrable **ecological validity,** that is, they do not relate to the real world at all. If FBI crime statistics tell us year in and year out, and all available cross-cultural, cross-species data converge in indicating that 80 to 90 percent of physical aggression is perpetrated by males, only a well-insulated ivory tower academician can insist that gender is unrelated to aggression.

The final and most crucial requirement for an evolutionary psychology of individual differences in personality concerns the genetic transmission of such traits. From this perspective, individual variation in personality traits must be shown to be heritable to some extent or the argument of a biological basis falls apart. Twin studies provide the critical test. In an extensive analysis of different types of kinships gathered from the entire world literature, Loehlin and colleagues provide compelling evidence for genetic influences on

Table 8.1 Parameter Estimates for Big Five Personality Dimensions

Dimension	Unshared Environment	Broad-Sense h^2	Narrow-Sense h^2	Siblings' Shared Environment
I. Extraversion	.49	.49	.32	.02
II. Agreeableness	.52	.39	.29	.09
III. Conscientiousness	.55	.40	.22	.05
IV. Emotional stability	.52	.41	.27	.07
V. Intellectual openness	.49	.45	.43	.06
Mean	.51	.43	.31	.06

NOTE: Adapted from Loehlin & Rowe (1992). Copyright 1992 by Harvester Wheatsheaf.

personality (Loehlin, 1992; Loehlin & Rowe, 1992). Their analysis includes a diverse range of behavior genetic research designs including MZ and DZ twins reared apart and together, and adoptive and biological parent–child and sibling resemblances. The advantages of such an extensive data set can be illustrated by comparing the following correlations for the FFM trait of extroversion: MZ twins reared together (.55); MZ twins reared apart (.38); biological siblings (.20); and unrelated siblings (–.06). Such a pattern is interpreted by behavior geneticists as indicating that individuals who share genes are alike in extroversion regardless of rearing environment, while unrelated individuals reared together show virtually no similarity in the trait (Rowe, 1994). The results of Loehlin and Rowe's analysis for all five of the FFM personality traits are shown in Table 8.1.

Best-fitting models have indicated that two major sources account for much of the individual variation in personality across traits: unshared environment and broad heritability. In contrast, the shared environment of siblings accounts for only 2 to 9 percent of the total variation. Finally, the least amount of influence on personality is the parent–child environmental influence, which is negligible. These findings (and others) should alert social scientists that the "social mold" model of personality development of the 1950s, in which the child's personality was seen as molded by parental behavior, is no longer tenable (Rowe, 1994). Clearly, correlations between child–rearing styles and child personality traits in biological families do not constitute unequivocal evidence for socialization effects, as is often presumed. By themselves correlations can never provide a convincing argument for cause and effect, and in some cases they may be very misleading.

Gene–Environment Interactions In the past, philosophers and scientists often pitted genetic and environmental factors against one another, as if a strong case for one resulted in a weak position for the other. Nativists battled empiricists, and psychologists reformulated these old debates in terms of nature versus nurture. An important theme of this book is that nature and nurture generally collaborate in producing the visible characteristics of the phenotype. Thus far we have presented a strong case for a biological basis of individual differences in personality and socioemotional behavior. But a solid case for heritability in no way undermines the belief that the environment critically influences the development of the child's personality. Rather than viewing genes and environment as separate forces acting on the child, most developmentalists now view genes and the environment as acting together.

An epigenetic perspective considers developmental change as an interactive function of existing structures and the ecology in which these structures are embedded. Behavioral development never takes place in the absence of ecological support. Because the action of genetic material is involved in the metabolic processes of every cell, genetic influence is also relevant to every developmental process. As the Zen Buddhist D. T. Suzuki commented, "once you have taken nature and nurture apart, how will you ever put them back together?" Such processes can be taken apart only in the mind of the theorist or on the page of a text, but never in the day-to-day functioning of the organism in its habitat.

In several influential papers, Sandra Scarr (Scarr, 1992; Scarr & McCartney, 1983) has developed a comprehensive model of the different types of **gene–environment interaction** that construct an individual's phenotypic characteristics like personality traits. The author begins with a position that is universally accepted by developmentalists: a child's phenotype (observable characteristics) is a product of the child's genotype and rearing environment. In Scarr's model, illustrated in Figure 8.2, the child is cast as an active agent in his or her own development, in addition to the genetic contributions of both parents and the shaping influence of the environment that they create for their child.

Three types of genotype–environment effects are proposed: passive, active, and evocative. A **passive effect** refers to the rearing environment provided by genetically related parents. The assumption here is that the parents' genetic characteristics influence what type of environment they create for themselves and their children. Rowe (1994) argues that genes can certainly influence variation in child-rearing styles via their organizing effects on the parents' central nervous systems. He cautions social scientists against overinterpreting environmental influences in studies using biological families that relate parental child rearing with childhood personality traits.

An **active effect** refers to the child's own choices to selectively attend to a specific aspect of the general environment. It is well known that individuals engage in a great deal of active "niche-picking," partly creating their own environment, which in turn influences the course of their development. Scarr proposes that the child's

Models of gene-environment interactions

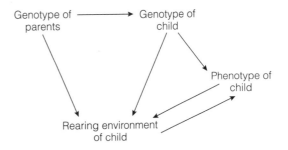

Figure 8.2 Gene-environment interactions

Source: Scarr and McCartney (1983). Adapted with permission from SRCD.

genotype contributes to the choices that the child makes.

Evocative effects refer to the various responses by a child's parents, teachers, peers, and others that are elicited by the child because of some aspect of his or her genotype. For example, if a child who is naturally shy by temperament is overprotected by well-intentioned parents, that child's environment may be substantially different from that of a bold child whose parents provide a wide range of social experiences. Peers as well may cease to initiate contact with a child who is unresponsive to social overtures out of shyness, creating a less stimulating social environment than that evoked by a more gregarious child. Again the question concerning evocative effects is not whether the child influences the responsive social environment (this should be obvious), but whether individuals are responding to *genetically* determined child characteristics.

As we noted earlier in our discussion of temperament, demonstrating stability in a child's temperament or personality does not rule out environmental explanations. Similarly, demonstrating associations between a biological parent's child-rearing style and childhood outcomes does not rule out a genetic contribution to the association, particularly via gene–environment interaction effects. Having established that inborn predispositions are likely to exert a substantial influence on a child's emotional and behavioral styles, let us now examine the environmental origins of individual differences.

ENVIRONMENTAL INFLUENCES: THE ROLE OF PARENTS

In this section on environmental influences, we shall consider the two primary socialization agents of early childhood: parents and peers. We begin our discussion with parents and consider their influence from three theoretical approaches: (1) an attachment model emphasizing primary relationships as the principal context of socioemotional development; (2) a social learning perspective on interaction processes emphasizing the role of reinforcement, punishment, and modeling on development; and (3) attributional models that examine the effects of parents' causal attributions of child behavior on affective expression and socialization.

Attachment Framework

Attachment theorists have proposed that patterns of coregulation established within early social relationships provide an **internal working model** (IWM) for later social relations (Bowlby, 1980, 1988; Sroufe, 1983, 1996). Although there is no firm consensus regarding the processes responsible for such linkages, most developmentalists agree that the infant's relationship with the primary caregivers lays a foundation for subsequent relationships because the attitudes, expectations, and interpersonal skills that the child acquires are carried forward and reintegrated into emerging developmental contexts (LaFreniere & Sroufe, 1985). Competence in one developmental period tends to promote adaptation within that period, while preparing the way for the formation of competence in the next (Sroufe & Rutter, 1984). Because homeostatic mechanisms are inherent to both the family system and the attachment subsystem, family environment and

quality of attachment both tend toward stability, though early deviations are likely to result in greater disturbances later on (Cicchetti, 1990). The child who shows persistent deviations may be assumed to be involved in a continuous maladaptive process. A transactional model implies that a stable manifestation of maladaptation depends on environmental support, while the child's characteristics, reciprocally, partially determine the nature of the environment (Cicchetti & Schneider-Rosen, 1986). Central questions have to do with where such stability resides and how positive change may be realized.

Attachment theorists believe that the child's representational model of the attachment figure is closely interwoven with the child's emerging self-concept, and the child's representation of relationships. For example, Bretherton (1985) argues that "if an attachment figure frequently rejects or ridicules the child's bids for comfort in stressful situations, the child may come to develop not only an internal working model of the parent as rejecting but also one of himself as not worthy of comfort or help" (p. 12). Alternatively, if a child experiences the attachment figure as trustworthy, loving, and sensitive, the child is likely to form a related model of the self as lovable and worthy of help and comfort from others. These inner representations or IWMs are thought to guide the processing of social information, as well as the child's beliefs, attitudes, and feelings about the self and expectations regarding social relationships. Although IWMs remain open to new input as the child encounters new people, they nevertheless tend toward stability because the child actively selects partners and forms new relationships that fit the existing model. According to Bowlby (1980), an IWM will be resistant to change once it is initially constructed, since it tends to operate outside the child's conscious awareness and because new information is assimilated to the existing model. In a new social milieu, the child actively elicits confirmation of the IWM, while often ignoring or discounting counterevidence. Such "self-fulfilling" prophecies may bias a child's socioemotional development positively or negatively by creating developmental pathways that originate with the caregiver's behavior toward the child.

Emotional Challenges of the Toddler Period During the toddler period, the care of children the world over often changes dramatically, typically presenting the child with a wider variety of social partners than during infancy when a few attachment figures dominate. Fathers, who are often much less involved with infant care than mothers, become more central to the socialization of toddlers. They typically provide a somewhat different style of interaction, often involving the child in vigorous physical play, creating new challenges while at the same time providing emotional support (Lamb, 1981; MacDonald, 1987; Parke & Stearns, 1993). In many societies, siblings take on added responsibilities in the care of a younger brother or sister, as well as the role of a sometimes challenging playmate (Dunn & Kendrick, 1982; Tronick, Morelli, & Ivey, 1992). Rudimentary peer interaction also begins during this period in Western societies, with much of the interaction centered around the interesting objects that attract the toddlers' attention in a typical day care center. Other adults besides the parents become more involved, including grandparents and other relatives, day care staff, baby-sitters, and other members of the adult community (Whiting & Edwards, 1988). Despite this increased diversity of social partners, central developmental tasks for this period still involve changes in the ongoing relationship with the primary caregivers.

Developmental theorists such as Ainsworth (Ainsworth et al., 1974), Erikson (1968), Kopp (1982), and Sroufe (1996) view this as a critically important period for the development of an autonomous self-system, capable of independence and initiative, as well as responsiveness and conformity to rules and expectations of others. Because human evolution is rooted in the basic primate patterns of group living and cooperation, Ainsworth believes that children naturally wish to conform to the wishes and expectations of their parents. Because this is a key developmental task,

it is important to examine the quality of its ongoing resolution within the parent–toddler relationship. In Erikson's psychosocial theory of development, successful resolution of the second major stage involving autonomy versus shame and doubt is forecast by the quality of adaptation in the first stage involving basic trust. Furthermore, autonomy is critical to later psychosocial tasks, in part because the newly emerging self is highly sensitive to parental approval/disapproval and emotionally vulnerable. Attachment theorists share this general framework and have begun to provide empirical evidence in support of it.

In contrast to temperament theorists, attachment theorists believe that a child's capacity for emotion regulation is shaped within the child's closest relationships. Sroufe (1996) employs the term *guided self-regulation* to capture the intermediate position of the toddler, between the earlier stage when the dyadic regulation provided mostly by the caregiver predominates, and the later stage when the preschooler achieves true self-regulation. In this intermediate stage, toddlers are learning how to regulate their own emotions and behavior within the limits and guidelines provided by their caregivers. Two important influences on the dynamics of this learning process have been clarified by research: (1) the overall quality of the parent's approach to discipline during the toddler period is more important than any specific child-rearing practice, and (2) the developmental history of the parent–child relationship has a profound impact on the transition toward more autonomous functioning. Let us examine both points in greater detail.

In an earlier era, researchers were primarily interested in knowing which specific child-rearing practices produced beneficial or deleterious results in the child. Freud's stages of psychosexual development viewed the specific issues of weaning and toilet training as critical, but generally researchers have not found that the age at which a child is weaned or toilet trained has any significant impact on personality development. In contrast, Erikson argued that these contexts may be important to the child's development because they provide a context in which the general responsiveness and quality of caregiving is manifest, rather than because of any specific practice per se. Indeed, substantial evidence demonstrates a link between general parenting styles involving warmth and control and later child outcomes (Arend, Gove, & Sroufe, 1979; Baumrind, 1967; Crockenberg & Litman, 1990; Maccoby & Martin, 1983).

In this research variables are often formulated to index qualitative dimensions of parenting that operate across a wide range of different contexts. For example, Sroufe and colleagues view emotional support and quality of assistance as key aspects of parental competence in a problem-solving situation that maximally challenges the 2-year-old's fledging abilities (Matas, Arend, & Sroufe, 1978). Their approach, now widely used by others (Bates et al., 1985; Spiker, Ferguson, & Brooks-Gunn, 1993), involves a series of different situations, each presenting the parent-toddler dyad with a different challenge. The first situation involving free play is minimally challenging, particularly with respect to the issue of autonomy. The next situation, in which the parent has been instructed to interrupt the child's play at a pre-arranged signal and get him or her to put away the toys, is designed to test how smoothly the pair can accommodate a potential conflict of wills. The third situation involves a graded series of physical problems presented from the simplest to the most difficult to ensure that at some point all the children will be taxed beyond their capabilities to solve the problem. This procedure is designed to assess the flexibility of the parent-child dyad, including parental support and guidance, and the child's emotion regulation and motivation.

Toddlers with a history of secure attachment with their mothers were found to be more enthusiastic in this context, expressing more positive affect and less frustration, and were more successful by virtue of their greater persistence, flexibility, and cooperation. Toddlers with a history of anxious attachment showed different patterns of maladaptation. An earlier pattern of anxious-resistant attachment was associated with poor emotional regulation. These toddlers were often clingy, and easily prone to emotional dysregulation, becoming frustrated and/or oppositional in the cleanup and problem-solving situations. Toddlers with an anxious-avoidant history were somewhat disengaged with the tasks, showing little pleasure or enthusiasm, and often ignoring their mothers' attempts to involve them. Historically, this research was important for demonstrating continuity in both the patterns of the child's emotional competence and maternal sensitivity across different developmental periods, at a time when researchers were questioning such continuites.

A number of studies provide convergent evidence for these results and the link between attachment in infancy and the quality of the parent-toddler relationship. Bates, Maslin, & Frankel (1985) also found that securely attached infants engaged in less conflict with their mothers at age 2 than toddlers with a history of insecure attachment. In particular, toddlers who were earlier assessed as anxious-avoidant were more prone to enter into conflict with their mothers. Reciprocally, their mothers were more restrictive and controlling. As with the attachment assessment, these studies reveal disturbances in the parent-child relationship, rather than problems that reside exclusively within the child. During the toddler years, however, the tensions and problems experienced with the primary attachment figure may be carried forward into other adult-child relationships, and several studies have shown this to be the case (Londerville & Main, 1981; Thompson & Lamb, 1983). It appears that the capacity for regulating affectively arousing stimulation is central to positive adaptation in both the family and peer system. For example, Easterbrooks and Lamb (1979) and Lieberman (1977) found secure attachment to be associated with positive, reciprocal exchanges with age-mates at 18 months and 3 years, respectively. These demonstrations of continuity and coherence in the child's adaptation and emotion regulation provide a key building block for theories of emotional development.

Preschool Adaptation During the preschool years, basic patterns of attachment are transformed, reflecting developments in language and cognition, as well as shifting issues in psychosocial adjustment. For the child experiencing a secure relationship, there is a new partnership with the caregiver that reflects these advances and allows for increased autonomy and **initiative** within and beyond the dyad (Erikson, 1963; Sroufe, 1983). Within the parent–child relationship, the secure strategy incorporates perspective-taking, mutual communication of affect and desires, and joint planning; however, a number of deviations from this pattern are possible (Crittendon, 1992; Sroufe, 1989). A transactional model casts the child as an active agent rather than a passive recipient of environmental input or a direct product of genetic determinism. A new social milieu, such as the preschool, may be constructed differently by different children according to their attachment history. This provides another possible response to the question posed at the beginning of this chapter, by suggesting that a child actively seeks out or avoids various resources and opportunities within the new niche according to expectations derived from previous relationships rather than inborn genetic traits.

During the past 20 years, considerable evidence for a direct link between an infant's primary attachment relationship and emotional qualities of the child's peer relations has been found. Using a variety of sources and measures, researchers report that compared to insecurely attached preschoolers, securely attached preschoolers behave more positively toward their peers and receive more positive behavior from them, are better liked by peers, enjoy more positive and synchronous friendships, and are more highly regarded by their teachers as helpful, cooperative, empathic, and socially competent (Belsky & Cassidy, 1994; Erickson, Sroufe, & Egeland, 1985; Jacobson & Wille, 1986; LaFreniere & Sroufe, 1985; Youngblade & Belsky, 1992).

Attachment history has also been related to emerging behavioral problems in preschoolers. In the **Minnesota Longitudinal Study,** attachment assessments in the strange situation at 12 and 18 months were related to behavior in the preschool classroom (Erickson, Sroufe, & Egeland, 1985). Results indicated that for this high-risk, inner-city sample, behavioral problems were evident (as assessed by teacher ratings) for 85 percent of infants with stable insecure attachments, 60 percent with unstable attachments (secure at one time, insecure at the other), and 29 percent with stable secure attachments. The investigators then examined other risk factors in the home in order to discover why some securely attached infants showed later behavioral problems and other insecurely attached infants did not. Compared to securely attached infants without later problems, the secure infants that did show problems had mothers who were less emotionally supportive and not as clear or consistent in their guidance and limit setting during the toddler and early preschool years. Other evidence suggested that these mothers experienced more confusion and disorganized mood states during this period and were less involved with their child than mothers of secure infants without behavior problems.

The comparison between insecure infants with and without behavior problems revealed that those without problems had mothers who were warmer, more supportive, and more appropriate in their limit setting at 42 months. Reciprocally, these children were more affectionate and compliant with their mothers in this latter assessment. These results are important in demonstrating continuity of child adaptation in stable environments and coherence in child adaptation in unstable environments. That is, when children with an earlier history of secure attachment were subsequently exposed to less than adequate maternal care and support, they were more likely to manifest behavior problems than secure infants in stable caregiving environments. Similarly, anxiously attached infants could become well-functioning preschoolers if their caregivers responded adequately to their needs during later developmental stages (Erickson, Egeland, & Sroufe, 1985).

The pattern of anxious-resistant attachment to the primary caregiver in infancy has been identified in longitudinal research as a risk factor for internalizing behavior problems, including anxiety, high dependency on adults, social withdrawal, passivity, and submissiveness with peers (Erikson, Sroufe, & Egeland, 1985; LaFreniere & Sroufe, 1985; Lewis, Feiring, McGuffog, & Jaskir, 1984; Sroufe, Fox, & Pancake, 1983). As infants and toddlers, children with this pattern were observed to be wary, easily upset, and difficult to settle. They were also characterized by a poverty of exploration, and at times they showed explicitly angry, tantruming behavior, all presumably based on a history of inconsistent or chaotic care (Ainsworth et al., 1978). In the Minnesota Longitudinal Study (LaFreniere & Sroufe, 1985; Sroufe, 1983), infants who were classified as anxious-resistant at 12 and 18 months were found to become low-status, peripheral members of their preschool peer group three years later. Some of these children exhibited extreme passivity and an infantile dependence on adults, while others were more forward with their peers but became easily overaroused and disorganized in the face of minor frustrations.

Children with a history of anxious-avoidant attachment have been shown to have a different pattern of strengths and weaknesses in their social adaptation and emotional adjustment to the preschool classroom. Their adoption of an avoidant behavioral style in order to cope with chronic insensitivity and rejection by their primary caregiver may lay the foundation for a defensive personality characterized by hostility and negative expectations of others. In a naturalistic observational study that directly compared the emotional expression of preschoolers with different attachment histories, those with anxious attachment histories were found to express more hostility and negative affect toward their peers and were more rejected by them than securely attached children (LaFreniere, 1982) (see Figure 8.3).

Other researchers have also found that preschoolers with a history of avoidant attachment appear to be vulnerable to externalizing problems (Cassidy & Kobak, 1988), which may be expressed in relational aggression. For example, Troy and Sroufe (1987) observed the development of peer relationships in pairs of preschoolers during a series of free play sessions. They found that a high percentage of children with avoidant histories took advantage of and mistreated their play partner. In all cases of victimization, the "exploiter" had an avoidant history, while the victim was often a child with a resistant history.

More recent evidence has linked the disorganized attachment pattern to specific forms of behavioral and emotional problems in preschoolers. Main and Solomon (1990) believe that these children respond to internal conflict by displaying contradictory or incomplete behavior patterns formed in response to chronic abusive or frightening parental behavior. As preschoolers, they appear to be inflexible and controlling, possibly as an attempt to bring some semblance of order to an otherwise chaotic network of close relationships. This pattern may also involve a role reversal between parent and child in caregiving and punishment. Such behaviors are believed to be mediated by deviant patterns of emotional regulation and communication in the parent–child relationship (Lyons-Ruth, Repacholi, McLeod, & Silva, 1991).

Preschool teachers often have distinct emotional reactions to children with different attachment histories. Several studies have shown that they often nurture and protect children with resistant histories, but sometimes react with anger to the open defiance and bullying of children with avoidant histories. These distinct emotional responses on the part of new caregivers underscore the transactional nature of these early emotional disorders.

Social Learning Framework

From a social learning perspective, great emphasis has been placed upon the primary role of

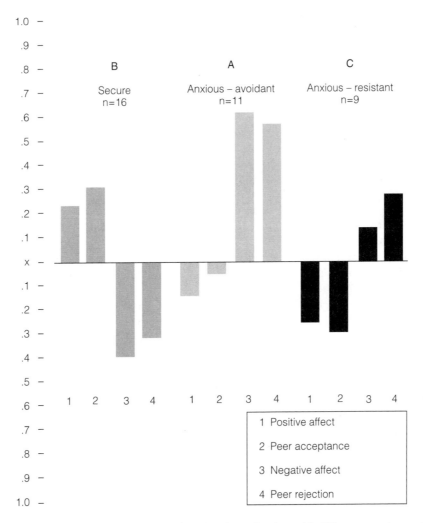

Figure 8.3 Affective expression and sociometric measures of preschoolers with different attachment histories.
Source: LaFreniere (1982).

parents in shaping and modeling competent social behavior. Classic developmental studies of parent–child socialization demonstrated that parental warmth combined with authoritative discipline is positively associated with the development of competence, while rejecting and authoritarian parenting is negatively related (Baumrind, 1967). This early view, which highlighted the parents' role in shaping the child, is now tempered by the recognition of child effects on the parent (Bell, 1968), completing a reciprocal view of parent–child interaction.

Many socialization studies can be cited that show a relationship between emotional qualities of child rearing and child outcomes. These studies converge with attachment research in implicating maternal sensitivity as a major factor in the socialization of competent behavior in early childhood. They also provide evidence of the cross-situational importance of emotionality in the parent–child relationship. For example, Denham, Renwick, and Holt (1991) found that maternal emotional expression was related to the child's expression of sadness in the preschool. Other researchers have begun to examine how parents respond to children's emotional expression. For example, Roberts and Strayer (1987) found that parents of competent children responded to negative affective displays in preschoolers with firmness while also acknowledging that they understood what had caused the child's distress. Putallaz (1987) found associations between peer sociometric status and maternal involvement and maternal affect, suggesting that mothers of socially competent children are more sensitive to their child's feelings and more likely to use reason rather than coercion when compared to mothers of less competent children, supporting similar conclusions drawn by Baumrind (1967) a generation earlier.

Perhaps the simplest explanation of the results of these studies is that children model parental behavior, particularly emotional behavior. Parental emotions capture the attention of the young child, and social learning theorists view observational learning or *modeling* as a key mechanism of emotion socialization. Barrett and Campos (1987) propose four ways that parental emotions serve as models for the young child. First, parental emotions as reactions to specific events may be directly imitated by the child, as we saw earlier in terms of social referencing. Should a parent display positive or negative emotions as a reaction to a particular person, the child is likely to respond with similar affect. Second, children learn the particular, even idiosyncratic expressions that a parent habitually uses. A child may copy a harsh, sarcastic intonation or even a specific phrase that is often used by the parent and transfer it to a new context. Third, parents model effective or ineffective coping responses, and children learn these patterns from watching the parents cope with emotionally challenging situations. Finally, parents provide an overall emotional climate in the home that may influence the child in subtle ways.

In an influential review, Dix (1991) examined the powerful role that emotions play in successful and problematic parenting. Although research on emotion and parenting is still in an early stage of development, Dix organizes current knowledge around four general conclusions. First, parenting arouses strong emotions, both positive and negative. In families with young children, conflicts between parents and children occur from 3 to 15 times per hour (Dunn & Munn, 1985), and even more often in families with children who are aggressive, sick, or disabled (Mednick & McNeil, 1968; Patterson, 1982). In most families, parents experience a much higher ratio of positive to negative emotion, though this can vary considerably between families. In one study of parent–child interaction, mothers of socially competent children (as judged by preschool teachers) expressed over 10 times more positive than negative affect, while mothers of anxious-withdrawn children expressed 1.5 times more negative than positive affect in the same situation (LaFreniere & Dumas, 1992). The average ratio of positive to negative affect for all parents was observed to be about 3:1, an estimate that also matches parental reports (Jersild, Woodyard, & del Solar, 1949).

A second conclusion is that the consistent patterns of parental emotion reflect the overall quality of the caregiving environment. This is because children are quite sensitive to parental expression of anger and affection from an early age (Cummings, Zahn-Waxler, & Radke-Yarrow, 1981). Considerable evidence exists to support the link between parental warmth and favorable child outcomes and the link between chronic parental hostility and negative outcomes (Grusec & Lytton, 1988; Maccoby & Martin, 1983). Third, sources of external stress and support influence the quality of caregiving because they alter the emotions parents experience with their children. In particular, high levels of stress and/or low levels of support are linked with harsh and erratic discipline (Belsky, 1984; Crockenberg, 1983; Hetherington & Camara, 1984; Patterson, 1982; Wahler & Dumas, 1989). Finally, research indicates that chronic and explosive negative emotion is a key marker of family dysfunction. For example, negative emotion is prominent in the parenting of (a) abusive mothers (Trickett & Kuczynski, 1986; Wolfe, 1985); (b) depressed mothers (Panacionne & Wahler, 1986; Radke-Yarrow, 1990); (c) mothers of aggressive boys (Patterson, 1982); (d) mothers of anxious-withdrawn preschoolers (LaFreniere & Dumas, 1992); (e) mothers of premature infants (Goldberg, Brachfield, & DiVitto, 1980); (f) teenage mothers (Hann et al., 1989); and (g) mothers living in poverty (McLoyd, 1990). Generally, researchers conclude that the parent's chronic negative emotions both reflect existing dysfunction and contribute to future deviation.

Deviations from an optimal goal-directed partnership involving mutuality and give-and-take between parent and child, as well as firm limit setting when necessary by the parent, may be viewed in terms of the balance of power in the parent–child relationship. Competent parenting requires a judicious balancing act between the pitfalls of overcontrolling, power-assertive responses and undercontrolling and ineffectual responses. Research has generally shown that mothers of aggressive children are often undercontrolling, permissive, or inconsistent in contexts that call for limit setting, acting predictably only by reliably failing to set firm limits when the child escalates, a pattern aptly described as "coercion training" (Dumas, LaFreniere, & Serketich, 1995; Patterson, Reid, & Dishion, 1992). In contrast, mothers of anxious-withdrawn preschoolers appear to be overcontrolling and intrusive, particularly in situations that call for mutuality and negotiation, rather than the exercise of parental authority (LaFreniere & Dumas, 1992; Verlaan & LaFreniere, 1994).

Understanding the *contingencies* operating between parent and child has proven to be a challenging task for researchers. Early behaviorist accounts of family functioning have often been criticized for their lack of a developmental perspective and their narrow focus on relatively molecular events occurring outside the person and in close spatial and temporal proximity to that person's behavior. In contrast, conceptions of parents' emotions have been so global and undifferentiated that the specific processes by which emotions influence parenting are poorly understood. For example, research on dysfunctional families has sometimes led to the oversimplified view that negative emotion is always harmful in its effects on children. However, more recent work reflects a broader perspective that includes an examination of contexts in which negative emotion may be seen as adaptive in some contexts, and maladaptive in others (Patterson, 1986; Wahler & Dumas, 1989; Zahn-Waxler, Radke-Yarrow, & King, 1979).

The child's relationship with the caregiver provides an example of such a context. Dumas (1989) has argued that the behavior of two interactants may be affected as much by the history of their relationship as by the immediate signals they exchange, and that this history may be reflected in each interactant's behavior outside of this relational context. In this view, the contingencies studied by family researchers (for example, a child's whining and a mother's sympathetic response) are part of a complex repertoire of responses that characterize both members of the dyad. To illustrate this more recent point of view, let us consider a typical conflict of wills between a mother and her preschooler. The probability that a child will comply to a maternal command will depend to a large extent on immediate factors such as the nature of the command, the mother's affect and willingness to enforce her instruction, and the child's extent of involvement in the activity. However, this probability will also depend on the history of command and compliance shared by both interactants. For example, a maternal command may give rise to a class of child responses characterized by whining, crying, and pleading that have reliably resulted in successful escape from maternal demands in the past. More importantly, this same class of responses may be generalized by the child to other social contexts in an attempt to deal with demands presented there by adults or peers.

A recent study by LaFreniere and Dumas (1992) suggests that the *meaning* of negative maternal affect may depend upon the relationship history of the dyad. In their observational research, mothers of competent and anxious-withdrawn children all responded reciprocally to their child's aversive behavior and negative affect. However, the context of this negative reciprocity was quite different for different children. For the competent child, maternal negative affect sent a strong message because it was embedded in a context of a coherent and contingent pattern of parenting with ample reward for positive behavior. The signal strength of an expression of negative affect is much greater when it is embedded in a context in which positive affect predominates over negative affect by a 10:1 ratio. In this relational context, children responded to maternal negativity with a significant *increase* in positive behavior, which may be interpreted as an effective means for the child to reestablish their more habitual pattern of positively toned interaction. On the mother's side of the interaction, if her child behaved positively, she was likely to immediately reciprocate with positive responses, in the short-term breaking the chain of negative reciprocity and in the long-term reinforcing competent behavior in her child.

Negative maternal affect had a completely different meaning for the anxious-withdrawn child because of stark differences in the emotional qualities characterizing this relational context. First, because of the chronically low base rate of positive affect of the mother, no signal could be sent to the child by lowering it still further. Only an increase in negative affect, from an already high base rate, could be used. Second, maternal negative affect had little signal value because it could not be distinguished from the general background pattern of negativity. Third, even a positive response by the child to the mother's signal was likely to result in a negative maternal response. From a behaviorist standpoint, the child's attempts to establish positive rapport are likely to be extinguished in the absence of reinforcement from the mother, and anxious re-

sponses are conditioned by repeated criticism, disapproval, and negative affect. Since even compliant behavior is likely to result in a negative maternal response, the child is caught in a no-win situation, producing frustration, conflict, and ultimately a sense of resignation on both sides of the relationship. A parenting style that fails to reciprocate positive affect and behavior directed by the child to the parent and instead places the child in a context of indiscriminate negativity coupled with high levels of superfluous controlling behavior constitutes an important *environmental* risk factor from either an attachment or a social learning perspective. From an attachment perspective, this lack of maternal sensitivity and positive regard for the child is part of a transactional process leading to low self-esteem and anxious patterns of social relations.

Recently, researchers have attempted to disentangle the effects of maternal and child characteristics (individual differences) from the effects of cumulative past interactions between mothers and their children (relationship dynamics). One research design involves placing mothers and their children in two interactive situations that are identical except that one involves the child's own mother (or mother's own child) and the other involves an unfamiliar adult female (or unfamiliar child). If mothers and children behave differently toward an unfamiliar than toward a familiar partner, such differences could be attributed to relationship dynamics that reflect the interactional history of the dyad. Using this design, Dumas and LaFreniere (1993) found that most children tended to be "nicer" to unfamiliar women than to their own mothers, as they were less aversive in behavior and affect toward the former. This is consistent with the observation that many children display more negative affect to their own mothers than to their female preschool teachers. However, anxious-withdrawn children ignored, rejected, or responded in an ambivalent manner to unfamiliar mothers. In a relationship perspective, this finding suggests that these children may be at risk when placed in novel social settings, such as a new day care. Ill-equipped to cope with social challenges by their relationships with their primary caregivers, anxious-withdrawn children may opt to deal with the demands arising in new social settings by responding ambiguously or actively rejecting the positive overtures of others and by ignoring their aversive behaviors. Although it may allow these children to cope in the short-term, this failure to reciprocate positive interactions is likely to deprive them of the relationships that facilitate the development of social skills in the new setting.

In the same study, mothers of anxious children were positive and reciprocal with a strange child but not with their own; all other mothers were positive and reciprocal with both their own and the unfamiliar child. This is a remarkable finding given that mothers of anxious children displayed high levels of aversive behavior and affect, intrusive behavior, and negative but not positive reciprocity with their own children. These same mothers appeared to change completely when interacting with an unfamiliar child by displaying the highest levels of positive affect of all mothers. Since the absence of a distressed relational context facilitated the display of much more functional interaction patterns in the unfamiliar condition, we believe that the behavior of mothers of anxious children cannot be accounted for solely in terms of limited parenting skills. These mothers obviously had the necessary skills to behave positively and contingently, but did not generally put these skills into practice with their own children.

Attributional Framework

Another important element of the parent–child relationship that influences the expression of emotions during social interaction is the cognitive appraisal of why the partner is behaving the way he or she is behaving. As discussed in Chapter 4, causal attributions of behavior and the appraisal of the situation provide a means for understanding the emotions of both interactants. In this sense attributions constitute an important part of the relationship; they reflect the past history of interaction and forecast probable future interaction.

The research program of Bugental and colleagues (Bugental, Blue, & Lewis, 1990; Bugental & Shennum, 1984) illustrates the importance of attributions to relationship dynamics, particularly in understanding strained parent–child relations. Across a number of different studies using different samples and methods, Bugental and colleagues have repeatedly demonstrated that preexisting attributions of low control, when confirmed by environmental cues, set into motion a broad defensive response system that may lead to dysfunctional interaction patterns in parent–child relations.

Bugental views the parent's sense of control or self-efficacy as a moderating variable that comes into play in situations involving difficult children rather than in all situations. For example, parents with attributions of high control are prepared to confront a difficult situation with effective and flexible problem solving that allows them to react to the difficult child with greater success than parents with low self-efficacy. Parents with low self-efficacy are likely to respond to the same difficult situation with pessimism and negative affect, responses that tend to lead toward a self-fulfilling prophecy.

A number of studies by Bugental and her colleagues lend support to her attributional-behavioral-transactional model, specifically to the role of maternal attributions as moderators of child effects rather than as direct causes of socialization outcomes. For example, Bugental and Shennum (1984) found that child responsiveness had a selective effect on mothers as a function of their perceived control. Mothers with low perceived control in their caregiver role reacted differently to boys who were responsive, as opposed to boys who ignored or were slow to respond to questions and suggestions.

Bugental interprets these results as manifestations of self-fulfilling prophecies that serve to maintain the mother's belief system. Mothers with attributions of low control perceived unresponsive children as difficult and reacted in ways that maintained difficult child behavior. The subsequent unresponsiveness that they elicited from the children could reasonably confirm their belief that they had little power to ensure successful interaction with these children. In contrast, mothers with high self-efficacy produced the best consequences with unresponsive children, by virtue of their failure to react to this behavior pattern. These mothers were impervious to child behavior that had the potential for weakening their sense of their own ability, and unresponsive children reacted to these mothers by behaving more like the responsive children. In essence, successful interactions were more likely when the mother attributed high ability to herself to ensure successful interaction with any child.

Subsequent studies by Bugental's team have found that low perceived control mothers send mixed messages to difficult children, such as smiles accompanied by frowns, negative messages presented in a kidding or sarcastic fashion, or positive messages delivered with deadpan affect (Bugental, Mantyla, & Lewis, 1989). These mothers may attempt to engage unresponsive children with an ingratiating style that serves to increase gaze aversion in the children (Bugental, Blue, & Lewis, 1989). Bugental interprets these displays of inappropriate affect as a "leakage of feelings of powerlessness" by the parent that only serves to confuse the child and leads to avoidance of the parent and further noncompliance. In turn, the child's noncompliance leads the parent to use more coercive forms of punishment that ultimately function to promote more negativity and noncompliance from the child. At a behavioral level, similar coercive cycles between mother and child have been described by Patterson (1982), who views negative reinforcement as a key mechanism for their maintenance and resistance to modification.

In contrast, Bugental's model views maternal attributions as the key factor. She has observed that low control mothers differ from high control mothers in their expression of sadness and increased negative ideation over the course of a difficult interaction, a pattern that is most evident

for low control mothers who perceive their child as having high control. Physiological data are consistent with the behavioral observations and show that when exposed to unresponsive children, low control mothers show increases in arousal as indexed by elevated heart rate and skin conductance. It may be that the elevated levels of autonomic reactivity found among abusive parents (Wolfe, Fairbank, Kelly, & Bradlyn, 1983) may be triggered by their cognitive construction of their relationships. Under intense levels of arousal, the responses of such persons are likely to exacerbate interactional problems. Moreover, there is reason to believe that high levels of autonomic and affective arousal may have implications for information processing. Generally, intense affect and defensive arousal are incompatible with broad and flexible attentional deployment and careful processing of information. Among mothers with low perceived control, the findings indicate less accurate information processing when they are confronted with threatening social cues, though high perceived control mothers maintain an orientation consistent with extensive information processing. While difficult to conduct, more experimental work is needed to investigate the intricate interplay of affect and cognition among parents in normal and dysfunctional families.

Integrating Perspectives

In this section, the contribution of parents to the socialization of emotion was examined from the perspective of attachment, behaviorist, and attributional theories. Despite important differences between these perspectives, several points of convergence provide a basis for integration. First, the recognition of the importance of relationships as a context for behavior and development has become an important point of intersection. Second, theoretical integration is possible only after reductionistic methodologies are discarded, allowing attachment, behaviorist, and attributional researchers to search for broader units of behaviors where the assumption of functional equivalence is more reasonable. Third, attachment constructs such as maternal sensitivity can be fruitfully integrated with operant concepts such as contingency to provide meaningful assessments of parental quality. Finally, all three approaches predict convergences between the quality of the child's functioning in the home and in the preschool or day care, though they invoke different processes to explain them.

In summary, more consensus than disagreement exists regarding the crucial impact of a contingently responsive environment on the emotional development of the child. The day-to-day contingencies provided by the responsive caregiver establish an expectation of control over the environment by the child (Seligman, 1975), lead to displays of positive affect (Watson, 1985), and enhance involvement with the environment (Lewis, Sullivan, & Brooks-Gunn, 1985). In their absence, neither child nor caregiver develops feelings of efficacy, and the establishment of a harmonious parent–child relationship is threatened (Ainsworth, Blehar, Waters, & Wall, 1978; Belsky, Rovine, & Taylor, 1984).

ENVIRONMENTAL INFLUENCES: THE ROLE OF PEERS

Thus far we have emphasized the role of parents in our account of environmental influences on children's personality and socioemotional development. In the final section of this chapter, we examine the contribution of peers to the socialization of emotion. Because of their equivalent status, peers make unique contributions to a child's socioemotional development. Ethologists emphasize the function of peers in shaping socially competent behavior, by providing experiences that promote affective development through vigorous play, facilitate the regulation of aggressive behavior by the establishment of dominance hierarchies and modes of conflict resolution, and provide for the acquisition of gender roles through same-sex play. Cognitive-developmental theorists view peers as promoting social competence

through decentration, perspective-taking, and social problem solving because of the sociocognitive conflict that results from peer interaction. Social learning theorists view peers as important socializing agents. They emphasize the social processes of reinforcement, punishment, and modeling to explain the acquisition of culturally defined social skills, emotional display rules, and gender roles. Whatever the theoretical orientation, developmentalists agree that peers serve important and unique functions for children's social and emotional development.

We begin this section with experimental research that demonstrates the functional significance of peers for the development of social competence in primates, with an emphasis on the importance of affective communication. Then we investigate the role of preschool peers in shaping emotional development by examining the nature of preschoolers' social interactions and relationships.

Function of Peer Interaction in Primates

In a series of influential experiments, the Harlows and colleagues provided compelling evidence for the function of peers in shaping competent behavior in rhesus monkeys (Harlow, 1969; Harlow & Harlow, 1962, 1965; Suomi & Harlow, 1972). These studies had an enormous impact on the field of child development during the 1960s and 1970s as the growth of the subfield of peer relations began its expansion (Hartup, 1983). Harlow's experiments involved various types of social deprivation by raising infant rhesus monkeys under conditions of total social isolation, only with mothers, or only with peers, as a means of identifying the possible functions served by parents and peers in social and emotional development. When denied the opportunity for contact with peers during early development, rhesus monkeys were generally avoidant in their response to peers and appeared to be threatened by peer contact and responded with unregulated aggression. These antisocial patterns of behavior often marked these monkeys as adults as well, and their adaptation to primate group life was jeopardized.

Subsequently, Harlow and colleagues raised infant monkeys entirely with peers and deprived them of all contact with their mothers. These infant rhesus monkeys compensated for the lack of an attachment figure by forming strong bonds with one another, though they remained insecure about the world around them. They would often exhibit attachment behaviors toward one another and cling to one another for long periods, and they were reluctant to explore and became highly agitated in the face of novelty. Like the "mother only" monkeys, they were threatened by outsiders and highly aggressive toward them. However, within the security of their peer group they appeared more competent in their social interaction and eventually displayed normal patterns of social and sexual behavior.

Monkeys raised in complete social isolation exhibited the most disturbed patterns of behavior affecting all aspects of their existence. They would stare vacantly into space for long periods and engage in self-stimulation (for example, repetitive rocking, self-clinging) and self-mutilation. When confronted with other monkeys, they were incapable of dealing with the arousal engendered by such stimulation and responded by mixing expressions of fear and threat, alternating between withdrawal and hyperaggressiveness. Mason (1960) hypothesized that these inabilities to engage in appropriate social interaction were due to deficiencies in their nonverbal communication of emotion.

In order to test this hypothesis, Miller, Caul, and Mirsky (1967) compared isolated and normal monkeys in a cooperative conditioning paradigm that assessed their ability to encode and decode facial expressions. This experiment involved placing a pair of monkeys in two separate cages, both of which delivered an aversive shock after the presentation of a flashing light as the conditioned stimulus (CS). However, the CS was presented in only one cage, while the lever for avoiding the shock was in the other. This arrangement required that the responder monkey (in the cage with the lever) read the facial expression of the stimulus monkey (in the cage with the flashing light) in order that both monkeys avoid the shock. Monkeys were paired in all possible combinations (isolate pairs, normal pairs, isolate-normal, and normal-isolate) in order to determine their respective abilities in sending and receiving effective nonverbal signals. Heart rate measures were recorded for all monkeys as a measure of their emotional responses.

When normal monkeys were paired together, they were able to effectively send and receive emotional cues and avoid the shock on 77 percent of the trials. Isolate pairs were minimally effective. Unlike normal pairs who both showed elevated heart rates, only the stimulus monkey in the isolate pair had an elevated heart rate, suggesting that the responder monkey did not receive the emotional cue, despite the heightened arousal of the stimulus monkey who saw the light flash. When normal responders were paired with isolate stimulus monkeys, they too did not learn to avoid the shock, nor did their heart rate show an increase. This demonstrates that effective emotional cues were not being sent by the isolates. Instead, isolate stimulus monkeys were expressing fear throughout the experiment and thus provided no discrete signal to the responder monkeys. However, when isolates were in the responder role and normals in the stimulus role, the isolates were also unable to decode the facial expressions of the normals. It is clear from this pattern of results that isolate monkeys were deficient in both tasks. They did not send clear emotional signals and they were unable to decode clear signals. This lack of competence in nonverbal communication of emotion in isolate reared monkeys directly contributed to their maladaptive social relations with peers.

The role of facial expressions in regulating harmonious social interaction in rhesus monkeys is further supported by experiments conducted by Izard (1975). He found that monkeys whose facial nerves had been bisected became the victims of aggression by other monkeys because of their inability to encode facial expressions. Both encoding and decoding skills contribute to the smooth flow of social interaction, and these important abilities to communicate and interpret emotional signals appear to be dependent on social interaction with parents and peers for their full development.

The pathological patterns of isolate reared monkeys were thought to be completely irreversible after the first six months of life in isolation until an experiment by Suomi and Harlow (1972) demonstrated that such early deprivation could be partially overcome. At six months, isolate reared monkeys were paired with normal 3-month-old peer "therapists" who were still in the phase of attachment. Abnormal patterns of rocking, self-clinging, and self-biting were gradually broken down by the experience of a younger peer who would cling to them, groom them, and provide other nonthreatening forms of social stimulation. As both monkeys developed, a number of aspects of normal social functioning were gradually built up, though the isolates remained highly reactive to stress or conflict. These experiments with rhesus monkeys served to inspire research on the rehabilitation of socially withdrawn preschoolers.

Preschool Peer Relations

Since the 1970s one of the most active subfields of research in child development has involved the investigation of the role of peers in social, cognitive, and emotional development (Hartup, 1983). In addition to adult ratings, which we have discussed in previous chapters, researchers have used a variety of methods to study the peer world, including (1) naturalistic observation, (2) standardized situations, and (3) peer sociometrics.

Naturalistic Observation A powerful means to analyze the emergence of individual differences in emotional expression and regulation is naturalistic observation of children's behavior and emotional expression in their everyday encounters with peers at home, in the classroom, and on

Figure 8.4 Monkeys show strong attachment toward peers when raised in isolation from adult caregivers.

(Photo from Harlow Primate Lab, University of Wisconsin)

the playground. While this methodology has a long history in developmental research on preschoolers, fewer studies have focused on affective expression between peers. Although many investigators regard middle childhood as the period when emotional display rules are learned, the groundwork for this is being laid during the preschool years. In particular, the relatively frequent conflicts observed to occur between friends during early childhood provide a salient context for learning affective perspective-taking and emotion management. Naturalistic research that examines the free flow of behavior during children's coordinated play with friends supports this idea (Parker & Gottman, 1989; Sroufe et al., 1984). Daily observations of preschoolers' struggles with this issue of emotion management in the often hurly-burly chaos of the classroom and playground make this evident:

> The more deeply we study social behavior in the free flow of the classroom, the more important affect and emotional modulation appear. . . . The centrality of affect—

of emotional control and expression—is most apparent in the free flow of behavior; that is, in chains of initiations, responses, adjustments, shared delight, protests, apologies, modifications, new directions, and further shared feeling. The place of affect in promoting, guiding, and perpetuating exchanges (or disrupting, disorganizing, or terminating them) is obvious to trained observers, but nonetheless very difficult to quantify. (Sroufe et al., 1984, p. 303)

For example, in the Minnesota Longitudinal Study, the association between affective balance (the frequency of positive minus negative affective expression during free play) and teacher rankings of social competence was .76 (Sroufe et al., 1984). But this does little to convey a qualitative understanding of the role of affect in social competence. A single example drawn from the unedited videotape records conveys much more:

As the scene begins, structured small-group activities are finished and the children are free to play as they wish. Seven children are present: Howard, John, Eddie, and Jerry (boys) and Tracy, Linda, and Alicia (girls).

With great positive affect Howard says, "Let's go to the movies!" Howard, John, Tracy, and Linda move off excitedly to a back corner of the room, while Jerry and Eddie watch them go. Alicia continues to work at a craft table. The four, with much shared excitement, set up a cardboard "screen" and line up chairs in front of it to "watch." John moves his chair to the front (very carefully so as not to hit anyone). When he notices that he is blocking Tracy's view, he moves his chair to the side. Led by Howard's improvised fantasies, all enjoy the "movie." Then, at one point in response to the "movie," Howard stands up and begins to dance. His enthusiasm spreads to the others and, at his suggestion, they all move joyously to

a larger play area and begin to dance. A teacher responds to their mood by providing a record player. All four children eagerly anticipate the music with broad smiles on their faces. A scene of uproarious glee follows, so affective that it cannot fully be captured with words.

At one point in the dancing, Linda pretends to fall down. Howard, at first not recognizing the pretense, stops all activity and looks on with open mouth and concerned expression. He then realizes the pretense and falls down himself. Soon all are laughing and dancing again.

It is interesting to note the behavior of the other three children in the group. Alicia, working at a nearby craft table, turns around to watch. Soon she is smiling. In time this becomes laughter and glee. Ultimately, she is up and dancing, showing great zest and joy. Eddie and Jerry were attracted to the area too. Eddie (who was depressed during much of the quarter) watches with great interest but makes only one tentative and incomplete movement to join. He cannot even respond to a rather explicit invitation by two girls, though he clearly is interested. He does occasionally smile slightly, and by the end is tapping his foot! In stark contrast, Jerry works with construction materials at the craft table, facing away from the group the entire time. In his world, it is as though this incredible scene was not even happening.

All four characters in this scene were ranked high on social competence, whereas Alicia, who at other times was very withdrawn from the group, and Eddie had moderate rankings. Jerry was low ranked. (Sroufe et al., 1984, p. 304)

During the 1980s when the study of emotion was still coming of age, it seemed as though scientific observers were allowing themselves to use adjectives and adverbs for the first time in their descriptions of children's behavior. While previously the content of peer interaction was studied, gradually investigators began to see the need to record qualitative aspects of peer interaction, though such work is still rare.

One research team embarked on a series of naturalistic, descriptive studies of peer interaction, choosing as their focus conversations among friends (Gottman, 1983; Gottman & Parker, 1986; Gottman & Parkhurst, 1980; Parker & Gottman, 1989). Friendships in early childhood are based upon achieving high levels of enjoyment and entertainment through coordinated play. Maintaining such interdependent activity is a significant challenge for preschoolers because it requires abilities that are still nascent, such as perspective-taking, give-and-take, conflict resolution, and affect management. Researchers who observe preschool peers in natural settings believe that friendships play a particularly crucial role in the socialization of competence, in part because children acquire unique information about their own emotional experiences and their partners' reactions to their emotional displays.

The following exchange between two 4-year-olds during fantasy play recorded by Gottman and colleagues illustrates the ability of preschool friends to respond to one another's emotional cues:

Eric: *[shouting]* Hold on there everyone! I am the skeleton! I'm the skeleton! Oh! Hee! Hugh, ha, ha! You're hiding.

Naomi: Hey, in the top drawer, there's the, there's the feet! *[makes clattering noise of "feet"]*

Eric: I'm the skeleton! Whoa! *[screams]* A skeleton, everyone! A skeleton!

Naomi: I'm your friend, the dinosaur.

Eric: Oh, hi dinosaur. *[subdued]* You know, no one likes me.

Naomi: *[reassuringly]* But I like you. I'm your friend.

Eric: But none of my other friends like me. They don't like my new suit. They don't

like my skeleton suit. It's really just me. They think I'm a dumb-dumb!

Naomi: I know what. He's a good skeleton.

Eric: *[yelling]* I am not a dumb-dumb!

Naomi: I'm not calling you a dumb-dumb. I'm calling you a friendly skeleton. (Parker & Gottman, 1989, p. 95)

As with any method, naturalistic observation offers a unique pattern of strengths and weaknesses for investigating children's emotional development. The chief disadvantage of naturalistic observation, particularly as the basis for measures of individual differences, is the fact that it is inconvenient and labor intensive. In addition, the naive application of this method invites observer bias, or the tendency to confirm the hypotheses or expectations that one brings to the observation. Researchers guard against this by adopting categories of behavior that require a minimum of subjective interpretation and can be verified against other independent observers.

The strengths of naturalistic research are most apparent in work with infants and young children who are less reactive to the observer than are older children, and whose verbal skills preclude the use of interviews and questionnaires. Since animals are not great talkers either, ethologists rely on naturalistic observation in order to ascertain the function of behavior in the ecology to which the animal is adapted, which may later be confirmed through experimentation. This emphasis on description in the natural sciences is far greater than in psychology, and perhaps because of this ethologists were the first to recognize the functional significance of emotional displays in regulating social exchanges (Charlesworth, 1982). According to Tinbergen (1963), "broad descriptive reconnaissance of the whole system of phenomena is necessary in order to see each individual problem in its perspective, it is the only safeguard for a balanced approach in which analytical and synthetical thinking can cooperate" (p. 130).

Naturalistic observation of humans is the only method that can inform us about how people behave in their everyday environment, and it is often the benchmark by which to judge the validity of other methods. Besides this important advantage of ecological validity, it is probable that young children's abilities are less likely to be underestimated than situations that place preschoolers in an unfamiliar setting, with an unfamiliar experimenter, or those that rely exclusively on verbal or abstract materials (Parke, 1994). For example, jealousy is typically viewed as an emotion that does not occur until relatively late in children's development (Harris, 1989). However, naturalistic observation by several investigator has revealed clear expressions of jealousy as early as age 2 or 3 in interaction at home with parents and siblings (Dunn, 1988). Similarly, the experience of close, supportive friendships, affective perspective-taking, and emotion management was considered by many to be an achievement of middle childhood (Piaget, 1965; Sullivan, 1953), and some experimental evidence supports this. However, the naturalistic work previously presented clearly reveals the presence of this experience in early childhood.

Analog Situations In contrast to the molar assessments and narrative descriptions generated by the naturalistic observations of children's expressions of emotion, more precise descriptions and tighter inferences regarding the relationship between children's emotional expression and their motivations, goals, actions, and outcomes can be generated by controlling key features of their environment and filming children's behavior and affective expression. Although decoding videotapes increases observer involvement tenfold over the real-time observations just described, the cost is often justified.

Several investigators have used this approach to investigate specific aspects of social and emotional behavior in peer dyads or small groups. For example, Putallatz and Gottman (1981) developed a standardized situation in which a child's group entry skills could be observed. Using this paradigm, researchers have found that children's ability to enter both familiar and unfamiliar peer groups by determining their frame of reference, making relevant comments, and engaging in group-oriented behaviors is related to their popularity with peers. The ability to assess how and when to join a group of peers requires both the encoding and decoding of expressive cues, in the same sense that we have previously discussed in reference to primate research.

Another important aspect of preschool peer competence is the ability to engage peers in sustained cooperative play without becoming a victim of their often egoistic orientation. Charlesworth and LaFreniere (1983) developed a standardized situation in which access to a desirable resource was limited and could be achieved only by cooperation. Preschoolers worked in four-child groups with a movie-viewer that required that one child crank the apparatus, and a second child hold down a light switch in order that a third child view the cartoon strip. Friends were able to generate more total viewing time for their group as a whole, and they were more harmonious, with more frequent turn-taking, than groups of familiar children who were not friends. Sex differences were evident in children's strategies to gain access to the movie-viewer in both mixed-sex and same-sex groups and dyads, particularly in the absence of adult monitoring (Charlesworth & Dzur, 1987; LaFreniere & Charlesworth, 1987; Powlishta & Maccoby, 1990).

Peer Sociometrics Sociometric approaches to the study of children's peer groups have been popular among developmental psychologists for over 50 years and show no signs of abating in the near future. **Sociometric measures** were designed to assess the network of relationships that exists in a stable group by asking the children themselves about their preferences for peer group members. Three basic techniques have been employed over the years—rating scales, paired-comparisons, and nominations. We shall describe in detail sociometric nominations and rating scales because they are the most widely used techniques in preschool peer groups.

When used with preschoolers, sociometric nominations and ratings require that each child in the group be interviewed separately by a familiar experimenter after the group has been together for a sufficient amount of time for group structures to have formed. The picture sociometric nomination involves presenting preschoolers with a set of photographs of all the children in the group and asking them to nominate three children that they really like and three other children that they do not like or that they like the least. Once each child in the group has been interviewed, the raw data may be used in several ways. The experimenter can use the data to produce a sociogram describing the social network of the group, identifying clique structures and social isolates. Alternatively, the experimenter may wish to assess individual differences by tallying the number of positive and negative nominations received as the basis for assessing each child's score in terms of peer acceptance (total positive nominations received), peer rejection (total negative nominations), social impact (all nominations), and sociometric status (positive minus negative nominations). These data may be used as continuous measures for correlational analyses, or a typology may be created by classifying the children into one of five categories as shown in Figure 8.5.

Sociometric rating procedures are often very similar to the nomination procedure just described, with the exception of not differentiating peer acceptance and peer rejection. Rather, a child's overall likability is assessed by having children rate each of their classmates on a Likert-type scale, and scores are computed by summing each child's ratings received from peers. Again preschoolers work with photographs of their classmates by placing each photo in one of three boxes labeled with line drawings of a smiling face if they like the peer "a lot," a neutral face if they "kinda" like the peer, and a frown if they "do not" like the peer (Asher, Singleton, Tinsley, & Hymel, 1979).

Most researchers have found acceptable levels of test–retest reliability and temporal stability

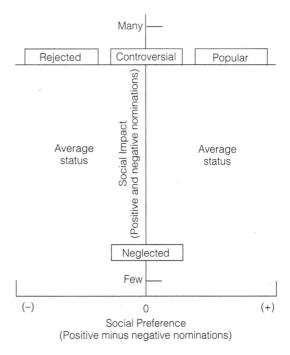

Figure 8.5 Five sociometric types based on different patterns of positive and negative nominations

Source: Shaffer (1994, p. 551). © 1997. Used by permission of McGraw-Hill.

when employing either of these sociometric techniques with children as young as 3 years (Denham & McKinley, 1993). As we shall see, although peer acceptance and peer rejection derived from nominations data are negatively related, they are not simply opposite ends of the same continuum. Rather each reflects a different aspect of a child's popularity with peers. In contrast, ratings are best conceptualized as a composite measure of popularity (Bukowski & Hoza, 1989).

The Role of Affect in Peer Competence

As interest on emotional processes began to rise during the 1980s, researchers attempted to directly observe preschoolers' positive and negative affective expressions during free play and to relate these observations to independent sources of data, particularly sociometric measures and teacher ratings of social competence (Denham, 1986; Denham, McKinley, Couchoud, & Holt, 1990; LaFreniere & Sroufe, 1985; Sroufe et al., 1984). Such broad categories had the advantage of offering high levels of observer agreement, temporal stability, and cross-situational stability, all important parameters of valid indices of individual differences. Individual rates of positive and negative affective expression are also substantially correlated with other important aspects of peer competence. Positive affect is related to both teacher ratings of social competence and peer sociometric measures of popularity because of its central role in initiating and regulating harmonious social interchanges among preschool peers (LaFreniere & Sroufe, 1985; Sroufe et al., 1984). In contrast, preschoolers who express chronically high or unusually intense negative emotions are viewed much less favorably by teachers and peers (LaFreniere & Sroufe, 1985; Rubin & Clark, 1983; Sroufe et al., 1984). Children who express a favorable balance of positive emotion over negative emotion are rated as more friendly and assertive and less aggressive or sad by their teachers (Denham et al., 1990).

More recent work has attempted to go beyond general indices of positive and negative emotion in order to provide a more differentiated view regarding the role of affective expression in children's social interaction. It is particularly important that different types of "negative affect" be discriminated. Observers recording affective expression of preschoolers' free play can reliably distinguish distress, sadness, and anger from one another based on vocal, facial, and postural cues (Werner & LaFreniere, 1998). However, because these emotions occur less frequently, it is not always possible to derive reliable and stable measures of individual differences from such data.

Recently, an observational study of preschoolers' expressions of anger during free play was conducted by Fabes and Eisenberg (1992). These researchers recorded the causes and consequences of children's anger and related these observations to measures of social competence and peer popularity. Most of these angry reactions were observed to be disputes among the children over objects, with other child causes, such as verbal teasing, social rejection, or physical actions, being less frequent for preschoolers. Consistent with the research cited earlier, children who were judged by peers as popular or by teachers as socially competent were less often involved in angry disputes. They were also more likely than less popular or competent children to deal directly and nonaggressively with the provocation, often using their greater sociometric status to retaliate by isolating the other child. In addition, children's responses to these provocations differed, depending on the age and sex of the child, the cause of the conflict, and the status of the person with whom the child was in conflict. This latter result suggests that preschoolers are beginning to alter their emotional expressions according to contextual cues. Among preschoolers it appears that this type of regulation involves verbal expressions prior to regulating facial expressions of emotion (Gnepp & Hess, 1986).

SUMMARY

In this chapter a wide range of biological and environmental factors influencing the emotional development of young children was explored. In the first section, longitudinal studies of behavioral inhibition in young children were described that examine the stability and different manifestations of this trait across time and in different settings. Next, an evolutionary account of personality differences was presented that postulates that gene complexes evolved to construct different types of personalities in order to serve adaptive functions. Five types of evidence in support of an evolutionary psychology of personality were noted: (1) comparative research on animals with similar systems that serve clear adaptive functions; (2) neurological research indicating a structural basis of these systems in the brain; (3) developmental research indicating the presence of recognizable precursors of adult personality traits in infancy; (4) cross-cultural personality research indicating that universal dimensions of personality may exist; and (5) behavioral genetics research that demonstrates significant heritability of personality traits. A model to explain the processes by which gene–environment interactions can account for individual differences in children's social, emotional, and personality development was presented describing active, passive, and evocative effects.

The second section on environmental influences presented three theoretical approaches: (1) attachment theory emphasizing primary relationships as the principal context of early emotional development; (2) a social learning theory emphasizing the role of reinforcement, punishment, and modeling on behavior and development; and (3) attributional models that examine the effects of parents' causal attributions of children's behavior.

Attachment research has consistently demonstrated links between the quality of the infant's attachment relationship with the primary caregiver and adaptation in other developmental periods' social contexts. Security of attachment in infancy has been linked with more prosocial, empathic behavior toward peers and greater acceptance and popularity in the peer group. Preschoolers with a history of secure attachment express more positive and less negative emotions when interacting with their peers. Preschoolers with avoidant attachment histories have been found to express more dependence toward teachers and greater hostility, negative affect, and aggression toward their peers. Preschoolers with anxious-resistant attachment histories have been found to be more anxious, withdrawn, passive, and immature with their peers. Preschoolers with disorganized attachment histories have been found to be inflexible and controlling, though more studies are needed to clarify the different patterns of psychosocial risks associated with specific anxious attachment histories.

Research from a social learning perspective confirms the importance of the emotional quality of the parent–child relationship as an impor-

tant influence on child development. Parenting arouses strong positive and negative emotions, and different patterns of parental emotion reflect the overall quality of caretaking. Research indicates that high levels of parenting stress and low levels of support are associated with negative emotion and harsh and erratic discipline. These patterns are in turn associated with greater levels of risk for the young child experiencing them. Chronic negative emotionality in the parent is thus a marker of existing dysfunction in the family and a predictor of future difficulties for the child.

Parental attributions about the causes of their child's behavior contribute to the dynamics of the parent–child relationship in an important way. Parents with a high sense of control or self-efficacy are more likely to persist and resolve difficulties that arise with their child. In contrast, parents with low self-efficacy, who view the child as controlling the outcome, are more likely to give up or give in during difficult exchanges with their child. Attribution theorists interpret these differences as manifestations of self-fulfilling prophecies that serve to maintain the parent's existing belief system.

In the final section of this chapter, we reviewed the contribution of peers to the socialization of emotion. Ethologists emphasize the function of peers in shaping socially competent behavior, by providing experiences that promote affective development through vigorous play, facilitate the regulation of aggressive behavior by the establishment of dominance hierarchies and modes of conflict resolution, and provide for the acquisition of gender roles through same-sex play. Cognitive-developmental theorists view peers as promoting social competence through decentration, perspective-taking, and social problem solving because of the sociocognitive conflict that results from peer interaction. Social learning theorists also view peers as critical socializing agents for the development of social competence. They emphasize the ways in which peers influence one another in terms of the social processes of reinforcement, punishment, and modeling to explain the acquisition of culturally defined social skills, emotional display rules, and gender roles.

The contribution of preschool peers in shaping emotional development was explored by highlighting various methods used to study the peer world, including (1) naturalistic observation, (2) analog situations, and (3) peer sociometrics. Researchers generally use these methods in combination to describe how children differ in the emotional qualities of their peer relations, as well as to discuss the processes of peer socialization that may contribute to these differences.

FURTHER READING

Bugental, D. B., & Shennum, W. A. (1984). Difficult children as elicitors and targets of adult communication patterns: An attributional-behavioral-transactional analysis. *Monographs of the SRCD, 49* (1, Serial No. 205).

This is an insightful analysis of the interconnections of emotion and attributions in mother–child relationships.

Geary, D. C. (1998). *Male, female: The evolution of human sex differences.* Washington, DC: American Psychological Association.

This book presents a comprehensive review of how males and females differ and why.

Saarni, C., Mumme, D. L., & Campos, J. J. (1998). Emotional development: Action, communication, and understanding. In W. Damon (Series Ed.) & N. Eisenberg (Vol. Ed.), *Handbook of child psychology: Vol. 3. Social, emotional, and personality development* (5th ed., pp. 237–309). New York: Wiley.

This is an up-to-date review of research on emotion socialization.

Sroufe, L. A., Schork, E., Motti, F., Lawroski, N., & LaFreniere, P. (1984). The role of affect in social competence. In C. E. Izard, J. Kagan, & R. B. Zajonc (Eds.), *Emotions, cognition, and behavior* (pp. 289–319). Cambridge, England: Cambridge University Press.

This groundbreaking work is based on a naturalistic study of the central role of emotions in promoting competence with peers.

9

Childhood, Society, and Emotions: A New Understanding

He who has eyes to see and ears to hear may
convince himself that no mortal can keep a secret.
If his lips are silent, he chatters with his fingertips:
betrayal oozes out of him at every pore.

FREUD (1925/1959)

COGNITIVE AND CULTURAL INFLUENCES

Throughout the transition from early to middle childhood, developmental advances in cognition, language, self-concept, and social relations set the stage for emotional communication that gradually begins to resemble that of adults. In this chapter we explore different aspects of this new awareness in a review of research on children's understanding of internal states called **theory of mind** (TOM). A "theory" of mind refers to an abstract causal system that allows one to explain and predict behavior through reference to unobservable mental states such as beliefs, intentions, desires, and emotions. We shall argue that the development of the child's theory about inner states underlies the increasing complexity of the child's social relations and emotional experience. This extends our discussion of the role of cognitive factors in emotional epigenesis, one of the central themes of this book.

Cognition provides the route by which culture enters the emotion process. Thus, a major goal of this chapter is to understand cultural universals and differences in emotional development as children assimilate the unique rules for emotional expression that operate within their culture of origin. Cross-cultural research on emotional development is one of the most exciting and theoretically significant domains of research in emotion science. Although there is a long tradition of work in this area, it is only recently that research questions and methods have been developed to explore developmental issues in cross-cultural perspective. In the last section of this chapter we shall review this recent work, but first we begin by making another type of comparison, between children and offspring of our next of kin—the chimpanzee.

THEORY OF MIND

Tactical Deception

In a landmark study in primatology that launched a new wave of research among developmental psychologists, David Premack and Guy Woodruff explored the question: Does the chimpanzee have a theory of mind? By this they meant, do apes attribute states of mind to others, and do they use these attributions to predict or explain others' behavior? Their ingenious experimental investigations of intentional communication in chimpanzees demonstrated that chimps are capable of clever deceptions that seem to rely upon an understanding of the desires, emotions, and intentions of their human trainers (Premack & Woodruff, 1978; Woodruff & Premack, 1979). They presented 3- to 4-year-old chimps with the following dilemma: the chimps knew the location of a hidden banana but could not reach it without the help of a trainer who could reach it, but did not know where it was hidden. During a number of trials, the chimps were exposed to two different trainers, a kind trainer who, when shown where the banana was hidden, would give it to them to eat, and a villainous trainer who, if shown the correct location, ate the banana himself. Faced with such duplicity, the chimps learned to direct honest communications to the kind trainer, but to deceive the villainous trainer by pretending not to know where the banana was hidden, or even by pointing to the wrong container. To distinguish such a strategy from other types of deception employed by animals (for example, based on instinct or conditioning), ethologists use the term **tactical deception.** By asking whether or not chimps possess a theory of mind, Premack and Woodruff were asking whether the chimps consciously employed the deceptive strategy based upon their understanding of the intentions of the villainous trainer.

How would children react to the type of problem Premack presented to his chimps?

To find out, we investigated the developmental aspects of tactical deception within a game context in which the child must try to conceal a hidden object from an adult interrogator. Sixty French-Canadian children from 3 to 8 years of age were filmed in the "hide-a-bear task" (LaFreniere, 1988). After hiding a toy bear in one of three hiding places, the child was instructed to try to "fool the hunter," an adult experimenter who questioned the child regarding the bear's location. With one exception, children younger than 4 years were always unsuccessful in their attempts to fool the adult, 5- and 6-year-olds were only occasionally successful, and 8-year-olds were successful significantly more often. Some 3-year-olds attempted to inhibit information by shrugging their shoulders and pretending that they did not know the location of the bear, but they were unable to fool the adult because they freely leaked information by glancing repeatedly at the location of the hidden object under questioning. Older children gained increasing control over nonverbal leaks and were more able (like Premack's chimps) to withhold this information from the interrogator. But nearly all the children under the age of 6 used a predictable hiding strategy in which the toy was hidden in each of the three locations for each of the three trials. Thus, by the third trial, they would give away the location of the bear. Only the 8-year-olds were able to correctly infer that such a regular hiding strategy would provide useful information to the adult interrogator; 80 percent of these older children employed an irregular hiding strategy.

In addition, only the 8-year-olds showed a significant increase in the use of the more effective strategy of intentionally misleading the interrogator when they were being questioned. This could take the form of quick glances at an incorrect location during questioning. Later they would state that they looked at a place where no bear was hidden because they thought that the adult would be fooled into thinking that the bear would be hidden there. They were right. I played

the hunter and I was occasionally taken in by their ruse! The strategy of these 8-year-olds closely parallels the behavior of 3-year-old Sarah, Premack's most intelligent chimp. In general, older children showed greater awareness of the effects of their own behavior on the experimenter's state of mind in the hide-a-bear task, demonstrating a recursive level of awareness of intentionality by providing misleading cues and by altering a regular hiding strategy so as not to provide inadvertently useful information to the experimenter. They were also the most successful in forestalling nonverbal leakage by successfully controlling their facial expression under mildly arousing conditions.

Subsequent research into the early development of children's deception has been lively with numerous studies of verbal and nonverbal deception in situations that range from naturalistic (Josephs, 1993, 1994; Lewis, Stranger, & Sullivan, 1989) to highly contrived (Chandler, Fritz, & Hala, 1989; Hala, Chandler, & Fritz, 1991; Sodian, Taylor, Harris, & Perner, 1991). In general, this work demonstrates that the early forms of deception enacted by preschoolers younger than 4 years are unsophisticated and consist of attempts to withhold information by not confessing to transgressions (Lewis, Stranger, & Sullivan, 1989) or by removing incriminating evidence (Chandler et al., 1989). Most studies have shown that more sophisticated forms of deception that rely upon a more mature theory of mind (that is, planting misleading evidence or adopting misleading expressive behavior) do not emerge until after 4 years. Not all acts of nonverbal deception rely upon the same cognitive capacities.

Sodian et al. (1991) used another version of a hiding game for children from 4 to 6 years inspired by Premack's work with chimpanzees. In this task, target pictures (for example, a police officer) could be hidden in places of strong (police station) or weak (sports arena) association under two conditions: cooperative (a nice king who is looking for the police officer) or competitive (a burglar). Success at the task involved demonstrating an understanding of the relevance of the cognitive cues by hiding the police officer in the sports arena, rather than the police station, in the competitive condition. Only a few 4-year-olds, half the 5-year-olds, and almost all the 6-year-olds chose the appropriate hiding place in relation to the cooperative/competitive condition.

Some theorists believe that children first learn to produce deceptive strategies and only afterward do they learn to detect the use of such strategies by others. Table 9.1 conveys the hierarchical progression that I believe to be implicit in both the development and evolution of communication. At the first level, information communicated from sender to receiver is taken at face value. At the second level, sender's strategy of providing a false signal to manipulate the behavior of receiver emerges. At the third level, receiver demonstrates a recursive awareness of intentionality by consciously considering that sender's message may be misleading. In this model, one hypothesizes that production precedes comprehension, or in other words, that the sender is capable of taking into account receiver's perspective, before receiver is able to take account of sender's taking-account-of-receiver's perspective. In subsequent levels this recursive cognition continues, much in the manner of chess players who may reason in the following manner: "Because I think my opponent thinks that I will try to capture his king, I will feint an attack on the king and try to capture the rook instead, using my knight," while the opponent may be thinking, "This attack is so clumsy it is obviously a trick. My opponent thinks I must be thinking that he will try to capture my king, but what are his true intentions?"

To investigate how well children can use expressive cues to detect ongoing deception in others, LaFreniere (1998) modified an experimental task previously used by Schultz and Cloghesy (1981) to explore children's recursive awareness of intentionality. In the original task, a card game was designed such that one player, after noting the color of the top card of the deck (lying face down), pointed to a red or black card (lying face up) as a cue to the other player, whose task

Table 9.1 Hierarchical Organization of Intentional Communication Systems

1. a believes b's signal
2. b believes that
   (a believes b's signal)
3. a believes that
   (b believes that
   (a believes b's signal))
4. b believes that
   (a believes that
   (b believes that
   (a believes b's signal)))
5. a believes that
   (b believes that
   (a believes that
   (b believes that
   (a believes b's signal))))
6. etc.

it was to guess the color of the top card. I modified the card game so that the truthfulness of the cue was contingent on the facial expression of the experimenter providing the cue. For example, every time I sent a false signal, I smiled slightly. Thus, the "contingency detection task" involved the detection of an expressive cue (smile) that was contingent upon the truthfulness of a social signal (pointing to a red or black card). Children from 4 to 8 years were instructed "to try to guess the color of the next card. I'm going to look at it first and then point to a red or black card to give you a hint about what color it might be. But be careful, because I might try to fool you sometimes." Children were tested in two age groups (preschoolers, first graders) under two conditions (smile = true, smile = false).

Preschoolers were rarely successful in solving the contingency detection task, with only 8 percent scoring significantly above chance levels across the 15 trials. Older children solved the contingency more often, with 50 precent scoring above chance. There was also a significant effect of condition in the older group. Three out of four of the older children solved the contingency task when the experimenter smiled while presenting a false cue (LaFreniere, 1998). In their own words, they knew when the experimenter was trying to fool them because of the "sneaky grin" on his face. However, only one of four was able to solve the task when the experimenter smiled while being truthful and kept a poker face while presenting a false cue. Although they had learned to associate the smile with attempts at deception, their "mind-reading" skills would need additional tuning before sitting in on high stakes poker games!

From Chimpanzees to Children

How can we compare the "mind-reading" abilities of chimpanzees and children? Although chimpanzees show some surprising abilities in deception, they make fewer attributions than humans, since they cannot attribute states of mind that they themselves do not possess. Naturalistic and experimental evidence suggests that apes make simple attributions of seeing, wanting, and expecting, rather than attributions about beliefs. Thus they appear to possess only a limited theory of mind. In a similar sense, 3-year-old children may possess a theory of mind that is also limited by their cognitive development. Premack's rule of thumb is that if a child of 3 1/2 years cannot do it, neither can the chimpanzee (Premack, 1988). This observation leads to an obvious question: What are the cognitive limitations shared by chimpanzees and young children?

Premack (1988) addressed this question by dividing states of mind into simple and complex states:

Simple states are those produced by processes that are hard-wired, automatic or reflex-like, and encapsulated . . . perception is the prototypic simple state, we may add others: first, certain basic motivational states; and secondly, somewhat more controversially, expectancy, a state that is produced by conditioning or simple learning. These three states—seeing, wanting, expecting—have in common a restricted and automatic production process that is independent of language both at the input level of the system and of internal representation. . . .

Complex states, of which belief is the prototype, are of course everything that simple states are not. Belief is not automatic, encapsulated, or hard-wired; moreover it definitely depends on language, most certainly at the level of internal representation though often also at the level of input to the system. (p. 172)

So the simple answer to the question we posed comparing the limitations shared by chimpanzees and young children leads us to the next question: How do chimpanzees and children process information about complex states of mind like beliefs?

Belief–Desire Psychology

By 3 years, both children and chimpanzees show a rudimentary understanding that the mind has connections to the external world. On the input side of this relation (behavior-to-mind), they know about hiding places, and if an object is well hidden in a box, they know that only someone who has looked inside knows where the toy is hidden (Flavell, Shipstead, & Croft, 1978; Premack, 1988). Hide-and-go-seek becomes a popular children's game beginning at this age. On the output (mind-to-behavior) side, children appear to connect desires and emotion to action prior to understanding the relation between beliefs and action. Henry Wellman (1990) proposes a developmental model of **belief–desire psychology,** as shown in Figure 9.1. In his developmental sequence, desire psychology emerges first and refers to the ability to explain and predict another person's behavior based on our assumptions about their emotions and desires. For example, most 3-year-olds can explain and predict action and emotional expressions based on desires. If a girl really wants a kitten for her birthday, 3-year-olds can tell you that she might ask her parents for one and that she will be happy if she opens her present and sees a kitten inside the box. But 3-year-olds appear to know less about how a person's beliefs might influence his or her behavior (Wellman & Wooley, 1990).

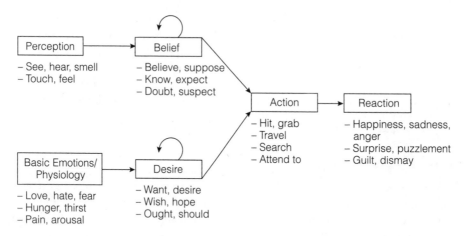

Figure 9.1 Wellman's model of belief–desire reasoning. This schematic diagram depicts the implicit theory of mind possessed by adults and young children.

Source: Wellman, 1990. Used by permission of MIT Press.

Because of advancing linguistic skills, children's (but not chimpanzees') understanding of the nature of the mind is revealed in their explanations about it, as well as their behavior. Preschoolers can inform us at an early age that thoughts cannot be seen or felt; that they happen inside your head. "How can you reach inside your head; besides it's not even there" (Wellman, 1990). Yet somehow the dividing line between imagination and reality is not altogether clear. During the hide-a-bear task, one 3-year-old girl burst into tears at the thought of the hunter capturing her bear who was hiding, and we needed to reassure her that she could take the bear home, that the hunter is really nice and not really a hunter, but just pretending, and so on. Research indicates that even older preschoolers are not too certain that an imaginary creature could not just possibly bite their finger off! In exploring the views of children aged 4 to 6 years, Harris and colleagues found that they all asserted that an imaginary monster was not real. However, when asked to pretend that an empty box contained the imaginary monster, they generally preferred to poke their finger into an empty box that contained an imaginary puppy instead and studiously avoided the box with an imaginary monster. In

addition, several 4-year-olds asked the experimenter not to leave them in the room with the empty box, even after verifying that it was empty. Although all the children "knew" that the monster was only pretend and not real, only about half the children were convinced that it was not in the box! (Harris, Brown, Whittall, & Harmer, 1991).

A major step forward in thinking about the mind that is beyond the understanding of most 3-year-olds entails the ability to reflect on the representational process and understand that a belief is a representation of reality, not reality itself. Unlike a desire, a belief may be true or false, and the external world may be represented accurately or inaccurately. By the age of 4, children, but not chimpanzees, generally pass **false-belief tasks** (Wellman's litmus test of belief–desire psychology), as demonstrated by Wimmer and Perner (1983) and others. In these tasks children may be told stories in which the protagonist is led to believe that an object was hidden in one place while they themselves knew it was actually hidden elsewhere. When asked where the protagonist would search, the 3-year-olds ignored the protagonist's false beliefs and predicted she would search the correct location, while 4- to 6-year-olds predicted she would search the incorrect location. A number of studies have now confirmed that 4-year-olds generally understand that another person may have beliefs that are different from their own—beliefs that may turn out to be incorrect. Of course false beliefs may be induced, not just about concrete things (like hidden objects), but also about more private phenomena, such as a person's internal state or feelings. We turn next to investigations of children's understanding of the distinction between appearances and reality, and particularly real versus apparent emotions.

Distinguishing Real Versus Apparent Emotion

John Flavell and his colleagues have developed a research program exploring how children come to learn that things are not always what they seem to be. They developed a series of **appearance–reality tasks** that required children to demonstrate their understanding that appearances can sometimes be misleading and not accurate representations of reality. In these tasks they showed children objects that looked liked other objects, such as a sponge that looked like a rock, or objects viewed through tinted glass. They consistently found that children younger than 4 years tended to equate reality with appearances. For example, if a glass of white milk is wrapped in a green filter, 3-year-olds will say that the milk not only "looks" green, but "really and truly is" green (Flavell, Green, & Flavell, 1986). Like the false-belief task, the appearance–reality distinction requires meta-representational skills or the ability to represent representations. And like the child's understanding of false beliefs, it is mostly absent in 3-year-olds and still quite fragile for children between 4 and 6 years of age.

Grasping the distinction between real and apparent emotion is similar from the standpoint of meta-representation, but even more difficult. For most 4-year-olds, this distinction is not clear, and most emotional expressions are taken at face value, though they understand the distinction between real and pretend. In contrast, most 6-year-olds understand that other people can be misled by displaying facial expressions that are different from what one actually feels (Gross & Harris, 1988). For example, they understand that someone may fall and hurt themselves, but try not to show that they are frightened, scared, or hurt if they think they might be teased as a result. Six-year-olds may have considerable difficulty deciding whether any given expression is real or apparent, but they understand the distinction and realize that expression and feeling need not coincide.

The understanding that physical appearances can be falsely represented with respect to an object's identity (green-looking white milk) and the understanding that reality can be represented in different ways depending on one's point of view (perspective-taking) share an underlying cognitive component with the child's ability to understand that expressive behaviors may not match inner feelings. Not only are these three abilities interrelated within subjects, but they all tend to emerge at about the same time, during the transition from early to middle childhood (Flavell, Miller, & Miller, 1993). After this period of relatively rapid cognitive growth, the emotional lives of children begin to change as children become increasingly aware of the subtleties of emotions in everyday life. Two aspects of this more subtle view of emotions that emerge during middle childhood involve (1) understanding that one may experience conflicting emotions as a single reaction and (2) learning the rules for emotional dissemblance that seem to be prescribed by one's culture.

NEW EMOTIONAL COMPLEXITIES

Understanding Mixed Emotions

During the preschool years the growth of children's social, cognitive, and linguistic abilities leads to significant advances in their understanding of emotions and their ability to communicate that understanding. It is clear that preschoolers can identify many different emotions, as well as typical situations that provoke them. This has been demonstrated in a variety of studies. Young children can listen to stories and identify what emotion would be felt in a number of familiar situations (Borke, 1971), and they can suggest specific situations that could make one feel happy, sad, surprised, scared, or angry (Trabasso, Stein, & Johnson, 1981).

It is less clear that they understand that certain events may simultaneously trigger conflicting emotions. When asked to describe emotional reactions or to imagine the reactions of a story character, preschoolers are likely to think in terms of just one emotion. For example, when they are asked how they might feel on the last day of school, or if invited from the audience to sing on stage, preschoolers are unable to imagine two different emotions being provoked. Between about 6 and 8 years, children will report that they would be sad or happy, excited or afraid, but never both emotions at the same time (Harris, 1993). By 9 or 10 years, children acknowledge that the last day of school may provide an occasion for mixed feelings, happiness at the prospect of summer vacation and sadness because they will miss their school friends or favorite teacher (Harter & Buddin, 1987; Harter & Whitesell, 1989). Not all researchers agree on the age at which children acquire the ability to comprehend mixed emotions, but the developmental question is: What has produced this change?

A plausible answer implicates advances in underlying cognitive structures that allow the child to consider simultaneously multiple aspects of a single event. This is similar to Piagetian demonstrations of increased abilities in conservation that stem from **decentration** or the ability to consider several aspects of a situation rather than centering on just one. Conservation tasks differ in their difficulty and the age at which the majority of children can solve them. For example, conservation of number is one of the easiest tasks passed by most 5-year-olds, while conservation tasks involving weight or volume are not

solved until 8 or 9 years (Gross, 1985). Preschoolers can recall all the elements of stories in which mixed emotional reactions would occur (Harris, 1983); however, they usually focus on just one element when asked to predict the emotional response of the story character. Researchers have shown that 5- and 6-year-olds can describe people who made them feel good and bad, or whom they liked and disliked, *sequentially*. For example, Stein and Trabasso (1989) found that older preschoolers can focus on one instance in which they responded emotionally to someone (for example, "I don't like him because he took my legos that I was building"), but can also recount another instance in which a different emotion was experienced ("I like him when we play together outside"). But when preschoolers are asked whether different people might have different emotional reactions to a given event, they consistently choose one possible reaction for everyone (Gnepp, McKee, & Domanic, 1987). It is as if they are unable to continue their analysis of the event from a different point of view once they have identified what appears to them as the one predominant aspect.

Research by Paul Harris and colleagues provides further support for this hypothesis (Peng, Johnson, Pollock, Glasspool, & Harris, 1992). They conducted a training study in which children listened to a story that contained two conflicting components. To ensure that the children were attending to the story, they were asked what emotion each component would provoke. At the story's end, the children were asked how the story character would feel overall. Children as young as 6 or 7 years, but not younger, demonstrated gains in their understanding of mixed emotions as a result of these simple prompts. Despite ignoring the possibility of mixed feelings at the outset, school-age children often reported that the story character could feel two opposing emotions simultaneously. They were also able to apply this gain in understanding to themselves when asked to recollect similar experiences in their own lives. The more complex understanding of emotional experience of middle childhood is an important developmental advance because it leads to increased understanding of social life in general, including conflicting motivations in ourselves and others, ambivalent interpersonal relationships, and a more complex conceptualization of the self (Arsenio & Kramer, 1992; Harter, 1986).

For example, imagine a boy of divorced parents who lives with his mother but is anticipating a monthly visit from his father. A common type of emotional conflict involves not wanting to see the father because of the pain of loss and anger at the family's breakup, while at the same time experiencing love and longing for the absent father. Donaldson and Westerman (1986) have explored whether children understand that strong, but conflicting feelings toward the same person can interact with one another in such circumstances. They report that only after the age of 10 do children understand this type of emotional conflict. In some cases, the children may choose to withdraw from it, but they can express their emotional awareness ("Well, I'd just get upset seeing him, so it was easier just not to, but then I feel guilty sometimes that I don't want to visit him," commented an 11-year-old).

Of course, researchers relying on verbal self-reports may underestimate the awareness of younger children or children with less cognitive or verbal skill. As discussed in previous chapters, attachment researchers have observed 1-year-olds expressing conflicting emotions in the strange situation (anger at being left behind, relief at the parent's return) in their nonverbal behavior. These children express their ambivalent emotions by mixing contact seeking with resistance to contact once it is achieved. Clearly, there is a significant gap between the child's emotional experience, and the child's ability to organize such experience cognitively and communicate it verbally. In some cases, children (or adults) may be consciously aware of only the most prominent emotion in a given situation, but as they attempt to cope with the situation or communicate their feelings, they may become aware of more complexity in their own emotional experience. In the next section we explore another aspect of that complexity, one that is critically shaped by the child's socialization within a given culture.

Emotional Dissemblance

A central goal in the socialization of children in widely diverse cultures involves shaping the infant's natural spontaneity and impulsive expression of emotion into more controlled forms deemed appropriate by the culture. Each culture informs the child through various socialization practices just how he or she is expected to respond expressively to a range of situations and for a wide range of emotions. These socialization experiences gradually shape the child's expressive behavior into culturally specific forms that often retain a universal quality, but add an element of control to how the individual presents the inner self to others (Ekman, 1973; Friesen, 1972; Goffman, 1959). This control, conceptualized in terms of **emotional dissemblance,** or the lack of correspondence between the internal affective state and its outward expression (Saarni, Mumme, & Campos, 1998), may be divided into two broad categories: cultural display rules and nonverbal deception. The study of emotional dissemblance was pioneered by Paul Ekman and Wallace Friesen in a series of studies beginning in the early 1970s.

The first category of emotional dissemblance involves the use of cultural **display rules,** such as the rule: "Look pleased when someone gives you a gift, even if you don't like it." The concept of cultural display rules evolved from the ethological concept of display. Recall from Chapter 2 that ethologists studying animal social behavior describe displays as ritualized expressions that are characteristic of a particular species and that have evolved to function as regulators of social interaction. From this origin, Paul Ekman coined the term *display rules* to account for the ways in which socialization within a particular culture can alter universal human facial expressions of emotion (Ekman & Friesen, 1971, 1975). Cultural display rules in humans serve similar functions as ritualized displays between members of the same species by promoting harmonious and scriptlike forms of social exchanges that are somewhat ritualized, making them predictable for members of the same culture.

Because display rules are chiefly products of sociocultural influences, they may be highly specific for a given culture, and quite different between cultures that have had little contact with one another. Each culture transmits to its members a wide variety of implicit and explicit rules regarding the display of emotion. Without this socialization, an individual entering a new culture might become acutely aware of the existence of a particular rule by transgressing it, and this can be a source of misunderstanding and friction when cultures collide. Peace Corps volunteers and others who experience such dislocations refer to this as "culture shock." Despite the incredible diversity of cultural display rules, harmony between members of different cultures can be readily established by genuine displays of warmth, consideration, caring, and politeness in difficult situations. The smile is universally appealing and very contagious.

The second category of emotional dissemblance involves the use of tactical deception to gain a strategic advantage or avoid a disadvantage, as in the original theory of mind tasks employed by Premack with chimpanzees. In Chapter 2 we outlined the view of evolutionary biologists regarding signal theory. Intentionality is central to their understanding of communication because signals that communicate one's intentions may be used by another to gain a strategic advantage, especially in situations of competition or conflict. As a result, false signals or deception could be advantageous to the sender on such occasions if others respond to them as true signals. Thus, ethologists argue that an evolutionary arms race ensues, resulting in more subtle forms of deception on the one hand, and more vigilance and subtle forms of detection on the other. This dynamic is currently seen as central to the evolution of primate intelligence as a key mechanism for promoting the adaptation of the individual within a social group (Dawkins & Krebs, 1978; Humphrey, 1976; Whiten & Byrne, 1988).

Ekman and Friesen's Theory of Nonverbal Deception

If young children are precocious in mimicking various emotions in play, they are less adept at an early age at concealing emotions, particularly when their emotions are intense. Classic theorists like Darwin and Freud were also convinced that emotional dissemblance at any age may be detected by careful inspection of nonverbal behavior.

However, Paul Ekman and Wallace Friesen (1969) were the first to formulate a broad theoretical and methodological framework for studying nonverbal deception. In addition to the concept of display rules, they also introduced the concepts of **deception cues** (which inform receiver that deception may be occurring, but do not reveal the concealed information) and **leakage** (the betrayal of the withheld information). According to Ekman and Friesen, in initiating a deceptive communication, sender has two basic choices: inhibition or simulation, though many times the result may be some blend of the two. Sender may choose to modulate or adjust the intensity of an emotion to show either more (exaggeration) or less (inhibition) than what is actually felt. The extreme form of the latter is neutralization. Although cutting off nonverbal signals is the surest means of forestalling leakage, it is usually taken as a strong cue that deception is being attempted. It is more strategic for sender to maintain the flow of signals, pretending that nothing has been concealed, while selectively inhibiting the expression of certain emotional reactions or states. This more fluid form of deception, involving simulation and masking, is more effective because (1) it fills gaps left by inhibition that if left unfilled would be obvious deception clues, (2) it erects a barrier against the breakthrough of the inhibited emotion, and (3) the substitution of the false emotion may be instrumental to the goal of the deception.

Ekman and Friesen identify the face as the focal point in affective expression; it has the greatest sending capacity. The legs/feet are viewed as the poorest nonverbal senders, while the hands are intermediate. Feedback from receiver closely parallels this order. Feedback from receiver that informs sender what receiver has perceived and evaluated is external. Internal feedback is defined as the sender's conscious awareness of what he or she is doing and the ability to recall, repeat, or enact a planned sequence of behavior.

Because people often look at the greatest source of information about a person's emotional state, the face, facial expressions are typically under the most conscious control of the sender. There are, however, limits to the extent to which one can attend to the face; too much looking can be uncomfortable and suggest a power struggle, intimacy, or interrogation. There are also taboos against too much looking at the hands. For example, hand acts that might involve emotional leakage, such as nervous gestures or unconscious touching of the body, clothing, or hair, are not usually reacted to by receiver. Even less commentary is reserved for sender's legs or feet. Thus, in terms of those behaviors with high information value—those that elicit scrutiny and evaluation, those that are subject to the most control—facial movements are first, then the hands, and lastly the feet. Ekman and Friesen argue that nonverbal leakage is expected to reverse this pattern. The face, which is equipped to betray the most emotion, can also conceal the most and can become the most confusing source of information during deception. The hands and other parts of the body, though they have less sending capacity, also receive less feedback, are less controlled, and are hypothesized to be a primary source of leakage during deception.

CULTURE, SOCIALIZATION, AND EMOTIONAL EXPRESSION

Development of Display Rules

Although it was not formulated as a developmental model, Ekman and Friesen's theory of nonverbal deception has been a fruitful source of ideas for developmental investigators, particularly the concept of cultural display rules. In his pioneering ethological studies of preschool children, Blurton-Jones (1967) reported that 3-year-olds are capable of exaggerating their displays of emotion. He observed children during playground activity and noted that they were more likely to cry after a mishap if they were aware that a teacher was watching, than if they thought they were unattended. Parents and teachers soon learn to distinguish between real and exaggerated displays of distress at about this time.

A number of studies have attempted to chart the development of children's strategies for managing the display of different types of emotion in different situations and at different ages from early childhood to adolescence (Casey, 1993; Cole, 1986; Feldman, Jenkins, & Popoola, 1979; Fuchs & Thelen, 1988; Gnepp & Hess, 1986; Malatesta & Haviland, 1982; Reissland & Harris, 1991; Saarni, 1979, 1984, 1988; Zeman & Garber, 1996; Zeman & Shipman, 1997). Several of these studies confirm Blurton-Jones's observations that even young children are capable of spontaneous management of emotional displays in some situations, and that this ability tends to improve with age.

Two early studies illustrate the use of an observational approach to understanding developmental advances in children's use of display rules. In the "sour fruit drink task," Robert Feldman and colleagues instructed first graders, seventh graders, and college students to display a pleased, positive expression while drinking sour fruit juice. Subsequently, naive raters more readily detected deception in the youngest age group (Feldman et al., 1979). These results would be predicted by Ekman and Friesen, since young children are the least experienced in using internal and external feedback to control their facial expressions. Similarly, Carolyn Saarni's research (Saarni, 1984) also shows a developmental progression in children's ability to manage emotional expression. In the "disappointing gift task," first, third, and fifth graders were presented with a disappointing gift when they expected to receive a desirable one. On two occasions, children were asked to help solve a problem in a textbook. After the first session, children were presented with an attractive toy, but after the second session they received an unappealing reward (for example, a plastic key on a ring). Videotapes of their reactions provide data on spontaneous attempts to control expressive behavior in a situation that calls for a conventional display of politeness. In contrast to the broad smiles and enthusiastic thank you's upon receiving the attractive toy, children typically produced muted positive reactions to the unattractive toy as if attempting to mask their genuine disappointment. Her results indicate that the youngest children (especially boys) were more likely to remain unsmiling when given a drab toy as a gift, while the older children (especially girls) were more likely to display a polite smile.

Subsequent researchers have elaborated both Feldman's and Saarni's original work using similar observational methods (Cole, 1986; Davies, 1995; Josephs, 1994). For example, Pamela Cole further explored emotion management in children as young as the age at which Blurton-Jones suggested that display rules are operative. In a study of preschool girls, Cole modified Saarni's disappointing gift task in two ways. She first had children rank order toys so that she could present them with the toy they liked least to ensure that it was disappointing. Second, she compared the facial displays of the girls in two situations. In one the experimenter was present (activating the display rule), while in the other the experimenter withdrew. The girls expressed more disappointment when the experimenter was absent, a finding that leaves little doubt that they were indeed masking their true feelings when the experimenter was present.

Much of the recent work on the development of display rules no longer involves actually observing children's expressive behaviors in emotion-eliciting situations, but favors instead self-report methods about hypothetical situations. Typically, children are asked either open-ended or structured questions about what they might express in a given situation. These methods are typical of studies of attitudes, cognitions, social-cognitions, and decision making in middle childhood or older age groups. They have the advantage of convenience of administration, and the experimenter can easily vary a number of theoretically interesting factors in an optimal design. However, they may be vulnerable to the influence of social desirability, experimenter effects, and other biases, and are less suitable for young children who are unable to engage in abstract, hypothetical thinking or whose verbal communication skills are insufficient for the task.

Of course, those investigators who choose observational methods to investigate developmental changes in children's real-life use of display rules must also confront methodological limitations. In particular, the generalizability of these studies is limited by the choice of the particular emotion-eliciting situation employed. Researchers have typically employed either the disappointing gift situation or sour fruit juice task, both of which call for masking a rather mild emotion. Despite these methodological limitations inherent in both self-report and observational studies of the development of children's display rules, a number of reasonably consistent findings have emerged when the literature is examined as a whole.

First, as most theories would predict, children's ability to engage in culturally appropriate emotional displays appears to increase with age from early childhood to adolescence, though a few studies report no age differences between adjacent developmental periods (Cole, 1986; Gnepp & Hess, 1986). Researchers have also demonstrated that older children are increasingly more likely to take into consideration the consequences of their expressive behavior on others (Meerum Terwogt, & Olthof, 1989). In particular, older children have learned to be more circumspect in their expression of negative emotions like anger and sadness, in part because they anticipate negative interpersonal consequences to overt expression of these emotions.

What types of consequences make children fearful of expressing negative emotions? Saarni (1979) interviewed American school children about when they would be likely to attempt to conceal their feelings of pain or fear and found that the children commonly cited embarrassment, avoiding ridicule, and getting attention or help as reasons for emotional dissemblance. In addition, school children of all ages recognized that they might be unable to conceal intense feelings even if they believed it desirable to do so. More recently, Saarni et al. (1998) listed four main types of motivation for managing emotional expression: (1) avoiding negative outcomes or enhancing positive ones, (2) protecting one's self-esteem, (3) maintaining relationships, and (4) respecting norms and conventions.

Second, social and cultural contexts emerge as important factors influencing the likelihood that a given emotion will be expressed, again because of children's expectations concerning interpersonal consequences. For instance, several studies have shown that predominantly white American school children report that they will more readily express negative emotions like anger and sadness to parents and adults, compared to age-mates (Saarni, 1988; Zeman & Garber, 1996). However, Underwood, Coie, and Herbsman (1992) found that African-American school children generally say that they would express anger more directly to peers than to teachers, revealing that they consider the consequences of their expressive behavior to be different in these situations. The important point is that these studies all demonstrate that children learn to distinguish between different social partners like mothers, fathers, teachers, peers, and siblings when considering how much of what they feel will be openly expressed. It is also likely that children will make different decisions depending upon the characteristics of the individual person within these categories of social partners, distinguishing between a friendly or derisive peer, or between a permissive or strict parent or teacher. A key factor that appears to govern this decision-making process is the

expected consequence of a given emotional display (recall Premack's chimpanzees).

Finally, the child's gender and type of emotion sometimes interact to produce gender-differentiated displays rules that are consistent with sex roles in a given culture. For example, a number of self-report studies demonstrate that American girls report expressing sadness, timidity, and fear more often than boys (Fuchs & Thelen, 1988; Zeman & Garber, 1996), while observational studies show that boys tend to express irritation, disappointment, frustration, and anger more openly than girls (Cole, 1986; Davies, 1995; Saarni, 1984), though self-reported anger does not appear to differ between girls and boys (Zeman & Garber, 1996). It remains to be seen how far one can generalize such findings about sex differences, since results are not always consistent within the same culture, may be different across cultures, and may be somewhat dependent upon choice of methodology in a manner similar to research on children's empathy (Lennon & Eisenberg, 1987), as discussed in Chapter 6. Because of the interest in the development of cultural display rules, it is likely that our knowledge base in this area will increase as multiple methods are used to replicate findings across different laboratories and different cultures in a concerted fashion.

Cross-Cultural Comparisons

In this section, we shall explore cultural universals and differences in emotional expression, regulation, and understanding. If no two snowflakes are exactly alike, it should be clear at the outset that no two people have equivalent emotional lives. Our emotional experiences may be quite similar to, or vastly different from, those of other people, including people from our own culture or even our own family.

In a recent review, Mesquita and Frijda (1992) examined the psychological and anthropological literature on cross-cultural similarities and differences with respect to situations that give rise to specific emotions, emotion appraisals, facial

Figure 9.2 Emotions are always determined by cultural and biological factors working together.

(Photo by Susie Fitzhugh/ Stock Boston)

expressions, and physiological reactions. For the most part, their review reveals a great deal of data showing cross-cultural similarities in these emotional processes, with relatively few data indicating cultural differences. However, their final sentence lends a note of caution to such a simple view: "The scope of cross-cultural emotion variations and the relationship between cultural variation and cultural consistency in emotions thus are as yet almost unexplored topics for research" (Mesquita & Frijda, 1992, p. 201).

It is noteworthy that Mesquita and Frijda (1992) reported only one cross-cultural comparison of emotions in childhood, a study comparing American and Chinese children (Borke & Su, 1972). Prior to this study, Borke established that American children seem to have a rather easy time when asked to listen to stories and identify what emotion would be felt in a number of familiar situations (Borke, 1971). The influence of culture on such emotion appraisal was subsequently explored by asking American and Chinese children to indicate what type of situa-

tions generally made them feel happy, sad, afraid, or angry, or what their parents or peers did that elicited these same basic feelings. Children in both cultures generated more situations that made them feel happy than any other emotion. However, American children mentioned situations that caused them to feel sad more often than did Chinese children (28 percent versus 18 percent), whereas Chinese children generated more situations that made them feel angry (27 percent versus 20 percent) or afraid (24 percent versus 18 percent). When asked to appraise ambiguous situations (that could possibly evoke sadness and anger), American children were more likely to make sad, rather than angry, attributions compared with Chinese children.

Mesquita and Frijda (1992) suggest that cultures may differ in appraisal tendencies or biases, but because of the relative paucity of data it is unclear how to interpret a single sample involving only a two-point cultural comparison. The study by Borke and Su represented an interesting start for cross-cultural comparisons of emotional processes in children. Nevertheless, citing just a single study in a comprehensive review of culture and emotion dramatically illustrates the relative neglect of the study of emotions in children and adolescents that appears to characterize much of the literature in this area with notable exceptions (for example, Whiting & Edwards, 1988; Whiting & Whiting, 1975). This is unfortunate, as anthropological studies of children's emotional development are such a potentially valuable source of information. Fortunately, a few cross-cultural studies of emotional development have been conducted, particularly in the area of managing emotional expression and distinguishing real versus apparent emotion.

A useful framework for orienting our discussion of cross-cultural universals and differences regarding the development of emotion management is provided by Shennum and Bugental (1982). They conceptualized a fourfold scheme of abilities necessary for effective emotion expression management: (1) knowledge concerning situations appropriate for expressing emotion, (2) ability to control expressive behavior, (3) motivation to do so, and (4) level of cognitive understanding. In reviewing research on these four aspects, I hypothesize that the impact of culture will be most clearly evident for 1 and 3, while the evidence for cross-cultural similarities will be strong for points 2 and 4. Knowledge concerning cultural display rules and the motivation to enact them is clearly tied to the socialization process—a process that can be highly variable across different cultures, particularly between Western and non-Western societies. In contrast, cognitive understanding of emotion and ability to control facial expression may be influenced primarily by maturational-developmental processes, and if that is true, the development of these abilities would be expected to progress according to a more universal timetable across different cultures.

A good illustration of the interplay between cognitive development and socialization practices concerns the relative spontaneity or restraint that is desirable in the cultural context of Western and Japanese societies. One of the first and most influential laboratory studies of the influence of culture on the use of emotional display rules was conducted by Ekman and Friesen (Ekman, 1973; Friesen, 1972). In this study (Friesen's doctoral dissertation), Japanese and American college students were shown two strikingly different films, a pleasant travelogue and a gruesome documentary showing a subincision ritual involving bodily mutilation. The facial expressions of the unsuspecting "moviegoers" were filmed as they watched the films in semidarkness. Subsequently the students were interviewed about the films by a member of their own culture.

The results showed a main effect for the type of film, but no discernible effect for culture on the facial expressions shown by the two groups of subjects as they were watching the film in private. In other words, even though the two films elicited very different emotional reactions, each film elicited the same basic emotions (in terms of facial expressions and physiological reactions) in both cultural groups—happiness while viewing the travelogue, but disgust and distress while viewing the mutilation. However, during the interview after the films, the Japanese students masked the discomfort and distress they had felt when watching the second film, whereas the American students displayed their negative emotions as they recounted the film to the interviewer. This study clearly shows the operation of cultural display rules (during the interview) and the universality of emotional appraisal, facial expression, and physiological reactions when the students felt no need to inhibit their emotional expressions in the safety of the dimly lit theater.

In view of these differences between Japanese and American adults, Hess and colleagues decided to explore the development of such differences by asking Japanese and American mothers the age at which they expected their children to master a number of basic developmental tasks. Although they generally had similar expectations, some interesting differences in their expectations were revealed. Japanese mothers expected their children to master their emotions several years earlier than did the American mothers, who in turn expected their children to assert themselves earlier than did the Japanese (Hess, Kashiwigi, Azuma, Price, & Dickson, 1980).

Harris and colleagues decided to see if such cultural expectations would influence the timing of the development of the ability to distinguish real versus apparent emotion between British and Japanese children. They hypothesized that early socialization pressures and the more explicit marking of the difference between inner experience and outer expression that characterizes Japanese society would lead Japanese children to grasp this distinction at an earlier age. Somewhat surprisingly, this prediction was not supported (Gardner, Harris, Ohmoto, & Hamazaki, 1988; Harris & Gross, 1988). These researchers examined how well children understood that facial expressions can sometimes be misleading and not accurate readouts of inner or felt emotion. For both British and Japanese children, 4-year-olds were unable to grasp this distinction, while 6-year-olds in both cultures generally recognized that outward appearances may not necessarily reveal how one feels on the inside.

In a related cross-cultural study, Joshi and MacLean (1994) reported both similarities and differences in their comparison of 4- and 6-year-olds in Bombay and England. Replicating Harris and colleagues, 6-year-olds in both cultures were found to be more proficient than 4-year-olds in their understanding of the distinction between real and apparent emotion. Indian and British boys were not different in their responses about whether or not children in stories would adopt misleading facial expressions in order to hide negative feelings. However, at age 4, more than triple the number of Indian girls compared to British girls endorsed the idea that children should try to hide their negative feelings from the adult. It may be that socialization pressures on girls in Indian society, more than in England, call for masking one's negative feelings while interacting with an adult, not out of concern for the adult's feelings, but because of fear of punishment for violating the display rules for their gender in their society (Joshi & MacLean, 1994).

Taken together, these studies suggest that the cognitive ability to understand the distinction between real and apparent emotion emerges between the ages of 4 and 6 in different cultures, but that knowledge about display rules and motivation to use them may be influenced by the socialization practices of a particular culture, and that certain display rules can apply for one gender but not the other. It also seems reasonable to postulate that the ability to enact cultural display rules, particularly when this involves concealing or minimizing a genuine emotion, emerges according to a relatively fixed developmental timetable. Clearly, young children the world over have less muscular control of the type that is necessary to manipulate their expressive behaviors, particularly when strong emotions are aroused (Charlesworth & Kreutzer, 1973). Thus, even very young Indian girls would not be expected to control their facial expressions, even though their society's rule system deems such control to be appropriate.

Several studies have shown that the capacity to minimize or suppress a felt emotion emerges during the latter preschool years, several years after the ability to mimic emotions in pretend play (Josephs, 1993; LaFreniere, 1988). Recall that French Canadian children younger than 4 years were unable to suppress repeated sidelong glances directly at where they hid a toy bear when asked, "Do you know where that bear is hiding?" Despite shrugging their shoulders and looking innocent, their nervous smiles and glances gave them away every time.

Apparently, German preschoolers behave in a similar fashion. In a variant of Feldman's sour fruit juice task designed to explore children's ability to conceal a positive emotion (glee at tricking a research assistant), Josephs (1993) arranged for the preschoolers to pretend that a glass of fruit juice was sweet, when it was actually quite sour. When the research assistant was gone, they all thought that this was quite a funny trick to play. When the assistant returned to drink the juice in front of the child, Josephs observed a number of tension-related behaviors, such as putting their hands over their mouths

Figure 9.3 Children's ability to pose convincing (but unfelt) facial expressions of emotion develops slowly during middle childhood.

(Photos by LaFreniere)

and incipient giggling, as well as smiling and sidelong glances at the confederate who shared in the joke. Recall that, using the same task, Feldman et al. (1979) found that naive raters more readily detected attempts at deception in first graders than in older groups. Future research involving different paradigms and more diverse cross-cultural comparisons is needed to complete our understanding of cultural differences and human universals in the emotional development of children.

SUMMARY

Throughout childhood, developmental advances in cognition, language, self-concept, and social relations set the stage for emotional communication that gradually begins to resemble that of adults. We began our discussion of these advances with a review of research on children's understanding of internal states called theory of mind (TOM). A "theory" of mind refers to an abstract causal system that allows one to explain and predict behavior through reference to unobservable mental states such as beliefs, intentions, desires, and emotions.

Research on TOM originated in experimental work on chimpanzee social intelligence. These experiments demonstrated that chimps are capable of clever deceptions that seem to rely upon an understanding of the desires, emotions, and intentions of their human trainers. Similarly, tactical deception in children that involves planting misleading evidence or adopting misleading expressive behavior relies upon an advanced theory of mind and does not emerge until after 4 years.

Although chimpanzees were found to possess some surprising abilities in TOM, they make fewer attributions about complex mental states than humans, since they cannot attribute states of mind that they themselves do not possess. Naturalistic and experimental evidence suggests that apes make simple attributions of seeing, wanting, and expecting, rather than attributions about beliefs.

Models of belief–desire psychology propose a two-step sequence of development that begins with a simple desire psychology. At this stage, children can explain and predict behavior. The next major step forward in thinking about the mind permits reflection on the representational process and the understanding that a belief is a representation of reality, not reality itself. Unlike a desire, a belief can be true or false, and the external world can be represented accurately or inaccurately.

Four-year-old children, but not chimpanzees, generally pass false-belief tasks, confirming their understanding that another person can hold beliefs that are different from their own—beliefs that could be incorrect, but which nevertheless determine their behavior.

Researchers have also been active in exploring how children come to learn that things are not always what they seem to be. These researchers employ appearance–reality tasks that require children to demonstrate their understanding that appearances can sometimes be misleading and not accurate representations of reality. Like the false-belief tasks, the appearance–reality distinction requires meta-representational skills or the ability to represent representations. This distinction is mostly absent in 3-year-olds and is still quite fragile for children between 4 and 6 years of age.

The understanding that physical appearances can be falsely represented with respect to an object's identity and the understanding that reality can be represented in different ways depending on one's point of view share an underlying cognitive component with the child's ability to understand that expressive behaviors may not match inner feelings. Not only are these three abilities interrelated within subjects, but they all tend to emerge at about the same time, during the transition from early to middle childhood. Most 6-year-olds understand that other people can be misled by displaying facial expressions that are different from what one actually feels, though they may have difficulty deciding whether any given expression is real or apparent.

With these advances in emotional understanding, children become more aware of the subtleties of emotions in everyday life. Two aspects of this more subtle view of emotions that emerge during middle childhood involve (1) understanding that one may experience ambivalent or conflicting emotions as a single reaction and (2) learning the rules for emotion management that seem to be prescribed by one's culture.

Children's understanding of emotional ambivalence does not appear to be well established before the age of 9. When preschoolers are asked how they might feel on the last day of school, they are unable to imagine two different emotions being provoked. Between about 6 and 8 years, children will report that they would be sad or happy, but never both emotions at the same time. By 9 years, children acknowledge that the last day of school may provide an occasion for mixed feelings—happiness at the prospect of summer vacation, and sadness because they will miss their school friends or favorite teacher.

Children's ability to engage in culturally appropriate emotional displays also appears to increase with age from early childhood to adolescence. Cultural display rules are implicitly taught through socialization within a particular culture. They serve similar functions as ritualized displays in animals by promoting harmonious and scriptlike forms of social exchanges that are somewhat ritualized, making them predictable for members of the same culture. Some display rules are learned in early childhood, though older children are increasingly more likely to take into consideration the consequences of their expressive behavior on others and to be more circumspect in their expression of negative emotions like anger and sadness, in part because they anticipate negative interpersonal consequences to overt expression of these emotions. Social and cultural factors also influence the likelihood that a given emotion will be expressed, again because of children's expectations concerning interpersonal consequences.

Four discrete abilities appear to be necessary for effective emotion expression management: (1) knowledge concerning situations appropriate for expressing emotion, (2) ability to control expressive behavior, (3) motivation to do so, and (4) level of cognitive understanding. Research suggests that cognitive understanding and the ability to enact cultural display rules, particularly when this involves concealing or minimizing a genuine emotion, emerge according to a relatively fixed developmental timetable. In contrast, knowledge about display rules and the motivation to use them are influenced by the socialization practices of a particular culture.

FURTHER READING

Ekman, P., & Friesen, W. V. (1975). *Unmasking the face.* Englewood Cliffs, NJ: Prentice-Hall.

An early and sophisticated treatment of emotional dissemblance, this book provides a detailed account of reliable clues to deception in facial expression.

Harris, P. L. (1989). *Children and emotion: The development of psychological understanding.* Oxford, England: Blackwell.

This very readable account of how children come to understand the complexities of emotional life includes some of the author's own insightful research on the topic.

10

Adolescence: Quest for Emotional Maturity

Coauthored with Jamie Walter

Adolescence begins in biology and ends in culture.

CONGER AND ADELSON (1984)

BIOSOCIAL PERSPECTIVE ON ADOLESCENCE

Adolescence is a period of dramatic changes in all aspects of development. With its origins in the latin word *adolescere,* meaning "to grow into adulthood," the period is initiated by the onset of puberty and comes to a close with the full transition to adult status. In many traditional societies, this transition is marked by culturally specific, but always sex-differentiated, **rites of passage.** This term was first used by the Belgian anthropologist Arnold van Gennep (1960), who noted that traditional societies practiced a three-part transitionary ritual involving (1) an initial isolation phase, (2) a phase of intentional confusion in which the identity of the adolescent is broken down, and (3) a phase of reinstatement in which the adolescent is incorporated into the adult community. These rites of passage signal to the individual and all others in the group that the transition to adult status is completed. Besides this signal value, human ethologists also suggest that puberty rites function to provide instruction in adult sex roles and to instill cultural loyalty (Weisfeld, 1997, 1999).

Unlike traditional societies, in contemporary Western society we can assert when adolescence begins but are much less clear about when it ends. It is certainly extended beyond the typical period seen in traditional societies. From a biosocial perspective, the form, the meaning, and even the duration of adolescence is primarily a cultural construction, though its onset and its functional significance appear to be universal, grounded in our common biology.

Historically, the conceptualization of a discrete developmental stage marking the transition from childhood to adulthood is of relatively recent origin, though Aristotle developed a view of adolescence that is remarkably similar to our conception today. He believed that children enter this period at puberty as emotionally unstable and impatient youths, but by about the age of 21 generally acquire greater self-control and maturity. Central to Aristotle's notion of maturity was the progressive movement toward self-determination involving independent decision making.

Twentieth-century psychological theorists have echoed these views to some extent. The American psychologist G. Stanley Hall is generally credited for the first comprehensive scientific treatment of adolescence (Hall, 1904). Influenced by Darwin, Hall characterized adolescence as a period of "storm and stress," a term that he chose to signify the passionate idealism and commitment to revolutionary principles that embodied the late eighteenth-century German literary and political movement known as "Sturm und Drang." This connection, and the connotation of zealous idealism and intense emotion, appears to have been lost somewhat in later characterizations of Hall's views. Mead (1928) challenged the view that adolescence is necessarily stressful by depicting the coming of age among Samoans as a peaceful and harmonious transition. More recently, Freeman (1983) has criticized Mead's findings as biased and essentially incorrect, concluding that adolescence in Samoa is more stressful than Mead was led to believe, and that juvenile delinquency exists in paradise in much the same way that it does in Western society.

Like all great debates, the truth probably lies in some middle ground between the views that adolescence is inherently stressful or largely harmonious and between the views that it is essentially biological or completely determined by culture. Many contemporary American psychologists believe that the "Sturm und Drang" of adolescence has been greatly exaggerated (Hill, 1980; Steinberg, 1990). However, few would disagree that this period is marked by a high point in emotional intensity, idealistic thinking, and passionate commitments to ideological causes. It is also clear that for too many American adolescents, the period poses grave risks and can be filled with interpersonal conflict, stress, violence, and even self-destruction, as FBI data attest. In this chapter we will attempt to reconcile these opposing views about the emotional lives of adolescents. In line with previous chapters, a biodevelopmental perspective will be integrated with a sociocultural view. Despite the activating influence of puberty, the balance of influence shifts to primarily sociocultural factors with increasing development. The role of emotions will be examined with respect to the development of the self, and with regard to the transformation of interpersonal relations in the family and the peer group. The most succinct and useful framework we have found for organizing our discussion is derived from the influential theories of Erik Erikson and John Hill.

PRIMARY CHANGES IN ADOLESCENCE

John Hill developed a framework for understanding adolescent development that incorporated Erikson's stage model and extended it by defining changes as primary and secondary. According to Hill's framework (Hill, 1980; Hill & Monks, 1977), adolescent development is set into motion by the primary changes in biology, cognition, and social relations that propel the individual toward new challenges or life tasks. These changes are considered primary because they are thought to be universal aspects of the adolescent experience, and because they have a reverberating impact on the secondary changes that are worked out within a specific cultural context.

Biological Changes

Puberty marks the onset of adolescence and represents the "one universal aspect of the adolescent experience, found in all primate species, in all cultures, throughout history" (Montemayor & Flannery, 1990). Virtually all scientific theories of adolescence, as well as most folk theories, are rooted in the ubiquitous fact of puberty. Due to the activating effects of hormones, at puberty dramatic morphological changes occur. These changes include growth spurts (timed earlier for girls, but more extensive in boys), qualitative changes in physical appearance, the emergence of primary and secondary sex characteristics, and a general increase in sexual **dimorphism.** It is well known that puberty accentuates the differences between men and women through the activating influence of the sex hormones—testosterone in men, and estrogen in women. However, the changes in morphology and behavior that are produced through the action of sex hormones are almost never discussed in functional terms. As Weisfeld and Billings (1988) noted:

> Textbooks on adolescent development have, through the years, faithfully detailed these morphological changes, but without acknowledging that these biological phenomena must necessarily possess identifiable adaptive functions . . . even the suggestion that some of the behavioral changes of adolescence might have an evolved basis virtually never appears in textbooks. Reading these accounts, one almost gets the impression that the sex drive itself appears because of television and "peer pressure" (other people's teenagers). (p. 207)

In humans, as in other animals, the adrenal glands produce a sex hormone that is the same for both sexes called dehydroepiandrosterone (DHEA). As shown in Figure 10.1, the amount of DHEA secreted by the adrenal glands peaks during the early teens. Similar to other sex hormones, DHEA is absorbed into the vascular system and reaches the brain where it influences activity in the hypothalamus. There are several lines of evidence suggesting that the onset of sexual attraction in early adolescence is due to the influence of DHEA, rather than the influence of testosterone or estrogen. Research indicates that people of both sexes recall the awakening of

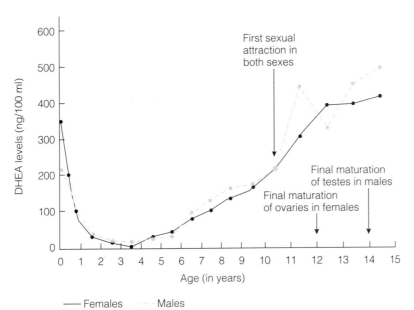

Figure 10.1 Blood levels of adrenal androgen DHEA in girls and boys as function of age

Source: McLintock and Herdt (1996). Used by permission of Blackwell Publishers.

sexual feelings toward another person as taking place between 10 and 12 years of age (McClintock & Herdt, 1996). If testosterone and estrogen were involved, these changes would be occurring at a later time, and they would be timed earlier in girls than boys by about two years. Instead, the timing of these changes is more consistent with the hypothesis that DHEA is the hormone linked to reproductive motivation.

Further evidence in support of this view comes from research in human ethology that has documented that both same-sex preferences and attraction to members of the opposite sex are based on a biologically programmed perceptual bias (Skrzipek, 1978, as reported in Eibl-Eibesfeldt, 1995). Given the choice between line drawings of female and male body contours, pre-pubertal children of both sexes prefer same-sex drawings. But beginning at about the age of 12 in both sexes, a dramatic reversal takes place, as shown in Figure 10.2, with female and male adolescents showing a clear preference for opposite-sex body profiles.

Further research is needed to clarify the role of puberty and sex hormones in the social and emotional development of human adolescents. In nonhuman primates, an increase in male aggressiveness during puberty is typical across many species, while female aggressiveness is largely unaffected by puberty and remains much lower than male levels. In humans, testosterone, a primarily male activating hormone, has been linked to gender differences in aggressive behavior (Geary, 1998), while estrogen, a primarily female activating hormone, has been linked to depression (Strober, 1985), though these relationships are not always found and are mediated by developmental history and other contextual factors.

Prevalence rates of depression and aggression are quite different between adolescent males and females. Depression is uncommon in childhood and sex differences are neglible. However, adolescent girls and women are significantly more likely to report suffering from depression than adolescent boys and men (Kessler et al., 1994). Similarly, homicide is relatively rare in childhood, but with the onset of adolescence, there is a remarkable increase in male rates of homicide. Year after year, throughout the world, between 80 and 90 percent of all homicides are committed by

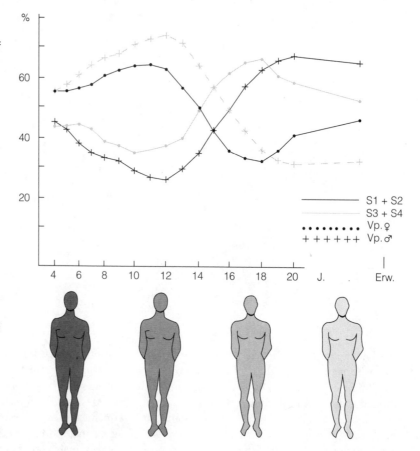

Figure 10.2 Masculine and feminine model choice by boys and girls as a function of age. The transition between preference for same-sex body contour and opposite-sex preference occurs between 12 and 18 years for both sexes.

Source: Adapted from Skrzipek, 1978 in Eibl-Eibesfeldt (1995).

men, mostly young men (excluding warfare, which is even more asymmetrical), and their victims are almost always men of the same age (Daly & Wilson, 1978; Wilson & Daly, 1985).

In the past, many psychologists insisted that these sex differences stemmed from purely environmental forces shaping the behavior of boys and girls through modeling, reinforcement, and other forms of social learning. Biologists disagree with such a one-sided view of human sociality, particularly biologists who study different animal species showing the same persistent asymmetries between the sexes across many different species. From an evolutionary perspective, the reproductive risks and rewards for competition and aggression are far greater for males than females in primates and mammals in general. This universal fact derives from simple logic: Unlike females, males can increase their reproductive success greatly through multiple matings (Daly & Wilson, 1978; Geary, 1998; Trivers, 1972).

Much greater variability among males in reproductive success was true for humans during the long formative period of our evolution, as supported by historical evidence and contemporary studies of preindustrial societies. For example, the anthropologist Napoleon Chagnon reports far higher variablity in reproductive success among males than females among the Yanomamö. The most reproductively successful man had 43 children, and his father had over 400 great-great grandchildren, modest attainments compared to history's most reproductive king, a Sharfian emperor of Morrocco who had 888

Figure 10.3 "From disdain to discovery"

(Top photo, by Eugene Richards/Magnum; bottom photo, by Susan Werner/Tony Stone Images)

children! (Chagnon, 1979; Daly & Wilson, 1978). In contrast, other Yanomamö men have had few or no children or grandchildren.

To summarize, it is clear that the number of potential offspring is far greater in males than females and more closely related to dominance status. Throughout human history, intermale competition and coalition based aggression has been related to reproductive success. In her historical analysis of the first six great civilizations, Laura Betzig makes the following generalization: "powerful men mate with hundreds of women,

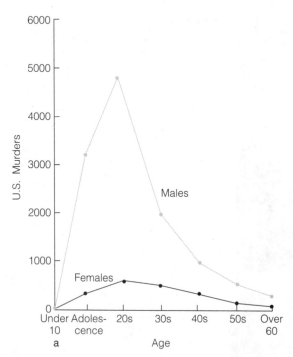

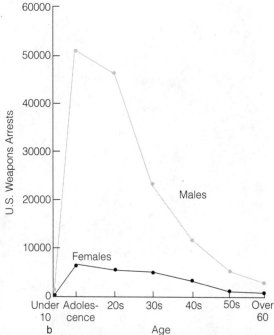

Figure 10.4a 1998 FBI data on murders as a function of age and gender

Figure 10.4b 1998 FBI data on weapons arrests as a function of age and gender

pass their power on to a son by one legitmate wife, and take the lives of men who get in their way" (Betzig, 1993, p. 37). The same generalization applies today in preindustrial societies. The motives for the high levels of intergroup conflict and violence among men in these societies include retaliation, economic gain, and capture of women and personal prestige, all of which may ultimately enhance reproductive success (Geary, 1998). For example, among the Yanomamö, 40 percent of adult males have killed at least once. They have more than twice as many wives and three times as many children as those men who have never killed (Chagnon, 1988).

These facts of life and death have led human ethologists Margo Wilson and Martin Daly (1985) to propose that the higher levels of risk-taking, violence, and aggression more commonly observed among adolescent males than females,

referred to as "the young-male syndrome," are a by-product of sexual selection. This simply means that throughout human evolution, males who took risks to achieve power and status produced more offspring *on average* than those who did not. Of course, one could argue that such evolutionary pressures are no longer operative in modern industrial societies due to the the extensive use of birth control. However, true or not, this would not have any impact on the phylogenetic adaptations rooted in biology. The scientific issue is whether or not contemporary observations are consistent with the thesis of the young-male syndrome.

An examination of United States Census Bureau data overwhelmingly confirms one aspect of the thesis. Male arrests for all categories of violent crimes consistently exceed females arrests (see Figures 10.4a and 10.4b). Not only do these statistics reveal a considerable gap between the sexes, with males exceeding females by margins that are typically as high as 10 to 1, but these rates are highest among younger than older males, and both findings are consistent in every year for which data are available (Uniform Crime Reports, Federal Bureau of Investigation 1997). Wilson and Daly (1985) also point out that many of the violent acts committed by young males are triggered by challenges to their status and other signs of disrespect. Acquiring status and respect is one of the foremost reasons for joining a street gang. Many violent acts are retaliations for perceived insults, they are more often performed when other young men are present, and young men who murder regularly choose to do so publicly as a means of proving their toughness and acquiring greater status.

It is quite clear that the behaviors reported in Figure 10.4 are committed by a tiny percentage of males in our society, but that does not contradict Wilson and Daly's hypothesis, since it is only designed to explain why certain differences between males and females are so ubiquitous across cultures and species. From a biosocial perspective, *individual differences* in the propensity for violence cannot be explained by biological or socialization factors acting alone, but rather by complex gene–environment interactions, as discussed in Chapter 8. Most psychologists believe that biological factors interact with a wide range of social factors, including the developmental history and gender of the individual, and stressful environmental conditions.

Cognitive Changes

The last of Piaget's stages, **formal operations,** characterizes the potential cognitive achievements and thought processes of the adolescent. Formal operations allow the adolescent to think logically, hypothetically, and to use deductive reasoning in abstract contexts. Piaget (1967) was the first to recognize that despite the superior power of formal operations in the realm of abstract problem solving, this cognitive advance brings with it potential risks and a new type of egocentrism:

> With the advent of formal intelligence, thinking takes wings and it is not surprising that at first this unexpected power is both used and abused. . . . Each new mental ability starts off by incorporating the world in a process of egocentric assimilation. Adolescent egocentricity is manifested by a belief in the omnipotence of reflection, as though the world should submit itself to idealistic schemes rather than to systems of reality. (pp. 63–64)

David Elkind (1967, 1976) has extended Piaget's conception of adolescent **egocentrism** and added several concepts of his own. Egocentrism at this stage is characterized by a belief that others are primarily focused and concerned with the issues that the adolescent feels are important. Elkind believes that such egocentric thinking may be a reaction to a kind of imaginary audience that is conjured up out of the heightened self-consciousness of the adolescent. The term **imaginary audience** refers to the subjective feeling that one's actions, appearance, and manners are constantly being scrutinized and criticized by others. While Shakespeare viewed all the world as a stage, adolescents view themselves as the principal characters; everyone else is perceived as members of the audience. Feeling the effects of this ever-present scrutiny, an adolescent girl may spend hours in front of the mirror trying to get her hair "just right." A boy may be equally concerned with hiding a pimple. Arriving at the prom, both of them may be mostly concerned that others are now scrutinizing the very same aspects of their appearance that have concerned them over the past few hours. This self-concern of both adolescent boys and girls carries over into their social relationships with parents, peers, and romantic interests, causing Philip Cowan to remark that "it is a wonder that authentic relationships do in fact begin to grow" (Cowan, 1978, p. 292).

Figure 10.5 David Elkind refers to the heightened self-consciousness of early adolescence as "imaginary audience."

(Photo by Christopher Brown/Stock Boston)

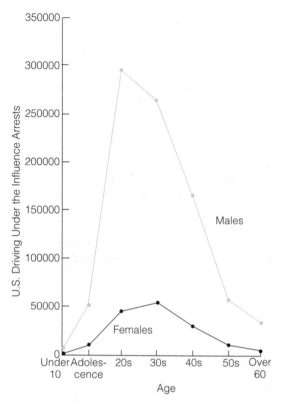

Figure 10.6 1998 FBI data on driving under the influence as a function of age and gender

Another aspect of adolescent egocentrism is the adolescent's sense of personal uniqueness, which Elkind has called the **personal fable.** A personal fable refers to the ongoing personal narrative that the adolescent is crafting, once again casting him- or herself in the lead. However, the adolescent is convinced that no one has ever had or ever could have the same kind of thoughts and feelings that he or she has experienced. Elkind provides an example of an adolescent girl who believes that her mother cannot possibly understand the hurt she has experienced because her boyfriend has broken up with her. She may tell her mother that she has no idea what it means to be in love, and drown herself in the misery of being forever misunderstood.

The personal fable also leads to the conviction that tragedies can happen only to others. This fiction may give rise to feelings of a sort of invulnerability to well-known risks and dangers. Reckless sex, driving while drunk, and risky experiments with powerful drugs are some exam-

ples of the types of risks that are run by adolescents who believe that "it could never happen to me." As shown in Figure 10.6, this type of risk-taking is about seven times more prevalent in teenage boys than teenage girls, which is consistent with the young-male syndrome presented earlier.

Social Changes

Many of the social changes occurring during adolescence stem directly from physical changes and sexual maturation. Parents, peers, and other socializing agents hold different assumptions, make different attributions, and have different expectations of the adolescent after the physical transformations of puberty. Given the variation in the timing of these changes between and within gender groups, this means that children of the same chronological age may receive quite different treatment according to their pubertal status (Hill, 1980).

In the context of family relations, Steinberg (1988; Steinberg & Hill, 1978) has demonstrated that pubertal maturation is often accompanied by greater emotional distance between parents and their adolescent children. According to Collins (1997), parent–adolescent interactions are mediated by their expectations of one another. If maturation gives rise to discrepancies between such expectations and actual behavior, the resulting conflict and disequilibrium experienced by both adolescents and parents may force a realignment in their attitudes and expectations, so that a new equilibrium may be established. Such changes in family relationships may take several years and create variable amounts of emotional tension and conflict between parents and their adolescent daughters and sons.

Different dynamics originating with the onset of puberty also influence changes in the structure and function of peer relationships. In Chapter 8 we noted that preschool children begin to prefer and interact with same-sex peers at about three years, and that this preference grows in magnitude throughout childhood. With the onset of puberty, this attraction to same-sex peers is reversed, and the structure of the peer group is gradually transformed. Based on extensive observation of peer interaction from preadolescence to young adulthood, Dexter Dunphy (1963) has formulated a well-known five-stage model of the structural changes in peer relations that occur during this period, as shown in Figure 10.7.

The first type of structure to emerge out of peer interaction is the clique. **Cliques** are small close-knit groups of mutual friends who spend a great deal of time interacting together. Clique structures are quite visible in preschool groups and from that time forward may be characterized as enclaves of same-age, same-sex peers—in short, children who are compatible with one another and share common interests. The preadolescent clique represents the apex of this social

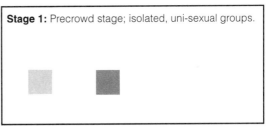

Stage 1: Precrowd stage; isolated, uni-sexual groups.

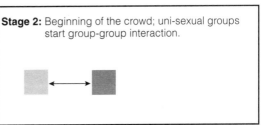

Stage 2: Beginning of the crowd; uni-sexual groups start group-group interaction.

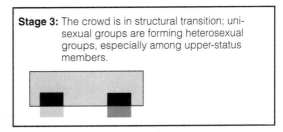

Stage 3: The crowd is in structural transition; uni-sexual groups are forming heterosexual groups, especially among upper-status members.

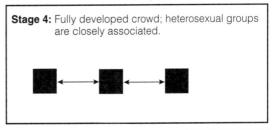

Stage 4: Fully developed crowd; heterosexual groups are closely associated.

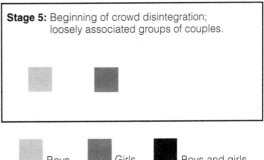

Stage 5: Beginning of crowd disintegration; loosely associated groups of couples.

Boys   Girls   Boys and girls

Figure 10.7 Dunphy's model of structural changes in peer groups during adolescence

structure. At this age, cliques may be as large as 10 or 12 members, but are typically composed of 5 or 6 same-age, same-sex peers.

A junior high school cafeteria is an excellent setting for a participant observer to witness uni-sex cliques in action. For example, one clique may be composed of a small group of girls who have lunch together every day, who interact with each other after school and on weekends, and who would not dream of sitting at the boys' table a few feet away. These boys may all be members of the junior high football team, and spend prac-tically all their free time together, practicing after school, watching sports on TV, hanging out on weekends, and discussing the girls at the table next to them during lunch hour. At this stage in Dunphy's model, gender boundaries prevail, though interest in members of the opposite sex may be on the rise as some individuals enter the early stages of puberty.

In the second stage, growing interest in members of the opposite sex leads to a structur-al change in peer interaction that is clearly tran-sitional in nature. At this stage, prior to actual dating, boys and girls come together in mixed-sex parties, but spend most of their time in the security of their same-sex clique while making an occasional foray across the gender divide. By the third stage, a new structure emerges, espe-cially in urban adolescent groups, which Dunphy refers to as crowds. **Crowds** are mixed-sex col-lectives that gather together semiregularly, and which are much larger, less exclusive, and less organized than same-sex cliques. Because crowds are based on individual reputations or labels, members of a crowd may not necessarily know each other well. In his initial study of this phe-nomenon, Dunphy (1963) described the struc-ture of a high school of 300 students as composed of 44 cliques, but just 12 crowds. At this stage, the crowd may be composed of sever-al same-sex cliques, in which high-status mem-bers begin to interact more frequently with opposite-sex peers. Gradually, as other members begin to follow this example, the same-sex clique dissolves.

This leads to the fourth stage in which the crowd has reached its apex, essentially transform-ing the same-sex cliques into heterosexual cliques. At this stage the fully developed crowd may be based more on reputation, style of dress, and stereotypes than on actual behavior (Brown, 1990), or in some American cities, the crowd may be organized by ethnic groups. The celebrated American play *West Side Story* provides a dramat-ic illustration of a fully developed crowd in New York City, and portrays all the universal themes (identity, autonomy, intimacy) as well as the unique cultural elements that make late adoles-cence an exciting and sometimes dangerous peri-od of development. Finally, in Dunphy's fifth stage, the crowd too begins to dissipate as couples form and move out into a larger, more anony-mous adult society. Couples may continue to associate together for a time but without the feel-ing of belonging to a crowd.

As implied in Dunphy's structural model, the nature of peer interactions also undergoes dra-matic change. In a naturalistic study of affective expression and physical contact in children between 6 and 18 years, Montemayor and Flannery (1989) unobtrusively observed children and adolescents in public settings as they interact-ed with either parents or peers. Significant age-related changes were apparent in social interaction, with early adolescents increasingly talking to their parents and opposite-sex peers, but by middle adolescence, opposite-sex peers engaged in more smiling, mutual gazing, and touching. Although young children rarely touched same-sex peers, adolescent girls increased their touching, while adolescent boys almost never touched each other. As many natu-ralistic observational studies have shown, the sex cleavage so apparent in middle childhood begins to break down with the onset of adolescence, and most high school students have had at least one romantic relationship by the time they graduate (Savin-Williams & Berndt, 1990). The essential point to be made now is that these primary changes in biological, cognitive, and social domains stimulate the secondary changes that we shall be discussing. They are secondary, not in importance, but because they arise from more fundamental developmental processes.

ERIKSON'S PSYCHOSOCIAL THEORY REVISITED

As we discussed in Chapter 4, Erikson's theory of psychosocial development has had considerable influence on developmental theory and research in both the conceptualization of normative trends and the search for meaningful constructs from which to assess individual differences. At no point in the life span is this impact more apparent than on research in adolescence. Erikson's psychosocial theory has provided the past two generations of developmental scholars with a heuristic sketch of the major developmental milestones from which one could develop empirical research programs to investigate the development of attachment relations in infancy, the emergence of autonomy in early childhood, and the development of a sense of personal identity and formation of intimate relations in adolescence and young adulthood. Similar to Piaget's status in cognitive development, Erikson may not have had the last word on these areas of research, but he clearly set the agenda for what has followed. Let us take a closer look at this influential theory, which was briefly introduced in Chapter 3.

In *Childhood and Society* (1963), Erikson sketched what he called "an epigenetic chart," as shown in Figure 10.8. In just five pages he elaborates the developmental and methodological implications of his epigenetic matrix of psychosocial development. This vision was so ambitious in its scope that researchers have barely begun to fill in the matrix after 50 years and thousands of empirical studies. The main lines of this research have clearly been established along the diagonal of the matrix. According to Erikson (1968):

The diagonal represents the normative sequence of psychosocial gains made as at each stage one more nuclear conflict adds a new ego quality, a new criterion for accruing human strength. Below the diagonal there is space for the precursors of each of these solutions, all of which begin with the beginning; above the diagonal there is space for the designation of the derivatives of these gains and their transformations in the maturing and immature personality.

. . . [W]e do not consider all development a series of crises: we claim only that psychosocial development proceeds by critical steps—"critical" being a characteristic of turning points, of moments of decision between progress and regression, integration and retardation.

It may be useful at this point to spell out the methodological implications of an epigenetic matrix. The more heavily-lined squares of the diagonal signify both a sequence of stages and a gradual development of component parts: in other words, the chart formalizes a progression through time of a differentiation of parts. This indicates (1) that each critical item of psychosocial strength discussed here is systematically related to all others, and that they all depend on the proper sequence of each item; and (2) that each item exists in some form before its critical time arrives.

An epigenetic diagram thus lists a system of stages dependent on each other; and while individual stages may have been explored more or less thoroughly or named more or less fittingly, the diagram suggests that their study be pursued always with the total configuration of stages in mind. The diagram invites, then, a thinking through all its empty boxes. (pp. 270–272)

In accepting this invitation, there is one more caveat to consider. Erikson warns against oversimplifying the model by assuming that the resolution of any given stage is an achievement

		1	2	3	4	5	6	7	8
Old Age	VIII								Integrity vs. Despair, Disgust WISDOM
Adulthood	VII							Generativity vs. Stagnation CARE	
Young Adulthood	VI						Intimacy vs. Isolation LOVE		
Adolescence	V					Identity vs. Confusion FIDELITY			
Middle Childhood	IV				Industry vs. Inferiority COMPETENCE				
Early Childhood	III			Initiative vs. Guilt PURPOSE					
Toddlerhood	II		Autonomy vs. Shame, Doubt WILL						
Infancy	I	Basic Trust vs. Mistrust HOPE							

Figure 10.8 Erikson's psychosocial stages

Source: Erickson, (1963).

"secured once and for all at a given state . . . impervious to new inner conflicts and to changing conditions." In this section we shall begin "thinking through the empty boxes." (p. 274)

In Figure 10.9, below the diagonal we note important precursors to the adolescent issues of identity and intimacy that occur in the company of peers throughout early and middle childhood. During the preschool years, the basic task of establishing a firm sense of one's gender identity is ubiquitous in all cultures, though sex roles may be more specific across culture. Equally universal is the formation and maintenance of close friendships, a central task during the preschool years that continues to evolve in emotional complexity throughout middle childhood. Such friendships, most often between same-sex peers, involve some, but not all, of the elements of affective perspective-taking and self-disclosure that characterize adolescent friendships with members of both sexes. It is these same-sex and later opposite-sex friendships that are precursors to intimate heterosexual relationships in adolescence. Attachment relations are also seen as precursors of

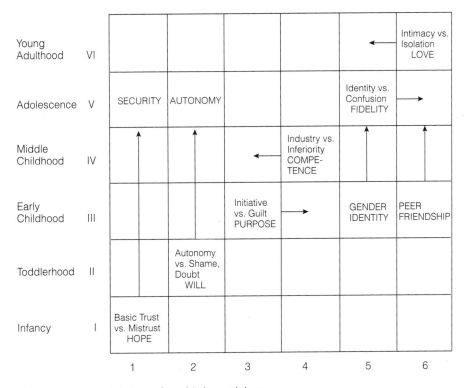

Figure 10.9 Erikson's psychosocial stages from birth to adolescence

intimate relations, and this influence is noted by the arrow running along the diagonal.

The diagonal itself is expanded in childhood to signify the joint, rather than stepwise, focus on initiative and industry (competence) as developmentally salient tasks throughout both early and middle childhood. In a similar sense, the joint issues of identity and intimacy are seen as simultaneous and salient throughout adolescence and young adulthood. Feminist writers have noted that some aspects of Erikson's vision of psychosocial development may be more appropriate for adolescent males than females. They argue persuasively that the task of establishing intimate relationships is more central at an earlier age among young women. For example, Schiedel and Marcia (1985) have suggested that intimacy and identity concerns merge for women rather than unfold in a stepwise progression. We have fused the two stages to indicate this possibility as well as to indicate that for

both sexes the two tasks are complementary. True intimacy would be unlikely without first establishing a firm sense of identity; reciprocally, the development of a close, intimate relationship affords a unique perspective from which a new understanding of one's self may emerge.

Derivatives are indicated above the diagonal and include (1) reworking the primary attachment bonds in the direction of greater symmetry and mutual empathy, and (2) reworking the basic issue of emotional autonomy, particularly with respect to parents. Peter Blos (1967) was among the first theorists to recognize the similarities in the emotional dynamics of separation-individuation in the toddler period, and the adolescent's quest for independence. We have carried forward both of Erikson's first two psychosocial stages to adolescence in order to highlight the developmental salience of these tasks for the adolescent. In this scheme it is not simply a question of separating

Table 10.1 Psychosocial Issues in Adolescent Development

Issue	Adolescent Change
Attachment	Transforming childhood social bonds to parents to bonds acceptable between parents and their adult children.
Autonomy	Extending self-initiated activity and confidence in it to wider behavioral realms.
Sexuality	Transforming social roles and gender identity to incorporate sexual activity with others.
Intimacy	Transforming acquaintanceships into friendships; deepening and broadening capacities for self-disclosure, affective perspective-taking, altruism.
Achievement	Focusing industry and ambition into channels that are future-oriented and realistic.
Identity	Transforming images of self to accommodate primary and secondary change; coordinating images to attain a self-theory that incorporates uniqueness and continuity through time.

Source: Adapted from Hill (1980).

from one's parents in order to achieve independence. Although independence and autonomy are crucial, they may be best achieved by transforming rather than negating close ties with the family.

SECONDARY CHANGES IN ADOLESCENCE

The psychosocial issues referred to as secondary changes in Hill's framework are shown in Table 10.1. As can be seen by comparing these issues with those introduced earlier in Erikson's model, there is more consensus than divergence between these two theorists regarding the psychosocial tasks of the adolescent period.

Transforming Family Relations

Emotional Autonomy The processes of individuation and identity exploration require the adolescent to become emotionally independent from the parent. In considering the emotional life of the adolescent, many theorists believe that children reenter a stage of autonomy struggles with parents. Although there may be similarities with the emotional dynamics of separation-individuation in the toddler period, the adolescent's quest for independence is different in many respects. We define **autonomy** in adolescence as increased self-reliance, initiative, resistance to peer pressure,

and responsibility for one's decisions and actions. For the American adolescent, increased autonomy occurs in the context of shifting priorities from parent-centered interactions to peer relationships (Steinberg, 1990). For example, in one study, the time adolescents spent with family members decreased from about 35 percent to only 14 percent of waking hours (Larson, Richards, Moneta, Holmbeck, & Duckett, 1996). In a review of the literature on parent–adolescent relationships, the relationship with parents was noted as becoming more egalitarian and peerlike as parents begin to expect, and the adolescent desires, more adultlike responsibility (Paikoff & Brooks-Gunn, 1991). With adolescents' increasing cognitive abilities and competencies, they are prone to detect flaws in their parents' behavior and strive for a more egalitarian relationship with them.

Steinberg (1990) believes that adolescents become less emotionally dependent on their parents for four reasons. First, older adolescents become less likely to turn to their parents in response to their emotional needs; second, they are more likely to have complex views of their parents as flawed and imperfect; third, they are often emotionally invested in relationships beyond the family; and finally, they are increasingly likely to interact with their parents in an egalitarian fashion. All of these cognitive and social reasons act to pull the adolescent toward the peer culture.

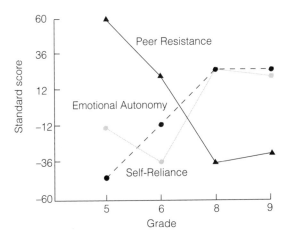

Figure 10.10 Age differences in three types of autonomy

Source: Steinberg & Silverberg (1986). Used by permission of the SRCD.

As seen in Figure 10.10, emotional autonomy and self-reliance steadily rise in early adolescence, and resistance to peer influence declines (Steinberg & Silverberg, 1986). In the course of adolescent development, these shifts to more autonomy and increases in peer influence may not always be smooth, but the nature of the parent–child relationship generally maintains a certain degree of cohesion in the midst of conflict and change.

In early adolescence it is difficult for children to see that their parents may act differently at home than at work or with friends. As Steinberg notes, adolescents develop critical attitudes toward their parents, detecting flaws where there was once uncritical identification. This may be an important step in the movement toward forging an independent identity. At this age they may often feel that it is better to seek the advice of a peer who "truly understands" them than a parent (Steinberg & Silverberg, 1986; Youniss & Smollar, 1985). Looking back on this period from young adulthood, one might conclude, as the joke goes, "that it is surprising how wise my parents have grown in just a few years!"

Daily Emotional Experiences In order to better understand the changing nature of family relations and the day-to-day emotional experiences of adolescents, Reed Larson has developed the **experience sampling method** (ESM) (Larson, 1989). In this approach, adolescents, and sometimes their parents, carry pagers that beep at semirandom intervals throughout the day. Participants are typically instructed to keep a journal with them so that when the pager beeps, they can write down information about their current social situation and emotional state (for example, who are they with, how they feel). The utility of the ESM is that we are given a glimpse of the changes in emotionality that can occur hour to hour that is highly descriptive. Possible limitations of the ESM include its exclusive reliance on self-report data and the generalizability of the samples that are tested.

The affective quality of adolescents' daily lives can be seen in their average mood states and in the lability of their emotional experiences. Greene (1990) found that junior high school students experience more negative affect than elementary school children. There is a slight decline in negative affect again in high school, but girls appear to remain in these negative states longer than boys, as the decrease in negative affect in high school is seen primarily in boys, not girls. Typical differences in adolescent emotionality are not found in the average mood state but in the variability in moods. For example, Larson and Richards (1994) found that adolescents reported more extreme positive and negative emotions, but less frequent neutral or mild affect than their parents. Adolescents reported being very happy six times more often and very unhappy three times more often than their parents. In addition to these more global emotional categories, adolescents were more likely than their parents to report that they felt embarrassed, awkward, nervous, as well as bored and apathetic.

Boredom may have a unique meaning in adolescence. For example, Larson and Richards (1991) found boredom to be associated with anger, frustration, and a lack of energy or motivation. Although boredom was most common in school, adolescents who were bored across different social contexts were rated by teachers as more disruptive. While often categorized as an emotion of indifference, these data suggest that boredom in adolescence may be more closely tied to negative emotional experiences such as frustration and anger.

When parents' and adolescents' emotional experiences are mapped across the course of several days, it appears that they report similar emotional experiences, with the intensity of the experience probably being greater for the adolescent. As seen in Figure 10.11, self-reported emotions during a typical weekend for an adolescent boy and his father follow a similar path. As Randy spends time with his friends, and his father with his wife, both report high levels of positive affect, a level of affect that remains throughout the course of the weekend. As descriptive accounts such as these attest, family life with an adolescent is not necessarily stormy and stressful, though some degree of conflict between adolescents and their parents is normative, and may contribute positively to adolescent psychosocial development.

Impact of Family Conflict Studies of the rate of family conflict range in estimates from an average of one argument every 3 days, with arguments lasting about 11 minutes, to 7 arguments per day when conflicts with peers are included (Laursen & Collins, 1994). Although it has been argued that findings of increased conflict in adolescence are an artifact of research methods, studies consistently find that verbal measures of conflict such as disagreements and interruptions show an increase in early adolescence and a decrease in later adolescence (Laursen & Collins, 1994; Montemayor, 1983; Steinberg, 1981; Steinberg & Hill, 1978). Conflicts with parents typically contain more negative affect than with either friends or dating partners, and the mother is more often involved in conflicts than the father.

The conflicts that develop in adolescence have historically been considered a process of detachment, where the adolescent is thought to break the parent–child attachment that was so

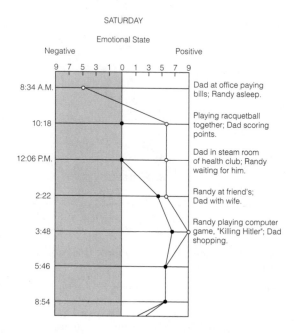

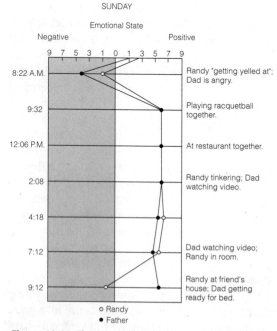

Figure 10.11 The emotions of a boy and his father over the course of a weekend

Source: From *Divergent Realities* by Reed Larson and Maryse H. Richards. Copyright © 1994 by Reed Larson and Maryse Richards. Reprinted by permission of Basic Books, a member of Perseus Books, L. L. C.

important for early development (A. Freud, 1958). The early psychoanalytic models of adolescent family conflict viewed such conflicts as healthy expressions of emotional development, and a lack of family discord was interpreted as potentially problematic for the developing adolescent. The alternative view of many contemporary theorists is that there is a considerable degree of harmony and stability in many families, and that high levels of conflict may indicate dysfunction.

Research has shown that families with an adolescent vary a great deal in their overall level of conflict. Three main patterns of development have been identified with respect to conflict and crisis in adolescent boys (Offer & Offer, 1975). About 25 percent of adolescent boys experience continuous growth, marked by mutual respect between the adolescent and his parents, a sense of purpose, and self-assurance. About 35 percent experience surgent growth, with periods of calm broken at times by anger, defiance, and immaturity. Finally another 25 percent show a pattern of tumultuous growth filled with stress and storm. The remaining 15 percent were unclassifiable within this system. A key question for developmental psychopathology concerns the origins and adult consequences of these different patterns of growth.

Many typical conflicts within middle-class families do not appear to be severe enough to drive the adolescent away. Rather, they amount to periodic bickering over daily life issues. Larson and Richards (1994) noted that

> adolescents' home time was also filled with repeated, often petty aggravations. Though chores were a small part of these teens' lives, they mentioned them frequently as a source of tension with their parents. One boy claimed to feel "horrible" because he had to help his dad cut wood. Another boy was happy taking care of his little brother until the child asked to go to a friend's house. "I wasn't supposed to let him go, so he got mad at me." The

result was that he felt "terrible, guilty, and grouchy." These parents regularly asked their teens to share part of the burden of necessary household labor, but their kids often experienced this request as harassment. Many of the adolescents, especially boys, felt little responsibility for their family's needs, and were therefore annoyed when asked to do their part. (pp. 99–100)

Conflict Resolution An important consideration in understanding adolescent conflicts within the family is how they are resolved. Unfortunately, these conflicts are sometimes handled poorly, with family members either submitting or detaching from the argument (Laursen & Collins, 1994). The importance of conflict resolution tactics within the family has been repeatedly associated with the adolescent's emotional and psychological functioning. A common methodology used to assess conflict resolution tactics is to tape-record family members discussing issues or problems together. In one such study, researchers found that adolescents who were encouraged by their parents to express their opinions and who remained emotionally attached to family members were more psychologically competent, and had higher self-esteem and more advanced coping strategies. Adolescents with less autonomy in the family reported more feelings of depression and were more likely to develop behavior problems across contexts (Allen, Hauser, Bell, & O'Connor, 1994; Allen, Hauser, Eickholt, Bell, & O'Connor, 1994; Silverberg, Tennenbaum, & Jacob, 1992).

In a longitudinal study by Capaldi, Forgatch, and Crosby (1994), adolescent males were observed in eighth and then tenth grade during a series of family interactions centered on resolving two high-conflict family issues. Raters coded affect, problem-solving efficiency, and the quality of the relationship; and a measure of self-esteem was also collected. Capaldi and colleagues found that families that did not stay problem focused and displayed high levels of negative affect, especially anger, or who displayed lower levels of tension regulation, often failed to solve the family dispute and had more distressed adolescents. The quality of the parent–child relationship was rated as lower in these families with low levels of emotion regulation. Over time, positive affect and humor diminished significantly, while negative emotions such as anxiety, tension, and contempt increased. Finally, families with more frequent positive affect also had boys with higher levels of self-esteem. It seems evident that the ability to regulate negative emotion in the family affects the adolescent's problem-solving ability and family relations.

Hill and Holmbeck (1986) found that although adolescents engage in more frequent conflicts with their parents, the conflicts do not significantly diminish the quality of the relationship. These conflicts may contribute in positive ways to adolescent development, particularly when these interactions occur in the context of a secure relationship with the parent (Paikoff & Brooks-Gunn, 1991). In a cross-sectional study of reported feelings of closeness to parents, college students and fourth graders reported similar levels of closeness. Thus, the increases in family conflict that occur during adolescence do not necessarily result in a severing of family ties, as was once thought (Hunter & Youniss, 1982).

Emotional Support Coping strategies on the part of the adolescent and emotional support by parents also seem to be important in determining adolescents' stress in the family. Wills (1990) theorized that parental support may promote positive affect in adolescents because they trust that a parent can be counted on in a time of need. Children who believe that their parents are there to support them are more likely to confide in their parents about problems, and also to learn more mature coping strategies. As a result, adolescents may have healthier perceptions about the impact of negative life events and spend less time ruminating about their problems. This literature suggests that the ability to regulate negative emotions in adolescence depends at least partly on practices within the family.

Adolescents' affective experiences and expressions within the family may be related to the child's gender as well as that of the parent. For boys and girls, reported affect with the family decreased in early adolescence and increased again in late adolescence, but girls and boys differed in the duration of these experiences. Girls tended to report this decrease in the affective quality of the family as lasting for a year or two longer than did boys. In addition, younger adolescents, especially girls, perceived their parents as being less friendly than did older adolescents. Additionally, mothers and fathers differed in the emotional support they gave to their adolescent children. An examination of social support networks revealed that mothers and siblings were equally important, but that fathers were viewed as less important for emotional support (Furman & Buhrmester, 1992). In a study of first semester college students, girls were more likely to turn to their mothers or their siblings to discuss feelings and to get help and guidance, whereas boys reported more often that their fathers told them what to do (Moser, Paternite, & Dixon, 1996). These findings suggest that throughout the course of adolescence, fathers may not be perceived by their children as providing as much emotional support as mothers.

Adolescents with higher self-reported emotional closeness to their family members were also found to have higher levels of self-esteem (Bell, Avery, Jenkins, Feld, & Shoenrock, 1985). The developing adolescent is exploring new social roles inside both the family and peer group, and dealing with the challenges these changes evoke. The understanding of a warm, supportive family appears to buffer them from the potentially negative impact of this transition. As discussed in Chapter 8, self-perceptions and peer relations can be strongly influenced by the quality of an individual's attachment relationship.

Similarly, in a sample of college students, Kobak and Sceery (1988) found that quality of attachment was related to affect regulation and social support from both parents and peers. Securely attached adolescents were perceived by their friends to be high in social competence, better adjusted, less distressed, and more able to constructively modulate their feelings. These adolescents also viewed their parents as supportive and felt loved by them, though they did not idealize them. They were able to see that their parents have flaws and could come to terms with the past. In contrast, adolescents who dismissed the importance of their attachment relationship were perceived to be more hostile and compulsively self-reliant by their friends. They reported feeling rejected and unloved by their parents, but also tended to idealize their relationships with their parents. When asked about these relationships, they often had trouble remembering details and felt that attachment relationships were unimportant. These adolescents also reported being unwilling to seek support or comfort from their parents. Finally, adolescents that were preoccupied with the attachment relationship were viewed by their friends as anxious as well as clingy to relationships that are unsuccessful at relieving this anxiety. Although their friends reported that these individuals thought of others as supportive, they felt that preoccupied adolescents were never able to get enough support from their relationships. Adolescents preoccupied with their attachment relationships also tended to reverse the parent–child role by hypervigilantly monitoring their parents. In addition, they showed little autonomy, as they would turn to their parents for support and verification of nearly every action. These findings suggest that the ability to successfully resolve the identity crisis and move confidently toward the emotional challenges of the peer world may depend, in part, on establishing secure relationships within a supportive family.

Transforming Peer Relations

At no time in the life cycle does the peer group play a more important role in social and emotional development than in adolescence. Adolescents spend more time in the company of peers and are more susceptible to peer pressure than at any other developmental period. Adolescents come to rely on peers, and especially friends, for emotional support as they struggle to transform their role in the family system (Savin-Williams & Berndt, 1990). These changes in the nature of peer relations may be seen in the increasing stability, loyalty, empathy, and support in same-sex friendships, and in the development of intimacy in sexual dating relationships.

Emotions of Adolescent Relationships

Adolescent peer relations contribute to healthy emotional development in a number of ways. First, peer relationships provide an important context for the expression and regulation of both positive and negative emotions because of their essentially egalitarian nature. Second, peers can offer effective emotional support and a sense of security in novel situations, which can be particularly important if family relations are strained or unsupportive. Third, peer friendships provide a source of self-esteem and validation from outside the family (Asher & Parker, 1989; Kelly & Hansen, 1987). Even in families that continue to provide the adolescent with advice and emotional support, peers are often seen as being more understanding of the adolescent's unique emotional needs (Savin-Williams & Berndt, 1990). Asher and Parker (1989) note that friends not only help with emotion management, but also allow adolescents the opportunity for self-disclosure and discovery in a nonthreatening environment. Intimacy in adolescent friendships stems from the realization that peers are equal and offer a special quality of closeness and emotional support.

However, not all adolescents experience emotional support from the peer group, or even have a close friend. The distinction between peer acceptance and friendship is important, as each is likely to contribute differently to an individual's social and emotional well-being (Bukowski & Hoza, 1989). Peer acceptance or popularity refers to the perception by the group of its individual members, whereas friendship refers to mutual liking between two people. Adolescents who are popular, for example, may have few close friends. However, it is more probable that adolescents who are disliked by their peer group have few or no friends. For example, Parker and Asher (1992) found that 91 percent of adolescents who were well liked by their peers also had a best friend, whereas only 54 percent of low accepted adolescents had a best friend. These low accepted adolescents also reported feeling more lonely, although those with a best friend were less lonely than those without a best friend.

These buffering effects of having a friend may depend upon the quality of the relationship itself. Low accepted adolescents' friendships had more frequent and longer lasting conflicts, conflict resolution was more difficult, and conflicts did not end amicably. These friendships were less intimate and less prosocial than friendships among average or well-liked peers. Although these adolescents may feel less lonely by having a friend, the quality of the friendship does not allow them to benefit from having a friendship as much as they could. In addition, low accepted adolescents view their friendships as less supportive, trustworthy, and loyal (Asher & Parker, 1989). Low peer acceptance is associated with dropping out of school, and aggressive adolescents with low levels of peer acceptance are more likely to commit both juvenile and adult crimes, whereas withdrawn adolescents with low levels of peer acceptance report the highest levels of loneliness of any group, suggesting that there is a considerable degree of variability among low accepted adolescents (Asher & Parker, 1989; Asher, Parkhurst, Hymel, & Williams, 1990). Across these studies, the function of friendships as well as positive peer regard appears to be in giving social and emotional support as well as a heightened sense of self-esteem.

Berndt and Perry (1990) have noted that children's friendships in middle childhood contain similar levels of positive emotional expression and conflict as in adolescence, but that "adolescents attach considerable emotional energy both to the problems and to the joys of their friendships" (p. 269). Larson and Richards (1991) found that

there is an increase in negative emotions like anxiety, distress, and anger from preadolescence to adolescence, and that this increase is primarily with friends. Both girls and boys report an increase in these negative emotions with opposite-sex friends, primarily because they are spending more time with these peers. Girls report an increase with same-sex friends as well. According to Savin-Williams (1987), "The best friend pairs so prevalent among early adolescent girls are still evident among the late adolescents; absent, however, are the constant changing of best friends and the backbiting, bickering, and cattiness" (p. 150). In late adolescence, girls show greater affective perspective-taking and can be quite sensitive to the needs and emotions of their friends.

Other developmental changes in social relationships can be seen in adolescents' definition of friendship. Whereas young children define friends as someone you like to play with and with whom you share toys, adolescents define friends as someone to whom they can disclose confidential information and whom they can admire (Selman & Schultz, 1990; Tedesco & Gaier, 1988). Berndt and Perry (1990) note that intimacy becomes an issue in early adolescents' conceptualizations of friendship and in their conversations with friends (Gottman & Mettetal, 1986, as cited in Berndt & Perry, 1990). Adolescent girls who perceive their best friends as being supportive, and their friendship as low in negative interactions, also feel that their needs match those of their best friend. It is not surprising that girls in these supportive relationships more often reported that their friends are better able to meet their needs than girls in unsupportive and more conflictual friendships (Gavin & Furman, 1996). These emotionally supportive friendships were also observed to be higher in positive affect, more attuned, and less jealous than those of girls with unsupportive friendships.

The effect of friendship on adolescent emotional development may depend partially on the amount of support or conflict that occurs within the relationship. In a longitudinal study of peer relations, Hightower (1990) found that adolescents who had positive peer relations and support along with close friendships were more psychologically healthy in adulthood. These findings can be interpreted in two ways. Positive peer relations in adolescence may have a lasting impact on mental health, or the characteristics that lead adolescents to develop positive friendships, including their past developmental history, are maintained throughout their lives.

Individuals differ in their ability to resolve conflicts once they arise. As a result they may have friends with similar social and emotional skills either by choice or because other more socially competent peers reject their friendship bids. Friendships of rejected adolescents often lack the prosocial behavior typically observed among friends. For example, in a study of the friendship quality of early adolescents, Dishion, Andrews, and Crosby (1995) found a strong correlation between adolescents' global ratings of social skills and the social skills of their nominated close friend. In a problem-solving situation between these friends, antisocial boys and their nominated close friend issued more commands, had more negative interactions, and displayed less positive reciprocity when compared to average peers. In addition, these friendships were initially formed in different settings. While most adolescents met at school, antisocial adolescents met in other contexts, and they chose friends with arrest records similar to their own. When interviewed one year later, antisocial adolescents' friendships were found to be of shorter duration than those of their peers, and the friendships tended to dissolve after conflicts.

Gender Differences in Adolescent Peer Relations With the onset of puberty, biological, cognitive, and social factors lead to a peak in sexual dimorphism even as adolescents reverse the childhood trend toward gender segregation and come to spend more time interacting with opposite-sex peers. As we discussed in Chapter 7, a number of sex differences have been found between same-sex cliques in childhood. Researchers have generally found that boys tend to play in larger groups, often in games involving physical assertion and competition, are more physically active, engage in more risk-taking and rough-and-tumble play, and exhibit more anger and aggression toward peers than girls. Girls tend to play in smaller, more exclusive groups, often interacting in a more intimate manner, and use direct and indirect verbal requests, rather than commands and physical dominance behaviors.

Social Status In an ethological study of same-sex peer relations in early adolescence, Savin-Williams (1987) reported findings that extend our view of the similarities and differences in the social interaction of same-sex cliques. This study was partially based on classic methods developed by Sherif and colleagues (1961) in their famous "robber's cave experiment" investigating the social structures and group dynamics in cliques of boys during summer camp. Savin-Williams chose to study eight same-sex cliques of 12- to 16-year-old girls and boys during the course of a five-week summer camp. The study represents a blend of naturalistic and experimental methodologies and provides a counterpoint to the questionnaire studies and self-report methodologies common to most psychological research on adolescence.

Both groups of girls and groups of boys who shared the same cabin over the five-week period established dominance hierarchies, traded insults, ridiculed low-status members, and competed for resources. However, they did all of these things in qualitatively different ways. For example, boys established highly stable status hierarchies on the day of their arrival at the cabin using very direct and overt strategies of physical dominance and verbal ridicule. In contrast, girls used physical assertion much less often, and were more indirectly manipulative in their verbal directives and ridicule. One of the girls who gradually took control of a cabin did so by ostracizing a high-status peer and undermining her through gossip, directing middle-status peers with "suggestions," and subtly ridiculing a low-status peer with "assistance." For example, she would put down a low-status girl by embarrassing her in front of the others: "Dottie, pass Opal a napkin so she can wipe the jelly off her face" (Savin-Williams, 1987, p. 92).

Dominance in boys' cabins was often anything but subtle. Almost 90 percent of the 1,600 recorded instances of dominance behavior in one cabin was overt rather than indirect. Quantitative analyses of all eight cabins reveal that the most overt female cabin (57 percent) was less overt than the least overt male cabin (67 percent). Not only was dominance behavior more overt among boys, it was also more frequent, occurring 16.25 times per hour, compared to 6.34 times per hour in the female cabins. Boys were often involved in rough play that could occasionally escalate to real fighting. When this happened, strained relations were quickly patched up with assertions that it was all "in fun." Whereas boys ordered, teased, argued, and dominated through physical play, girls gossiped, ostracized, and provided unsolicited advice. In cabins of girls, in some cases conflicts were dealt with by giving the other the "silent treatment," which could last for days on end. Status in girls' groups was also revealed in terms of the lower-status girl recognizing the higher-status girl by giving compliments, asking favors and advice, and by imitation much more often than in groups of boys (Savin-Williams, 1987).

Friendships In adolescence, girls value intimacy in their relationships; mutual disclosures, shared secrets, and talk about feelings characterize close friendships among adolescent girls more than boys. Girls often use their friends as a means of managing initially anxiety-arousing experiences, and can be on the phone for hours sorting out the events of the day (Douvan & Adelson, 1976; Hill, 1980). For example, Apter (1990) found that girls turn to their friends for advice on emotion management when they feel hurt or disappointed by friends and dating partners. Rather than being passive listeners, these girls are actively helping each other cope with the more complex emotions of the adolescent world. In addition, LeCroy (1988) found that girls not only report

that they value emotional support from their friends, but they also turn to a smaller group of close friends or one best friend for emotional support.

Boys value friendships for quite different reasons in which social support may take on different meanings. Like girls, boys derive security and status from belonging to a close-knit clique or group of friends. However, unlike girls, emotional support does not take the form of long intimate discussions of their feelings. Instead, emotional support might be provided by active assistance (for example, helping a friend repair his car), by coming to the aid of a friend in a physical conflict, or by being with the friend and enjoying high-spirited fun in a free and easy manner, with a notable absence of tension or conflict. Perhaps because of the group dynamics of adolescent males, the characteristic that boys value the most in their friendships is loyalty, and friendships between boys tend to remain stable. In general, friendships that are perceived as supportive are highly valued by both adolescent boys and girls (Berndt & Perry, 1990).

Gender differences in friendship intimacy also develop during adolescence, as mixed-sex friendships and dating relationships become increasingly common. For example, early adolescent girls report that their same-sex friendships are more intimate than their opposite-sex friendships. By late adolescence, girls report that their opposite-sex friendships are just as intimate as their same-sex ones. For late adolescent boys, these opposite-sex friendships are more intimate than same-sex friendships, suggesting that boys are becoming more conversational and girls less wary of boys (Maccoby, 1998). There is also much evidence that boys and girls differ in their communication styles. For example, in opposite-sex friendships and dating relationships, boys tend to use more active and girls more tentative speech. As boys and girls begin to develop heterosexual relationships after spending much of middle childhood apart, it is not surprising that they will have to adjust their behavior and learn the communication styles of the opposite sex.

Sexuality, Dating, and Intimacy Although dating can be an important arena for adolescents to gain independence outside the family, middle adolescents reported that parental approval is important to them in their dating relationships and attempt to highlight their dating partners' positive qualities (Guerney & Arthur, 1984; Leslie, Huston, & Johnson, 1986). In addition, parental support appears to be an important factor in the degree of intimacy felt between adolescents. For example, in a study of support in first year college students' dating relationships, quality of parental attachment was related to the amount of support given and received within the couple (Simpson, Rholes, & Nelligan, 1992). In an anxiety-provoking situation, securely attached females were more likely to seek and to get emotional support and reassurance from their partners than any other group. In addition, the more anxious she was, the more comfort she sought and the more supportive her partner was. As anxiety increased, these couples engaged in more physical contact and more kissing. In contrast, avoidantly attached adolescents sought and received less emotional support and comforting in situations of high anxiety. These couples engaged in less smiling and less eye contact as anxiety increased. Still, adolescent dating relationships are typically short-lived, lasting only about four months (Feiring, 1996). These short-lived romances can be a source of great self-esteem and status within the peer group, but also the cause of much turmoil (Larson & Asmussen, 1991; Skipper & Nass, 1966).

Conflict in dating relationships does not always have a negative effect on the relationship, and in some cases may strengthen it (Laursen, 1993). Still, "as children move into the adolescent years, a larger portion of their anger, frustration, and worry emanates from the area of heterosexual concerns, including real relationships and fantasized ones" (Larson & Asmussen, 1991, p. 28). The emotional upheaval of romantic love may be the result of adolescents' trying out fledgling skills of intimacy and opening themselves to more emotional vulnerability. According to traditional stereotypes, girls are expected to enter these rela-

tionships with the ability to handle the emotional nature of dating and love, whereas boys are expected to behave more sexually (Hill, 1980). A recent study found that girls and boys did differ in their descriptions of dating relationships, with girls emphasizing interpersonal qualities and boys valuing physical attraction in their partners (Feiring, 1996).

Adolescents of both sexes may not be fully prepared to handle dating relationships, since more complex aspects of emotional reasoning are only just appearing. As discussed in the preceding chapter, preadolescents do not yet understand that a given situation or person may elicit multiple, conflicting emotions. Early in adolescence, children understand that they can feel two opposing emotions at the same time, but they cannot yet experience them toward the same person. By about age 11, adolescents begin to understand that conflicting emotions may be evoked by the same person. They can feel excited about a first date, but scared that they will do something wrong. Still, these cognitive appreciations of complex emotion states are not fully developed, and adolescents who are dating report greater emotional lability than those not in a romantic relationship (Larson & Richards, 1994). In addition, adolescents are prone to attributional errors when trying to determine the intent of a romantic partner. When cognitive errors occur in such emotionally charged social relationships, negative emotions such as jealousy are inevitable. These misattributions may also be responsible for the confusing experience of the adolescent "crush." Being unable to accurately understand that an opposite-sex friend can have feelings of affection but not of romantic love may be difficult for the adolescent to perceive, especially as opposite-sex friendships are first emerging.

As adolescents explore the emotional experiences involved in developing intimate relations of a sexual nature, they are at the same time transforming and deepening their understanding of themselves. We turn next to research on the nature of the adolescent's search for a personal identity.

(a)   (b)   (c)

Figure 10.12 "A smile is just a smile"

(Photos by I. Eibl-Eibesfeldt, 1989)

Transforming the Self

Marcia's Contribution to the Study of Identity Expanding on Erikson's identity versus role confusion stage of adolescence, James Marcia (1966, 1980) has been the central figure in developing the methodology of research on adolescent identity. In this sense he occupies a position with respect to Erikson that is like that which Ainsworth occupies with respect to Bowlby. Just as Ainsworth's paradigm provided Bowlby's concept of attachment an empirical focus, Marcia's strategy for investigating Erikson's concept of **identity crisis** has provided the foundation for 25 years of systematic research on identity formation. As always, once this empirical process begins in earnest, the theory, too, must change and grow.

To assess individual differences in the identity construct, Marcia developed the identity status paradigm in which the different types of identity status may be defined with respect to two major dimensions: commitment and exploration. These orthogonal dimensions yield four categories of ego development that can be used to characterize any individual in terms of his or her current state of identity formation (see Figure 10.13). According to Marcia's scheme:

(a) **Identity diffusion** is the least developmentally advanced status, although, like all of the statuses, it has adaptive aspects, and may be the most adaptive mode of functioning under certain conditions.

Commitment to an internally consistent set of values and goals is absent, and exploration is either missing or shallow. People in identity diffusion tend to follow the path of least resistance, and may present as having a carefree, cosmopolitan lifestyle, and/or as being empty and dissatisfied.

(b) **Identity foreclosure** represents a high level of commitment following little or no exploration. For some, identity foreclosure is a developmental starting point from which a period of exploration will ensue. However, as an identity resolution, foreclosure is considered by Marcia to represent a less developed state than that of moratorium or identity achievement. People who follow the foreclosure pattern adopt a single set of values and goals without a period of questioning or exploration.

(c) **Moratorium** is arguably considered a stage rather than a resolution of the identity formation process, although some people apparently remain in moratorium for many years. Marcia's moratorium status refers to the process of forging an identity—occupational, interpersonal, and ideological commitments—from the myriad of possibilities available. The person in moratorium is intensely preoccupied with exploring options and working toward commitment.

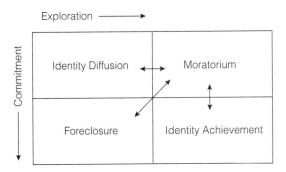

Figure 10.13 Marcia's model of different types of identity status

(d) **Identity achievement** represents an autonomous resolution of identity, incorporating a set of commitments adopted after a period of exploration (moratorium). It is the exploration of the moratorium period that distinguishes the flexible strength of identity achievement from the rigid strength of identity foreclosure. (Patterson, Sochting, & Marcia, 1992, pp. 10–12)

In Erikson's theory, the development of a personal sense of identity is a lifelong process with roots in the development of primary attachments in infancy, autonomy and self-control in toddlerhood, gender identity in early childhood, and social competence and self-efficacy in later childhood. During the period of adolescence the search for a new sense of identity is thus never completely new, but rather a continuation of cycles of exploration and consolidation in relation to one's sense of self. As a pivotal stage in the life cycle, Erikson viewed **identity** as "the accrued confidence that the inner sameness and continuity prepared in the past are matched by the sameness and continuity of one's meaning for others, as evidenced in the tangible promise of a 'career'" (Erikson, 1968, p. 261). According to this view, three aspects appear to be central to the process of identity achievement. First, the individual must experience integrity from within. Well-defined values and principles determine

Figure 10.14 Teenagers' norms and values often mirror those of the adult society.

(Photo by Deborah Davis/Tony Stone Images)

one's action and choices. Second, relationships and community are central to defining and validating one's sense of integrity. Finally, the sense of identity is experienced as continuous over time. Past achievements, as well as future aspirations, are linked to the present (Patterson, Sochting, & Marcia, 1992).

Using Marcia's paradigm, researchers have consistently found that it is not until late adolescence that this type of identity achievement can be observed, though younger individuals may be high in specific domains of identity (Adams & Jones, 1983; Archer, 1982; Marcia, 1980). Most studies have shown that variation in identity status becomes most prominent between 18 and 21 years, suggesting that the crisis and exploration of identity that characterize the adolescent experience in Western societies may not be clearly evident among high school students. Rather, identity issues and crises may be propelled by the transition of graduating from high school, going to college, or starting a first job, at least in middle-class American society. These choices and changing roles associated with late adolescence may force adolescents to more fully examine themselves and their commitments.

In a recent review of research on adolescence, Grotevant (1997) notes that the identity status construct has been more useful for understanding individual differences than in tracing normative developmental patterns. Moreover, research on individual differences in identity is quite limited with respect to developmental issues, particularly antecedent-consequent relations. Finally, much of the literature on identity status is dominated by self report methodologies and correlational designs. This leaves the empirical literature weakened by problems of self-report method bias, including social desirability problems and inflated intercorrelations due to shared method variance, or an overreliance on a single type of method. Despite these methodological weaknesses, a number of interesting findings have emerged from systematic research, particularly research on the behavioral correlates of identity status. In our review of this literature, we have chosen to highlight studies that explore some of the emotional and behavioral correlates of identity status, as shown in Table 10.2.

Emotion and Identity Two recent reviews of the literature by Marcia (1993) and Grotevant (1998) have shown that identity status is related to stable patterns of individual differences in psychological and emotional development. As shown in Table 10.2, identity achievers show a pattern of positive adaptation across a wide variety of domains. Identity achievers' greater empathy is reflected in their high levels of compassion and moral judgment. Academically, these adoles-

cents want to challenge themselves, and often choose difficult majors and have better study habits and higher GPA scores than other adolescents. Identity achievers are not simply studying more or studying better, though. These adolescents are creative and self-motivated in other domains as well. With peers, they are popular and are less likely to be influenced by peer pressure. Identity achievers are less likely to succumb to social pressures probably because they have made a commitment that was grounded in crisis and exploration. Across social contexts, these adolescents are less antagonistic and are able to find effective ways of regulating emotion and releasing tension. They achieve personal closeness and a sense of belonging with others, so that they are able to seek other people's opinions when they need help. Identity achievers are able to approach the challenges of adolescence with an internal locus of control and confidence that they can cope with stressful situations should they arise.

In contrast to the self-assurance of the identity achiever, individuals in moratorium report the highest levels of anxiety of any identity group and score higher on measures of internalizing and externalizing behavior. Marcia (1993) argues individuals in moratorium have more difficulty in regulating intense emotional experiences because they are already in a chronic state of high stress. Moratorium is characterized as a state of exploration, which is reflected in both thoughts and behaviors of individuals. Moratorium tends to be the least stable identity status, as individuals in this state of crisis are actively seeking to make a commitment. These adolescents are open to experience, are actively exploring, and have high levels of moral reasoning. This crisis of identity may be reflected in their active exploration of sexuality and moderate level of drug use. Although they report marijuana use, they do not appear to have high levels of abuse or addiction, as their drug use probably reflects their curiosity. In addition, individuals in moratorium are less cooperative with authority figures than with peers, but they also tend to be conforming to both. These findings suggest that individuals in moratorium are

Table 10.2 Emotional and Behavioral Correlates of Identity Status

Status	Emotional and Behavioral Correlates
Identity Achievement Commitment after exploration	Internal locus of control[b] Moral, empathic, and compassionate[b] Popular with peers, less conforming[b] More creative and reflective[b] Better study habits, higher GPAs, and more difficult majors[b] Able to release tension, less antagonistic[a] Shows solidarity, asks for others opinions[a]
Moratorium No commitment Actively exploring	More reflective, open to experience[b] More exploration and the least temporally stable status[a] High levels of anxiety[b] Sexual exploration, marginal marijuana use[a] High in internalizing and externalizing[a] High levels of moral reasoning[a]
Foreclosure Commitment without exploration	Cognitive inflexibility, reliance on social stereotypes, obedient to authority[b] High in social desirability[b] Females use manipulative strategies[a] Males are more antagonistic[a]
Identity Diffusion No commitment Not exploring	External locus of control[b] Least liked by peers, likely to conform to peer pressure[b] Frequent drug use[a] Moderate drug use[a] Moderate levels of anxiety[b] Withdrawal from cognitively difficult tasks[b] Least difficult majors[b]

Sources: [a]Grotevant, 1998; [b]Marcia, 1993.

moving away from authority figures, but are not yet sure just where they are going.

According to Marcia, foreclosed individuals have made a commitment without exploring many options, typically adopting the values of their parents. The families of such individuals tend to be child-centered and conformist (Adams, Gullotta, & Adams-Markstrom, 1994), and their children tend to be close to and feel highly valued by their parents. Foreclosed adolescents also tend to be more authoritarian and view the world in terms of stereotypes. They have a strict sense of what is right and wrong, and rarely question the correctness of their position. Foreclosed individuals report the lowest levels of anxiety of any identity status. It may be that an adolescent who conforms to the roles and values

promoted by parents would be less likely to experience the anxiety and conflict of the adolescent who questions authority. Their need to respond in ways that they think people will want is reflected in their high social desirability scores and their willingness to follow instructions from an authority figure. Although foreclosed individuals show a clear pattern of obeying authority, they also attempt to assert themselves in more subtle ways. Finally, foreclosed individuals, particularly females, often appear to be well adjusted with high levels of self-esteem.

In contrast, identity diffused adolescents' developmental difficulties resonate across many domains. Their family situation is the polar opposite of foreclosed individuals: they have generally experienced harsh, negative relationships with parents and show little identification with their parents' values. Their academic goals are generally low, as they choose the least difficult majors and withdraw from cognitive challenge. Identity diffused adolescents may not attribute these outcomes to be personal failures; rather, they blame circumstances or make other self-serving attributions typical of an external locus of control. Identity diffused adolescents also have difficulty with their social relations, possibly for the same reason. For example, they tend to be unpopular with their peers, especially identity achievers. They do show high levels of conformity to peer pressure, for example, they have high levels of drug use. They often display a casual lifestyle that belies their moderately high level of anxiety. In general, they may appear bored and apathetic, with a lack of motivation that may reflect their lack of commitment to any coherent values. In general, this group appears to be at risk for adult psychopathology.

SUMMARY

From a biosocial perspective, the form, the meaning, and even the duration of adolescence is primarily a cultural construction, though its onset at puberty and its functional significance appear to be universal. Many psychologists believe that the idea that adolescence is necessarily stressful has been exaggerated; however, few would disagree that this period is marked by a high point in emotional intensity, idealistic thinking, and passionate commitments to ideological causes. It is also clear that for too many American adolescents, the period poses grave risks, as both headlines and FBI data attest.

John Hill developed a framework for understanding adolescent development that incorporated Erikson's psychosocial stage model and extended it by defining changes as primary and secondary. According to Hill's framework, adolescent development is set into motion by the primary changes in biology, cognition, and social relations that propel the individual toward new challenges or life tasks.

Due to the activating effects of hormones, at puberty dramatic morphological changes occur. These changes include growth spurts, qualitative changes in physical appearance, the emergence of primary and secondary sex characteristics, and a general increase in sexual dimorphism. In addition, the adrenal glands produce a sex hormone that is believed to trigger the onset of sexual attraction, and research indicates that people of both sexes recall the awakening of sexual feelings toward another person as taking place between 10 and 12 years of age. Hormones may also be implicated in differential prevalence rates of depression and aggression between adolescent males and females.

Cognitive advances in adolescence lead to a new form of egocentrism characterized by a belief that others are primarily focused and concerned with the issues that the adolescent feels are important. The term *imaginary audience* refers to the subjective feeling that one's actions, appearance, and manners are constantly being scrutinized and criticized by others. Another aspect of adolescent egocentrism is the adolescent's sense of personal uniqueness, or personal fable. A personal fable refers to the uniqueness of the ongoing personal narrative, and the belief that tragedies can happen only to others. This fiction may give rise to feelings of a sort of invulnerability to well-known risks and dangers.

Social changes in the peer group involve the gradual dissolution of the clique and the rise of the crowd. The preadolescent clique is typically composed of five or six same-age, same-sex peers, a structure that originated in early childhood. In midadolescence, a new structure emerges, especially in urban adolescent groups, which Dunphy refers to as a crowd. Crowds are mixed-sex collectives that gather together semiregularly, and which are much larger, less exclusive, and less organized than same-sex cliques.

Social changes in the family involve the adolescent's search for personal freedom and independence. Autonomy may be defined as increased self-reliance, initiative, resistance to peer pressure, and responsibility for one's decisions and actions. Increased autonomy occurs in the context of shifting priorities from parent-centered interactions to peer relationships, and conflicts arise as the adolescent pushes for more freedom than parents are willing to give. Research has shown that families with an adolescent vary a great deal in their overall level of conflict. Three main patterns of development have been identified. About 25 percent experience continuous growth, marked by mutual respect between the adolescent and his or her parents, a sense of purpose, and self-assurance. About 35 percent experience surgent growth, with periods of calm broken at times by anger, defiance, and immaturity. Finally another 25 percent show a pattern of tumultuous growth filled with stress and storm.

An important consideration in understanding adolescent conflicts within the family is how they are resolved. Conflict resolution tactics are closely linked with the adolescent's emotional and psychological functioning. Although adolescents engage in more frequent conflicts with their parents, these conflicts may contribute in positive ways to adolescent development, particularly when these interactions occur in the context of a secure relationship with the parent. Adolescents with higher self-reported emotional closeness to their family members also have higher levels of self-esteem. The understanding of a warm, supportive family appears to buffer adolescents from the potentially negative impact of this stage.

Adolescent peer relations also contribute to healthy emotional development in a number of ways. First, peer relationships provide an important context for the expression and regulation of both positive and negative emotions because of their essentially egalitarian nature. Second, peers can offer effective emotional support and a sense of security in novel situations, which can be particularly important if family relations are strained or unsupportive. Third, peer friendships provide a source of self-esteem and validation from outside the family. Even in families that continue to provide the adolescent with advice and emotional

support, peers are often seen as being more understanding of the adolescent's unique emotional needs.

Peers also provide a unique set of challenges and growth experiences. In an ethological study of early adolescence, Savin-Williams found that groups of girls and groups of boys who shared the same cabin over a five-week period established dominance hierarchies, traded insults, ridiculed low-status members, and competed for resources. However, they did all of these things in qualitatively different ways. Whereas boys ordered, teased, argued, and dominated through physical play, girls gossiped, ostracized, and provided unsolicited advice. In cabins of girls, in some cases conflicts were dealt with by giving the other the "silent treatment," which could last for days on end. Status in girls' groups was also revealed by giving compliments, asking favors and advice, and by imitation much more often than in groups of boys.

In adolescence, girls value intimacy in their relationships; mutual disclosures, shared secrets, and talk about feelings characterize their relationship dynamics. Girls often use their friends as a means of managing initially anxiety-arousing experiences. Like girls, boys derive security and status from belonging to a close-knit clique or group of friends. Emotional support for boys might be provided by active assistance or by simply being with the friend and enjoying high-spirited fun in a free and easy manner. Perhaps because of the group dynamics of adolescent males, the characteristic that boys value the most in their friendships is loyalty.

Adolescents of both sexes may not be fully prepared to handle dating relationships, since more complex aspects of emotional reasoning are still maturing. As boys and girls begin to develop heterosexual relationships after spending much of middle childhood apart, it is not surprising that they will have to adjust their behavior and learn the communication styles of the opposite sex. The emotional experiences involved in developing intimate relations of a sexual nature transform and deepen their understanding of themselves or personal identity.

To assess individual differences in the identity construct, Marcia developed the identity status paradigm in which the different types of identity status may be defined with respect to two major dimensions: commitment and exploration. According to Marcia's scheme:

1. Identity diffusion is the least developmentally advanced status. Commitment to an internally consistent set of values and goals is absent, and exploration is either missing or shallow.

2. Identity foreclosure represents a high level of commitment following little or no exploration. People who follow the foreclosure pattern adopt a single set of values and goals, usually those of their parents.

3. Moratorium refers to the process of forging an identity—occupational, interpersonal, and ideological commitments—from the myriad of possibilities available. The person in moratorium is intensely preoccupied with exploring options and working toward commitment.

4. Identity achievement represents an autonomous resolution of identity, incorporating a set of commitments adopted during a period of exploration (moratorium). It is the exploration of the moratorium period that distinguishes the flexible strength of identity achievement from the rigid strength of identity foreclosure.

FURTHER READING

Grotevant, H. D. (1998). Adolescent development in family contexts. In N. Eisenberg (Ed.), *Handbook of child psychology* (5th ed., Vol. 3). New York: Wiley.

This is an up-to-date review of research on adolescence from an experienced scholar in the field.

Larson, R., & Richards, M. H. (1994). *Divergent realities: The emotional lives of mothers, fathers, and adolescents.* New York: Basic Books.

This book explores the emotional world of adolescents and their parents.

Marcia, J. E. (1993). The status of the statuses: Research review. In J. E. Marcia, A. S. Waterman, D. R. Matteson, S. L. Archer, & J. L. Orlofsky (Eds.), *Ego identify: A handbook for psychological research* (pp. 22–41). New York: Springer-Verlag.

This article provides a review of literally thousands of studies exploring individual differences in identity achievement.

Savin-Williams, R. C. (1987). *Adolescence: An ethological perspective.* New York: Springer-Verlag.

This is an innovative and exciting study of how adolescents relate to one another that is based not on what they say but on what they do.

Weisfeld, G. (1999). *Evolutionary principles of human adolescence.* New York: Basic Books.

This book provides a comprehensive treatment of adolescence from a modern evolutionary perspective including comparisons of adolescence across cultures. historical periods, and other species.

Glossary

action potentials Neural impulses; consisting of discrete electrical bursts that begin at one end of the axon on a neuron and travel to the other end.

active genotype/environment interaction The notion that genotypes affect the types of environments that people prefer and will seek out.

adaptation Close functional fit between a character and aspects of the environment achieved gradually by a process of natural selection.

adaptationist approach In evolutionary psychology, a strategy involving the search for adaptive design; adaptations "designed" by natural selection to solve problems of organism–environment interaction.

adaptive problem In evolutionary psychology, any of numerous problems arising from organism–environment interactions, the solution to which results in enhancement or facilitation of reproduction of the organism.

adaptive radiation Extensive evolutionary diversification from a parental taxon into several new taxa having different adaptations (*e.g.*, several new species originating from one ancestral population, as in Darwin's finches or New World warblers).

affective perspective-taking The ability to accurately infer the feelings or emotions that others are experiencing.

Age of Reason The period spanning the seventeenth and eighteenth centuries that shaped the modern intellectual tradition of the West, including the concept of the university and its three major branches of learning—the natural sciences, the social sciences, and the humanities; sometimes referred to as the Enlightenment. Enlightenment scholars were defiantly secular and skeptical of all forms of religious and civil authority, and embraced instead a spirit of free inquiry into all branches of knowledge.

alleles Different genes that occupy the same locus on a pair of chromosomes and thus can potentially pair with one another.

altricial Species that are relatively immature at birth and require substantial parental care for survival.

amygdala An almond-shaped structure that is part of the limbic system. Experimental lesions of this region have been shown to produce profound emotional changes, leading some researchers to consider it to be the emotion center of the brain.

analogy An ethological term for similar characteristics in two different species, where the similarity is achieved through convergent evolution (*i.e.,* similar adaptation) rather than through descent from a common ancestral form. Compare *homology*

anthropomorphic The attribution of human form or personality to a nonhuman.

antidepressant A drug used to treat depression by making certain transmitter substances, such as serotonin, more available for use at synapses.

appearance–reality tasks In these tasks children are shown objects that look like other objects, such as a sponge that looks like a rock, requiring an understanding that appearances can sometimes be misleading and not an accurate representation of reality.

appraisal Evaluation of a salient event in a given context. Many theorists view appraisals as central to the process of determining the individual's emotional response to the event.

arousal Alert state, with the autonomic nervous system activated, and the body prepared for action.

attachment An enduring emotional bond that leads the infant to experience pleasure, joy, and safety in the principal caregiver's company, and distress when temporarily separated.

attribution Evaluation of the causes of an event. An internal attribution assigns the cause to oneself; an external attribution assigns it to an outside factor. Causes may be attributed to be stable or unstable, controllable or uncontrollable.

autonomic nervous system (ANS) The portion of the peripheral nervous system inside the body of vertebrates that innervates smooth muscles and glands.

autonomy The capacity to make decisions independently, to serve as one's own source of emotional strength, and to otherwise manage one's life tasks without depending on others for assistance; an important developmental task of adolescence.

autonomy versus shame and doubt The second of Erikson's psychosocial stages, in which toddlers either assert their wills and attend to their own basic needs or else become passive, dependent, and lacking in self-confidence.

avoidant attachment An insecure infant/caregiver bond, characterized by little separation protest and a tendency of the child to avoid or ignore the caregiver when stressed.

axon A thin, tubelike extension from a neuron that is specialized to carry neural impulses (action potentials) to other cells.

Baldwin effect Incorporation (hardwiring) into the brain of behavioral traits acquired through natural selection.

basic emotions A small set of emotions including fear, joy, and anger that is considered primary because of these emotions' (1) universal expression, (2) quick onset, (3) comparable expressions in other animals, (4) emotion-specific physiology, (5) universal antecedent events, (6) coherence in response systems, (7) brief duration, (8) automatic appraisal mechanism, and (9) unbidden occurrence. See *primary emotions*

behavioral approach systems (BAS) Refers to a cluster of tendencies involving dominance/sensation-seeking, risk-taking, and impulsivity.

behavioral ecology The study of the evolutionary functions of behavior.

behavioral inhibition A temperamental characteristic reflecting one's tendency to withdraw from unfamiliar people or situations.

behavioral inhibition systems (BIS) Refers to a cluster of tendencies involving fear, wariness, caution, and safety-seeking.

behavior genetics The scientific study of how one's hereditary endowment interacts with environmental influences to determine such attributes as intelligence, temperament, and personality.

belief–desire psychology A developmental model in which desire psychology emerges first and refers to the ability to explain and predict another person's behavior based on assumptions about their desires, prior to understanding the relation between beliefs and action.

biological function The relatively immediate consequence or end accomplished by an individual's behavior or other characteristic. Compare *fitness*

bonobo A pygmy chimpanzee.

Brazelton Neonatal Behavioral Assessment Scale (NBAS) An evaluation of a neonate's neurological status and responsiveness to environmental stimuli.

causation Unless further modified, used here to mean proximate causation, one of Tinbergen's four questions; underlying mechanism.

central nervous system (CNS) The brain and spinal cord.

cerebral cortex The outermost, newest in evolutionary terms, and (in humans) by far the largest portion of the brain; it is divisible into two hemispheres (right and left), and each hemisphere is divisible into four lobes—the occipital, temporal, parietal, and frontal.

chromosomes The structures within the cell nucleus that contain the genetic material (DNA).

Circadian rhythm Occurring or functioning in approximately twenty-four-hour periods or cycles (from circa, about + dias, day). The circadian rhythm provides for greater energy in the morning hours, and stimulates the appetite for carbohydrates. It can be influenced by inputs from the limbic system due to salient events such as naps, meals, and exposure to light.

classical conditioning (or Pavlovian conditioning) Learning to associate a neutral stimulus with something pleasurable or painful.

clique A small, tightly knit group of peers who share common interests and viewpoints and who set themselves apart from other peers.

closed system A system that is isolated from the matter in its environment. Although energy can be exchanged, matter cannot (as in a closed pot of water over heat).

coevolution Evolution of two or more entities (species; variants within a species; organism and habitat/environment) that are joined as a system.

cognitive-motivational-relational theory Lazarus's theory of emotion in which *cognitive* refers to the appraisal process, *motivational* refers to the fact that events are appraised from the standpoint of a person's goals and desires, and *relational* emphasizes the person's continuous negotiation with the physical and social world.

concordance In behavioral genetics research, an index of heritability that is found by identifying a set of individuals who have a particular trait and then determining the percentage of some specific class of their relatives (such as identical twins) who have the same trait.

conditioned response (CR) A learned response to a stimulus that was not originally capable of producing the response (*e.g.*, a dog salivating at the sound of a bell).

conditioned stimulus (CS) An initially neutral stimulus that comes to elicit a particular response after being paired with an unconditioned stimulus (UCS) that always elicits the response (*e.g.,* ringing a bell paired with the presentation of food).

conspecific Member of the same species.

constraint Applied to both development and evolution, a factor or set of factors that either restricts particular changes from happening or makes them more likely.

control parameter In dynamic systems theory, a parameter to which the system is particularly sensitive.

convergent evolution The development of similar traits that have similar functions from differing evolutionary origins.

corpus callosum A large fiber tract that connects the two cerebral hemispheres.

correlational design A type of research design that indicates the strength of associations among variables; although correlated variables are systematically related, these relationships are not necessarily causal.

cortex The most recently evolved outer layer of the forebrain of mammals that is so prominent in humans; sometimes referred to as the neocortex or cerebral cortex.

cortisol The primary stress hormone produced by the *hypothalamic-pituitary-adrenocortical (HPA) system*. This system is a *neuroendocrine* system that is regulated by outputs from the amygdala to the hypothalamus, which in turn regulates the production and release of stress hormones into the bloodstream.

critical period A brief period in the development of a human being or animal that is the optimal time of readiness for responding to particular stimuli or acquiring particular skills or abilities.

critical realism An important philosophical foundation of classic ethology that assumes that species-typical adaptations mirror external reality. Kant understood that an organism's knowledge of the external world is determined not so much by the features of external reality, but by its perceptual faculties. Evolutionary scientists add that the organism's perceptual faculties evolved in response to those features of external reality critically involved in the organism's survival and reproduction.

cross-cultural comparison A study that compares the behavior and/or development of people from different cultural or subcultural backgrounds.

cross-foster The experimental procedure of fostering the young of one strain (or species) onto a mother from a second strain (or species).

cross-sectional design A research design in which subjects from different age groups are studied at the same point in time.

crowd A mixed-sex adolescent collective that gathers together semi-regularly and is much larger, less exclusive, and less organized than a clique.

cybernetics The scientific study of methods of control and communication common to organisms and certain machines like computers.

Darwinism The evolutionary theory proposed by Charles Darwin that all currently living organisms have evolved from earlier forms in accordance with the principle of natural selection.

decentration In Piaget's theory, the ability to consider several aspects of a situation rather than centering on just one.

deception cues Inadvertent expressive behaviors that inform the receiver that deception may be occurring, but do not reveal the concealed information.

defense mechanisms In psychoanalytic theory, self-deceptive means by which the mind defends itself against anxiety, including displacement, projection, rationalization, reaction formation, repression, and sublimation.

dendrites The thin, tubelike extensions of a neuron that typically branch repeatedly near the neuron's cell body and are specialized for receiving signals from other neurons.

deprivation study An experimental procedure in which an organism is removed from a normal environmental input so as to measure the importance of the input to its development.

differential emotion theory (DET) Izard's evolutionary theory of emotion that postulates a set of universal discrete emotions, each with a specific neurophysiological basis, adaptive function, and facial expression.

differentiation The progression from a generalized beginning to more specialized form as development proceeds.

difficult temperament Temperament in which the child is irregular in his or her daily routines and adapts slowly to new experiences, often responding negatively and intensely.

dimorphism Two variants of a characteristic found in a population; most often used with respect to sexual dimorphism.

disorganized/disoriented attachment An insecure infant/caregiver bond, characterized by the infant's dazed appearance on reunion or a tendency to first seek and then abruptly avoid the caregiver.

display rules A theoretical term implying that a particular society has implicit rules about what emotions can be displayed to others, and when.

dizygotic twins See *fraternal twins*

DNA Deoxyribonucleic acid; a molecule that is capable of self-replication during cell division as well as the regulated replication (transcription) of small portions of itself onto RNA as a step in protein synthesis.

dominant In Mendelian genetics, the allele that is expressed in the heterozygous condition.

Duchenne smiles Broad smiles readily identified by others as expressions of happiness that involve the action of multiple muscles and include the crinkling of the eyes as the mouth is pulled into a grin. They are called Duchenne smiles after the French scientist who first described them.

dynamic systems theory Modern systems theory that postulates qualitative changes in systems and nonlinear causation. Emotions are viewed as complex systems that become organized with development. See also *organizational approach*

dynamic tension model Sroufe's model that hypothesizes a dynamic threshold range for affective response in which tension is viewed as a natural by-product of actively engaging the environment. The critical feature of the tension model is that thresholds for inciting a given emotional response are not stationary but vary as a function of the meaning of an event in a given context.

easy temperament Temperament in which the child quickly establishes regular routines in infancy, is generally good-natured, and adapts easily to new experiences.

ecological validity A type of external validity that describes how well a measure relates to data derived from everyday contexts and events.

ego A psychoanalytic term for the rational component of the personality.

egocentrism The tendency to view the world from one's own perspective while failing to recognize that others may have different points of view.

ego control Refers to the child's developing capacity to manage strong feelings, impulses, wishes, or desires, while *ego resiliency* refers to the flexibility of such emotion management.

electroencephalography (EEG) A technique used to measure electrical activity emanating from the cerebral cortex or outer layer of the brain.

electromyography (EMG) A technique used to record muscle activation of posed and spontaneous facial expressions.

elicitor An event that initiates some emotion, or some action.

emergent A property of one level in a system that arose from interactions of elements at a lower level but that cannot be identified in those elements, taken either singly or collectively.

emotion A state usually caused by an event of importance to the subject. It typically includes (1) a conscious mental state with a recognizable quality of feeling; (2) a bodily sensation and physiological change of some kind; (3) recognizable expressions of the face, tone of voice, and gesture; and (4) a readiness for certain kinds of action.

emotional dissemblance The lack of correspondence between the internal affective state and its outward expression; may be divided into two broad categories: cultural display rules and nonverbal deception.

emotion regulation The implicit and explicit strategies that one uses to increase or decrease the intensity and duration of emotional experiences and their expression.

endocrine system Glands that are specialized to secrete hormones into the circulatory system.

endogenous smiles The earliest smiles to appear in the neonate, they are spontaneous or reflexive and seem to depend on the infant's internal state. These first smiles, which involve simply turning up the corners of the mouth, do not occur when the infant is awake, but only when the infant is asleep, most often in periods characterized by low levels of cortical activity.

enlightenment See *Age of Reason*

environment of evolutionary adaptedness (EEA) The ancestral human environment in which selection pressures caused the design of a particular adaptation to be favored over alternatives.

epigenesis The conception of development as qualitative change, not reducible to genes or programs in genes, involving interactions within and among many levels of the organism and its external milieu.

equivalence Cross-cultural construct validation requires evidence for three distinct types of equivalence: (1) functional, (2) conceptual, and (3) metric. The first two are considered to be necessary preconditions for comparison, while the latter can be established only after data has been collected and analyzed. *Functional equivalence* exists when behavioral units or behavioral systems serve the same function across comparison groups. *Conceptual equivalence* refers to the similarity in the meaning of research materials, procedures, and situations across comparison groups. *Metric equivalence* implies consistent statistical relationships among dependent variables as well as stable patterns of covariation among independent and dependent variables.

ethogram A general profile of species-typical behavior patterns that have evolved to promote the organism's adaptation to its ecological niche.

ethology The scientific study of animal behavior, including humans, especially under natural conditions. Aims at understanding development, causation, function, and evolution of species-typical behavior patterns.

evocative genotype/environment interaction The notion that our heritable attributes will affect others' behavior toward us and thus will influence the social environment in which development takes place.

experience sampling method (ESM) In this approach, adolescents, and sometimes their parents, carry pagers that beep at semi-random intervals throughout the day. Participants are typically instructed to keep a journal with them so that when the pager beeps, they can write down information about their current social situation and emotional state.

experimentation A research design for testing hypotheses about cause–effect relationships, in which the researcher manipulates one variable (the independent variable) in order to assess its effect on another variable (the dependent variable).

expression Charles Darwin's term for the more-or-less involuntary changes of face, voice, and posture that are observable signs of an emotion.

extroversion See *introversion/extroversion*

eyebrow flash A momentary raising of the eyebrows, lasting about one-sixth of a second, which is a nonverbal sign of greeting in cultures throughout the world.

facial feedback hypothesis The idea, introduced by Darwin and developed by Tomkins and Ekman, that information from facial movements creates or intensifies emotions.

false-belief tasks Tasks in which children are told stories in which the protagonist is led to believe that an object has been hidden in one place while they themselves know it has been hidden elsewhere. By the age of 4, children generally understand that false beliefs may be induced in others and that these beliefs will guide their behavior.

fitness A measure of response to natural selection in an individual, stated in terms of probable contribution to future gene pools.

five-factor model (FFM) The view that the major dimensions of personality can be accounted for by just five factors. These "Big Five" personality dimensions are usually named for one end of the continuum they represent:

1. *Extroverted:* gregarious, sociable, dominant, adventurous
2. *Agreeable:* affectionate, warm, kind, friendly
3. *Conscientious:* organized, planful, reliable
4. *Stable:* calm, worry-free, stable
5. *Open:* original, insightful, inventive, wide-ranging interests

fixed action pattern In classical ethology, a term for a behavior that occurs in essentially identical fashion among most members of a species (though it may be limited to one sex or the other), is elicited by a specific environmental stimulus, and is typically more complex than a reflex.

forebrain Most recently evolved part of the vertebrate brain.

foreclosure Identity status characterizing individuals who have prematurely committed themselves to occupations or ideologies without really thinking about these commitments.

formal operations Piaget's fourth stage of cognitive development characterized by the ability to think logically, hypothetically, and to use deductive reasoning in abstract contexts.

fraternal twins Two individuals who developed simultaneously in the same womb, but who originated from separate zygotes (fertilized eggs) and are therefore no more genetically similar to one another than are nontwin siblings; also called dizygotic twins. Compare *identical twins*

game theory An ethological model for conceptualizing conditional strategies in which the optimal strategy is not fixed, but requires a consideration of the strategies most likely to be encountered by other gameplayers.

gender identity One's awareness of one's gender and its implications.

gene A construct used to explain heredity, variously defined as a unit of inheritance identified by an associated phenotype; a location on a chromosome; and a transcribable sequence of nucleotides within a DNA molecule.

genotype The complete set of genes possessed by an individual.

genotype/environment interactions The notion that genotypes influence the environment in which an individual develops. See *active, passive,* and *evocative genotype/environment interaction*

goal-corrected partnership Bowlby's term for the partnership that develops between child and parent, based on each being able to represent the goals of the other.

goal relevance theories Theories of emotion in which the determinant of emotion is the person's evaluation of whether a goal is being approached or violated.

habitat The effective environment of an animal described in terms of resources and challenges that affect survival and reproduction.

heart rate A measure often assumed to indicate emotional arousal.

heredity The sum of the qualities and potentialities genetically derived from parents.

heritability The extent to which a pattern of behavior is attributable to hereditary factors.

heritability coefficient A measure of heritability, which can vary from 0 (no heritability) to 1 (complete heritability); defined as variance due to genes divided by total variance.

heuristic value The quality of a theory that stimulates new research and discovery.

hindbrain The lower portion of the brainstem.

holism A conception of behavioral development that considers behavior to be a property of the whole organism rather than of its constituent parts.

homology An ethological term for structures (or behavioral patterns) that have descended from a common ancestral structure or pattern, owing any similarity to that fact. Compare *analogy*

hormone A chemical substance that travels in the blood to affect the brain or other parts of the body.

hunter–gatherer society A small nomadic group of humans that relies on hunting animals and gathering plants for its food supply.

hypothalamic-pituitary-adrenocortical (HPA) system Neuroendocrine system that is regulated by outputs from the amygdala to the hypothalamus, which in turn regulates the production and release of stress hormones into the bloodstream.

hypothalamus Part of the forebrain responsible for controlling the autonomic nervous system, and the pituitary gland; also implicated in species-characteristic behavior of eating, drinking, sex, and attack.

id a psychoanalytic term for the inborn component of the personality that is driven by the instincts.

identical twins Two individuals who are genetically identical to one another because they originated from a single zygote (fertilized egg); also called monozygotic twins. Compare *fraternal twins*

identification Freud's term for the child's tendency to emulate another person, usually the same-sex parent.

identity One's mature self-definition; a sense of who one is, where one is going, and how one fits into society.

identity achievement Identity status characterizing individuals who have carefully considered identity issues and have made firm commitments to an occupation and a set of personal values.

identity crisis Erikson's term for the uncertainty and discomfort that adolescents experience when they become confused about their present and future roles in life.

identity diffusion Identity status characterizing individuals who are not questioning who they are and have not yet committed themselves to an identity or a consistent set of personal values.

identity foreclosure Identity status that represents a high level of commitment following little or no exploration. For some, identity foreclosure is a developmental starting point from which a period of exploration will ensue. Others may simply adopt a single set of values and goals, usually those of their parents.

imaginary audience A form of adolescent egocentrism that involves confusing your own thoughts with those of a hypothesized audience and concluding that others have your preoccupations.

imprinting An instinctual restriction of social responses to familiar objects that is learned during a critical period in infancy of some species. Lorenz illustrated imprinting by demonstrating that goslings will follow and become attached to large moving objects.

inclusive fitness The fitness of an individual combined with the fitness of its relatives, weighted by the extent of genetic sharing between the individual and its relatives.

industry versus inferiority The fourth of Erikson's psychosocial stages (grade-school years), in which children must acquire important social and intellectual skills or else will view themselves as incompetent.

initiative versus guilt The third of Erikson's psychosocial stages, in which preschool children either develop goals and strive to achieve them or feel guilty when their ambitions are thwarted by others.

innate Characteristics that are present at birth and assumed to be genetically predetermined.

instinct Species-typical behavior that is unlearned, and genetically programmed.

instrumental conditioning A form of learning in which behaviors become either more or less probable, depending on the consequences they produce; also called operant conditioning.

integration The progression toward increased organization of more complex structures as development proceeds.

internalization The process of adopting the attributes or standards of other people, taking these standards as one's own.

internal working models Cognitive representations of self, others, and relationships that infants construct from their interactions with caregivers.

intimacy versus isolation The sixth of Erikson's psychosocial conflicts, in which young adults must commit themselves to a shared identity with another person (that is, intimacy) or else remain aloof and unconnected to others.

introversion/extroversion The opposite poles of a personality dimension: introverts are shy, anxious around others, and ready to withdraw from social situations; extroverts are highly sociable and enjoy being with others.

kindchenschema An ethological term (literally baby-schema) used to refer to the relatively large head, large eyes, and soft, rounded features of the typical infant's face, which are thought to elicit an emotionally based caregiving response from the adult.

kin selection An evolutionary term whereby natural selection favors traits that improve the reproductive success of relatives, mediated by shared genes.

lateralization Greater representation of a function on one side of the brain than on the other.

leakage In Ekman's theory of nonverbal deception, leakage refers to the inadvertent betrayal of withheld information.

learned helplessness A feeling of helplessness arising from a lack of control over situations, due to previous exposure to uncontrollable events in similar situations.

lesion Damage to a part of the brain.

limbic system Part of the forebrain, including the amygdala, that is thought to be especially important for emotions.

linear causation The conception that causes have effects in a direct, linear fashion.

localization of function The concept that different, localizable parts of the brain serve different, specifiable functions in the control of mental experience and behavior.

longitudinal design A design in which repeated measurements of the same individuals are taken at two or more points in time over a period of months or years.

magnetic resonance imaging (MRI) A technique that uses magnetic detectors to measure the amounts of hemoglobin, with and without oxygen. Brain areas that have been highly active can be identified because they have used up the oxygen bound to hemoglobin, allowing scientists to study the living brain by viewing it at different depths as if in slices.

magnetoencephalography (MEG) A brain imaging technique that provides a color image of the brain at work that is based on electromagnetic fields that are created as electrochemical information passes between neurons.

maturation Developmental changes in the body or behavior that result from the aging process rather than from learning, experience, or some specific environmental agent.

midbrain The upper portion of the brainstem, bounded at its lower end by the pons and at its upper end by the thalamus, that organizes basic movement patterns.

Minnesota Longitudinal Study A longitudinal study of developmental psychopathology and resilience initiated by Sroufe and Egeland in a large, high-risk, inner-city Minneapolis sample. Attachment assessments in the strange situation at 12 and 18 months have been consistently related to outcomes in early childhood through adolescence.

monozygotic twins See *identical twins*

mood A disposition to respond emotionally in a particular way that may last for hours, days, or even weeks, perhaps at a low level, and perhaps without the person knowing what started the mood.

moratorium Identity status characterizing individuals who are currently experiencing an identity crisis and are actively exploring occupational and ideological positions in which to invest themselves.

motivation A state of having some goal, aim, or purpose.

naturalistic observation Any data-collection procedure in which the researcher records subjects' ongoing behavior in a natural setting, without interfering with that behavior.

natural selection Darwin's explanation of evolution based on the differential reproductive success or survival of individuals or groups possessing characteristics that promoted adaptation to the environment.

neocortex See *cortex*

neonate A newborn infant from birth to approximately 1 month of age.

neoteny A particular type of heterochrony in which the juvenile form of some character is retained in adulthood.

neurochemicals A genetic term for substances such as transmitters, peptides, and hormones that affect nerve function.

neurocultural theory Ekman's theory of biologically based emotions and cultural display rules.

neuroendocrine system See *endocrine system*

neurohormone A chemical substance that is similar to a neurotransmitter in that it is secreted from the axon terminals of neurons but is classed as a hormone because it is secreted into blood vessels rather than onto other neurons.

neuron A nerve cell, the fundamental functional unit of nervous tissue.

neurotransmitter A chemical substance released from the axon terminal of a neuron, at a synapse, that influences the activity of another neuron, a muscle cell, or a glandular cell; also called a transmitter.

New York Longitudinal Study (NYLS) The longitudinal research program of Thomas,

Chess, and Birch, in which parental descriptions of infant temperament were studied during infancy and followed up with assessments that extended into adulthood.

nonlinear causation Causation having multidirectional, looping, often unexpected, and nonobvious pathways and effects that may be disproportionate in size.

nonshared environmental influence An environmental influence that people living together do not share and that makes these individuals different from one another.

normative development Refers to the general or idealized developmental sequences that describe the average growth patterns in a given area (*e.g.,* cognition, emotion) without reference to individual differences.

object permanence Piaget's term for the understanding that an object still exists even when it is out of view.

object relations Refers to the dynamic interplay between the inner images of the infant's emerging sense of self and its unique experience of the early caretaking environment. The child creates a template for the significant other from his or her interpersonal experiences that is imbued with great emotional energy.

ontogeny A synonym for development; one of Tinbergen's four questions.

open system A system that can exchange both matter and energy with its environment.

operant conditioning See *instrumental conditioning*

organizational approach An approach based on systems theory that emphasizes the role of emotions as regulators and determinants of both intrapersonal and interpersonal behaviors. It highlights the adaptive role of emotions by considering their meaning to the individual within a given context.

orienting reflex An involuntary behavioral and physiological response to a sudden, novel, or unexpected event that includes a wide range of instrumental responses, such as heightened sensitivity of the sense organs, directing sense receptors toward stimuli, rapid inhibition of ongoing behaviors, and changes in respiration and HR.

Parasympathetic division of the ANS A system composed of neurons linking the spinal cord to the internal organs. Its function is to maintain the body's state in nonemergency situations. Compare *sympathetic division of the ANS*

parental investment theory In evolutionary psychology, the theory that gender differences in personality systems may be understood as evolved affective-motivational systems that represent a range of alternative strategies for attaining universal human goals related to enhancing survival and reproduction. For example, the theory predicts that males will generally pursue relatively high-risk strategies compared to females.

parsimony A criterion for evaluating the scientific merit of theories; a parsimonious theory is one that uses relatively few explanatory principles to explain a wide range of facts.

passive genotype/environment interaction The concept that the rearing environments that biological parents provide are influenced by the parents' genes and, hence, are correlated with the child's own genotype.

peptide A substance with large molecules made up of several amino acids that diffuses to affect the function of the brain or other parts of the body.

peripheral In neuroanatomy, this term is used in contrast to "central"; thus, the peripheral nervous system is made up of the nerves running from the brain or spinal cord to muscles, and from the sensory endings to the brain or spinal cord.

peripheral nervous system The entire set of cranial and spinal nerves that connect the central nervous system (brain and spinal cord) to the body's sensory organs, muscles, and glands.

personal fable A form of adolescent egocentrism in which the individual thinks his or her thoughts and feelings are unique and that negative events can happen only to others.

phenotype An observable, measurable feature of an individual that identifies its correlated genotype; a trait; a characteristic.

phylogenetic approach The conception that if all organisms are related to one another by common evolutionary descent, similarities should be expected between closely related species such as humans and their closest primate relatives.

phylogeny The genealogy of a species (or other taxon) or of a trait; evolutionary history; one of Tinbergen's four questions.

pituitary gland An endocrine gland having a vascular connection to the hypothalamic region of the brain, from which it receives regulatory hormones. Hormones produced by the pituitary, in turn, regulate many other glands in the body.

polymorphism The existence of more than one qualitatively distinct variant of a trait (or type) in a population.

positron emission tomography (PET scan) A brain imaging technique that provides a color image of brain activity on the screen of a computer monitor that is based upon the uptake of a radioactive form of oxygen into active areas of the brain.

precocial Species that are relatively mature at birth. Compare *altricial*

primary emotions The small set of emotions present at birth in rudimentary form and emerging early in the first year that evolutionary theorists believe to be biologically programmed in terms of early expression and recognition. See *basic emotions*

prototype In an organization approach, a characteristic example of a concept.

proximate explanations Explanations of behavior that state the immediate environmental conditions or the mechanisms within the individual that cause the behavior to occur. Compare *ultimate explanations*

psychoanalysis The method of therapy initially developed by Freud, in which emotional problems are understood in light of unconscious processes that have developed through childhood experience. The therapist listens and occasionally offers interpretations to make sense of what the patient is saying.

psychodynamic theories of personality Theories that describe personality and its development in terms of inner mental forces that are often in conflict with one another and are shaped by experiences in early childhood.

psychosocial theory Erickson's theory describing personality development in terms of the resolution of a series of developmental tasks. The resolution of prior tasks provides a basis for predicting the resolution of later developmental tasks.

puberty The activation of sex hormones that marks the onset of adolescence and produces dramatic morphological changes. These changes include growth spurts (timed earlier for girls, but more extensive in boys), qualitative changes in physical appearance, the emergence of primary and secondary sex characteristics, and a general increase in sexual dimorphism related to male and female reproductive strategies.

radical behaviorism A movement in American psychology in the early twentieth century toward the study of objective stimuli and behavioral responses, relegating emotion, along with cognition, to a "black box" of phenomena unsuitable for scientific inquiry.

recessive In Mendelian genetics, the allele that is expressed only in the homozygous condition (*i.e.,* when paired with its counterpart).

reciprocal determinism The conception that the flow of influence between children and their environments is a two-way street: the environment may affect the child, but the child's behavior will also influence the environment.

recognitory assimilation When the infant is presented with a challenging stimulus, such as a stationary face, there is strong effort leading to assimilation of the schema, followed by tension release and smiling. If there is no successful assimilation, the infant may turn away or cry.

reductionism An explanatory mode that seeks to explain phenomena at one level of a system in terms of events and components at lower levels.

reflex A fairly discrete action, based on a neural pathway that connects a stimulus to a response.

reification A fallacy in scientific thought wherein the naming of a concept has the effect of making it seem like a concrete thing.

REM (rapid eye movement) sleep The recurring stage of sleep during which the EEG resembles that of an alert person, rapid eye movements occur, the large muscles of the body are most relaxed, and true dreams are most likely to occur.

resistant attachment An insecure infant/caregiver bond characterized by strong separation protest and a tendency by the child to resist contact initiated by the caregiver, particularly after a separation.

rite of passage A three-part ritual practiced in traditional societies to mark the adolescent's transition to adult status.

ritualization An ethological term for the process by which signals evolved from incidental and involuntary expressions of emotions (*i.e.,* a facial expression or erection of hair or feathers).

romanticism The philosophical, literary, and artistic movement founded by Rousseau that flowered for about one hundred years as a reaction to the formal and impersonal style of the rational and classical movements that preceded it. During this period, poets, novelists, and musicians explored emotion, nature, and everyday life as their principal themes, and were critical of high culture as artificial.

rouge test A test of infants' self-recognition; if they have achieved self-recognition, infants whose faces are marked with rouge will, when placed before a mirror, touch their own faces rather than the mirror image.

scaffolding Actions of parents and teachers that provide an external framework or support around the child's actions that stretches the limits of the child's competence.

script A stored outline of a sequence of actions that achieves a goal.

secure attachment An infant/caregiver bond in which the child actively seeks contact with the caregiver as a secure base from which to explore the environment, especially if distressed.

selection pressure Any condition or process that causes some individuals to leave more descendants than others as a result of differences in genetic makeup.

self-awareness Emerges in humans during the transition from infancy to toddlerhood. Research based on the mirror self-recognition paradigm reveals that most human infants recognize themselves in a mirror by the age of 22 months.

self-conscious emotions The feelings of guilt, shame, embarrassment, and pride, which are linked to thoughts about the self or one's own actions in reference to internalized standards.

self-regulation Internal processes by which one monitors and controls actions, thoughts, and emotions for the purpose of achieving a goal.

separation anxiety A wary or fretful reaction that infants and toddlers often display when separated from the persons to whom they are attached, especially in an unfamiliar environment.

shared environmental influence An aspect of environment that is experienced (shared) by people living together that is often assumed to make them similar to one another.

sign stimuli Ethologists' term for a stimulus that reliably elicits a behavior that occurs in essentially identical fashion among most members of a species (though it may be limited to one sex).

skin conductance An electrical measurement of the minute amounts of sweat being produced by the skin. It indicates changes in the autonomic nervous system which in turn indicate emotional changes.

slow-to-warm-up temperament Temperament in which the child is inactive and moody and displays mild passive resistance to new routines and experiences.

sociability One's willingness to interact with others and to seek their attention or approval.

socialization The process by which children acquire the beliefs, values, and behaviors considered desirable or appropriate by the society to which they belong.

social referencing The use of others' emotional expressions to infer the meaning of otherwise ambiguous situations.

sociobiology The comparative study of social organization in animals, including humans, especially with regard to its genetic and evolutionary history.

socioemotional A term used in development to imply the association between emotions and close relationships with others.

sociometric measures Assessments of the network of relationships that exists in a stable group by asking the children themselves about their preferences for peer group members. Three basic techniques may be employed: rating scales, paired-comparisons, and nominations.

species A population of organisms that can in principle reproduce with one another but that are reproductively isolated from those in other populations. This definition does not cover all populations that one would, on other grounds, want to designate as species.

species-characteristic pattern An extended pattern of goal-directed behavior that is acquired genetically and is characteristic of a species.

stranger anxiety A wary or fretful reaction that infants and toddlers often display when approached by an unfamiliar person.

strange situation A laboratory test situation developed by Ainsworth to examine infants' reactions to separation from and reunion with their caregivers in order to determine the quality of their attachments to the caregivers.

striatal system The part of the forebrain concerned with scheduling daily activities.

subcortical Relating to or involving nerve centers below the cerebral cortex.

superego A psychoanalytic term for the component of the personality that consists of one's internalized moral standards.

sympathetic division of the ANS The set of motor neurons that act upon visceral muscles and glands and mediate many of the body's responses to stressful stimulation, preparing the body for possible "fight or flight." Compare *parasympathetic division of the ANS*

synapse The space between the axon terminal of one neuron and the dendrites of its neighbor across which a nervous impulse jumps from one neuron to another.

tabula rasa The conception of the mind of an infant as a "blank slate" and that all knowledge, abilities, behaviors, and motives are acquired through experience.

tactical deception The term used by ethologists to distinguish a conscious strategy of deception from other types of deception employed by animals (*e.g.,* based on instinct or conditioning).

temperament An individual's characteristic mode of response or disposition that is constitutional in origin, shows stability over time, and has a genetic basis.

temporal lobe The lobe of the cerebral cortex that lies in front of the occipital lobe and below the parietal and frontal lobes that contains the auditory area of the brain.

thalamus Brain nuclei providing the major source of inputs to the cortex.

theory A set of concepts and propositions designed to organize, describe, and explain an existing set of observations.

theory of mind (TOM) The attribution of an unobservable mental state (*e.g.,* a belief, a desire, or knowledge) to another individual.

trait An aspect of personality that shows some stability over time and across situations.

transmitter substance A chemical substance secreted by nerve cells to communicate with other nerve cells that may diffuse outside synapses to affect nerve cells over a local region.

tree of life A branching representation depicting the relatedness of different species based on comparison of the composition of their DNA.

trust versus mistrust The first task in Erikson's psychosocial theory corresponding to Freud's oral stage or what is now described as the establishment of a secure or insecure attachment. In Erikson's theory, the resolution of the first task provides a basis for predicting the resolution of later developmental tasks.

twin study A study in which sets of twins differing in zygosity (kinship) are compared to determine the heritability of an attribute or attributes.

two-factor theory Schachter's theory of emotion that states that the individual's cognitive appraisal of physiological arousal determines which emotion is felt. These two factors, arousal and its interpretation, construct the emotion.

ultimate explanations Functional explanations of behavior that state the role that the behavior plays or once played in survival and reproduction, that is, explanations of why the potential for the behavior was favored by natural selection. Compare *proximate explanations*

unconditioned response (UCR) The unlearned response elicited by an unconditioned stimulus.

unconditioned stimulus (UCS) A stimulus that elicits a particular response without any prior learning.

vagal tone An index based on the time period between heartbeats, rather than heart rate which measures the number of heartbeats per minute. This more precise measure takes into consideration the rhythmic increase and decrease of heart rate with respiration.

vagus A complex system of bi-directional neural pathways linking the brain stem to various bodily organs, such as the heart and the digestive system.

validity The extent to which a measuring instrument accurately reflects what the researchers intend to measure.

Washoe A bonobo (pygmy chimpanzee), the first nonhuman primate to learn to communicate with humans using signs from the vocabulary of American Sign Language for the hearing impaired.

zone of proximal development Vygotsky's term for the difference between what a child can do alone and what the child can do in collaboration with a more competent partner.

References

Achenbach, T. M., & Edelbrock, C. S. (1981). Behavioral problems and competencies reported by parents of normal and disturbed children aged four through sixteen. *Monographs of the Society for Research in Child Development, 46*(1).

Achenbach, T. M., & Edelbrock, C. S. (1986). *Child behavior checklist and youth self-report*. Burlington: University of Vermont, Department of Psychiatry.

Achenbach, T. M., Edelbrock, C. S., & Howell, C. T. (1987). Empirically based assessment of the behavioral/emotional problems of 2- and 3-year-old children. *Journal of Abnormal Child Psychology, 15*, 629–650.

Adams, G. R., Gullotta, T. P., & Adams-Markstrom, C. (1994). *Adolescent life experiences,* (3d ed.). Pacific Grove, CA: Brooks/Cole.

Adams, G. R., & Jones, R. M. (1983). Female adolescents' identity development: Age comparisons and perceived childrearing experiences. *Developmental Psychology, 19*, 249–256.

Ahrens, R. (1954). Beitrag zur entwicklun des physionomie und mimikerkennens. *A.F. Exp. U. Angew, Psychologie, 2*, 599–633.

Ainsworth, M. D. S. (1963). The development of infant–mother attachment among the Ganda. In D. M. Foss (Ed.)., *Determinants of infant behavior* (Vol 2, pp. 67–104). New York: Wiley.

Ainsworth, M. D. S. (1967). *Infancy in Uganda: Infant care and the growth of love.* Baltimore: Johns Hopkins University Press.

Ainsworth, M. D. S. (1977). Infant development and mother–infant interaction among Ganda and American families. In P. H. Leiderman, S. R. Tulkin, & A. Rosenfeld (Eds.), *Culture and infancy: Variations in the human experience.* New York: Academic Press.

Ainsworth, M. D. S., Bell, S., & Stayton, D. (1974). Infant–mother attachment and social development: Socialization as a product of reciprocal responsiveness to signals. In M. Richards (Ed.), *The integration of the child into the social world.* Cambridge, England: Cambridge University Press.

Ainsworth, M. D . S., Blehar, M., Waters, E., & Wall, S. (1978). *Patterns of attachment: A psychological study of the strange situation.* Hillsdale, NJ: Erlbaum.

Allen, J. P., Hauser, S. T., Bell, K. L., & O'Connor, T. G. (1994). Longitudinal assessment of autonomy and relatedness in adolescent–family interactions as predictors of adolescent ego development and self-esteem. *Child Development, 65*(1), 179–194.

Allen, J. P., Hauser, S. T., Eickholt, C., Bell, K. L., & O'Connor, T. G. (1994). Autonomy and relatedness in family interactions as predictors of expressions of negative adolescent affect. *Journal of Research on Adolescence, 4*(4), 535–552.

Amsterdam, B. (1972). Mirror self-mage reactions before age two. *Developmental Psychobiology, 5,* 297–305.

Apter, T. (1990). Mothers on a seesaw: Friends and peers. *Altered loves: Mothers and daughters during adolescence.* New York: St. Martin's Press.

Archer, S. L. (1982). The lower age boundaries of identity development. *Child Development, 53,* 1551–1556.

Arend, R., Gove, F., & Sroufe, L. A. (1979). Continuity of individual adaptation from infancy to kindergarten: A predictive study of ego-resiliency and curiosity in preschoolers. *Child Development, 50,* 950–959.

Aristotle. (1941). *The basic works of Aristotle* (R. McKeon, Ed.; J. I. Beare, Trans.). New York: Random House.

Armon-Jones, C. (1986). The thesis of constructionism. In R. Harré (Ed.), *The social construction of emotions* (pp. 32–56). Oxford: Blackwell.

Arnold, M. B. (1960). *Emotion and personality: Vol. I. Psychological aspects.* New York: Columbia University Press.

Arsenio, W. F., & Kramer, R. (1992). Victimizers and their victims: Children's conceptions of the mixed emotional consequences of moral transgression. *Child Development, 63,* 915–927.

Asher, S. R., & Dodge, K. A. (1986). Identifying children who are rejected by their peers. *Developmental Psychology, 22,* 444–449.

Asher, S. R., Parhurst, J. T., Hymel, S., & Williams, G. A. (1990). Peer rejection and loneliness in childhood. In S. R. Asher & J. D. Coie (Eds.), *Peer rejection in childhood* (pp. 253–273). New York: Cambridge University Press.

Asher, S., & Parker, J. (1989). Significance of peer relationship problems in childhood. In B. Schneider, G. Attili, J. Nadel, & R. Weissberg (Eds.), *Social competence in developmental perspective* (pp. 5–23). Dordrecht, Holland: Kluwer.

Asher, S., Singleton, L., Tinsley, R., & Hymel, S. (1979). A reliable sociometric measure for preschool children. *Developmental Psychology, 15,* 443–444.

Aslin, R. (1987). Visual and auditory development in children. In J. Osofsky (Ed.), *Handbook of infant development* (2d. ed.). New York: Wiley.

Averill, J. R. (1968). Grief: Its nature and significance. *Psychological Bulletin, 70,* 721–748.

Averill, J. (1980). Emotion and anxiety: Sociocultural, biological, and psychological determinants. In A. O. Rorty (Ed.); *Explaining emotions.* Berkeley, CA: University of California Press.

Averill, J. R. (1985). The social construction of emotion: With special reference to love. In K. J. Gergen & K. E. Davis (Eds.), *The social construction of the person* (pp. 89–109). New York: Springer-Verlag.

Ax, A. F. (1953). The physiological differentiation between fear and anger in humans. *Psychosomatic Medicine, 15,* 433–442.

Axelrod, R. (1984). *The evolution of cooperation.* New York: Basic Books.

Banks, M. S., & Salapatek, P. (1981). Infant pattern vision: A new approach based on contrast-sensitivity function. *Journal of Experimental Child Psychology, 31,* 1–45.

Banks, M. S., & Salapatek, P. (1983). Infant and visual perception. In P. H. Mussen (Ed.), *Handbook of child psychology* (4th ed.): Vol. 2. M. M. Haith and J. J. Campos (Eds.), *Infancy and developmental psychobiology.* New York: Wiley.

Bard, P. (1928). A diencephalic mechanism for the expression of rage with special reference to the sympathetic nervous system. *American Journal of Physiology, 84,* 490–513.

Barrera, M. E., & Maurer, D. (1981a). Recognition of mother's photographed face by the three-month-old. *Child Development, 52,* 558–563.

Barrera, M. E., & Maurer, D. (1981b). The perception of facial expressions by the three-month-old infant. *Child Development, 52,* 203–206.

Barrett, K., & Campos, J. (1987). Perspectives on emotional development: 2. A functionalist approach to emotions. In J. Osofsky (Ed.), *Handbook of infant development* (2d ed., pp. 555–578). New York: Wiley.

Barrett, K. C., Zahn-Waxler, C., & Cole, P. M. (1993). Avoiders vs. amenders: Implications for the investigation of guilt and shame during toddlerhood? *Cognition and Emotion, 7,* 481–505.

Bates, J. E. (1980). The concept of difficult temperament. *Merrill-Palmer Quarterly, 26,* 299–319.

Bates, J. E. (1987). Temperament in infancy. In J. D. Osofsky (Ed.), *Handbook of infant development* (2d ed., pp. 1101–1149). Mew York: Wiley.

Bates, J. E. (1989). Concepts and measures of temperament. In G. A. Kohnstamm, J. E. Bates, & M. K. Rothbart (Eds.), *Temperament in childhood.* New York: Wiley.

Bates, J., Maslin, C., & Frankel, K. (1985). Attachment security, mother–child interaction, and temperament as predictors of behavior problem ratings at age three years. In I. Bretherton & E. Waters (Eds.), *Growing points in attachment theory and research. Monographs of the Society for Research in Child Development, 50*(209), 167–193.

Baumrind, D. (1967). Child care patterns anteceding three patterns of preschool behavior. *Genetic Psychology Monographs, 75,* 43–88.

Bell, N. J., Avery, A. W., Jenkins, D., Feld, J., & Shoenrock, C. J. (1985). Family relations and social competence during adolescence. *Journal of Youth and Adolescence, 14,* 109–114.

Bell, R. (1968). A reinterpretation of the direction of effects in studies of socialization. *Psychological Review, 75,* 81–95.

Belsky, J. (1984). Determinants of parenting: A process model. *Child Development, 55,* 83–96.

Belsky, J., & Cassidy, J. (1994). Attachment: Theory and evidence. In M. L. Rutter, D. F. Hay, & S. Baron-Cohen (Eds.), *Development through life: A handbook for clinicians.* Oxford: Blackwell.

Belsky, J., & Isabella, R. (1988). Maternal, infant and social-contextual determinants of attachment security: A process analysis. In J. Belsky & T. Nezworski (Eds.), *Clinical implications of attachment* (pp. 41–94). Hillsdale, NJ: Erlbaum.

Belsky, J., Rovine, M., & Taylor, D. G. (1984). The Pennsylvania Infant and Family Development Project: 2. The origins of individual differences in infant–mother attachment: Maternal and infant contributions. *Child Development, 55,* 718–728.

Benenson, J. F. (1993). Greater preference among females than males for dyadic interaction in early childhood. *Child Development, 64,* 544–555.

Benenson, J. F. (1996). Gender differences in the development of relationships. In G. Noam & K. Fischer (Eds.), *Development and vulnerability in close relationships.* Hillsdale, NJ: Erlbaum.

Berndt, T. J., & Perry, T. B. (1990). Distinctive features and effects of early adolescent friendships. In R. Montemayor (Ed.), *Advances in adolescent research.* Greenwich, CT: JAI Press.

Berry, J. W. (1980). Introduction to methodology. In H. C. Triandis & J. W. Berry (Eds.), *Handbook of cross-cultural psychology: Vol. 2. Methodology.* Boston: Allyn & Bacon.

Bertenthal, B., Campos, J., & Barrett, K. (1984). Self-produced locomotion: An organizer of emotional, cognitive, and social development in infancy. In R. Emde & R. Harmon (Eds.), *Continuities and dis-*continuities in development (pp. 175–210). New York: Plenum.

Betzig, L. (1993). Sex, succession, and stratification in the first six civilizations: How powerful men reproduced, passed power on to their sons, and used power to defend their wealth, women, and children. In L. Ellis (Ed.), *Social stratification and socioeconomic inequality: Vol. 1. A comparative biosocial analysis* (pp. 37–74). Westport, CT: Praeger.

Bjorkland, D. F. (1995). *Children's thinking: Developmental function and individual differences* (2d ed.). Pacific Grove, CA: Brooks/Cole.

Blakemore, J. E., LaRue, A. A., & Olejnik, A. B. (1979). Sex appropriate toy preference and the ability to conceptualize toys as sex-role related. *Developmental Psychology, 15,* 339–340.

Blehar, M., Lieberman, A., & Ainsworth, M. (1977). Early face to face interaction and its relation to later infant–mother attachment. *Child Development, 48,* 182–194.

Block, J. H., & Block, J. (1980). The role of ego-control and ego-resiliency in the organization of behavior. In W. A. Collins (Ed.), *Minnesota symposia on child psychology* (Vol. 13, pp. 39–101). Hillsdale, NJ: Erlbaum.

Blos, P. (1967). The second individuation process of adolescence. *Psychoanalytic Study of the Child, 22,* 162–186.

Blurton-Jones, N. (1967). An ethological study of some aspects of social behaviour of children in nursery school. In D. Morris (Ed.), *Primate ethology.* London: Weidenfeld and Nicolson.

Blurton-Jones, N. G. (Ed.). (1972). *Ethological studies of child behaviour.* Cambridge, England: Cambridge University Press.

Borke, H. (1971). Interpersonal perception of young children: Egocentrism or empathy? *Developmental Psychology, 5,* 263–269.

Borke, H., & Su, S. (1972). Perception of emotional responses to social interactions by Chinese and American children. *Journal of Cross Cultural Psychology, 3,* 309–314.

Bouchard, T. J., Jr. (1996). The genetics of personality. In K. Blum & E. P. Noble (Eds.), *Handbook of psychoeurogenetics.* Boca Raton, FL: CRC Press.

Bouchard, T. J., Jr. (1997). Twin studies of behavior: New and old findings. In A. Schmitt et al. (Eds.), *New aspects of human ethology.* New York: Plenum.

Bouchard, T. J., Jr., Lykken, D. T., McGue, M., Segal, N. L., & Tellegen, A. (1990). Sources of human psychological differences: The Minnesota study of twins reared apart. *Science, 250,* 223–228.

Bouchard, T. J., Jr., & McGue, M. (1981). Familial studies of intelligence: A review. *Science, 212,* 1055–1059.

Bowlby, J. (1951). *Maternal care and mental health.* Geneva: World Health Organization.

Bowlby, J. (1960). Grief and mourning in infancy and early childhood. *Psychoanalytical Study of Children, 15,* 9–52.

Bowlby, J. (1969). *Attachment and loss: Vol. I. Attachment.* New York: Basic Books.

Bowlby, J. (1973). *Attachment and loss: Vol. II. Separation, anxiety, and anger.* New York: Basic Books.

Bowlby, J. (1980). *Attachment and loss: Vol. III. Loss.* New York: Basic Books.

Bowlby, J. (1988). *A secure base: Parent–child attachment and healthy human development.* New York: Basic Books.

Brannigan, C. R., & Humphries, D. A. (1972). Human nonverbal behavior, a means of communication. In N. G. Blurton-Jones (Ed.), *Ethological studies of child behaviour.* Cambridge, England: Cambridge University Press.

Brazelton, T. B. (1969). *Infants and mothers.* New York: Delacorte.

Brazelton, T. B. (1984). *Neonatal Behavioral Assessment Scale* (2d ed.). Philadelphia: Lippincott.

Bretherton, I. (1985). Attachment theory: Retrospect and prospect. In I. Bretherton & E. Waters (Eds.), Growing points of attachment theory and research. *Monographs of the Society for Research in Child Development, 50.*

Bretherton, I., Fritz, J., Zahn-Waxler, C., & Ridgeway, D. (1986). Learning to talk about emotions: A functionalist perspective. *Child Development, 57,* 529–548.

Brewster Smith, M. (1995). Introduction. In E. V. Demos (Ed.), *Exploring affect: The selected writings of Silvan S. Tomkins.* Cambridge, England: Cambridge University Press.

Bridges, K. M. B. (1930). A genetic theory of the emotions. *Journal of Genetic Psychology, 37,* 514–527.

Bridges, K. M. B. (1932). Emotional development in early infancy. *Child Development, 3,* 325–341.

Bridges, L., & Grolnick, W. (1995). The development of emotional self-regulation in infancy and early childhood. In N. Eisenberg (Ed.), *Social development: Review of child development research,* (Vol. 15, pp. 185–211). Thousand Oaks, CA: Sage.

Broca, P. (1878). Anatomie comparée des circonvolutions cérébrales: Le grand lobe limbique et la scissure limbique dans la série des mammiferes. *Revue d'Anthropologie, 1,* 385–498.

Bronson, G. W. (1972). Infants' reactions to unfamiliar persons and novel objects. *Monographs of the Society for Research in Child Development, 32* (3, Serial No. 148).

Brown, B. B. (1990). Peer groups and peer culture. In S. S. Feldman & G. R. Elliot (Eds.), *At the threshold: The developing adolescent.* Cambridge, MA: Harvard University Press.

Brown, J. R., & Dunn, J. (1991). "You can cry, mum": The social and developmental implications of talk about internal states. *British Journal of Developmental Psychology, 9,* 237–256.

Bruner, J. (1975). The ontogenesis of speech acts. *Journal of Child Language, 2,* 1–19.

Bugental, D. B., Blue, J., & Cruzcosa, M. (1989). Perceived control over caregiving outcomes: Implications for child abuse. *Developmental Psychology, 25,* 532–539.

Bugental, D. B., Mantyla, S. M., & Lewis, J. (1989). Parental attributions as moderators of affective communications to children at risk for physical abuse. In D. Cichhetti & V. Carlson (Eds.), *Current research and theoretical advances in child maltreatment* (pp. 254–279). New York: Cambridge University Press.

Bugental, D. B., & Shennum, W. A. (1984). "Difficult" children as elicitors and targets of adult communication patterns: An attributional-behavioral-transactional analysis. *Monographs of the Society for Research in Child Development, 49* (1, Serial No. 205).

Bukowski, W., & Hoza, B. (1989). Popularity and friendship: Issues in theory, measurement and outcome. In T. J. Berndt & G. W. Ladd (Eds.), *Peer relationships in child development* (pp. 15–45). New York: Wiley.

Bureau of Justice sourcebook of criminal statistics. (1997). New York: The Hindelang Criminal Justice Research Center.

Buss, A. H., & Plomin, R. (1975). *A temperament theory of personality development.* New York: Wiley.

Buss, A. H., & Plomin, R. (1984). *Temperament: Early developing personality traits.* Hillsdale, NJ: Erlbaum.

Buss, D. M. (1995). Evolutionary psychology: A new paradigm for psychological science. *Psychological Inquiry, 6,* 1–49.

Buss, D. M. (1996). Social adaptation and five major factors in personality. In J. S. Wiggins (Ed.), *The five-factor model of personality: Theoretical perspectives* (pp. 180–207). New York: Guilford.

Byrne, R. W., & Whitten, A. (1988). *Machiavellian intelligence: Social expertise and the evolution of intellect in monkeys, apes and humans.* Oxford: Oxford University Press.

Caldera, Y. M., Huston, A. C., & O'Brien, M. (1989). Social interactions and play patterns of parents and toddlers with feminine, masculine, and neutral toys. *Child Development, 60,* 70–76.

Calkins, S. D., & Fox, N. A. (1992). The relations among infant temperament, security of attachment, and behavioral inhibition at twenty-four months. *Child Development, 63,* 1456–1472.

Campos, J. J., & Barrett, K. C. (1984). Toward a new understanding of emotions and their development. In C. E. Izard, J. Kagan, & R. B. Zajonc (Eds.), *Emotions, cognition, and behavior* (pp. 229–263). New York: Cambridge University Press.

Campos, J. J., Barrett, K. C., Lamb, M. E., Goldsmith, H. H., & Sternberg, C. (1983). Socioemotional development. In M. Haith & J. J. Campos (Eds.), *Handbook of child psychology: Vol. 2. Infancy and developmental psychobiology.* New York: Wiley.

Campos, J. J., Emde, R., Gaensbauer, T., & Henderson, C. (1975). Cardiac and behavioral interrelationships in the reactions of infants to strangers. *Developmental Psychology, 11,* 589–601.

Campos, J. J., Hiatt, S., Ramsay, D., Henderson, C., & Svejda, M. (1978). The emergence of fear on the visual cliff. In M. Lewis & L. A. Rosenblum (Eds.), *The development of affect: Vol. I. Genesis of behavior* (pp. 149–182). New York: Plenum.

Campos, J., Mumme, D., Kermoian, R., & Campos, R. (1994). A functionalist perspective on the nature of emotion. In N. Fox (Ed.), The development of emotion regulation: Biological and behavioral considerations. *Monographs of the Society for Research in Child Development, 59*(2/3, Serial No. 240).

Camras, L. A. (1992). Expressive development and basic emotions. *Cognition and Emotion, 6,* 269–283.

Camras, L., Holland, E., & Patterson, M. (1993). Facial expression. In M. Lewis & J. Haviland (Eds.), *Handbook of emotions* (pp. 199–208). New York: Guilford.

Camras, L. A., Malatesta, C., & Izard, C. (1991). The development of facial expressions in infancy. In R. Feldman & B. Rime (Eds.), *Fundamentals of nonverbal behavior.* New York: Cambridge University Press.

Cannon, W. (1927). The James–Lange theory of emotions: A critical examination and alternative theory. *American Journal of Psychology, 39,* 106–124.

Capaldi, D. M., Forgatch, M. S., & Crosby, L. (1994). Affective expression in family problem-solving discussions with adolescent boys. *Journal of Adolescent Research, 9,* 28–49.

Carlson, V., Cicchetti, D., Barnett, D., & Braunwald, K. (1989). Disorganized, disoriented attachment relationships in maltreated infants. *Developmental Psychology, 25,* 525–531.

Casey, R. (1993). Children's emotional experience: Relations among expression, self-report, and understanding. *Developmental Psychology, 29,* 119–129.

Cassidy, J. (1994). Emotion regulation: Influences of attachment relationships. In N. A. Fox (Ed.), The development of emotion regulation. *Monographs of the Society for Research in Child Development, 59*(2–3), 228–283.

Cassidy, J., & Kobak, R. (1988). Avoidance and its relation to other defensive processes. In J. Belsky & T. Nezworski (Eds.), *Clinical implications of attachment* (pp. 300–317). Hillsdale, NJ: Erlbaum.

Chagnon, N. A. (1968). *Yanomamö: The fierce people.* New York: Holt, Rinehart & Winston.

Chagnon, N. A. (1979). Mate competition, favoring close kin, and village fissioning among the Yanomamö Indians. In N. A. Chagnon & W. Irons (Eds.), *Evolutionary biology and human social behavior: An anthropological perspective.* North Scituate, MA: Duxbury Press.

Chagnon, N. A. (1988). Life histories, blood revenge, and warfare in a tribal population. *Science, 239,* 985–992.

Chandler, M., Fritz, A., & Hala, S. (1989). Small-scale deceit: Deception as a marker of two-, three-, and four-year-olds' early theories of mind. *Child Development, 60,* 1263–1277.

Charlesworth, W. R. (1969). The role of surprise in cognitive development. In D. Elkind & F. Flavell (Eds.), *Studies in cognitive development* (pp. 257–314). London: Oxford University Press.

Charlesworth, W. R. (1974). General issues in the study of fear: Section IV. In M. Lewis & L. A. Rosenblum (Eds.), *The origins of fear* (pp. 254–258). New York: Wiley.

Charlesworth, W. R. (1982). An ethological approach to research on facial expressions. In C. E. Izard (Ed.), *Measuring emotions in infants and children.* Cambridge, England: Cambridge University Press.

Charlesworth, W. R. (1996). Co-operation and competition: Contributions to an evolutionary and developmental model. *International Journal of Behavioural Development, 19,* 25–38.

Charlesworth, W. R., & Dzur, C. (1987). Gender comparisons of preschoolers' behavior and resource utilization in group problem solving. *Child Development, 58,* 191–200.

Charlesworth, W. R., & Kreutzer, M. A. (1973). Facial expressions of infants and children. In P. Ekman (Ed.), *Darwin and facial expression: A century of research in review* (pp. 91–168). New York: Academic Press.

Charlesworth, W. R., & LaFreniere, P. (1983). Dominance, friendship and resource utilization in preschool children's groups. *Ethology and Sociobiology, 4,* 175–186.

Chevalier-Skolnikoff, S. (1973). Facial expression of emotion in nonhuman primates. In P. Ekman (Ed.), *Darwin and facial expression* (pp. 11–90). New York: Academic Press.

Christopherson, E. R. (1989). Injury control. *American Psychologist, 44,* 237–241.

Cicchetti, D. (1990). The organization and coherence of socio-emotional cognitive and representational development: Illustrations through a developmental psychopathology perspective on Down's syndrome and child maltreatment. In R. Thompson (Ed.), *Nebraska Symposium on Motivation* (Vol. 36). Lincoln, NE: University of Nebraska Press.

Cicchetti, D., & Beeghly, M. (1990). *Down syndrome: A developmental perspective.* Cambridge, England: Cambridge University Press.

Cicchetti, D., Ganiban, J., & Barnett, D. (1991). Contributions from the study of high risk populations to understanding the development of emotion regulation. In J. Garber & K. Dodge (Eds.), *The development of emotion regulation* (pp. 15–48). New York: Cambridge University Press.

Cicchetti, D., & Hesse, P. (1983). Affect and intellect: Piaget's contributions to the study of infant emotional development. In R. Phluchik & H. Kellerman (Eds.), *Emotion: Theory, research and experience: Vol. 2. Emotion in early development* (pp. 115–170). New York: Academic Press.

Cicchetti, D., & Schneider-Rosen, K. (1986). An organizational approach to childhood depression. In M. Rutter, C. E. Izard, & P. B. Read (Eds.), *Depression in young people.* New York: Guilford.

Cohn, D. A. (1990). Child–mother attachment of six-year-olds and social competence at school. *Child Development, 61,* 152–162.

Cohn, J. F., Matias, R., Tronick, E. Z., Connell, D., & Lyons-Ruth, D. (1986). Face-to-face interactions of depressed mothers and their infants. In E. Z. Tronick & T. Field (Eds.), *Maternal depression and infant disturbance.* San Francisco: Jossey-Bass.

Cohn, J. F., & Tronick, E. Z. (1983). Three-month-old infants' reaction to simulated maternal depression. *Child Development, 54,* 185–193.

Coie, J. D., Dodge, K. A., & Kupersmidt, J. B. (1990). Peer group behavior and social status. In S. R. Asher & J. D. Coie (Eds.), *Peer rejection in childhood: Origins, consequences, and intervention* (pp. 17–59). New York: Cambridge University Press.

Cole, P. (1986). Children's spontaneous control of facial expression. *Child Development, 57,* 1309–1321.

Cole, P. J., Barrett, K., & Zahn-Waxler, C. (1992). Emotional displays in two-year-olds during mishaps. *Child Development, 63,* 314–324.

Coll, C. G., Kagan, J., & Reznick, J. S. (1984). Behavioral inhibition in young children. *Child Development, 56,* 1005–1019.

Collaer, M. L., & Hines, M. (1995). Human behavioral sex differences: A role for gonadal hormones during early development? *Psychological Bulletin, 118,* 55–107.

Collins, W. A. (1997). Relationships and development during adolescence: Interpersonal adaptation to individual change. *Personal Relationships, 4,* 1–14.

Columbo, J. (1982). The critical period concept: Research, methodology, and theoretical issues. *Psychological Bulletin, 91,* 260–275.

Cornelius, R. R. (1996). *The science of emotion.* Upper Saddle River, NJ: Prentice-Hall.

Cowan, P. (1978). *Piaget with feeling.* New York: Holt, Rinehart & Winston.

Crittenden, P. M. (1988). Distorted patterns of relationships in maltreating families: The role of internal representational models. *Journal of Reproductive and Infant Psychology, 6,* 183–199.

Crittenden, P. M. (1992). Treatment of anxious attachment in infancy and early childhood. *Development and Psychopathology, 4*(4), 575–602.

Crockenberg, S. (1981). Infant irritability, mother responsiveness, and social support influences on the security of infant–mother attachment. *Child Development, 52,* 857–865.

Crockenberg, S., & Litman, C. (1990). Autonomy as competence in 2-year-olds: Maternal correlates of child defiance, compliance, and self-assertion. *Developmental Psychology, 26,* 961–970.

Cronbach, L. J., & Meehl, P. E. (1955). Construct validity in psychological tests. *Psychological Bulletin, 52,* 281–302.

Cummings, E. M., Zahn-Waxler, C., & Radke-Yarrow, M. (1981). Young children's responses to expressions of anger and affection by others in the family. *Child Development, 52,* 1274–1282.

Daly, M., & Wilson, M. (1978). Sex, evolution, and behavior. North Scituate, MA: Duxbury Press.

Damasio, A. R., Damasio, H., & Tranel, D. (1990). Impairments of visual recognition as clues to the processes of memory. In G. M. Edelman, W. E. Gall, & W. M. Cowan (Eds.), *Signal and sense: Local and global order in perceptual maps* (pp. 451–473). New York: Wiley.

Dannemiller, J. L., & Stephens, B. R. (1988). A critical test of infant pattern preference models. *Child Development, 59,* 210–216.

Darwin, C. (1859). *On the origin of species.* London: Murray.

Darwin, C. (1872/1965). *The expression of the emotions in man and animals.* Chicago: University of Chicago Press.

Davidson. R. J. (1993). The neuropsychology of emotion and affective style. In M. Lewis & J. M. Haviland (Eds.), *Handbook of emotions* (pp. 143–154). New York: Guilford.

Davidson, R. J., Ekman, P., Saron, C., Senulis, R., & Friesen, W. V. (1990). Approach-withdrawal and cerebral asymmetry: 1. Emotional expression and brain physiology. *Journal of Personality and Social Psychology, 58,* 330–341.

Davidson, R. J., & Fox, N. A. (1982). Asymmetrical brain activity discriminates between positive versus negative affective stimuli in human infants. *Science, 218,* 1235–1237.

Davies, T. (1995). Gender differences in masking negative emotions: Ability or motivation? *Developmental Psychology, 31,* 660–667.

Dawkins, R. (1976). *The selfish gene.* New York: Oxford University Press.

Dawkins, R., & Krebs, J. R. (1978). Animal signals: Information or manipulation? In J. R. Krebs & N. B. Davies (Eds.), *Behavioral ecology.* Oxford: Blackwell.

DeCasper, A. J., & Fifer, W. (1980). Of human bonding: Newborns prefer their mothers' voice. *Science, 208,* 1174–1176.

DeCasper, A. J., & Spence, M. J. (1986). Prenatal maternal speech influences newborn's perception of speech sounds. *Infant Behavior and Development, 9,* 133–150.

Deese, J. (1985). *American freedom and the social sciences.* New York: Columbia University Press.

de Kloet, E. R. (1991). Brain corticosteroid receptor balance and homeostatic control. *Frontiers in Neuroendocrinology, 12*(2), 95–164.

Delgado, J. (1969). Offensive-defensive behavior in free monkeys and chimpanzees induced by radio stimulation of the brain. In S. Garattini & E. B. Sigg (Eds.), *Aggressive behavior.* Amsterdam: Excerpta Medica.

Denham, S. A. (1986). Social cognition, social behavior, and emotion in preschoolers: Contextual validation. *Child Development, 57,* 194–201.

Denham, S., & Auerbach, S. (1995). *Mother–child dialogue about emotions and preschoolers' emotional competence.* Paper presented at the biennial meeting of the Society for Research in Child Development, Indianapolis, IN.

Denham, S., Cook, M., & Zoller, D. (1992). "Baby looks very sad": Implications of conversations about feelings between mother and preschooler. *British Journal of Developmental Psychology, 10,* 301–315.

Denham, S. A., & McKinley, M. (1993). Sociometric nominations of preschoolers: A psychometric analysis. *Early Education and Development, 4,* 109–122.

Denham, S. A., McKinley, M., Couchoud, E. A., & Holt, R. (1990). Emotional and behavioral predictors of preschool peer ratings. *Child Development, 61,* 1145–1152.

Denham, S., Renwick, S., & Holt, R. (1991). Working and playing together: Prediction of preschool social-emotional competence from mother–child interaction. *Child Development, 62,* 242–249.

Dennis, W. (1940). Does culture appreciably affect patterns of infant behavior? *Journal of Social Psychology, 12,* 305–317.

Descartes, R. (1649/1989). On the passions of the soul. In E. S. Haldane & C. R. T. Ross (Eds.), *Philosophical works of Descartes* (pp. 332–427). New York: Dover.

Dimond, S., Farrington, L., & Johnson, P. (1976). Differing emotional response from right and left hemispheres. *Nature, 261,* 690–692.

DiPietro, J. A. (1981). Rough and tumble play: A function of gender. *Developmental Psychology, 17,* 50–58.

Dishion, T. J., Andrews, D. W., & Crosby, L. (1995). Antisocial boys and their friends in early adolescence: Relationship characteristics, quality, and interactional process. *Child Development, 66,* 139–151.

Dix, T. (1991). The affective organization of parenting: Adaptive and maladaptive processes. *Psychological Bulletin, 110,* 3–25.

Dobzhansky, T. (1973) Nothing in biology makes sense except in the light of evolution. *American Biology Teacher, 35,* 125–129.

Dollard, J., Miller, N. E., Doob, L. W., Mowrer, O. H., & Sears, R. R. (1939). *Frustration and aggression.* New Haven, CT: Yale University Press.

Donaldson, S. K., & Westerman, M. A. (1986). Development of children's understanding of ambivalence and causal theories of emotion. *Developmental Psychology, 22,* 655–662.

Douvan, E., & Adelson, J. (1966). *The adolescent experience.* New York: Wiley.

Duffy, E. (1934). Emotion: An example of the need for reorientation in psychology. *Psychological Review, 41,* 184–198.

Dumas, J. E. (1989). Let's not forget the context in behavioral assessment. *Behavioral Assessment, 11,* 231–247.

Dumas, J. E., & LaFreniere, P. J. (1993). Mother–child relationships as sources of support or stress: A comparison of competent, average, aggressive, and anxious dads. *Child Development, 64*(4).

Dumas, J. E., LaFreniere, P. J., & Serketich, W. J. (1995). Balance of power: A transactional analysis of control in mother–child dyads involving socially competent, aggressive, and anxious children. *Journal of Abnormal Psychology, 104*(1), 104–113.

Dumas, J. E., Martinez, A., & LaFreniere, P. J. (1998). The Spanish version of the Social Competence and Behavior Evaluation: Translation and field testing. *Hispanic Journal of Behavioral Development, 20*(2), 255–269.

Dunn, J., Bretherton, I., & Munn, P. (1987). Conversations about feeling states between mothers and their children. *Developmental Psychology, 23,* 132–139.

Dunn, J., & Brown, J. (1991). Relationships, talk about feelings, and the development of affect regulation in early childhood. In J. Garber & K. Dodge (Eds.), *The development of emotion regulation and dysregulation* (pp. 89–108). Cambridge, England: Cambridge University Press.

Dunn, J., & Kendrick, C. (1982). *Siblings.* Cambridge, MA: Harvard University Press.

Dunn, J., & Munn, P. (1985). Becoming a family member: Family conflict and the development of social understanding in the second year. *Child Development, 56,* 480–492.

Dunphy, D. C. (1963). The social structure of urban adolescent peer groups. *Society, 26,* 230–246.

Durkheim, E. (1912 /1960). *Les formes elementaires de la vie religieuse* (4th ed.). Paris: Presses Universitaires de France.

Durrett, M. E., Otaki, M., & Richards, P. (1985). Attachment and mother's perception of support from the father. *International Journal of Behavioral Development.*

Eagly, A. H., & Crowley, M. (1986). Gender and helping behavior: A meta-analytic review of the social psychological literature. *Psychological Bulletin, 100,* 283–308.

Easterbrooks, M. A., & Lamb, M. E. (1979). The relationship between quality of infant–mother attachment and infant competence in initial encounters with peers. *Child Development, 50,* 380–387.

Eaton, W. O., & Yu, A. P. (1989). Are sex differences in child motor activity level a function of sex differences in maturational status? *Child Development, 60,* 1005–1011.

Eder, D., & Hallinan, M. (1978). Sex differences in children's friendships. *American Sociological Review, 43,* 237–250.

Egeland, B., & Farber, E. (1984). Infant–mother attachment: Factors related to its development and changes over time. *Child Development, 55,* 753–771.

Egeland, B., & Sroufe, L. A. (1981). Developmental sequelae of maltreatment in infancy. In D. Cicchetti & R. Rizle (Eds.), *Developmental approaches to child maltreatment: New directions for child development* (pp. 77–91). San Francisco: Jossey-Bass.

Eibl-Eibesfeldt, I. (1972). Similarities and differences between cultures in expressive movements. In R. A. Hinde (Ed.), *Nonverbal communication* (pp. 297–311). Cambridge, MA: Cambridge University Press.

Eibl-Eibesfeldt, I. (1973). The expressive behavior of the deaf-and-blind-born. In M. Von Cranach & I. Vine (Eds.), *Social communication and movement* (pp. 163–194). New York: Academic Press.

Eibl-Eibesfeldt, I. (1989). *Human ethology.* New York: Aldine de Gruyter.

Eibl-Eibesfeldt, I. (1995). The evolution of familiality and its consequences. *Futura, 4,* 253–264.

Eibl-Eibesfeldt, I. (1997). Human ethology: Origins and prospects of a new discipline. In A. Schmitt et al. (Eds.), *New aspects of human ethology.* New York: Plenum.

Eisenberg, N. (1992). *The caring child.* Cambridge, MA: Harvard University Press.

Eisenberg, N., & Fabes, R. (1992). Emotion, regulation, and the development of social competence. In M. S. Clark (Ed.), *Emotion and social behavior: Vol. 14.*

Review of personality and social psychology (pp. 119–150). Newbury Park, CA: Sage.

Eisenberg, N., Fabes, R., Nyman, M., Bernzweig, J., & Pinuelas, A. (1994). The relations of emotionality and regulation to children's anger-related reactions. *Child Development, 65,* 109–128.

Eisenberg, N., & Lennon, R. (1983). Sex differences in empathy and related capacities. *Psychological Bulletin, 94,* 100–131.

Eisenberg, N., Schaller, M., Fabes, R., Bustamante, D., Mathy, R., Sheel, R., & Rhodes, K. (1988). Differentiation of personal distress and sympathy in children and adults. *Developmental Psychology, 24,* 766–775.

Ekman, P. (1971). Universal and cultural differences in facial expression of emotion. In J. R. Cole (Ed.), *Nebraska Symposium on Motivation.* Lincoln, NE: University of Nebraska Press.

Ekman, P. (1973). *Darwin and facial expression.* New York: Academic Press.

Ekman, P. (1989). The argument and evidence about universals in facial expressions of emotion. In H. Wagner & A. Manstead (Eds.), *Handbook of social psychophysiology* (pp. 143–163). New York: Wiley.

Ekman, P. (1992). An argrument for basic emotions. *Cognition and Emotion, 6,* 169–200.

Ekman, P. (1995). Silvan Tomkins and facial expression. In E. V. Demos (Ed.), *Exploring affect: The selected writings of Silvan S. Tomkins.* Cambridge, England: Cambridge University Press.

Ekman, P., & Friesen, W. V. (1969). Nonverbal leakage and clues to deception. *Psychiatry, 32,* 88–106.

Ekman, P., & Friesen, W. V. (1971). Constants across cultures in face and emotion. *Journal of Personality and Social Psychology, 17,* 124–129.

Ekman, P., & Friesen, W. V. (1975). *Unmasking the face.* Englewood Cliffs, NJ: Prentice-Hall.

Ekman, P., & Friesen, W. V. (1982). Felt, false, and miserable smiles. *Journal of Nonverbal Behavior, 6*(4), 238–252.

Ekman, P., & Friesen, W. V. (1986). A new pan-cultural facial expression of emotion. *Motivation and Emotion, 10,* 159–168.

Ekman, P., Friesen, W. V., & Davidson, R. J. (1990). The Duchenne's smile: Emotion expression and brain physiology: 2. *Journal of Personality and Social Psychology, 58,* 342–353.

Ekman, P., Friesen, W., & Simons, R. (1985). Is the startle reaction an emotion? *Journal of Personality and Social Development, 49,* 1416–1426.

Ekman, P., Levenson, R. W., & Friesen, W. V. (1983). Autonomic nervous system activity distinguishes between emotions. *Science, 221,* 1208–1210.

Eldredge, N., & Gould, S. J. (1972). Punctuated equilibria: An alternative to phyletic gradualism. In T. J. M. Schopf (Ed.), *Models in paleobiology* (pp. 82–115). San Francisco: Freeman.

Elkind, D. (1967). Egocentrism in adolescence. *Child Development, 38,* 1025–1034.

Elkind, D. (1976). *Child development and education: A Piagetian perspective.* New York: Oxford University Press.

Emde, R. (1980a). Toward a psychoanalytic theory of affect: Part I. The organizational model and its propositions. In S. Greenspan & G. Pollock (Eds.), *The course of life: Psychoanalytic contributions toward understanding personality and development* (pp. 63–83). Adelphi, MD: Mental Health Study Center, NIMH.

Emde, R. (1980b). Toward a psychoanalytic theory of affect: Part II. Emerging models of emotional development in infancy. In S. Greenspan & G. Pollock (Eds.), *Psychoanalysis and development, current perspectives* (pp. 85–112). Washington, DC: U.S. Government Printing Office.

Emde, R. (1992). Social referencing research: Uncertainty, self, and the search for meaning. In S. Feinman (Ed.), *Social referencing and the social construction of reality* (pp. 79–94). New York: Plenum.

Emde, R., & Buchsbaum, H. (1990). "Didn't you hear my mommy?" Autonomy with connectedness in moral self-emergence. In D. Cicchetti & M. Beeghly (Eds.), *The self in transition* (pp. 35–60). Chicago: University of Chicago Press.

Emde, R., Gaensbauer, T., & Harmon, R. (1976). Emotional expression in infancy: A biobehavioral study. *Psychological Issues Monograph Series, 10* (37), 1–198.

Emde, R. N., Harmon, R. J., & Good, W. V. (1986). Depressive feelings in children. A transactional model for research. In M. Rutter, C. Izard, & P. Read (Eds.), *Depression in young people: Developmental and clinical perspectives* (pp. 135–160). New York: Guilford.

Emde, R. N., Izard, C., Huebner, R., Sorce, J. F., & Klinnert, M. (1985). Adult judgments of infant emotions: Replication studies within and across laboratories. *Infant Behavior and Development, 8,* 79–88.

Emde, R., & Koenig, K. L. (1969). Neonatal smiling and rapid eye movement states. *American Academy of Child Psychiatry, 8,* 57–67.

Emde, R. N., McCartney, R. D., & Harmon, R. J. (1971). Neonatal smiling in REM states: Part 4. Premature study. *Child Development, 42,* 1657–1661.

Emde, R. N., Plomin, R., Robinson, J., Corley, R., DeFries, J., Fulker, D. W., Reznick, J. S., Campos, J., Kagan, J., & Zahn-Waxler, C. (1992). Temperament, emotion, and cognition at fourteen months: The MacArthur Longitudinal Twin Study. *Child Development, 63,* 1437–1455.

Engen, T. L., Lipsitt, L., & Peck, M. B. (1974). Ability of newborn infants to discriminate sapid substances. *Developmental Psychology, 10,* 741–744.

Eppinger, H., & Hess, L. (1910). *Die Vagotonie* (Nervous and Mental Disease Monograph, No. 20). N.p.

Erickson, M., Egeland, B., & Sroufe, L. A. (1985). The relationship between quality of attachment and behavior problems in preschool in a high risk sample. In I. Bretherton & E. Waters (Eds.), Growing points in attachment theory and research. *Monographs of the Society for Research in Child Development* (209), 147–186.

Erickson, M. F., Korfmacher, J., & Egeland, B. R. (1992). Attachments past and present: Implications for therapeutic intervention with mother–infant dyads. *Development and Psychopathology, 4,* 495–507.

Erikson, E. H. (1950). *Childhood and society* (1st ed.). New York: Norton.

Erikson, E. H. (1963). *Childhood and society* (2d ed.). New York: Norton.

Erikson, E. H. (1968). *Identity: Youth and crisis.* New York: Norton.

Escalona, S. K. (1968). *The roots of individuality: Normal patterns of development in infancy.* Chicago: Aldine de Gruyter.

Eysenck, H. J. (1967). *The biological basis of personality.* Springfield, IL: Thomas.

Fabes, R. A., & Eisenberg, N. (1992). Young children's coping with interpersonal anger. *Child Development, 63,* 116–129.

Fabes, R. A., Eisenberg, N., & Eisenbud, L. (1993). Behavioral and physiological correlates of children's reactions to others in distress. *Developmental Psychology, 29,* 655–663.

Fabes, R. A., Eisenberg, N., Nyman, M., & Michealieu, Q. (1991). Young children's appraisals of others' spontaneous emotional reactions. *Developmental Psychology, 27,* 858–866.

Fagot, B. I., Leinbach, M. D., & Hagan, R. (1986). Gender labeling and the adoption of sex-typed behaviors. *Developmental Psychology, 22,* 440–443.

Fairbairn, W. R. D. (1952). *An object-relations theory of personality.* New York: Basic Books.

Fantz, R. L. (1961). The origin of form perception. *Scientific American, 204*(5), 66–72.

Federal Bureau of Investigation. (1998). *Uniform crime reports for the United States, 1997: Crime in the United States.* Washington, DC: U.S. Government Printing Office.

Feinman, S., & Lewis, M. (1983). Social referencing and second order effects in ten-month-old infants. *Child Development, 54,* 878–887.

Feiring, C. (1996). Concepts of romance in 15-year-old adolescents. *Journal of Research on Adolescence, 6,* 181–200.

Feldman, R. S., Jenkins, L., & Popoola, O. (1979). Detecting of deception in adults and children via facial expressions. *Child Development, 50,* 350–355.

Felleman, E. S., Barden, R. C., Carlson, C. R., Rosenberg, L., & Masters, J. C. (1983). Children's and adults' recognition of spontaneous and posed emotional expressions in young children. *Developmental Psychology, 19,* 405–413.

Field, T. (1984). Early interactions between infants and their post-partum depressed mothers. *Infant Behavior and Development, 7,* 517–522.

Field, T. (1994). The effects of mother's physical and emotional unavailability on emotion regulation. In N. A. Fox (Ed.), The development of emotion regulation. *Monographs of the Society for Research in Child Development, 59* (2–3, Serial No. 240), 208–227.

Field, T., & Fogel, A. (1982). *Emotional and early interaction.* Hillsdale, NJ: Erlbaum.

Field, T., Woodson, R., Greenberg, R., & Cohen, D. (1982). Discrimination and imitation of facial expressions by neonates. *Science, 218,* 179–181.

Finkel, D., Pedersen, N. L., McGue, M., & McClearn, G. E. (1995). Heritability of cognitive abilities in adult twins: Comparison of Minnesota and Swedish data. *Behavior Genetics, 25,* 421–431.

Fischer, K. W., Shaver, P. R., & Carnochan, P. (1990). How emotions develop and how they organise development. *Cognition and Emotion, 4*(2), 81–127.

Flavell, J. H., Green, F. L., & Flavell, E. R. (1986). Development of knowledge about the appearance–reality distinction. *Monographs of the Society for Research in Child Development, 51* (Serial No. 212).

Flavell, J. H., Miller, P. H., & Miller, S. A. (1993). *Cognitive development* (3d ed.). Englewood Cliffs, NJ: Prentice-Hall.

Flavell, J. H., Shipstead, S. G., & Croft, K. (1978). Young children's knowledge about visual perception: Hiding objects from others. *Child Development, 49,* 1208–1211.

Fouts, R. (1997). *Next of kin: What chimpanzees have taught me about who we are.* New York: William Morrow.

Fox, N. A. (1994). Dynamic cerebral processes underlying emotion regulation. In N. Fox (Ed.), The development of emotion regulation: Biological and behavioral considerations. *Monographs of the Society for Research in Child Development, 59*(2/3, Serial No. 240), 152–166.

Fox, N. A., & Calkins, S. D. (1993). Multiple measure approaches to the study of emotion. In M. Lewis & J. M. Haviland (Eds.), *Handbook of emotions* (pp. 167–184). New York: Guilford.

Fox, N. A., & Davidson, R. J. (1984). Hemispheric substrates of affect: A developmental model. In N. A. Fox & R. J. Davidson (Eds.), *The psychobiology of affective development* (pp. 353–381). Hillsdale, NJ: Erlbaum.

Fox, N. A., & Davidson, R. J. (1988). Patterns of brain electrical activity during the expression of discrete emotions in ten-month-old infants. *Developmental Psychology, 24,* 230–236.

Fox, N. A., & Gelles, M. (1984). Face to face interaction in term and preterm infants. *Infant Mental Health Journal, 5,* 192–205.

Fox, N. A., Kimmerly, N. L., & Schafer, W. D. (1991). Attachment to mother/attachment to father: A meta-analysis. *Developmental Psychology, 62,* 210–225.

Fox, R., Aslin, R. N., Shea, S. L. & Dumais, S. T. (1980). Stereopsis in human infants. *Science, 207*(4428), 323–324.

Frankenhaeuser, M. (1980). Psychobiological aspects of life stress. In S. Levine & H. Ursin (Eds.), *Coping and health.* New York: Plenum.

Freedman, D. (1974). *Human infancy: An evolutionary perspective.* Hillsdale, NJ: Erlbaum.

Freeman, D. (1983). *Margaret Mead and Samoa.* Cambridge, MA: Harvard University Press.

Freud, A. (1936/1958). *The ego and the mechanisms of defense.* New York: International Universities Press.

Freud, S. (1895/1966). Project for a scientific psychology. In J. Strachey (Ed. & Trans.), *The standard edition of the complete psychological works of Sigmund Freud.* London: Hogarth Press.

Freud, S. (1925/1959). Fragment of an analysis of a case of hysteria. *Collected Papers, 3.* New York: Basic Books.

Freud, S. (1930). *Civilization and its discontents.* London: Hogarth Press.

Freud, S. (1936). Inhibitions, symptoms, and anxiety. In J. Strachey (Ed.), *The standard edition of the complete psychological works of Sigmund Freud* (Vol. 20, pp. 77–175). London: Hogarth Press.

Fridlund, A. J. (1994). Human facial expression: An evolutionary view. San Diego: Academic Press.

Friesen, W. V. (1972). *Cultural differences in facial expressions in a social situation. An experimental test of the concept of display rules.* Unpublished dissertation, University of California, San Francisco, CA.

Fuchs, D., & Thelen, M. (1988). Children's expected interpersonal consequences of communicating their affective states and reported likelihood of expression. *Child Development, 59,* 1314–1322.

Furman, W., & Buhrmester, D. (1992). Age and sex differences in perceptions of networks of personal relationships. *Child Development, 63,* 103–115.

Gallup, G. G. (1977). Self-recognition in primates: A comparative approach to the bi-directional properties of consciousness. *American Psychologist, 32,* 329–338.

Gardner, D., Harris, P. L., Ohmoto, M., & Hamazaki, T. (1988). Japanese children's understanding of the distinction between real and apparent emotion. *International Journal of Behavioral Development, 11*(2), 203–218.

Gavin, L. A., & Furman, W. (1996). Adolescent girls' relationships with mothers and best friends. *Child Development, 67,* 375–386.

Gazzaniga, M. S. (1970). *The bisected brain.* New York: Appleton-Century-Crofts.

Gazzaniga, M. S. (1985). *The social brain: Discovering the networks of the mind.* New York: Basic Books.

Gazzaniga, M. S. (1988). Brain modularity: Towards a philosophy of conscious experience. In A. J. Marcel & E. Bisiach (Eds.), *Consciousness in contemporary science* (pp. 218–238). Oxford: Oxford University Press.

Gazzaniga, M. S., & LeDoux, J. E. (1978). *The integrated mind.* New York: Plenum.

Geary, D. C. (1998). *Male, female: The evolution of human sex differences.* Washington, DC: American Psychological Association.

Geppert, U. (1986). *A coding system for analyzing behavioral expressions of self-evaluative emotions.* Munich: Max-Planck-Institute for Psychological Research.

Geppert, U., & Gartmann, D. (1983). *The emergence of self-evaluative emotions as consequences of achievement actions.* Paper presented at the biennial meeting of the International Society for the Study of Behavioral Development, Munich, Germany.

Gesell, A. (1928). *Infancy and human growth.* New York: Macmillan.

Gewirtz, J. L. (1965). The course of infant smiling in four child-rearing environments in Israel. In B. M. Foss (Ed.), *Determinants of infant behavior* (Vol. 3, pp. 205–248). London: Methuen.

Gibbs, E. L., Gibbs, F. A., & Fuster, B. (1948). Psychomotor epilepsy. *Archives of Neurology and Psychiatry, 60,* 331–339.

Gilligan, C. (1982). *In a different voice: Psychological theory and women's development.* Cambridge, MA: Harvard University Press.

Ginsburg, H. J., & Miller, S. M. (1982). Sex differences in children's risk-taking behavior. *Child Development, 53,* 426–428.

Gnepp, J., & Hess, D. L. R. (1986). Children's understanding of verbal rules. *Developmental Psychology, 22,* 103–108.

Gnepp, J., McKee, E., & Domanic, J. A. (1987). Children's use of situational information to infer emotion: Understanding emotionally equivocal situations. *Developmental Psychology, 23,* 114–123.

Goffman, E. (1959). *The presentation of self in everyday life.* New York: Doubleday.

Goldberg, S., Brachfeld, S., & DiVitto, B. (1980). Feeding, fussing, and play: Parent-infant interaction in the first year as a function of prematurity and perinatal medical problems. In T. M. Field, S. Goldberg, D. Stern, & A. M. Sostek (Eds.), *High-risk infants and children: Adult and peer interactions* (pp. 133–153). San Diego, CA: Academic Press.

Goldsmith, H. H. (1989). Behavior-genetic approaches to temperament. In G. A. Kohnstamm & M. K. Rothbart (Eds.), *Temperament in childhood* (pp. 111–132). Chichester, England: Wiley.

Goldsmith, H. H. (1993). Temperament: Variability in developing emotion systems. In M. Lewis & J. M. Haviland (Eds.), *Handbook of emotion* (pp. 353–364). New York: Guilford.

Goldsmith, H. H., & Alansky, J. A. (1987). Maternal and infant temperamental predictors of attachment: A meta-analytic review. *Journal of Consulting and Clinical Psychology, 55,* 805–816.

Goldsmith, H. H., & Campos, J. J. (1986). Fundamental issues in the study of early temperament: The Denver Twin Temperament Study. In M. E. Lamb, A. L. Brown, & B. Rogoff (Eds.), *Advances in devel-*

opmental psychology (Vol. 4, pp. 231–283). Hillsdale, NJ: Erlbaum.

Goldsmith, H. H., Losoya, S. H., Bradshaw, D. L., & Campos, J. J. (1994). Genetics of personality: A twin study of the five factor model and parental–offspring analyses. In C. Halverson, R. Martin, & G. Kohnstamm (Eds.), *The developing structure of temperament and personality from infancy to adulthood* (pp. 241–265). Hillsdale, NJ: Erlbaum.

Goldsmith, H. H., & Rothbart, M. K. (1991). Contemporary instruments for assessing early temperament by questionnaire and in the laboratory. In J. Strelau & A. Angleitner (Eds.), *Explorations in temperament: International perspectives on theory and measurement* (pp. 249–272). New York: Plenum.

Goodall, J. (1986). *The chimpanzees of Gombe.* Harvard: Belknap

Goodall, J. (1971). *In the shadow of man.* London: Collins.

Goodenough, F. L. (1931). *Anger in young children.* Minneapolis, MN: University of Minnesota Press.

Gottman, J. M. (1983). How children become friends. *Monographs of the Society for Research in Child Development, 48*(3, Serial No. 201).

Gottman, J. M., & Parker, J. G. (Eds.). (1986). *Conversations among friends: Speculations on affective development.* New York: Cambridge University Press.

Gottman, J. M., & Parkhurst, J. T. (1980). A developmental theory of friendship and acquaintanceship processes. In W. A. Collins (Ed.), *Minnesota symposia on child development: Vol. 13. Development of cognition, affect, and social relations* (pp. 197–253). Hillsdale, NJ: Erlbaum.

Gould, S. J. (1980). *The panda's thumb.* New York: Norton.

Gould, S. J. (1989). *Wonderful life.* New York: Norton.

Gowers, W. R. (1881). *Epilepsy and other chronic convulsive diseases: Their causes, symptoms, and treatment.* New York: William Wood.

Graham, F. K., & Clifton, R. K. (1966). Heart rate changes as a component of the orienting response. *Psychological Bulletin, 65,* 305–320.

Gray, J. A. (1971). *The psychology of fear and stress.* New York: McGraw-Hill.

Gray, J. A. (1982). *The neuropsychology of anxiety.* Oxford: Oxford University Press.

Gray, J. A. (1987). *The psychology of fear and stress* (2d ed.). Cambridge, England: Cambridge University Press.

Gray, P. (1999). *Psychology* (3rd. ed.). New York: Worth.

Greenberg, J. R. & Mitchell, S. A. (1983). *Object relations in psychodynamic theory*. Cambridge, MA: Harvard University Press.

Greene, A. L. (1990). Patterns of affectivity in the transition to adolescence. *Journal of Experimental Child Psychology, 50*, 340–356.

Greeno, C. G. (1989). *Gender differences in children's proximity to adults*. Unpublished doctoral dissertation, Stanford University, Stanford, CA.

Gross, D., & Harris, P. L. (1988). False beliefs about emotion: Children's understanding of misleading emotional displays. *International Journal of Behavioral Development, 11*, 475–488.

Gross, T .F. (1985). *Cognitive development*. Monterey, CA: Brooks/Cole.

Grossman, K., Grossman, K. E., Spangler, G., Suess, G., & Unzer, L. (1985). Maternal sensitivity and newborn orienting responses as related to quality of attachment in northern Germany. In I. Bretherton & E. Waters (Eds.), Growing points in attachment theory and research. *Monographs of the Society for Research in Child Development* (209), 233–356.

Grossman, K., Grossman, K. E., Huber, F., & Wartner, U. (1981). German children's behavior toward their mothers at 12 months and their fathers at 18 months in Ainsworth's Strange-Situation. *International Journal of Behavioral Development, 4*, 157–181.

Grotevant, H. D. (1997). Adolescent development in family contexts. In N. Eisenberg (Ed.), *Handbook of child psychology* (5th ed., Vol. 3). New York: Wiley.

Grusec, J. E., & Lytton, H. (1988). *Social development*. New York: Springer-Verlag.

Guerney, L., & Arthur, J. (1984). Adolescent social relationships. In R. Lerner & N. L. Galambos (Eds.), *Experiencing adolescents: A sourcebook for parents, teachers and teens* (pp. 87–118). New York: Teachers College Press.

Gunnar, M. (1980). Control, warning signals and distress in infancy. *Developmental Psychology, 16*(4), 281–289.

Gunnar, M., Mangelsdorf, S., Larson, M., & Herstgaard, L. (1989). Attachment, temperament, and adrenocortical activity in infancy: A study of psychoendocrine regulation. *Developmental Psychology, 25*, 355–363.

Gunnar, M., Marvinney, D., Isensee, J., & Fisch, R. O. (1989). Coping with uncertainty: New models of the relations between hormonal behavioral and cognitive processes. In D. Palermo (Ed.), *Coping with uncertainty: Biological, behavioral, and developmental perspectives*. Hillsdale, NJ: Erlbaum.

Gunnar, M. R., Porter, F. L., Wolf, C. M., Rigatuso, J., & Larson, M. C. (1995). Neonatal stress reactivity: Predictions to later emotional temperament. *Child Development, 66*, 1–13.

Gunnar, M., & Stone, C. (1984). The effects of positive maternal affect on infant responses to pleasant, ambiguous, & fear-provoking toys. *Child Development, 55*, 1231–1236.

Hala, S., Chandler, M., & Fritz, A. S. (1991). Fledgeling theories of mind: Deception as a marker of 3-year-olds' understanding of false beliefs. *Child Development, 61*, 83–97.

Hall, G. S. (1904). *Adolescence: Its psychology and its relations to physiology, anthropology, sociology, sex, crime, religion, and education* (Vols. 1, 2). New York: Appleton.

Hamilton, N. G. (1989). A critical review of object relations theory. *American Journal of Psychiatry, 146*, 1552–1560.

Hamilton, W. D. (1963). The evolution of altruistic behavior. *American Naturalist, 97*, 354–356.

Hamilton, W. D. (1964). The genetical evolution of social behaviour: I and II. *Journal of Theoretical Biology, 7*, 1–52.

Hann, D. M., Osofsky, J. D., & Carter, S. L. (1989, April). *A comparison of affects between infants of adolescent and older mothers*. Paper presented at the meetings of the Society for Research in Child Development, Kansas City, MO.

Harlow, H. F. (1969). Age-mate or peer affectional system. In D. S. Lehrman, R. A. Hinde, & E. Shaw (Eds.), *Advances in the study of behavior* (Vol. 1). New York: Academic Press.

Harlow, H. F. (1971). *Learning to love*. San Francisco, Albion.

Harlow, H. F., & Harlow, M. K. (1962). Social deprivation in monkeys. *Scientific American, 207*, 136–146.

Harlow, H. F., & Harlow, M. K. (1965). The affectional systems. In A. M. Schier, H. F. Harlow, & F. Stollnitz (Eds.), *Behavior of nonhuman primates* (Vol. 2). London: Academic Press.

Harlow, H. F., & Harlow, M. K. (1966). Learning to love. *American Scientist, 54*, 244–272.

Harlow, H. F., & Zimmerman, R. R. (1959). Affectional responses in the infant monkey. *Science, 130*, 421–432.

Harlow, J. M. (1868/1963). Recovery from the passage of an iron bar through the head. Reprinted in *History of Psychiatry, 4*, 274–281.

Harmon, R. J., & Emde, R. N. (1972). Spontaneous REM behaviors in a macrocephalic infant. *Perceptual and Motor Skills, 34,* 827–833.

Harré, R. (1986). The social constructionist viewpoint. In R. Harré (Ed.), *The social construction of emotions* (pp. 2–14). Oxford: Blackwell.

Harrigan, J. A. (1984). The effects of task order on children's identification of facial expressions. *Motivation and Emotion, 8,* 157–169.

Harris, P. L. (1983). Children's understanding of the link between situation and emotion. *Journal of Experimental Child Psychology, 36,* 490–509.

Harris, P. L. (1989). *Children and emotion: The development of psychological understanding.* Oxford: Blackwell.

Harris, P. L. (1993). Understanding of emotions. In M. Lewis & J. Haviland (Eds.), *Handbook of emotions* (pp. 237–246). New York: Guilford.

Harris, P. L., Brown, E., Marriot, C., Whittall, S., & Harmer, S. (1991). Monsters, ghosts, and witches: Testing the limits of fantasy–reality distinctions in young children. *British Journal of Developmental Psychology, 9,* 105–123.

Harris, P. L., & Gross, D. (1988). Children's understanding of real and apparent emotion. In J. W. Astington, P. L. Harris, & D. R. Olson (Eds.), *Developing theories of mind* (pp. 295–314). Cambridge, England: Cambridge University Press.

Harter, S. (1986). Cognitive-developmental processes in the integration of concepts about emotions and self. *Social Cognition, 4,* 119–151.

Harter, S., & Buddin, B. J. (1987). Children's understanding of the simultaneity of two emotions: A five-stage developmental acquisition sequence. *Developmental Psychology, 23,* 388–399.

Harter, S., & Whitesell, N. R. (1989). Developmental changes in children's understanding of single, multiple, and blended emotion concepts. In C. Saarni & P. Harris (Eds.), *Children's understanding of emotion* (pp. 81–116). Cambridge, England: Cambridge University Press.

Hartup, W. (1983). Peer relations. In P. H. Mussen (Ed.), *Handbook of child psychology* (Vol. 4), E. M. Hetherington (Vol. Ed.). New York: Wiley.

Hartup, W. (1989). Behavioral manifestations of children's friendships. In T. Berndt & G. Ladd (Eds.), *Peer relationships in child development* (pp. 46–70). New York: Wiley.

Hass, H. (1968). *Wir Menschen.* Wien, Austria: Molden.

Hauser, M. D. (1997). *The evolution of communication.* Cambridge, MA: MIT Press.

Haviland, J. M., & Lelwica, M. (1987). The induced affect response: 10-week-old infants' responses to three emotional expressions. *Developmental Psychology, 23,* 97–104.

Hayden-Thomson, L., Rubin, K. H., & Hymel, S. (1987). Sex preferences in sociometric choices. *Developmental Psychology, 23,* 558–562.

Hebb, D. (1946). On the nature of fear. *Psychological Review, 53,* 259–276.

Heckhausen, H. (1984). Emergent achievement behavior: Some early developments. In J. Nicholls (Ed.), *Advances in motivation and achievement: Vol 3. The development of achievement motivation* (pp. 1–32). Greenwich, CT: JAI Press.

Hess, R. D., Kashiwagi, K., Azuma, H., Price, G. G., & Dickson, W. P. (1980). Maternal expectations for mastery of developmental tasks in Japan and the United States. *International Journal of Psychology, 15,* 259–271.

Hetherington, E. M., & Camara, K. A. (1984). Families in transition: The processes of dissolution and reconstitution. In R. D. Parke (Ed.), *The family* (pp. 398–439). Chicago: University of Chicago Press.

Hiatt, S., Campos, J., & Emde, R. (1979). Facial patterning and infant emotional expression: Happiness, surprise, and fear. *Child Development, 50,* 1020–1035.

Hightower, E. (1990). Adolescent interpersonal and familial precursors of positive mental health at midlife. *Journal of Youth and Adolescence, 19*(3), 257–275.

Hill, J. P. (1980). *Understanding early adolescence: A framework.* Chapel Hill, NC: Center for Early Adolescence.

Hill, J. P., & Holmbeck, G. N. (1986). Attachment and autonomy during adolescence. In G. W. Whitehurst (Ed.), *Annals of child development* (Vol. 3). Greenwich, CT: JAI Press.

Hill, J. P., & Monks, F. J. (1977). Some perspectives on adolescence in modern societies. In J. P. Hill & F. J. Monks (Eds.), *Adolescence and youth in prospect* (pp. 28–78). Guilford, England: IPC Science and Technology Press.

Hinde, R. A. (1974). *Biological bases of human social behavior.* New York: McGraw-Hill.

Hinde, R. A., Titmus, G., Easton, D., & Tamplin, A. (1985). Incidence of friendship and behavior toward strong associates versus nonassociates in preschoolers. *Child Development, 56,* 234–245.

Hodos, W., & Campbell, C. B. G. (1969). *Scala naturae*: Why there is no theory in comparative psychology. *Psychological Review, 76,* 337–350.

Hoffman, M. (1970). Moral development. In P. H. Mussen (Ed.), *Carmichael's manual of child psychology* (3d ed., Vol. 2, pp. 261–360). New York: Wiley.

Hoffman, M. (1979). Development of moral thought, feeling, and behavior. *American Psychologist, 34,* 958–966.

Hoffman, M. L. (1984). Interaction of affect and cognition in empathy. In C. E. Izard, J. Kagan, & R. B. Zajonc (Eds.), *Emotions, cognition, and behavior* (pp. 103–131). Cambridge, England: Cambridge University Press.

Hooff, J.A.R.A.M. van. (1972). A comparative approach to the phylogeny of laughter and smiling. In R. A. Hinde (Ed.), *Nonverbal communication.* New York: Cambridge University Press.

Horner, A. J. (1989). *The wish for power and the fear of having it.* Northvale, NJ: Jason Aronson.

Horner, A. J. (1991). *Psychoanalytic object relations theory.* Northvale, NJ: Jason Aronson.

Huebner, R. R., & Izard, C. E. (1988). Mothers' responses to infants' facial expressions of sadness, anger and physical distress. *Motivation and Emotion, 12*(2), 185–196.

Huffman, L. C., Bryan, Y. E., del Carmen, R., Petersen, F. A., & Porges, S. W. (1992). *Autonomic correlates of reactivity and self-regulation at twelve weeks of age.* Unpublished manuscript, National Institute of Mental Health, Rockville, MD.

Hughlings-Jackson, J. (1878/1959). *Selected writings of John Hughlings-Jackson,* J. Taylor (Ed.). New York: Basic Books.

Hume, D. (1739/1972). *A treatise on human nature.* London: Fontana/Collins.

Humphrey, N. K. (1976). The social function of intellect. In P. P. G. Bateson & P. A. Hinde (Eds.), *Growing points in ethology.* Boston: Cambridge University Press.

Humphreys, A. P., & Smith, P. K. (1987). Rough and tumble, friendship, and dominance in school children: Evidence for continuity and change with age. *Child Development, 58,* 201–212.

Hunter, F. T., & Youniss, J. (1982). Changes in functions of three relations during adolescence. *Developmental Psychology, 18*(6), 806–811.

Huston, A. C. (1983). Sex-typing. In P. H. Mussen (Series Ed.) & E. M. Hetherington (Vol. Ed.), *Handbook of child psychology: Vol 4. Socialization, personality, and social development* (pp. 387–468). New York: Wiley.

Huxley, J. S. (1966). A discussion on the ritualization of behavior in animals and man. *Philosophical Transcripts of the Royal Society* (London), 251.

Huxley, L. (1898). Grandmother's tale. *Macmillan's Magazine, 78,* 423–435.

Hwang, C. P. (1986). Behavior of Swedish primary and secondary caretaking fathers in relation to mother's presence. *Developmental Psychology, 22,* 749–751.

Irvine, S. H., & Carroll, W. K. (1980). Testing and assessment across cultures: Issues in methodology and theory. In H. C. Triandis & J. W. Berry (Eds.), *Handbook of cross-cultural psychology* (Vol. 1). Boston: Allyn & Bacon.

Isabella, R. (1993). Origins of attachment: Maternal interactive behavior across the first year. *Child Development, 64,* 605–621.

Isabella, R. A., & Belsky, J. (1991). Interactional synchrony and the origins of infant–mother attachment: A replication study. *Child Development, 62,* 373–384.

Izard, C. E. (1975). Patterns of emotion and emotion communication in hostility and aggression. In P. Pliner, L. Kranes, & T. Alloway (Eds.), *Advances in the study of communication and affect* (Vol. 2, pp. 77–102). New York: Plenum.

Izard, C. E. (1978). On the ontogenesis of emotions and emotion-cognition relationships in infancy. In M. Lewis & L. A. Rosenblum (Eds.), *The development of affect* (pp. 389–413). New York: Plenum.

Izard, C. E. (1979). *The maximally discriminative facial movement coding system (Max).* Newark, NJ: University of Delaware, Instructional Resources Center.

Izard, C. E. (1991). *The psychology of emotions.* New York: Plenum.

Izard, C. E., Hembree, E. A., & Huebner, R. R. (1987). Infants' emotion expressions to acute pain: Developmental change and stability of individual differences. *Developmental Psychology, 23,* 105–113.

Izard, C. E., & Malatesta, C. Z. (1987). Perspectives on emotional development: I. Differential emotions theory of early emotional development. In J. D. Osfsky (Ed.), *Handbook of infant development* (2d ed., pp. 494–554). New York: Wiley-Interscience.

Jacklin, C. N., & Maccoby, E. E. (1978). Social behavior at 33 months in same-sex and mixed-sex dyads. *Child Development, 49,* 557–569.

Jacobson, J. L. & Wille, D. E. (1986). The influence of attachment pattern on developmental changes in peer interaction from the toddler to the preschool period. *Child Development, 57,* 338–347.

Jacobson, S. W., & Frye, K. F. (1991). Effect of maternal social support on attachment: Experimental evidence. *Child Development, 62,* 572–582.

James, W. (1884). What is an emotion? *Mind, 9,* 188–205.

James, W. (1890/1950). *The principles of psychology.* New York: Dover.

Janosz, M., & LaFreniere, P. J. (1991). Affectivé, amitié et competence sociale chez des garcons d'age préscolarie en situation de ressource limitée. *Enfance, 1–2,* 59–81.

Jersild, A. T., Woodyard, & del Solar. (1949). *Joys and problems of childrearing.* Cambridge, England: Cambridge University Press.

Josephs, I. (1993). *The regulation of emotional expression in preschool children.* New York: Waxmann Verlag.

Josephs, I. (1994). Display rule behavior and understanding in preschool children. *Journal of Nonverbal Behavior, 18,* 301–326.

Joshi, M. S., & MacLean, M. (1994). Indian and English children's understanding of the distinction between real and apparent emotion. *Child Development, 65,* 1372–1384.

Kagan, J. (1971). *Change and continuity in infancy.* New York: Wiley.

Kagan, J. (1994). *Galen's prophecy: Temperament in human nature.* New York: Basic Books.

Kagan, J., Keasley, R. B., & Zelazo, P. R. (1980). *Infancy: Its place in human development.* Cambridge, MA: Harvard University Press.

Kagan, J., Reznick, J. S., & Gibbons, J. (1989). Inhibited and uninhibited types of children. *Child Development, 60,* 838–845.

Kagan, J., Reznick, J. S., & Snidman, N. (1986). The physiology and psychology of behavioral inhibition in children. *Child Development, 58,* 1459–1473.

Kagan, J., Reznick, J. S., & Snidman, N. (1988). Biological bases of childhood shyness. *Science, 240,* 167–171.

Kagan, J., Reznick, J. S., Snidman, N., Gibbons, J., & Johnson, M. O. (1988). Childhood derivatives of inhibition and lack of inhibition to the unfamiliar. *Child Development, 59,* 1580–1589.

Kalat, J. W. (1999). *Introduction to psychology* (5th ed.). Pacific Grove, CA: Brooks/Cole.

Karen, R. (1994). *Becoming attached: Unfolding the mystery of the infant–mother bond and its impact on later life.* New York: Warner Books.

Kelly, J. A., & Hansen, D. J. (1987). Social interactions and adjustment. In V. B. Van Hasselt & M. Hersen (Eds.), *Handbook of adolescent psychology.* New York: Pergamon Press.

Kessen, W. (1965). *The child.* New York: Wiley.

Klinnert, M. D. (1984). The regulation of infant behavior by maternal facial expression. *Infant Behavior and Development, 7,* 447–465.

Klinnert, M. D., Campos, J. J., Sorce, J. F., Emde, R. N., & Svejda, M. (1983). Emotions as behavior regulators: Social referencing in infancy. In R. Plutchik & H. Kellerman (Eds.), *Emotion: Theory, research and experience* (pp. 57–86). New York: Academic Press.

Kluver, H., & Bucy, P.C. (1937). "Psychic blindness" and other symptoms following bilateral temporal lobectomy. *American Journal of Physiology, 119,* 352–353.

Kobak, R. R., & Sceery, A. (1988). Attachment in late adolescence: Working models, affect regulation, and representation of self and others. *Child Development, 59,* 135–146.

Kochanska, G. (1993). Toward a synthesis of parental socialization and child temperament in early development of conscience. *Child Development, 64,* 325–347.

Konner, M. (1982a). *The tangled wing: Biological constraints on the human spirit.* New York: Henry Holt.

Konner, M. (1982b). Biological aspects of the mother–infant bond. In R. N. Emde & R. J. Harmon (Eds.), *The development of attachment and affiliative systems* (pp. 137–160). New York: Plenum.

Konner, M. (1991). Childhood. Boston: Little, Brown.

Kopp, C. B. (1982). Antecedents of self-regulation: A developmental perspective. *Developmental Psychology, 18,* 199–214.

Kopp, C. (1989). Regulation of distress and negative emotions: A developmental view. *Developmental Psychology, 25,* 343–354.

Kopp, C., Krakow, J., & Vaughn, B. (1983). The antecedents of self-regulation in young handicapped children. In M. Perlmutter (Ed.), *Minnesota Symposia on Child Psychology* (Vol. 17, pp. 93–128). Hillsdale, NJ: Erlbaum.

Korner, A. F., Hutchinson, C. A., Koperski, J., Kraemer, H. C., & Schneider, P. A. (1981). Stability of individual differences of neonatal motor and crying patterns. *Child Development, 52,* 83–90.

Kövecses, Z. (1990). *Emotion concepts.* New York: Springer-Verlag.

Krystal, H. (1978). Trauma and affects. *Psychoanalytic Study of the Child, 33,* 81–116.

Kuchuk, W., Vibbert, M., & Bornstein, M. H. (1986). The perception of smiling and its experiental correlates in 3-month-old infants. *Child Development, 57,* 1054–1061.

Kuczynski, L., & Kochanska, G. (1990). Children's noncompliance from toddlerhood to age five. *Developmental Psychology, 26,* 398–408.

Kuhn, D., Nash, S., & Burcken, L. (1978). Sex role concepts of two- and three-year-olds. *Child Development, 49,* 445–451.

Kummer, H. (1971). *Primates societies.* Arlington Heights, IL: AHM.

LaBarbera, J. D., Izard, C. E., Vietze, P., & Parisi, S. A. (1976). Four- and six-month-old infants' visual responses to joy, anger, and neutral expressions. *Child Development, 47,* 535–538.

Lacey, J. I. (1967). Somatic response patterning and stress: Some revisions of activation theory. In M. H. Appley & R. Trumbull (Eds.), *Psychological stress.* New York: Appleton-Century-Crofts.

LaFreniere, P. (1982). *From attachment to peer relations. An analysis of individual patterns of social adaptation during the formation of a preschool peer group.* Unpublished doctoral dissertation, University of Minnesota, Minneapolis, MN.

LaFreniere, P. J. (1985, April). *Assessing parent–child attachment across cultures: A comparison of the strange-situation and Q-sort methods.* Paper presented at the Society for Research in Child Development, Toronto, Canada.

LaFreniere, P. J. (1988). The ontogeny of tactical deception in humans. In R. W. Byrne & A. Whiten (Eds.), *Machiavellian intelligence: Social expertise and the evolution of intelligence in monkeys, apes, and humans.* Oxford: Oxford University Press.

LaFreniere, P. J. (August, 1998). *Card sharks and poker faces: Links between developmental research on deception and evolutionary models.* Paper presented at the International Society for Human Ethology, Vancouver, BC.

LaFreniere, P. J., & Charlesworth, W. R. (1983). Dominance, affiliation and attention in a preschool group: A nine-month longitudinal study. *Ethology and Sociobiology, 4,* 1–14.

LaFreniere, P., & Charlesworth, W. R. (1987). Effects of friendship and dominance status on preschooler's resource utilization in a cooperative/competitive situation. *International Journal of Behavioral Development, 10*(3), 345–358.

LaFreniere, P. J., & Dumas, J. E. (1992). A transactional analysis of early childhood anxiety and social with-drawal. *Development and Psychopathology, 4*(4), 385–402.

LaFreniere, P. J., & Dumas, J. E. (1995). *Social Competence and Behavior Evaluation, preschool edition.* Los Angeles: Western Psychological Services.

LaFreniere, P. J., & Dumas, J. (1996). Social Competence and Behavior Evaluation in children aged three to six: The short form (SCBE-30). *Psychological Assessment, 8,* 369–377.

LaFreniere, P. J., Dumas, J., Capuano, F., & Dubeau, D. (1992). The development and validation of the preschool socio-affective profile. *Psychological Assessment: Journal of Consulting and Clinical Psychology, 4*(4), 442–450.

LaFreniere, P. J., & MacDonald, K. (1996). Evolutionary perspectives on children's resource-directed behaviour in peer relationships: An introduction. *International Journal of Behavioural Development, 19,* 1–7.

LaFreniere, P. J., & Sroufe, L. A. (1985). Profiles of peer competence: Interrelations among measures, influence of social ecology, and relation to attachment history. *Developmental Psychology, 21,* 56–69.

LaFreniere, P., Strayer, F. F., & Gauthier, R. (1984). The emergence of same-sex preferences among preschool peers: A developmental ethological perspective. *Child Development, 55,* 1958–1965.

Lamb, M. (1981). The development of father–infant relationships. In M. E. Lamb (Ed.), *The role of the father in child development* (2d ed.). New York: Wiley.

Lamb, M. (1986). *The father's role: Cross-cultural perspectives.* Hillsdale, NJ: Erlbaum.

Lamb, M., Thompson, R., Gardner, W., Charnov, E., & Estes, D. (1984). Security of infantile attachment as assessed in the strange situation: Its study and biological interpretation. *Behavioral and Brain Sciences, 7,* 127–147.

Lange, C. (1885/1922). The emotions. In E. Dunlap (Ed.), *The emotions.* Baltimore: Williams & Wilkins.

Langlois, J. H., Roggman, L. A., Casey, R. J., Ritter, J. M., Reisser-Danner, L. A., & Jenkins, V. Y. (1987). Infant preferences for attractive faces: Rudiments of a stereotype? *Developmental Psychology, 23,* 363–369.

Langsdorf, P., Izard, C. E., Rayias, M., & Hembree, E. (1983). Interest expression, visual fixation, and heart rate changes in 2- to 8-month-old infants. *Developmental Psychology, 19*(3), 375–386.

Larson, R. (1989). Beeping children and adolescents: A method for studying time use and daily experience. *Journal of Youth and Adolescence, 6,* 511–530.

Larson, R., & Asmussen, L. (1991). Anger, worry, and hurt in early adolescence: An enlarging world of negative emotions. In M. E. Colton & S. Gore (Eds.), *Adolescent stress, social relationships, and mental health.* New York: Aldine de Gruyter.

Larson, R., & Richards, M. H. (1991). Daily companionship in late childhood and early adolescence: Changing developmental contexts. *Child Development, 62,* 284–300.

Larson, R., & Richards, M. H. (1994). *Divergent realities: The emotional lives of mothers, fathers, and adolescents.* New York: Basic Books.

Larson, R. W., Richards, M. H., Moneta, G., Holmbeck, G., & Duckett, E. (1996). Changes in adolescents' daily interactions with their families from 10 to 18: Disengagement and transformation. *Developmental Psychology, 32,* 744–754.

Lashley, K. S. (1930). Basic neural mechanisms in behavior. *Psychological Review, 37,* 1–24.

Lashley, K. S. (1951). The problem of serial order in behavior. In L. A. Jeffres (Ed.), *Cerebral mechanisms in behavior.* New York: Wiley.

Laursen, B., & Collins, W. A. (1994). Interpersonal conflict during adolescence. *Psychological Bulletin, 115,* 197–209.

Lazarus, R. S. (1966). *Psychological stress and the coping process.* New York: McGraw-Hill.

Lazarus, R. S. (1991). *Emotion and adaptation.* Oxford: Oxford University Press.

Lazarus, R. S., & Folkman, S. (1984). *Stress, appraisal and coping.* New York: Springer.

LeCroy, C. (1988). Parent-adolescent intimacy: Impact on adolescent functioning. *Adolescence, 23*(89), 137–147.

LeDoux, J. E. (1986). The neurobiology of emotion. In J. E. LeDoux & W. Hirst (Eds.), *Mind and brain: Dialogues in cognitive neuroscience.* Cambridge, England: Cambridge University Press.

LeDoux, J. E. (1993). Emotional networks in the brain. In M. Lewis & J. Haviland (Eds.), *Handbook of emotions* (pp. 109–118). New York: Guilford.

LeDoux, J. E. (1996). *The emotional brain: The mysterious underpinnings of emotional life.* New York: Simon & Schuster.

Lee, G. P., Loring, D. W., Meader, K. J., & Brooks, B. B. (1990). Hemispheric specialization for emotional expression: A reexamination of results from intracarotid administration of sodium amobarbital. *Brain and Cognition, 12,* 267–280.

Lennon, R., & Eisenberg, N. (1987). Gender and age differences in empathy and sympathy. In N. Eisenberg & J. Strayer (Eds.), *Empathy and its development* (pp. 195–217). New York: Cambridge University Press.

Leslie, L., Huston, T., & Johnson, M. (1986). Parental reactions to dating relationships: Do they make a difference? *Journal of Marriage and the Family, 48*(2), 57–66.

LeVine, R. A. (1982). Culture, context, and the concept of development. In W. A. Collins (Ed.), *The concept of development. Minnesota Symposia on Child Psychology* (Vol. 15). Hillsdale, NJ: Erlbaum.

LeVine, R., Dixon, S., LeVine, S., Richman, A., Leiderman, P. H., Keefer, C. H., & Brazelton, T. B. (1994). *Child care and culture: Lessons from Africa.* New York: Cambridge University Press.

Lewin, K. (1949). Cassirer's philosophy of science and the social sciences. In P. A. Schlipp (Ed.), *The philosophy of Ernst Cassirer.* Evanston, IL: Library of Living Philosophers.

Lewis, M. (1993a). The emergence of human emotions. In M. Lewis & J. M. Haviland (Eds.), *Handbook of emotions* (pp. 223–236). New York: Guilford.

Lewis, M. (1993b). Self-conscious emotions: Embarrassment, pride, shame, and guilt. In M. Lewis & J. Haviland (Eds.), *The handbook of emotions* (pp. 563–573). New York: Guilford.

Lewis, M., Alessandri, S. M., & Sullivan, M. W. (1990). Violation of expectancy, loss of control, and anger expressions in young infants. *Developmental Psychology, 26,* 745–751.

Lewis, M., Alessandri, S., & Sullivan, M. (1992). Differences in shame and pride as a function of children's gender and task difficulty. *Child Development, 63,* 630–638.

Lewis, M., Feiring, C., McGuffog, C., & Jaskir, J. (1984). Predicting psychopathology in six-year-olds from early social relations. *Child Development, 55,* 123–136.

Lewis, M., & Haviland, J. M. (1993). *Handbook of emotions.* New York: Guilford.

Lewis, M., & Michalson, L. (1983). *Children's emotions and moods.* New York: Plenum.

Lewis, M., Stanger, C., & Sullivan, M. W. (1989). Deception in 3-year-olds. *Developmental Psychology, 25,* 439–443.

Lewis, M., Sullivan, M., & Brooks-Gunn, J. (1985). Emotional behavior during the learning of a contingency in early infancy. *British Journal of Developmental Psychology, 3,* 307–316.

Lewis, M., Sullivan, M., Stanger, C., & Weiss, M. (1989). Self-development and self-conscious emotions. *Child Development, 60,* 146–156.

Lieberman, A. F. (1977). Preschoolers' competence with a peer: Relations with attachment and peer experience. *Child Development, 48,* 1277–1287.

Lieberman, A. F., Weston, D. R., & Pawl, J. H. (1991). Preventive intervention and outcome with anxiously attached dyads. *Child Development, 62,* 199–209.

Linnemeyer, S. A., & Porges, S. W. (1986). Recognition memory and cardiac vagal tone in 6-month-old infants. *Infant Behavior and Development, 9,* 43–56.

Loehlin, J. C. (1992). *Genes and environment in personality development.* Newbury Park, CA: Sage.

Loehlin, J. C. & Rowe, D. C. (1992). Genes, environment, and personality. In G. Capara & G. L. Van Heck (Eds.), *Modern personality psychology: Critical reviews and new directions* (pp. 352–370). New York: Harvester Wheatsheaf.

Loewi, O. (1960). An autobiographic sketch. *Perspectives in Biology, 4,* 3–25.

Londerville, S., & Main, M. (1981). Security of attachment, compliance, and maternal training methods in the second year of life. *Developmental Psychology, 17,* 289–299.

Lorenz, K. (1935). Der Kumpan in der Umwelt des Vogels [The Companion in the Bird's World]. *Journal of Ornitbology, 83,* 137–213. In C. Schiller (Ed. & Trans.), *Instinctive behavior: Development of a modern concept* (pp. 83–128). London: Methuen.

Lorenz, K. (1941). Kants lehre vom apriorischen im lichte gegenwärtiger biologie. *Blätter für Deutsche philosophie, 15.*

Lorenz, K. (1943). Die angeborenem Formen moglicher Erfahrung. *Zeitschrift für Tierpsychologie, 5,* 235–409.

Lorenz, K. (1965). Introduction. In C. Darwin, *The expression of emotions in man and animals* (1872/1965). Chicago: University of Chicago Press.

Lorenz, K. (1973). *Die ruckseite des spiegels.* Munich and Zurich: Piper.

Lorenz, K., & Tinbergen, N. (1938). Taxis und Instinkthandlung in der Eirolbewegung der Graugans [Taxis and instinctive action in the egg-retrieving behavior of the greylag goose]. *Zeitschrift für Tierpsychologie, 2,* 1–29. In C. Schiller (Ed. & Trans.), *Instrinctive behavior: Development of a modern concept* (pp. 176–208). London: Methuen.

Ludemann, P. M. (1991). Generalized discrimination of positive facial expressions by seven- and ten-month-old infants. *Child Development, 62,* 55–67.

Ludemann, P. M., & Nelson, C. A. (1988). Categorical representation of facial expressions by 7-month-old infants. *Developmental Psychology, 24,* 492–501.

Luria, A. R. (1980). *Higher cortical functions in man* (2d ed.). New York: Basic Books.

Lyons-Ruth, K., Connell, D. B., Grunebaum, H. U., & Botein, S. (1990). Infants at social risk: Maternal depression and family support services as mediators of infant development and security of attachment. *Child Development, 61,* 85–98.

Lyons-Ruth, K., Connell, D., Zoll, D., & Stahl, J. (in press). Infants' maltreatment, maternal behavior, and infant attachment behavior. *Developmental Psychology.*

Lyons-Ruth, K., Repacholi, B., McLeod, S., & Silva, E. (1991). Disorganized attachment behavior in infancy: Short-term stability, maternal and infant correlates, and risk-related subtypes. *Development and Psychopathology, 3*(4), 377–396.

Maccoby, E. E. (1988). Gender as a social category. *Developmental Psychology, 24,* 755–765.

Maccoby, E. E. (1990). Gender and relationships: A developmental account. *American Psychologist, 45,* 513–520.

Maccoby, E. E. (1998). *The two sexes: Growing up apart, coming together.* Harvard: Belknap.

Maccoby, E. E., & Jacklin, C. N. (1974). *The psychology of sex differences.* Stanford, CA: Stanford University Press.

Maccoby, E., & Martin, J. (1983). Socialization in the context of the family. In E. M. Hetherington (Ed.), *Handbook of child psychology: Socialization, personality, and social development* (Vol. 4, pp. 1–101). New York: Wiley.

MacDonald, K. (1987). Parent–child physical play with rejected, neglected, and popular boys. *Developmental Psychology, 23* (5), 705–711.

MacDonald, K. (1998). Evolution, culture, and the five-factor model. *Journal of Cross-Cultural Psychology, 29* (1), 119–149.

MacDonald, K., & Parke, R. D. (1984). Bridging the gap: Parent–child play interaction and peer interactive competence. *Child Development, 55,* 1265–1277.

MacLean, P. D. (1967). The brain in relation to empathy and medical education. *Journal of Nervous and Mental Disease, 144,* 374–382.

MacLean, P. D. (1990). *The triune brain in evolution: Role in paleocerebral functions.* New York: Plenum.

MacLean, P. D. (1993). Cerebral evolution of emotion. In M. Lewis & J. M. Haviland (Eds.), *Handbook of emotions* (pp. 67–86). New York: Guilford.

Mahler, M., Pine, F., & Bergman, A. (1975). *The psychological birth of the human infant.* New York: Basic Books.

Main, M., & Cassidy, J. (1988). Categories of response to reunion with the parent at age 6: Predictable from infant attachment classifications and stable over a 1-month period. *Developmental Psychology, 24*(3), 415–526.

Main, M., & Solomon, J. (1990). Procedure for identifying infants as disorganized/disoriented during the Ainsworth Strange Situation. In M. Greenberg, D. Cicchetti, & M. Cummings (Eds.), *Attachment in the preschool years: Theory, research, and intervention* (pp. 121–160). Chicago: University of Chicago Press.

Main, M., & Weston, D. R. (1981). The quality of the toddler's relationship to mother and father as related to conflict behavior and readiness to establish new relationships. *Child Development, 52,* 932–940.

Main, M., & Weston, D. R. (1982). Avoidance of the attachment figure in infancy: Descriptions and interpretations. In C. M. Parkes & J. Stevenson-Hinde (Eds.), *The place of attachment in human behavior* (pp. 31–59). New York: Basic Books.

Malatesta, C. Z. (1990). The role of emotions in the development and organization of personality. In R. A. Thompson (Ed.), *Socioemotional development* (Nebraska Symposium on Motivation, Vol. 36). Lincoln, NE: University of Nebraska Press.

Malatesta, C. Z., Culver, C., Tesman, J. R., & Shepard, B. (1989). The development of emotion expression during the first two years of life. *Monographs of the Society for Research in Child Development, 54*(1–2, Serial No. 219).

Malatesta, C. Z., & Haviland, J. M. (1982). Learning display rules: The socialization of emotion expression in infancy. *Child Development, 53,* 991–1003.

Malthus, T. R. (1798/1826). *An essay on the principle of population, as it affects the future improvement of society* (6th ed.). London: Murray.

Mandler, G. (1975). *Mind and emotions.* New York: Wiley.

Mangelsdorf, S., Gunnar, M., Kestenbaum, R., Lang, S., & Andreas, D. (1990). Infant proneness-to-distress temperament, maternal personality, and mother–infant attachment: Associations and goodness of fit. *Child Development, 61,* 820–831.

Marcia, J. E. (1966). Development and validation of ego identity status. *Journal of Personality and Social Psychology, 3,* 551–558.

Marcia, J. E. (1980). Identity in adolescence. In J. Adelson (Ed.), *Handbook of adolescent psychology* (pp. 159–187). New York: Wiley.

Marcia, J. E. (1993). The status of the statuses: Research review. In J. E. Marcia, A. S. Waterman, D. R. Matteson, S. L. Archer, & J. L. Orlofsky (Eds.), *Ego identity: A handbook for psychological research* (pp. 22–41). New York: Springer-Verlag.

Marcus, J., Maccoby, E. E., Jacklin, C. N., & Doering, C. H. (1985). Individual differences in mood in early childhood: Their relation to gender and neonatal sex steroid. *Developmental Psychobiology, 18,* 327–340.

Marler, P. (1959). Developments in the study of animal communication. In P. R. Bell (Ed.), *Darwin's biological work.* New York: Cambridge University Press.

Marshall, G. D., & Zimbardo, P. G. (1979). Affective consequences of inadequately explained physiological arousal. *Journal of Personality and Social Psychology, 37,* 970–988.

Maslach, C. (1978). The emotional consequences of arousal without reason. In C. E. Izard (Ed.), *Emotion and psychopathology.* New York: Plenum.

Mason, W. A. (1960). The effects of social restriction on the behavior of rhesus monkeys: I. Free social behavior. *Journal of Comparative and Physiological Psychology, 53,* 582–589.

Mason, W. A. (1997). Discovering behavior, *American Psychologist, 52*(7), 713–720.

Masters, J., & Wellman, H. (1974). Human infant attachment: A procedural critique. *Psychological Bulletin, 81,* 218–237.

Matas, L., Arend, R., & Sroufe, L. (1978). Continuity of adaptation in the second year: The relationship between quality of attachment and later competence. *Child Development, 49,* 547–556.

Matheny, A. (1989). Children's behavioral inhibitions over age and across situations: Genetic similarity for a trait change. *Journal of Personality, 57,* 215–235.

Matias, R., & Cohn, J. (1993). Are max-specified infant facial expressions during face-to-face interaction consistent with differential emotions theory? *Developmental Psychology, 29,* 524–531.

Maurer, D., & Salapatek, P. (1976). Developmental changes in the scanning of faces by young infants. *Child Development, 47,* 523–527.

Maynard Smith, J. (1982). *Evolution and the theory of games.* Cambridge, England: Cambridge University Press.

Mayr, E. (1942). *Systematics and the origin of species.* New York: Columbia University Press.

Mayr, E. (1974). Behavior programs and evolutionary strategies. *American Scientist, 62,* 650–659.

Mayr, E. (1982). *The growth of biological thought: Diversity, evolution, and inheritance.* Cambridge, MA: Harvard University Press.

McClintock, M. K., & Herdt, G. (1996). Rethinking puberty: The development of sexual attraction. *Current Directions in Psychological Science, 6,* 178–183.

McDougall, W. (1926). *An introduction to social psychology.* Boston: Luce.

McGrew, W. C. (1972). *An ethological study of children's behavior.* New York: Academic Press.

McGue, M., Bouchard, T. J., Jr., Iacono, W. G., & Lykken, D. T. (1993). Behavior genetics of cognitive ability: A life-span perspective. In R. Plomin & G. E. McClearn (Eds.), *Nature, nurture and psychology* (pp. 59–76). Washington, DC: American Psychological Association.

McLoyd, V. C. (1990). The impact of economic hardship on black families and children: Psychological distress, parenting, and socioemotional development. *Child Development, 61,* 311–346.

Mead, M. (1928). *Coming of age in Samoa.* New York: Morrow.

Mebert, C. J. (1991). Dimensions of subjectivity in parents' ratings of infant temperament. *Child Development, 62,* 352–361.

Meerum Terwogt, M., & Olthof, T. (1989). Awareness and self-regulation of emotion in young children. In J. Saarni & P. Harris (Eds.), *Children's understanding of emotion* (pp. 209–240). Cambridge, England: Cambridge University Press.

Mesquita, B., & Frijda, N. (1992). Cultural variations in emotion: A review. *Psychological Bulletin, 112,* 179–204.

Meyer, M. F. (1933). That whale among the fishes—The theory of emotions. *Psychological Review, 40,* 292–300.

Miller, R. E., Caul, W. F., & Mirsky, A. (1967). Communication of affects between feral and socially isolated monkeys. *Journal of Personality and Social Psychology, 7,* 231–239.

Mineka, S., Davidson, M., Cook, M., & Keir, R. (1984). Observational conditioning of snake fear in rhesus monkeys. *Journal of Abnormal Psychology, 93*(4), 355–372.

Miyake, K., Chen, S., & Campos, J. (1985). Infant temperament, mother's mode of interaction, and attachment in Japan. In I. Bretherton & E. Waters (Eds.), Growing points in attachment theory and research. *Monographs of the Society for Research in Child Development, 50*(1/2, Serial No. 209), 276–297.

Money, J., & Ehrhardt, A. A. (1972). *Man and woman, boy and girl.* Baltimore: John Hopkins University Press.

Montemayor, R. (1983). Parents and adolescents in conflict: All families some of the time and some families most of the time. *Journal of Early Adolescence, 3,* 83–103.

Montemayor, R., & Flannery, D. J. (1989). A naturalistic study of the involvement of children and adolescents with their mothers and friends: Developmental differences in expressive behavior. *Journal of Adolescent Research, 4,* 3–14.

Montemayor, R., & Flannery, D. J. (1990). Making the transition from childhood to early adolescence. In R. Montemayor, G. R. Adams, & T. P. Gulotta (Eds.), *From childhood to adolescence: A transitional period?* Newbury Park, CA: Sage.

Moser, R. M., Paternite, C. E., & Dixon, Jr., W. E. (1996). Late adolescents' feelings toward parents and siblings. *Merrill-Palmer Quarterly, 42,* 537–553.

Muir, D., & Clifton, R. (1985). Infants' orientation to location of sound sources. In G. Gottlieb & N. Krasnegor (Eds.), *Measurement of audition and vision in the first year of life: A methodological overview.* Norwood, NJ: Ablex.

Nathanson, D. L. (1987). Shaming systems in couples, families, and institutions. In D. L. Nathanson (Ed.), *The many faces of shame* (pp. 246–270). New York: Guilford.

Nelson, C. A. (1987). The recognition of facial expression in the first two years of life: Mechanisms of development. *Child Development, 58,* 889–909.

Nelson, C. A., & De Haan, M. (1997). A neurobehavioral approach to the recognition of facial expressions in infancy. In J. A. Russell & J. M. Fernández-Dols (Eds.), *The psychology of facial expression.* Cambridge, England: Cambridge University Press.

Oatley, K. (1993). Social construction in emotions. In M. Lewis & J. M. Haviland (Eds.), *Handbook of emotions* (pp. 341–352). New York: Guilford.

Oatley, K., & Jenkins, J. M. (1996). *Understanding Emotions.* Cambridge, MA: Blackwell.

Oatley, K., & Johnson-Laird, P. N. (1987). Towards a cognitive theory of emotions. *Cognition and Emotion, 1,* 29–50.

Odom, R., & Lemond, C. (1972). Developmental differences in the perception and production of facial expressions. *Child Development, 43,* 359–369.

Offer, E., & Offer, J. (1975). *From teenage to young manhood.* New York: Basic Books.

Ortony, A., Clore, G. L., & Collins, A. (1988). *The cognitive structure of emotions.* Cambridge, England: Cambridge University Press.

Ortony, A., & Turner, T. J. (1990). What's basic about basic emotions? *Psychological Review, 74,* 431–461.

Owings, D., & Morton, E. S. (1998). *Animal vocal communication: A new approach.* New York: Cambridge University Press.

Paikoff, R. L., & Brooks-Gunn, J. (1991). Do parent–child relationships change during puberty? *Psychological Bulletin, 110,* 47–66.

Paikoff, R. L., Brooks-Gunn, J., & Warren, M. P. (1991). Effects of girls' hormonal status on depressive and aggressive symptoms over the course of one year. *Journal of Youth and Adolescence, 20,* 191–215.

Paley, V. G. (1984). *Boys and girls: Superheroes in the doll corner.* Chicago: University of Chicago Press.

Panksepp, J. (1982). Toward a general psychobiological theory of emotions. *The Behavioral and Brain Sciences, 5,* 407–467.

Panksepp, J. (1998). *Affective neuroscience: The foundations of human and animal emotions.* New York: Oxford University Press.

Panoccione, V. F., & Wahler, R. G. (1986). Child behavior, maternal depression, and social coercion as factors in the quality of child care. *Journal of Abnormal Child Psychology, 14,* 263–278.

Papez, J. W. (1937). A proposed mechanism of emotion. *Archives of Neurology and Psychiatry, 38,* 725–743.

Papousek, M., Papousek, H., & Bornstein, M. (1985). The naturalistic vocal environment of young infants: On the significance of homogeneity and variability in parental speech. In T. Field & N. Fox (Eds.), *Social perception in infants* (pp. 82–105). New York: Academic Press.

Parke, R. D. (1981). *Fathers.* Cambridge, MA: Harvard University Press.

Parke, R. D., & Slaby, R. G. (1983). The development of aggression. In P. H. Mussen (Series Ed.) & E. M. Hetherington (Vol. Ed.), *Handbook of child psychology: Vol. 4. Socialization, personality and social development* (pp. 547–641). New York: Wiley.

Parke, R. D., & Stearns, P. (1993). Fathers and childrearing: A historical analysis. In G. Elder, Jr., J. Modell, & R. D. Parke (Eds.), *Children in time and place: Developmental and historical insights.* New York: Cambridge University Press.

Parker, J., & Asher, S. (1993). Friendship and friendship quality in middle childhood: Links with peer group acceptance and feelings of loneliness and social dissatisfaction. *Developmental Psychology, 29,* 611–621.

Parker, J., & Gottman, J. M. (1989). Social and emotional development in a relational context: Friendship interaction from early childhood to adolescence. In T. Berndt & G. Ladd (Eds.), *Peer relationships in child development* (pp. 95–131). New York: Wiley.

Patterson, G. R. (1976). The aggressive child: Victim and architect of a coercive system. In E. J. Mash, L. A. Hamerlynck, & L. C. Handy (Eds.), *Behavior modification and families* (pp. 267–316). New York: Brunner/Mazel.

Patterson, G. R. (1980). Mothers: The unacknowledged victims. *Monographs of the Society for Research in Child Development, 45* (5, Serial No. 186).

Patterson, G. R. (1982). *Coercive family processes.* Eugene, OR: Castalia.

Patterson, G. R., Reid, J. B., & Dishion, T. J. (1992). *Anti-social boys.* Eugene, OR: Castalia.

Patterson, S. J., Sochting, I., & Marcia, J. E. (1992). The inner space and beyond: Women and identity. In G. R. Adams, T. P. Gullotta, & R. Montemayor (Eds.), *Adolescent identity formation.* Newbury Park, CA: Sage.

Pavlov, I. P. (1927/1960). *Conditioned reflexes* (G. V. Anrep, Trans.). New York: Dover.

Penfield, W., & Jasper, H. (1954). *Epilepsy and the functional anatomy of the human brain.* Boston: Little, Brown.

Peng, M., Johnson, C. N., Pollock, J., Glasspool, R., & Harris, P. L. (1992). Training young children to acknowledge mixed emotions. *Cognition and Emotion, 6,* 387–401.

Peterson, D. R. (1961). Behavior problems of middle childhood. *Journal of Consulting Psychology, 25,* 205–209.

Piaget, J. (1952). *The origins of intelligence in children.* New York: Routledge & Kagan Paul.

Piaget, J. (1962). *Play, dreams and imitation in childhood.* New York: Norton.

Piaget, J. (1965). *The moral judgement of the child.* New York: Free Press.

Piaget, J. (1967). The mental development of the child. In D. Elkind (Ed.), *Six psychological studies by Piaget.* New York: Random House.

Plomin, R., Chipuer, H. M., & Loehlin, J. C. (1990). Behavioral genetics and personality. In L. A. Pervin

(Ed.), *Handbook of personality* (pp. 225–243). New York: Guilford.

Plomin, R., & DeFries, J. C. (1985). *Origins of individual differences in infancy: The Colorado adoption project.* Orlando, FL: Academic Press.

Plomin, R., Emde, R. N., Braungart, J. M., Campos, J., Corley, R., Fulker, D. W., Kagan, J., Reznick, J. S., Robinson, J., Zahn-Waxler, C., & DeFries, J. C. (1993). Genetic change and continuity from fourteen to twenty months: The MacArthur Longitudinal Twin Study. *Child Development, 64,* 1354–1376.

Plomin, R., McClearn, G. E., Pedersen, N. L., Nesselroade, J. R., & Bergeman, C. S. (1988). Genetic influence on childhood family environment perceived retrospectively from the last half of the life span. *Developmental Psychology, 24,* 738–745.

Plutchik, R. (1980). *Emotion: A psychoevolutionary synthesis.* New York: Harper & Row.

Plutchik, R. (1991). Emotions and evolution. In K. T. Strongman (Ed.), *International review of studies on emotion* (Vol. 1, pp. 37–58). Chichester, England: Wiley.

Popper, K. (1968). *The logic of scientific discovery* (2d ed.). New York: Harper & Row.

Porges, S. W. (1986). Respiratory sinus arrhythmia: Physiological basis, quantitative methods, and clinical implications. In P. Grossman, K. Janssen, & D. Vaitl (Eds.), *Cardiorespiratory and cardiosomatic psychophysiology* (pp. 101–115). New York: Plenum.

Porges, S. (1991). Vagal tone: An autonomic mediator of affect. In J. Garber & K. Dodge (Eds.), *The development of emotion regulation and dysregulation* (pp. 111–128). New York: Cambridge University Press.

Porges, S. W. (1992). Autonomic regulation and attention. In B. A. Campbell, H. Hayne, & R. Richardson (Eds.), *Attention and information processing in infants and adults.* Hillsdale, NJ: Erlbaum.

Porges, S. W., & Doussard-Roosevelt, J. A. (in press). The psychophysiology of temperament. To appear in J. D. Noshpitz (Ed.), *Handbook of child and adolescent psychiatry.* New York: Wiley.

Porges, S. W., Doussard-Roosevelt, J. A., & Maiti, A. K. (1994). Vagal tone and the physiological regulation of emotion. In N. A. Fox (Ed.), Emotion regulation: Behavioral and biological considerations (pp. 167–186). *Monograph of the Society for Research in Child Development, 59*(Serial No. 240).

Portales, A. L., Doussard-Roosevelt, J. A., Lee, H. B., & Porges, S. W. (1992). Infant vagal tone predicts 3-year child behavior problems [Abstract]. *Infant Behavior and Development, 15,* 636.

Porter, F., Porges, S. W., & Marshall, R. E. (1988). Newborn pain cries and vagal tone: Parallel changes in response to circumcision. *Child Development, 59,* 495–505.

Powlishta, K. K., & Maccoby, E. E. (1990). Resource utilization in mixed-sex dyads: The influence of adult presence and task type. *Sex Roles, 23*(5/6), 223–240.

Premack, D. (1988). Does the chimpanzee have a theory of mind? Revisited in R. W. Byrne & A. Whiten (Eds.), *Machiavellian intelligence: Social expertise and the evolution of intelligence in monkeys, apes, and humans.* Oxford: Oxford University Press.

Premack, D., & Woodruff, G. (1978). Does the chimpanzee have a theory of mind? *Behavioral and Brain Sciences, 1,* 515–526.

Price, D. A., Close, G. C., & Fielding, B. A. (1983). Age of appearance of circadian rhythm in salivary cortisol values in infancy. *Archives of Disease in Childhood, 58,* 454–456.

Pryce, C. R. (1995). Determinants of motherhood in human and nonhuman primates: A biosocial model. In C. R. Pryce, R. D. Martin, & D. Skuse (Eds.), *Motherhood in human and nonhuman primates: Bioscial determinants* (pp. 1–15). Basel, Switzerland: Karger.

Putallaz, M. (1987). Maternal behavior and children's sociometric status. *Child Development, 58,* 324–340.

Putallaz, M., & Gottman, J.M. (1981). Social skills and group acceptance. In S. R. Asher & J. M. Gottman (Eds.), *The development of children's friendships.* Cambridge, England: Cambridge University Press.

Quay, H. C. (1979). Classification. In H. C. Quay & J. Werry (Eds.), *Psychopathological disorders of childhood* (2d ed.). New York: Wiley.

Quay, H. C. (1983). A dimensional approach to behavior disorder: The revised behavior problem checklist. *School Psychology Review, 12,* 244–249.

Radke-Yarrow, M. (1990). Family environments of depressed and well parents and their children: Issues of research methods. In G. R. Patterson (Ed.), *Depression and aggression in family interaction* (pp. 169–184). Hillsdale, NJ: Erlbaum.

Radke-Yarrow, M., & Zahn-Waxler, C. (1984). Roots, motives, and patterns in children's pro-social behavior. In E. Staub, D. Bartal, J. Karylowski, & J. Reykowski (Eds.), *The development and maintenance of pro-social behaviors.* New York: Plenum.

Reisenzein, R. (1983). The Schachter theory of emotion: Two decades later. *Psychological Bulletin, 94,* 239–264.

Reissland, J., & Harris, P. (1991). Children's use of display rules in pride-eliciting situations. *British Journal of Developmental Psychology, 9,* 431–435.

Reissland, N. (1994). The socialization of pride in young children. *International Journal of Behavioral Development, 17,* 541–552.

Richman, N., Stevenson, J. S., & Graham, P. J. (1982). *Preschool to school: A behavioral study.* London: Academic Press.

Ridgeway, D., Waters, E., & Kuczaj, S. A. (1985). Acquisition of emotion-descriptive language: Receptive and productive vocabulary norms of ages 18 month to 6 years. *Developmental Psychology, 21,* 901–908.

Roberts, W., & Strayer, J. (1987). Parent responses to the emotional distress of their children: Relations with children's competence. *Developmental Psychology, 23,* 415–425.

Robertson, J. (1952). *A two-year-old goes to hospital* (film). New York: New York University Film Library.

Robinson, R. G., Kubos, K. L., Starr, L. B., Rao, K., & Price, T. R. (1984). Mood disorders in stroke patients. *Brain, 107,* 81–93.

Rosenblum, L. A., Coe, L. L., & Bromley, L. J. (1975). Peer relations in monkeys: The influence of social structure, gender, and familiarity. In. M. Lewis & L. A. Rosenblum (Ed.), *Friendship and peer relations.* New York: Wiley.

Rothbart, M. K. (1981). Measurement of temperament in infancy. *Child Development, 52,* 569–578.

Rothbart, M. K. (1989). Temperament in childhood: A framework. In G. Kohnstamm, J. Bates, & M. Rothbart (Eds.), *Temperament in childhood* (pp. 59–73). New York: Wiley.

Rothbart, M. K., & Bates, J. E. (1998). Temperament. In W. Damon (Series Ed.) & N. Eisenberg (Vol. Ed.), *Handbook of child psychology: Vol. 3. Social, emotional, and personality development* (5th ed.). New York: Wiley.

Rothbart, M. K., & Mauro, J. A. (1990). Questionnaire approaches to the study of infant temperament. In J. W. Fagen & J. Colombo (Eds.), *Individual differences in infancy: Reliability, stability and prediction* (pp. 411–429). Hillsdale, NJ: Erlbaum.

Rousseau, J. J. (1762/1956). *Emile.* New York: Teachers College Press.

Rowe, D. C. (1994). *The limits of family influence: Genes, experience, and behavior.* New York: Guilford.

Rubin, K. D., & Clark, M. L. (1983). Preschool teachers' ratings of behavioral problems: Observational, sociometric, and social-cognitive correlates. *Journal of Abnormal Child Psychology, 11,* 273–286.

Rubin, R. T., Reinisch, J. M., & Haskett, R. F. (1981). Postnatal gonadal steroid effects on human behavior. *Science, 211*(4488), 1318–1324.

Rutter, M., & Garmezy, N. (1983). Developmental psychopathology. In P. H. Mussen (Ed.), *Handbook of child psychology* (4th ed., Vol. 4, pp. 776–911). New York: Wiley.

Saarni, C. (1979). Children's understanding of display rules for expressive behavior. *Developmental Psychology, 15,* 424–429.

Saarni, C. (1984). An observational study of children's attempts to monitor their expressive behavior. *Child Development, 55,* 1504–1513.

Saarni, C. (1988). Children's understanding of the interpersonal consequences of dissemblance of nonverbal emotional-expressive behavior. *Journal of Nonverbal Behavior, 12,* 275–294.

Saarni, C., Mumme, D. L., & Campos, J. J. (1998). Emotional development: Action, communication, and understanding. In W. Damon (Series Ed.) & N. Eisenberg (Vol. Ed.), *Handbook of child psychology: Vol. 3. Social, emotional, and personality development* (5th ed., pp. 237–309). New York: Wiley.

Sackeim, H. A., Greenberg, M., Weiman, A., Gur, R. C., Hungerbuhler, J. P., & Geschwind, N. (1982). Hemispheric asymmetry in the expression of positive and negative emotions: Neurological evidence. *Archives of Neurology, 39,* 210–218.

Sackett, G. P. (1966). Monkeys reared in isolation with pictures as visual input: Evidence for an innate releasing mechanism. *Science, 154,* 1468–1470.

Sackett, G. P. (1970). Unlearned responses, differential rearing environments, and the development of social attachments by rhesus monkeys. In L. A. Rosenblum (Ed.), *Primate behavior: Developments in field and laboratory research.* New York: Academic Press.

Sander, L. (1975). Infant and caretaking environment. In E. J. Anthony (Ed.), *Explorations in child psychiatry* (pp. 129–165). New York: Plenum.

Santrock, J. W. (1997). *Children* (5th ed.). Dubuque, IA: Brown & Benchmark.

Savin-Williams, R. C. (1987). *Adolescence: An ethological perspective.* New York: Springer-Verlag.

Savin-Williams, R. C., & Berndt, T. J. (1990). Friendship and peer relations. In S. S. Feldman & G. R. Elliott (Eds.), *At the threshold: The developing adolescent* (pp. 277–307). Cambridge, MA: Harvard University Press.

Scarr, S. (1992). Developmental theories for the 1990's: Development and individual differences. *Developmental Psychology, 63,* 1–19.

Scarr, S., & McCartney, K. (1983). How people make their own environments: A theory of genotype–environment effects. *Child Development, 54,* 425–435.

Schachter, S. (1966). The interaction of cognitive and physiological determinants of emotional state. In C. D. Spielberger (Ed.), *Anxiety and behavior* (pp. 193–224). New York: Academic Press.

Schachter, S., & Singer, J. E. (1962). Cognitive, social and physiological determinants of emotional state. *Psychological Review, 69,* 379–399.

Schaffer, H., & Callender, M. (1959). Psychological effects of hospitalization in infancy. *Pediatrics, 24,* 528–539.

Scherer, K. R. (1986). Vocal affect expression: A review and model for further research. *Psychological Bulletin, 98,* 143–165.

Scherer, K. R. (1989). Vocal correlates of emotional arousal and affective disturbance. In H. Wagner & A. Manstead (Eds.), *Handbook of social psychophysiology* (pp. 165–197). New York: Wiley.

Schiedel, D. G., & Marcia, J. E. (1985). Ego identity, intimacy, sex role orientation, and gender. *Developmental Psychology, 21*(1), 149–160.

Schneirla, T. C. (1959). An evolutionary and developmental theory of biphasic processes underlying approach and withdrawal. In M. R. Jones (Ed.), *Nebraska symposium on motivation* (Vol. 7, pp. 297–339). Lincoln, NE: University of Nebraska Press.

Schore, A. N. (1991). Early superego development: The emergence of shame and narcissistic affect in the practicing period. *Psychoanalysis and Contemporary Thought, 14,* 187–250.

Schore, A. N. (1994). *Affect regulation and the origin of self: The neurobiology of emotional development.* Hillsdale, NJ: Erlbaum.

Schwartz, G. E., Ahern, G. L., & Brown, S. L. (1979). Lateralized facial muscle response to positive and negative emotional stimuli. *Psychophysiology, 16,* 561–571.

Schwartz, G. M., Izard, C. E., & Ansul, S. E. (1985). The 5-month-old's ability to discriminate facial expression of emotion. *Infant Behavior and Development, 8,* 65–77.

Segal, N. L. (1999). *Entwined lives: Twins and what they tell us about human behavior.* New York: Dutton.

Seifer, R., Sameroff, A. J., Barrett, L. C., & Krafchuk, E. (1994). Infant temperament measured by multiple observations and maternal report. *Child Development, 65,* 1478–1490.

Seligman, M. E. P. (1975). *Helplessness: On depression development and death.* San Francisco: Freeman.

Selman, R. L., & Schultz, L. H. (1990). *Making a friend in youth: Developmental theory and pair therapy.* Chicago: University of Chicago Press.

Selye, H. (1950). *Stress: The physiology and pathology of exposure to stress.* Montreal, Canada: Acta.

Semenza, C., Pasini, M., Zettin, M., Tonin, P., & Portolan, P. (1986). Right hemisphere patients' judgements on emotions. *Acta Neurologica Scandinavica, 74,* 43–50.

Serbin, L. A., Moller, L. C., Gulko, J., Powlishta, K. K., & Colburne, K. A. (1994). The emergence of gender segregation in toddler playgroups. In C. Leaper (Ed.), *Child gender segregation: Causes and consequences* (pp. 7–17). San Francisco: Jossey-Bass.

Sergent, J., Ohta, S., & MacDonald, B. (1992). Functional neuroanatomy of the face and object processing: A positron emission tomography study. *Brain, 115,* 15–36.

Shaffer, D. R. (1998). *Social and personality development* (3d ed.). Pacific Grove, CA: Brooks/Cole.

Shennum, W. A., & Bugental, D. B. (1982). The development of control over affective expression in nonverbal behavior. In R. S. Feldman (Ed.), *Development of nonverbal behavior in children* (pp. 101–118). New York: Springer-Verlag.

Sherif, M., Harvey, O., White, B., Hood, W., & Sherif, C. (1961). Intergroup conflict and cooperation: The Robbers Cave experiment. Norman, OK: University of Oklahoma Press.

Shirley, M. M. (1933). *The first two years: A study of 25 babies.* Minneapolis, MN: University of Minnesota Press.

Shultz, T. R., & Cloghesy, K. (1981). Development of recursive awareness of intention. *Developmental Psychology, 17,* 465–471.

Shultz, T. R., & Zigler, E. (1970). Emotional concomitants of visual mastery in infants: The effects of stimulus movement on smiling and vocalizing. *Journal of Experimental Child Psychology, 10,* 390–402.

Silverberg, S. B., Tennenbaum, D. L., & Jacob, T. (1992). Adolescence of family interaction. In V. B. Van Hasselt & M. Hersen (Eds.), *Handbook of social devel-*

opment: A lifespan perspective. Perspectives in developmental psychology (pp. 347–370). New York: Plenum.

Simpson, J. A., Rholes, W. S., & Nelligan, J. S. (1993). Support seeking and support giving within couples in an anxiety-provoking situation: The role of attachment styles. *Journal of Personality and Social Psychology, 62,* 434–446.

Skipper, J. K., & Nass, G. (1966). Dating behavior: A framework for analysis and an illustration. *Journal of Marriage and the Family, 29,* 412–420.

Skinner, B. F. (1953). *Science and human behavior.* New York: Appleton.

Smith, P., & Dagliesh, L. (1977). Sex differences in parent and infant behavior in the home. *Child Development, 48,* 1250–1254.

Smuts, B., & Levine, S. (1977). Limbic system regulation of ACTH. *Acta Physiologica Pololica, 28,* 93–108.

Snyder, S. (1985, October). The molecular basis for communication between cells. *Scientific American,* pp. 132–141.

Sodian, B., Taylor, C., Harris, P. L., & Perner, J. (1991). Early deception and the child's theory of mind: False trails and genuine markers. *Child Development, 62,* 468–483.

Solomon, R. C. (1993). The philosophy of emotions. In M. Lewis & J. Haviland (Eds.), *The handbook of emotions* (pp. 3–15). New York: Guilford.

Sorce, J. F., Emde, R. N., Campos, J., & Klinnert, M. D. (1985). Maternal emotional signaling: Its effect on the visual cliff behavior of 1-year-olds. *Developmental Psychiatry, 21,* 195–200.

Spiker, D., Ferguson, J., & Brooks-Gunn, J. (1993). Enhancing maternal interactive behavior and child social competence in low birth weight, premature infants. *Child Development, 64,* 754–768.

Spitz, R. A. (1946). *The first year of life.* New York: International Universities Press.

Spitz, R. (1965). *The first year of life.* New York: International Universities Press.

Spitz, R. A., Emde, R. N., & Metcalf, D. R. (1970). Further prototypes of ego formation: A working paper from a research project on early development. *Psychoanalytic Study of the Child, 25,* 417–441.

Sroufe, L. A. (1977). Wariness of strangers and the study of infant development. *Child Development, 48,* 731–746.

Sroufe, L. A. (1979). Socioemotional development. In J. D. Osofsky (Ed.), *Handbook of infant development* (pp. 462–516). New York: Wiley.

Sroufe, L. A. (1983). Infant–caregiver attachment and patterns of adaptation in preschool: Roots of maladaption and competence. In M. Perlmutter (Ed.), *Minnesota symposia on child psychology, 16.* Hillsdale, NJ: Erlbaum.

Sroufe, L. A. (1985). Attachment classification from the perspective of infant–caregiver relationships and infant temperament. *Child Development, 56,* 1–14.

Sroufe, L. A. (1989). Relationships, self, and individual adaptation. In A. J. Sameroff & R. N. Emde (Eds.), *Relationship disturbances in early childhood: A developmental approach.* New York: Basic Books.

Sroufe, L. A. (1996). *Emotional development: The organization of emotional life in the early years.* Cambridge, England: Cambridge University Press.

Sroufe, L. A., Fox, N. E., & Pancake, V. R. (1983). Attachment and dependency in developmental perspective. *Child Development, 54,* 1615–1627.

Sroufe, L. A., & Rutter, M. (1984). The domain of developmental psychopathology. *Child Development, 55,* 1184–1199.

Sroufe, L. A., Schork, E., Motti, F., Lawroski, N., & LaFreniere, P. J. (1984). The role of affect in social competence. In C. E. Izard, J. Kagan, & R. B. Zajonc (Eds.), *Emotions, cognition, and behavior* (pp. 289–319). Cambridge, England: Cambridge University Press.

Sroufe, L. A., & Waters, E. (1977a). Attachment as an organizational construct. *Child Development, 48,* 1184–1199.

Sroufe, L. A., & Waters, E. (1977b). Heart rate as a convergent measure in clinical and developmental research. *Merrill-Palmer Quarterly, 23,* 3–27.

Sroufe, L. A., & Wunsch, J. P. (1972). The development of laughter in the first years of life. *Child Development, 43,* 1326–1344.

Stansbury, K., & Gunnar, M. R. (1994). The adrenocortical system and the study of emotion regulation: A multi-level perspective. In N. A. Fox (Ed.), Emotion regulation: Behavioral and biological considerations. *Monographs of the Society for Research in Child Development, 59*(2–3), 108–134.

Stein, N., & Trabasso, T. (1989). Children's understanding of changing emotional states. In C. Saarni & P. Harris (Eds.), *Children's understanding of emotion* (pp. 50–80). Cambridge, England: Cambridge University Press.

Steinberg, L. D. (1981). Transformation in family relations at puberty. *Developmental Psychology, 17,* 833–840.

Steinberg, L. D. (1988). Reciprocal relation between parent–child distance and pubertal maturation. *Developmental Psychology, 24,* 122–128.

Steinberg, L. (1990). Autonomy, conflict, and harmony in the family relationship. In S. Feldman & G. Elliott (Eds.), *At the threshold: The developing adolescent* (pp. 255–276). Cambridge, MA: Harvard University Press.

Steinberg, L. D., & Hill, J. P. (1978). Patterns of family interaction as a function of age, the onset of puberty, and formal thinking. *Developmental Psychology, 14,* 683–684.

Steinberg, L. D., & Silverberg, S. B. (1986). The vicissitudes of autonomy. *Child Development, 57,* 841–851.

Stenberg, C. R., & Campos, J. J. (1983). The development of the expression of anger in human infants. In M. Lewis & C. Saarni (Eds.), *The socialization of affect.* New York: Plenum.

Stenberg, C. R., & Campos, J. J. (1990). The development of anger expressions in infancy. In N. Stein, B. Leventhal, & T. Trabasso (Eds.), *Psychological and biological approaches to emotion* (pp. 247–282). Hillsdale, NJ: Erlbaum.

Stern, D. N. (1985). *The interpersonal world of the infant.* New York: Basic Books.

Stifter, C., & Fox, N. (1987). Preschoolers' ability to identify and label emotions. *Journal of Nonverbal Behavior, 10,* 255–266.

Stifter, C. A., & Fox, N. A. (1990). Infant reactivity: Physiological correlates of newborn and five month temperament. *Develomental Psychology, 26,* 582–588.

Stifter, C. A., Fox, N. A., & Porges, S. W. (1989). Facial expressivity and vagal tone in five- and ten-month-old infants. *Infant Behavior and Development, 12,* 127–137.

Stipek, D. (1995). The development of pride and shame in toddlers. In J. P. Tangney & K. W. Fischer (Eds.), *Self-conscious emotions; the psychology of shame, guilt, embarrassment, and pride* (pp. 343–367). New York: Guilford.

Stipek, D., Recchia, S., & McClintic, S. (1992). Self-evaluation in young children. *Monographs of the Society for Research in Child Development, 57*(1, Serial No. 226).

Story, S. (1979). *Rodin.* New York: Dutton.

Strayer, F. F., & Strayer, J. (1976). An ethological analysis of social agonism and dominance relations among preschool children. *Child Development, 47,* 980–989.

Strober, M. (1985). Depressive illness in adolescence. *Psychiatric Annals, 15*(6), 375–378.

Sullivan, H. S. (1953). *The interpersonal theory of psychiatry.* New York: Norton.

Suomi, S. J., & Harlow, F. (1972). Social rehabilitation of isolate-reared monkeys. *Developmental Psychology, 6,* 487–496.

Tangney, J., & Fischer, K. (Eds.). (1995). *Self-conscious emotions: The psychology of shame, guilt, embarrassment, and pride.* New York: Guilford.

Tedesco, L., & Gaier, E. (1988). Friendship bonds in adolescence. *Adolescence, 89,* 127–136.

Termine, N. T., & Izard, C. E. (1988). Infants' responses to their mothers' expressions of joy and sadness. *Developmental Psychology, 24,* 223–229.

Thomas, A., Chess, S., Birch, H. G., Hertzig, M. E., & Korn, S. (1963). *Behavioral individuality in early childhood.* New York: New York University Press.

Thompson, R. A. (1990). Emotion and self-regulation. *Nebraska Symposium on Motivation* (pp. 367–467).

Thompson, R. A. (1994). Emotion regulation: A theme in search of definition. In N. Fox (Ed.), Emotion regulation: Behavioral and biological consideration. *Monographs of the Society for Research in Child Development, 59*(Serial No. 240), 25–52.

Thompson, R. A., & Lamb, M. E. (1983). Individual differences in dimensions of socio-emotional development in infancy. In R. Plutchik & H. Kellerman (Eds.), *Emotion: Theory, research and experience: Vol. 2. Emotions in early development.* New York: Academic Press.

Thompson, R. A., & Lamb, M. E. (1984). Assessing qualitative dimensions of emotional responsiveness in infants: Separation reactions in the strange situation. *Infant Behavior and Development, 7,* 423–445.

Tieger, T. (1980). On the biological basis of sex differences in aggression. *Child Development, 51*(4), 943–963.

Tinbergen, N. (1951). *The study of instinct.* London: Oxford University Press.

Tinbergen, N. (1952). Derived activities: Their causation, biological significance, origin and emancipation during evolution. *Quarterly Review of Biology, 27,* 1–32.

Tinbergen, N. (1963). On aims and methods of ethology. *Z. Tierpsychol., 20,* 410–433.

Tinbergen, N. (1968). On war and peace in animals and man. *Science, 160,* 1411–1418.

Tomkins, S. S. (1962). *Affect, imagery, consciousness: Vol. 1. The positive affects.* New York: Springer.

Tomkins, S. S. (1963). *Affect, imagery, consciousness: Vol. 2. The negative affects.* New York: Springer.

Tomkins, S. S. (1981). The quest for primary motives: Biography and autobiography of an idea. *Journal of Personality and Social Psychology, 41,* 306–329.

Tomkins, S. S., & McCarter, R. (1964). What and where are the primary affects? Some evidence for a theory. *Perceptual and Motor Skills, 18,* 119–158.

Trabasso, T., Stein, N., & Johnson, L. R. (1981). Children's knowledge of events: A causal analysis of story structure. In G. Bower (Ed.), *Learning and motivation* (Vol 15). New York: Academic Press.

Trevarthen, C. (1984). Emotions in infancy: Regulators of contact and relationships with persons. In K. R. Scherer & P. Ekman (Eds.), *Approaches to emotion* (pp. 129–161). Hillsdale, NJ: Erlbaum.

Trickett, P. K., & Kuczynski, L. (1986). Children's misbehaviors and parental discipline strategies in abusive and nonabusive families. *Developmental Psychology, 22*(1), 115–123.

Trivers, J. (1971). The evolution of reciprocal altruism. *Quarterly Review of Biology, 46,* 35–57.

Trivers, J. (1972). Parental investment and sexual selection. In B. Campbell (Ed.), *Sexual selection and the descent of man* (pp. 136–179). Chicago: Aldine Press.

Tronick, E. Z. (1989). Emotions and emotional communication in infants. *American Psychologist, 44,* 112–119.

Tronick, E. Z., Morelli, G. A., & Ivey, P. K. (1992). The Efe forager infant and toddler's pattern of social relationships: Multiple and simultaneous. *Developmental Psychology, 28,* 568–577.

Troy, M., & Sroufe, L. A. (1987). Victimization among preschoolers: Role of attachment relationship history. *Journal of the American Academy of Child and Adolescent Psychiatry, 26,* 166–172.

Underwood, M. K., Coie, J., & Herbsman, C. (1992). Display rules for anger and aggression in school-age children. *Child Development, 63,* 366–380.

Ursin, H., Baade, E., & Levine, S. (1978). *Psychobiology of stress.* New York: Academic Press.

van den Boom, D. C. (1991). The influence of infant irritability on the development of the mother–infant relationship in the first six months of life. In J. K. Nugent, B. M. Lester, & T. B. Brazelton (Eds.), *The cultural context of infancy* (Vol. 2, pp. 63–89). Norwood, NJ: Ablex.

van den Boom, D. C. (1994). The influence of temperament and mothering on attachment and exploration: An experimental manipulation of sensitive responsiveness among lower-class mothers with irritable infants. *Child Development, 65,* 1457–1477.

van Gennep, A. (1960). *The rites of passage.* Chicago: Chicago University Press.

Van Ijzendoorn, M. H., Juffer, F., & Duyvesteyn, M. G. C. (1995). Breaking the intergenerational cycle of insecure attachment: A review of the effects of attachment-based interventions on maternal sensitivity and infant security. *Journal of Child Psychology and Psychiatry, 36,* 225–248.

Van Ijzendoorn, M. H., & Kroonenberg, P. M. (1988). Cross-cultural patterns of attachment: A meta-analysis of the Strange Situation. *Child Development, 59,* 147–156.

Vaughn, B., Bradley, C., Joffe, L., Seifer, R., & Barglow, P. (1987). Maternal characteristics measured prenatally are predictive of ratings of temperamental "difficulty" on the Carey Infant Temperament Questionnaire. *Developmental Psychology, 23,* 152–161.

Vaughn, B., Egeland, B., Waters, E., & Sroufe, L. A. (1979). Individual differences in infant–mother attachment at twelve and eighteen months: Stability and change in families under stress. *Child Development, 59,* 971–975.

Vaughn, B. E., Lefever, G. B., Seifer, R., & Barglow, P. (1989). Attachment behavior, attachment security, and temperament during infancy. *Child Development, 60,* 728–737.

Vaughn, B., & Sroufe, L. A. (1979). The temporal relationship between infant HR acceleration and crying in an aversive situation. *Child Development, 50,* 565–567.

Verlaan, P., & LaFreniere, P. J. (1994). Adaptation des enfants anxieux-isolés à la garderie. Caractéristiques comportementales et affectives de la relation mère-enfant. *Canadian Journal of Behavioral Sciences, 26*(1), 52–67.

Von Bertalanffy, L. (1968). *General systems theory.* New York: Braziller.

Vygotsky, L. (1978). *Mind and society.* Cambridge, MA: Harvard University Press.

de Waal, F. B. M. (1982). *Chimpanzee politics.* London: Jonathon Cape.

de Waal, F. B. M. (1986). Deception in the natural communication of chimpanzees. In R. W. Mitchell & N. S. Thompson (Eds.), *Deception: Perspectives on human and nonhuman deceit.* Albany, NY: State University of New York Press.

de Waal, F. B. M. (1996). *Good natured: The origins of right and wrong in humans and other animals.* Cambridge, MA/London: Harvard University Press.

Wahler, R. G. (1967). Infant social attachments: A reinforcement theory interpretation and investigation. *Child Development, 38,* 1079–1088.

Wahler, R. G., & Dumas, J. E. (1989). Attentional problems in dysfunctional mother–child interactions: An interbehavioral model. *Psychological Bulletin, 105,* 116–130.

Walden, T. A., & Ogan, T. A. (1988). The development of social referencing. *Child Development, 59,* 1230–1240.

Washburn, S. L. (1960). Tools and human evolution. *Scientific American, 203,* 3–15.

Waters, E., & Deane, K. (1985). Defining and assessing individual differences in attachment relationships: Q-methodology and the organization of behavior in infancy and early childhood. *Monographs of the Society for Research in Child Development, 50,* 209.

Waters, E., Matas, L., & Sroufe, L. A. (1975). Infant's reactions to an approaching stranger: Description, validation and functional significance of wariness. *Child Devleopment, 46,* 348–356.

Waters, E., & Sroufe, L. A. (1983). A developmental perspective on competence. *Developmental Review, 3,* 79–97.

Watson, J. B. (1924/1970). *Behaviorism.* New York: Norton.

Watson, J. B. (1928). *Psychological care of infant and child.* New York: Norton.

Watson, J. B., & Raynor, R. (1920). Conditioned emotional reactions. *Journal of Experimental Psychology, 3,* 1–14.

Watson, J. S. (1985). Contingency perception in early social development. In T. M. Field & N. M. Fox (Eds.), *Social perception in infants* (pp. 157–165). Norwood, NJ: Ablex.

Weiner, B. (1985). An attributional theory of achievement motivation and emotion. *Psychological Review, 89*(4), 548–573.

Weiner, B. (1986). *An attributional theory of motivation and emotion.* New York: Springer-Verlag.

Weiner, B., & Graham, S. (1989). Understanding the motivational role of affect: Life-span research from an attributional perspective. *Cognition and Emotion, 3*(4), 401–419.

Weisfeld, G. E. (1997). Puberty rites as clues to the nature of human adolescence. *Cross-Cultural Research, 31*(1), 27–54.

Weisfeld, G. E. (1999). *Evolutionary principles of human adolescence.* New York: Basic Books.

Weisfeld, G. E., & Billings, R. L. (1988). Observations on adolescence. In K. MacDonald (Ed.), *Sociobiological perspectives on human development* (pp. 207–233). New York: Springer-Verlag.

Weiskrantz, L. (1956). Behavioral changes associated with ablation of the amygdaloid complex in monkeys. *Journal of Comparative and Physiological Psychology, 49,* 381–391.

Wellman, H. M. (1990). *The child's theory of mind.* Cambridge, MA: MIT Press.

Wellman, H., & Wooley, J. (1990). From simple desires to ordinary beliefs: The early development of everyday psychology. *Cognition, 35,* 245–275.

Werner, J., & LaFreniere, P. J. (1998, February). *A naturalistic study of affective expression, social competence, and sociometric status in preschoolers.* Poster presented at the 69th Annual Meeting of the Eastern Psychological Association, Boston, MA.

Whiten, A., & Byrne, R. W. (1988). Tactical deception in primates. *Behavioral and Brain Sciences, 11,* 233–273.

Whiting, B. B., & Edwards, C. P. (1988). *Children of different worlds.* Cambridge, MA: Harvard University Press.

Whiting, B., & Whiting, J. (1975). *Children of six cultures: A psycho-cultural analysis.* Cambridge, MA: Harvard University Press.

Williams, G. C. (1966). *Adaptation and natural selection.* Princeton, NJ: Princeton University Press.

Wills, T. A. (1990). Social support and the family. In E. A. Blechman et al. (Eds.), *Emotions and the family: For better or for worse* (pp. 75–98). Hillsdale, NJ: Erlbaum.

Wilson, E. O. (1992). *The diversity of life.* Cambridge, MA: Harvard University Press.

Wilson, M., & Daly, M. (1985). Competitiveness, risk taking, and violence: The young male syndrome. *Ethology and Sociobiology, 6,* 59–73.

Wimmer, H., & Perner, P. (1983). Beliefs about beliefs; representation and constraining function of wrong beliefs in young children's understanding of deception. *Cognition, 13,* 103–128.

Wolfe, D. A., Fairbank, J. A., Kelly, J. A., & Bradlyn, A. S. (1983). Child abusive parents' physiological responses to stressful and non-stressful behavior in children. *Behavioral Assessment, 5*(4), 363–371.

Wolff, P. (1963). Observations on the early development of smiling. In B. M. Foss (Ed.), *Determinants of infant behavior* (Vol. 1). London: Methuen.

Woodruff, G., & Premack, D. (1979). Intentional communication in the chimpanzee: The development of deception. *Cognition, 7,* 333–362.

Worobey, J., & Lewis, M. (1989). Individual differences in the activity of young infants. *Developmental Psychology, 25,* 663–667.

Yonas, A. (1981). Infants' responses to optical information for collision. In R. Aslin & L. Pettersen (Eds.), *Development of perception: Psychobiological perspectives* (Vol. 2, pp. 313–334). New York: Academic Press.

Yonas, A., Cleaves, W., & Pettersen, L. (1978). Development of sensitivity to pictorial depth. *Science, 200,* 77–79.

Youngblade, L. M., & Belsky, J. (1992). Parent–child antecedents of five-year-olds' close friendships: A longitudinal analysis. *Developmental Psychology, 28*(4), 700–713.

Younge-Browne, G., Rosenfeld, H. M., & Horowitz, F. D. (1977). Infant discrimination of facial expressions. *Child Development, 48,* 555–562.

Youniss, J., & Smollar, J. (1985). *Adolescent relations with mothers, fathers, and friends.* Chicago: University of Chicago Press.

Zahn-Waxler, C., & Kochanska, G. (1990). The origins of guilt. In R. A. Thompson (Vol. Ed.), *Nebraska Symposium on Motivation 1988: Vol. 36. Socioemotional development* (pp. 183–258). Lincoln, NE: University of Nebraska Press.

Zahn-Waxler, C., & Radke-Yarrow, M. (1982). The development of altruism: Alternative research strategies. In N. Eisenberg-Berg (Ed.), *The development of pro-social behavior* (pp. 109–137). New York: Academic Press.

Zahn-Waxler, C., & Radke-Yarrow, M. (1990). The origins of empathic concern. *Motivation and Emotion, 14,* 107–130.

Zahn-Waxler, C., Radke-Yarrow, M., & King, R. A. (1979). Child rearing and children's prosocial initiations towards victims of distress. *Child Development, 50,* 319–330.

Zahn-Waxler, C., Radke-Yarrow, M., Wagner, E., & Chapman, M. (1992). Development of concern for others. *Developmental Psychology, 28,* 126–136.

Zahn-Waxler, C., & Robinson, J. (1995). Empathy and guilt: Early origins of feelings of responsibility. In J. Tangney & K. Fischer (Eds.), *Self-conscious emotions: The psychology of shame, guilt, embarrassment, and pride* (pp. 143–173). New York: Guilford.

Zajonc, R. B. (1980). Feeling and thinking: Preferences need no inferences. *American Psychologist, 35*(2), 151–175.

Zeanah, C. H., Keener, M. A., Thomas, F., & Viera-Baher, C. C. (1987). Adolescent mother's perceptions of their infants before and after birth. *American Journal of Orthopsychiatry, 57,* 351–360.

Zelazo, P. R. (1972). Smiling and vocalizing: A cognitive emphasis. *Merrill-Palmer Quarterly, 18,* 349–365.

Zelazo, P. R., & Komer, M. J. (1971). Infant smiling to non-social stimuli and the recognition hypothesis. *Child Development, 42,* 1327–1339.

Zeman, J., & Garber, J. (1996). Display rules for anger, sadness, and pain: It depends on who is watching. *Child Development, 67,* 957–973.

Zeman, J., & Shipman, K. (1997). Social-contextual influences on expectancies for managing anger and sadness: The transition from middle-childhood to adolescence. *Developmental Psychology, 33,* 917–924.

Zivin, G. (1977). On becoming subtle: Age and social rank changes in the use of facial gestures. *Child Development, 48,* 1314–1321.

Zuckerman, M. (1995). Good and bad humors: Biochemical bases of personality and its disorders. *Psychological Science, 6,* 325–332.

Zuckerman, M., & Przewuzman, S. (1979). Decoding and encoding facial expressions in preschool-age children. *Environmental Psychology and Nonverbal Psychology, 3,* 147–163.

Name Index

Subject Index